Returns of Marxism

Returns of Marxism

Marxist Theory in a Time of Crisis

Edited by Sara R. Farris

Acknowledgments

Financial assistance for the copy editing of this volume was provided by Roland Boer's Australian Research Council project, "Unfinished Business: On Marxism and Religion". Special thanks to Sean Durbin for his copy editing assistance.

Many thanks also to the International Institute for Research and Education (IIRE) Team that allowed the usage of the IIRE premises for the whole duration of the seminar and provided precious help in all stages of the preparation of the seminar and this volume. Thanks in particular to Antonio Carmona Báez, Alex de Jong, Eva Ferraren, Joost Kircz, Alex Merlo, Eng Que, Murray Smith, Bertil Videt and Jakob Wedemeijer.

Special thanks also go to Marijke Colle for her help in the translation of Michael Heinrich's text into English and to Dan Hartley for the linguistic revision of the text.

First published in 2014 by the International Institute for Research and Education (IIRE)
© 2014 IIRE

Published in paperback in 2016 by
Haymarket Books
P.O. Box 180165
Chicago, IL 60618
773-583-7884
www.haymarketbooks.org

ISBN: 978-1-60846-574-3

Trade distribution:
In the US, Consortium Book Sales, www.cbsd.com
In Canada, Publishers Group Canada, www.pgcbooks.ca
In the UK, Turnaround Publisher Services, http://www.turnaround-uk.com
In all other countries, Publishers Group Worldwide, www.pgw.com

Cover design by Eric Kerl.

This book was published with the generous support of Lannan Foundation and the Wallace Global Fund.

Printed in Canada by union labor.

10 9 8 7 6 5 4 3 2 1

Library of Congress Cataloging-in-Publication data is available.

CONTENTS

Historicising Historical Materialism

Feminist and Queer Marxisms

Many Marxisms

Notes on contributors

INTRODUCTION

Sara R. Farris

Returns of Marxism was the name given to the seminar series that took place at the International Institute for Research and Education (IIRE) between 2007 and 2009. The title of the series was not casual, for we wanted to highlight the return in Amsterdam of a cycle of public encounters devoted to the discussion of Marxist themes, after their long absence in the Dutch city. Yet, the returns also refer to the compensations, or rewards of the Marxist tradition itself when that wealth of ideas and practices inspired by Marx's thought are re-appropriated and re-interpreted by a new generation of activists in their own struggles. This entails a return *to* Marx, a return that is never simple or innocent, for it demands the abandonment of a 'dogmatic' approach to the texts and the willingness to strive in the present for an understanding of Marx's analyses of capitalism.

In recent years we have witnessed a renewed interest in Marx's thought, as a younger generation of scholars and activists have rediscovered Marx as a crucial source for the critique of the neo-liberal face of capitalism. On the one hand, the actuality of Marx's *Capital* itself has been reassessed through a wealth of publications directly attempting a re-reading of his magnum opus in light of capitalism's most recent developments. David Harvey, Fredric Jameson and David McNally – only to name the most well-known figures – figure prominently here. On the other hand, the Marx *Renaissance* of the last few years is due to the renewed interest in the idea of communism, reproposed as a crucial theme for research and as a terrain of political experimentation by prominent contemporary critical thinkers, from Alain Badiou, Slavoj Žižek, and Antonio Negri, to Bruno Bosteels and Jodi Dean. Marx's critique of the inherent and insuperable disfunction of capital have thus become dramatically contemporary.

The contributions collected in this volume are all revised texts originally presented as papers for discussion during the two year seminar series. The division of the texts in six different sections has the aim to propose a path for reading them as contributions to broader significant problematics within the Marxist tradition.

Reading Capital.

The first section is comprised of essays directly engaging with specific aspects of Marx's *Das Kapital* and representing different readings of Marx's theory of value. Guglielmo Carchedi's chapter proposes a reading of the theory of value as the necessary framework to articulate a theory of subjectivity and knowledge production. For Carchedi, the understanding of the subjective manifestations of the contradictory objective foundations and movement of the economy is the necessary step for the exploration of the production of knowledge as the production of value and surplus value. As a result, Carchedi considers the development of a Marxist theory of knowledge itself as the condition of possibility for a theory of crises. Riccardo Bellofiore's text, on the other hand, attempts to assess the nature of contemporary capitalism in terms of 'centralisation' without 'concentration', whereby financial capital is increasingly central to valorisation and workers' organisation and struggles are made more difficult by the schizophrenic emergence of the labourer as a 'traumatised' worker, a 'manic-depressive' saver and an 'indebted' consumer. In this scenario, Bellofiore argues that we can exit from this situation only by taking up again the instruments of analysis individuated by Marx's theory of value: money as capital, living labour as source of new value. The text by Michael Heinrich aims to reopen and critique the discussion that framed the reading of *Capital* as the mature work of an older Marx more interested in a critique of political economy to be contrasted with a younger more philosophically oriented one. For Heinrich, instead, we need to see in Marx's work a series of attempts, discontinuations, shifts, new concepts and new beginnings. All of Marx's central projects, Heinrich argues, remain unfinished and incomplete; the return to Marx, therefore, cannot be understood as the return to an oeuvre, which has all answers to our concerns. Geert Reuten interprets part one of Marx's *Capital, Volume I* concerning 'abstract labour', or the *ideal introversive form of value*, as inseparable from money, or the *ideal extroversive form of value*. Reuten thus links the absence of the term 'abstract labour' from subsequent parts of Marx's volume as proof that money is the only actual ideal measure of value. Finally, Frieder Otto-Wolf's text reads Marx's critique of political economy as establishing a clear distinction between theory and history. For Wolf, Marx's critical theory of the capitalist mode of production is not to be understood as a recounting of historical events, and therefore, it cannot be taken to propose a deterministic reading of history. This element, for Wolf, leads to the recognition that the workings of history should not be searched within the general structure of the capitalist mode of production, but rather within 'modern bourgeois societies' and their global constellations.

Re-reading Marx.

The contributions to this section of the volume attempt a re-reading of Marx's texts through thematic focuses on key issues of his elaboration. Tom Rockmore's text traces Marx's theory of human activity back to Fichte's theory in reaction against Kant. According to Rockmore, Marx inherited Fichte's theory through the influence the latter had on the specific critique of Hegel carried out by the Young Hegelians. The second text in the section by Wei Xiaoping asks whether Marx has a principle of distributive justice. According to Xiaoping, Marx's approach to the process of the liberation of humanity presents two steps: the first is that of justice in distribution, rewarding according to effort; the second is that of distribution beyond justice that rewards according to needs. According to Xiaoping it is only in the second stage that the difference between Marx's theory of justice on the one hand, and Nozick's and Rawls' theory of justice on the other, can be fully grasped. At this second stage people can express and develop themselves fully, and thus be organised into a social community. Finally, Joost Kircz deals with the relation between Marxism and modern science. According to Kircz the Marxist goal of a better world is grounded in knowledge of the understanding of nature and, in particular, of the conscious element therein; that is to say, human society. Understanding the world in order to change it means, according to Kircz, to have a programme of how modern bourgeois thinking understands that same world and to what extent the most advanced thinking in that camp is developing.

Marxism and international politics.

This section collects those texts devoted to discussing Marxist concepts in the field of international relations and international politics. The first essay by Jan Drahokoupil, Bastiaan Van Apeldoorn and Laura Horn analyses the economic and political tensions at the heart of the European integration project. By exploring the actual manifestations of neoliberal restructuring in the EU and the concomitant contradictions and social struggles emanating from them, the authors aim to unravel the recent transformations of capitalism and capitalist societies with the

9

lenses provided by the critical political economy approach. The second text by Gal Kirn focuses on the specificity of post-socialist ideology in the post-Yugoslav context. Here Kirn explores in particular the ideology of 'national reconciliation' and its role in legitimizing the ethnic divisions in ex-Yugoslavia. By examining the politics of memory, particularly the management of monuments as an expression of such politics, Kirn interrogates the national reconciliation discourse in relation to its implications for post-Yugoslav politics. Jeffery Webber's text discusses the complex dynamics of Ecuador's social and political configuration under Rafael Correa. Webber's analysis highlights in particular the contradictions of Correa's development model and their implications for the politics of the popular movements in the country.

Historicising Historical materialism.

This section includes all papers that in different ways addressed Marx's and Marxist concepts of history and historiography, or that analyse important concepts of the Marxist tradition from an historical perspective. Against the 'revisionist' readings that have criticized social interpretations of revolutions in general and Marxist interpretations in particular, Nygaard attempts to re-open the debate on the relevance of the Marxist tradition for the understanding of bourgeois revolutions. By focusing on the historiography of the French revolution, Nygaard discusses the category of 'bourgeois revolution' through an outline of the main points in its conceptual development and proposes a model for reconstructing the important issues involved in such categorisation. In the second essay of the section, Marcel Van Der Linden critically interrogates the concept of working class within much of the Marxist tradition. By analysing in particular the distinctions between free and unfree labor, and self-employment, Van der Linden contends that the boundaries between the 'free' wage labourers and other kinds of subaltern workers in capitalist society are less cut-edged than a certain Marxist tradition has assumed. They thus need to be continually interrogated and grounded in empirical and historical analyses. Finally, in the last text of the section Peter D. Thomas puts forward a reading of Antonio Gramsci's thought as a source from which fertile tools and concepts for research into the 'macro- or meta-narrative' of modernity and modernization can be drawn. For Thomas, the concept of 'passive revolution' and Gramsci's reading of the Base/Superstructure metaphor in particular allows for a reassessment of the foundational concepts of historical materialism that both breaks with various 'determinist' deformations of Marx's thought while at the same time insisting upon the integrity of Marxist theory, as a tradition of thought capable of renewal through self-criticism.

Feminist and queer Marxisms.

This section brings together the two papers in the seminar series that addressed the relationship between Marxism, Feminism and Queer activism and theory.

In the first text, Chiara Bonfiglioli looks at the ways in which Marxist texts influenced the practices of communist parties and organisations in Western and South-Eastern Europe as 'women-friendly' policies or 'state feminism'. Bonfiglioli explores in particular second wave feminist critiques of Marxism within capitalist and socialist countries, taking as a case study the international feminist conference 'Comrade Woman. The Woman's Question: A New Approach?', held in Belgrade in 1978. In the second text of the section Peter Drucker speaks of his experience as a socialist and feminist gay man vis-à-vis the questions posed by queer activism. Here Drucker provides a brief reconstruction of the historical social origins of queer activism, in light of which he attempts in particular to explain its present formation. He then discusses its strengths and limitations and highlights the need for the emergence of a radical queer activism that fully embraces the challenges of the revolutionary traditions: organisation, engagement with the broad LGBT movement, ethnic and racial diversity, and materialism. Such engagement, for Drucker, 'can lay the basis for a powerful queer anti-capitalism and feminism'.

Many Marxisms.

This section of the book brings together the papers of the seminar that discussed some of the different traditions, readings and schools that sprang from Marxism in the twentieth century. In the first essay of the section, Steve Wright discusses his encounter with the tradition of Italian Marxism known as Workerism (Operaismo). Wright discusses in particular the centrality of the category of class composition within the tradition. The centrality given to deciphering class composition as the foundation of anti-capitalist politics is, for Wright, the most useful legacy that remains from the workerist experience. By understanding the trajectories of this category, it is possible to unravel the strengths and weaknesses of the workerist experience. The second text by Katja Diefenbach continues to debate the workerist legacy. Diefenbach analyses in particular how post-workerism, emerging at the beginning of the 1990s, discussed the relation between valorisation, bio-power and law within capitalism. By interrogating the meaning of the concepts of politics and living labour within Italian post-workerism, Diefenbach illustrates the trajectory of post-workerism from its origins.

Finally, in the final essay of the section, Roland Boer discusses the relationship between Marxism and theology. In particular Boer addresses questions such as: Why are Marxism and theology so close? Why do they argue so much? Is it something that weakens each one, holding the other back? Or are they, perhaps, stronger and sharper because of that tense connection?

***

As the above brief overview shows, ultimately the collection of essays presented in this volume aims to demonstrate the richness, rigour and importance of Marx's thought for developing alternative worldviews and politics in the present. We hope the reader will find these texts interesting and useful not only in her efforts to make sense of the world that surround us, but also in her fight against the many forms of injustice brought about by capitalism.

READING CAPITAL

THE CRISIS AND MARX'S THEORY OF KNOWLEDGE[1]

Guglielmo Carchedi

Introduction

Since the explosion of the most recent crisis in 2007, the number of works analysing this recurrent phenomenon from a Marxist perspective has kept increasing. Many of these works contribute to the understanding of the crisis-prone nature of capitalism and some of them illuminate aspects left hitherto unexplored. But all of them focus exclusively on the crises' objective causes and operations without considering how this contradictory objectivity emerges at the level of the consciousness of individuals and classes.

A complete theory of crises requires the development of a theory of knowledge consistent with Marx's wider theoretical opus, suitable for the development of an account of those aspects left unexplored by Marx, in tune with contemporary reality, and appropriate to fostering radical social change. This essay relates the objective working of the economy to the subjectivity of social agents, that is, to the subjective manifestations of the contradictory objective foundations and movement of the economy. This theory, in turn, will be the necessary background for the exploration of a much-debated issue, namely whether and when the production of knowledge is the production of value and surplus-value. This issue is of great importance for a theory of crises, since there is today a widespread notion that in contemporary capitalism the economy rests more on the production of knowledge (mental production) than on 'material', or, better said, objective production.[2] The Marxian theory of knowledge advanced here hinges upon two fundamental distinctions, between concrete individuals and abstract individuals and thus between individual and social phenomena. Let us then begin by briefly examining these notions.

1. This article is part of Chapter 4 of Carchedi (2010).
2. The term material has been put within quotation marks for reasons that will become clear in Section 3.

Individual and social phenomena

As Engels once said: '*History* does *nothing* ... history is *nothing but* the activity of man pursuing his aims'.[3] This is true. However, there is a difficulty here: categories such as 'people' or 'man' are too generic. The proper focus hinges upon a new distinction, between *concrete and abstract individuals*. This distinction is implicit in Marx: 'here individuals are dealt with only insofar as they are the personifications of economic categories, embodiments of particular class relations and class interest ... the individual [cannot be made] responsible for relations whose creature he socially remains, however much he may subjectively raise himself above them'.[4] This distinction is similar to the one Marx makes between concrete and abstract labour and plays the same fundamental role here as Marx's distinction does in his value-theory.

Individuals can be considered in their uniqueness, as unique individuals. As such, they are referred to as *concrete* individuals. But they can also be considered as possessing some common features (for example, they are all Catholic), irrespective of the specific, individual forms taken by those common features (for example, somebody's specific way of being a Catholic). It is because of these common features that individuals are considered to be members of a certain group. From this angle, they are considered not in their individuality and specificity, but as members of a group who share certain characteristics. As members of social groups, individuals are *abstract* individuals, since abstraction is made of their specific features, of their concrete forms of existence. The basic difference between abstract and concrete individuals is that the former are replaceable (on account of their common features), while concrete individuals, being unique, are not. This is in line with Marx's notion of commodities as replaceable due to their common social substance, abstract labour: 'As *values*, the commodities are expressions of the *same unity*, of abstract human labour ... Their *social relationship* consists exclusively in counting with respect to one another as expressions of this social substance of theirs which differs only quantitatively, but which is qualitatively equal and hence replaceable and interchangeable with one another'.[5] *In reality*, individuals are *always both* concrete *and* abstract. I am a teacher in the abstract because I belong to the group of teachers, and at the same time

3. Marx and Engels 1975, p. 92; emphasis in the original.
4. Marx 1967a, p. 10.
5. Marx 1967b, pp. 28–9; emphasis in the original.

I am a teacher with features that are only my own. However, *analytically*, individuals are *either* concrete *or* abstract. If we consider their unique features we disregard their common features, and vice versa. While concrete features differentiate, general features unify.

As concrete individuals, people engage in individual relations and processes, that is, in *individual phenomena*. Individual phenomena depend for their inception, continuation, transformation or termination only on the uniqueness of those individuals and on their capacity and will to engage (either freely or not) in that relation. This should not be interpreted as if other 'external' factors do not play a role: they do, but only inasmuch as they change the specific and unique features of those individuals and thus of their individual relation. On the other hand, as abstract individuals people engage in social relations and processes, that is, in *social phenomena*. Social phenomena are relations and processes among abstract individuals, namely, individuals seen from the point of view of having some common features and as such individuals are replaceable in those phenomena. The relationship between concrete individuals and individual phenomena is one of *determination*, in the specific sense that concrete individuals determine individual phenomena, since the former, due to their specificity, contain within themselves the latter as a potentiality, thus being the latter's *condition of existence*. In turn, individual phenomena are the *conditions of reproduction or supersession* of concrete individuals, since concrete individuals can reproduce themselves only due to those relations and processes. Similarly, for abstract individuals and social phenomena.

In individual phenomena, concrete individuals, being unique, are not replaceable. For example, two friends engage in an individual relation because they are unique, and thus irreplaceable. If one of the friends were replaced by someone else, then the relation would be replaced by another one, rather than a specific and unique individual being replaced by another within the same relation. One can speak of friendship in general, but this is merely a verbal category that disregards the specific, irreplaceable, characteristics of each relation of friendship. It does not indicate a social relation in which friends are replaceable. In social phenomena, on the other hand, individuals are replaceable. Therefore, social phenomena can *continue* to exist and reproduce themselves *irrespective* of the concrete individuals who, as abstract individuals, carry those specific social relations and engage in those processes.

The categories of concrete and abstract individuals (individual and social phenomena) are not simply categories of thought: they pertain to the same social reality. These categories find their objective basis in the fact that there are really two dimensions in social reality: that of concrete individuals (individual phenomena) and that of abstract individuals (social phenomena). There is no third dimension. There is no location of individuals outside these two dimensions. Individuals exist only in relation to each other, and these relations (and processes) constitute the social space.

The social space is not something that exists even given the absence of social and individual phenomena. Relations and processes *do not fill* a social space: they *are* the social space. It follows that it is futile to ask whether relations and processes pre-exist individuals or the other way around. It is as futile as asking what was there before the Big Bang. Neither is the social space something static. It exists only because social phenomena exist in their mutual determination, and is an ever-changing entity. But there is mutual determination not only among social phenomena, but also between social and individual phenomena. Let us see how.

Similar to social phenomena, individual phenomena are both potential and realised. Realised individual phenomena can become realised social phenomena if the individuals engaging in them become substitutable. For instance, in the case of two friends setting up an enterprise in which they, as economic agents, become substitutable. This implies that this realised social phenomenon (the enterprise) was already potentially present in the realised individual phenomenon (the relation of friendship) as one of its potentialities. Vice versa, social phenomena can revert to a state of potential if these agents become irreplaceable. In other words, *individual phenomena are potentially present in the concrete individuals engaging in relations and processes; potential individual phenomena, upon their realisation as realised individual phenomena, become potential social phenomena* (just as, for Marx, individual values are potential social values). It follows that *concrete individuals are potentially abstract individuals and that the former engage in realised individual phenomena which are formless potential social phenomena* (a relation of friendship can originate an array of social relations and processes). This is the bridge between the individual and the social dimension of reality.

These two dimensions of reality are different. What holds in one dimension does not hold in the other, due to their radical differences. However, they are related to each other, rather than unbridgeable. The bridge

18

is the potential aspects of individual and social phenomena. Within the dimension of individual phenomena, social phenomena are internalised by concrete individuals and become potential individual phenomena, having been reduced to a state of potential. This internalisation is part of the process of mental (knowledge) production to be discussed in Section 4. It is because of this that, upon their realisation, these individual phenomena become potential social phenomena.

Within this dimension, individual phenomena determine social phenomena, since the latter are contained potentially within the former. This is the bridge from the individual to the social dimension of society. But within the dimension of social phenomena, it is realised social phenomena that determine individual phenomena. Realised social phenomena must manifest themselves in a personal, concrete form. Thus, they contain within themselves a variety of personal forms, depending upon the specific features of those individuals. Social phenomena determine individual phenomena as potential social phenomena, and not in their individual specificity. And this is the bridge from the social to the individual dimension. Thus, the mutual determination (and thus connection) between realised individual and realised social phenomena takes place through their potentials. It is the realm of potentials, rather than that of the realised, that connects the two dimensions of social reality.

Individual knowledge

The distinction between concrete and abstract individuals is the basis for the theorisation of individual and social knowledge. *Individual knowledge* is the view of reality from the perspective of the concrete individual, her specific view of reality. This will be the topic of the present section. Social knowledge is the view of reality of social groups. This will be analysed in the next section.

Characterisations such as 'intellectual labour' versus 'manual labour' are inadequate and theoretically unfounded. All labour is intellectual, as it involves the working of the brain, and all labour is manual, including writing down one's thoughts on a piece of paper. Likewise for the distinction between 'mental' and 'material' labour. As we will soon see, all labour is material because the expenditure of human energy is itself a material entity. At the same time, all labour is intellectual, the result of conception, because conception is produced by the whole body (without which the

19

brain could not work) and humans are not automatons who can act without thinking. We must change our perspective. The following paragraph introduces the basic notions and definitions that will guide the analysis in this and the following section.

Here, let us introduce the notion of transformations. We can distinguish between two types, namely objective transformations and mental transformations. *Objective transformations* are the transformation of objective reality, of reality existing outside our consciousness, while *mental transformations* are the transformations of knowledge, be it knowledge of objective reality or of previous knowledge.

It might be thought that objective transformations are material and that mental transformations are non-material. However, b*oth objective and mental transformations require the expenditure of human energy and are thus material processes*. To hold to the thesis of the immateriality of mental transformations is tantamount to denying the results of the medical science of the last centuries, namely its inquiries into human metabolism. Given that – as we will soon see – transformations are the basis of labour, the opposition between material and mental labour is incorrect.[6] It follows that, for the same reason, material labour cannot be contrasted to immaterial labour.

The latter does not exist. Marx does refer to 'immaterial labour' – to the best of my knowledge, only once[7] – but it is clear from his opus that this should not be taken literally. Alternatively, one could hold that mental transformations are material processes, but that the new knowledge produced is not. This thesis would imply that the first law of thermodynamics, that is, that energy can neither be created nor destroyed but can only change form, can be dispensed with. As such, we can only conclude that new knowledge, too, must be material.

More specifically, the reason why knowledge is material is that thinking, the learning process, is an expenditure of human energy that causes a change in the nervous system. This is a change in synapses, the functional connections between neurons in the brain, namely information from one neuron flowing to another neuron across a synapse. 'Recent studies have shown that synapse and spine densities are altered following learning ... Synaptic change clearly occurs with learning'.[8] This

6. I, too, used this incorrect terminology in my previous writings.
7. Marx 1976a, pp. 1047–8.
8. Woolf 2006, pp. 66–7.

is a material change. New knowledge is the *outcome of a material process, of* synaptic changes. *It is this synaptic modification that changes our perception of the world*, that is, our knowledge of it. To deny materiality to knowledge-production and to knowledge means to ignore the results of neuroscience.

In short, objective transformations are material transformations of the reality outside us, and mental transformations are also material transformations, synaptic changes, occurring with learning, through changes in human cognition and consciousness both of the reality outside us and of our previous knowledge.

Let us consider these two types of transformations in more detail. Objective transformations, for example the production of a car, are the transformations by labour-power of the *means of objective transformation*, for example machines, and of the *objects of objective transformation*, for example iron and plastic. In this case, labour-power is the capacity to transform material inputs into material outputs. Mental transformations, or transformations of knowledge, are the transformations by labour-power of the knowledge contained in the workers' labour-power, their *subjective knowledge*, and of *objective knowledge*, into new knowledge.

Objective knowledge is both the knowledge contained in the objective means of mental transformations, for example the information stored in computers, books, and so on, and the knowledge contained in other mental producers' labour-power inasmuch as it has not (yet) become an input of our subjective knowledge, that is, inasmuch as we have not (yet) known it. The knowledge contained in labour-power is both the *means* of mental transformation and one of the two mental *objects* of mental transformation (the other being objective knowledge). Mental transformations are the self-transformation of knowledge. Here, labour-power is the capacity to transform knowledge. Mental transformations can be either individual or social. *Individual mental transformations* transform our individual knowledge and consciousness into a different individual knowledge. They transform individual subjectivities. This is the topic of this section. *Social mental transformations* transform social knowledge, the knowledge shared by the members of a social group, into a different social knowledge. They transform social subjectivities. They will be analysed in the next section.

It follows that individual knowledge is only one of the two inputs of subjective knowledge. The other is social knowledge, insofar as it is appropriated in thought by the individual producer of knowledge. In other words, from a person's or a group's perspective, the (individual or social) knowledge of other individuals or social groups is objective knowledge inasmuch as that person does not know it. However, from the point of view of other persons, our knowledge, inasmuch as it is unknown to them, is objective knowledge, which they transform into their own subjective knowledge when they use it as an input in their production of knowledge.

The moment that we transform objective knowledge by making it our own, we transform it into our individual or social knowledge, into our individual or social subjectivity. But when we interact with other individuals, our subjective knowledge (which, up to this point, was for them objective knowledge) becomes part (an input) of their subjective knowledge, which then exists outside us and, from that moment on, becomes independent of our knowledge and thus for us becomes objective knowledge. Thus, mental transformations are a two-way process: they are transformations of objective knowledge into subjective (individual or social) knowledge and back from (individual or social) subjective knowledge into objective knowledge, according to who the producer of knowledge is.

Table 1. Three categories of transformations.

OBJECTIVE TRANSFORMATIONS

    Individual transformations (individual knowledge)
     /
Mental transformations
  \
    Social transformations (social knowledge)

The distinction between objective and mental transformations is only analytical. In reality, objective transformations require mental transformations, and vice versa. However, when dealing with objective transformations, we disregard the mental transformations needed for them; conversely, when dealing with mental transformations, we disregard the necessary objective transformations. The distinction between objective transformations and mental transformations is only the first step in the analysis. *Labour*, and thus a labour-process, is *always* the combination of *both* types of transformations. These two types of transformations cannot exist independently, and can realise themselves as a labour-process only in conjunction and contemporaneously. But a labour-process and thus labour is *either* an objective labour-process or a mental labour-process *depending upon which type of transformation is determinant* (in the sense spelt out above).

Given that it is not possible to observe which of the two types of transformations is determinant during the labour-process, we can trace back the nature of this process by considering the outcome. Usually, this nature is empirically given. Thus, in the production of a car it is the objective aspect of the output that is empirically given (and, on this basis, we know that the production-process has been an objective one, one in which the objective transformation has been determinant) and in the production of a concert it is the mental aspect that is empirically apparent (such that we can deduce that it is the mental aspect which has been determinant).

However, this rule is not always accurate. What decides the issue is the *social validation of the product*. This social validation occurs at the moment of exchange. Thus, for example, a book is produced and exchanged primarily because of its mental content, while its objective features (clearly printed, graphically attractive, with as few printing mistakes as possible, and so on) are necessary, but subordinate to (determined by) the mental content inherent in the book. Both aspects are potentially present in the outcome before exchange, but only one realises itself and then becomes the determinant aspect. As a short-cut, we can say that the outcome of an objective labour-process is an objective product (commodity) and that of a mental labour-process is new knowledge. But we should be aware that these are the determinant, and not the only aspects of this outcome.

It is well-known that labour is both concrete (the expenditure of human energy in the specific modalities needed to produce the specificity of the products) and abstract (the expenditures of undifferentiated human energy, such as calories, needed to produce value and surplus-value). As a consequence, both concrete and abstract labour can be both mental and objective. For example, the labour of a researcher is mental labour, which is both concrete, according to the object and the outcome of her research, and abstract, because it is at the same time the expenditure of undifferentiated human energy. The labour of a shoe-maker is objective labour. It, too, is both concrete and abstract. The relation between objective and mental, concrete and abstract labour is set out in Table 2 below.

23

Table 2. Four categories of labour

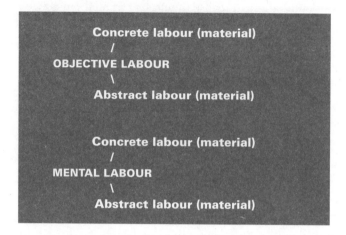

Concrete labour (material)
/
OBJECTIVE LABOUR
\
Abstract labour (material)

Concrete labour (material)
/
MENTAL LABOUR
\
Abstract labour (material)

It is thus clear that abstract labour is not equivalent to mental labour: abstract labour is always material (an expenditure of material human energy in the abstract) and is an aspect of both objective and mental labour. The same holds for concrete labour, which is also always material and an aspect of both objective and mental labour.

The theory here advanced, according to which all labour is material, be it objective or mental, be it concrete or abstract, calls for a definition of material, that is, of what is matter. The concept of matter is a contentious question that goes back to the origin of philosophical thought. In what follows, it will be touched upon only tangentially. It will suffice to mention that matter should not be confused with anything physical, tangible. The identification of matter with physical, tangible reality goes back to Descartes. As McMullin recounts,

> The Cartesian usage of the term 'matter' proved so useful in an age when mechanics was revealing its possibilities that soon the older, more technical senses were forgotten, save by philosophers. In this way, 'matter' passed into general use in Western languages, no longer as a clearcut technical term, but rather as a vague practical label for a varied array of things that the physicist speaks about, one that does not commit the speaker to any particular theory about the nature of these things. This is the sense it retains in ordinary usage today.[9]

9. McMullin 1978, pp. 18–19.

This notion is insufficient for our present purposes, not least because it leaves open the question as to whether knowledge and society are material. Consonant with the theory advanced above, and from a truly materialist standpoint, *matter* is here defined as anything that can be proven to *exist*, that can be proven to be (the outcome of) a *process*, physical, biological, neurological, and so on: *something that comes to be, develops and passes away within a spatial-temporal dimension.* From this perspective, matter is the only form of existence: only matter is real. For example, the notion of God, a specific form of knowledge, is material because it is the outcome of a specific, material process. However, God is not material and thus does not exist since it cannot be proven that God is the outcome of a process, that it came to be, developed and will eventually die. As for society, it, too, is material, given that individual and social relations are processes, interactions among individuals.

This position can be criticised on the following grounds. First, as Lobkowicz submits, 'if *matter* is an all-embracing, absolutely universal concept, then the statement "everything is material" cannot be proven'.[10] The notion of matter here advanced is, however, left unscathed by this objection, since it requires an empirical verification of the existence of a process. Second, 'if whatever exists, is material, what does this tell us of what exists? If nothing but matter exists, what are, then, the properties of whatever exists?'[11] This question is easily answered. Each form of existence of matter has its own specific features. Moreover, all forms of existence of matter share four specific features. Matter, being a process, is movement. Since movement implies space and time, these latter dimensions are also an essential feature of matter. But movement also implies change, and change in social reality implies the contradiction of what has become realised and what exists potentially. Reality and thus matter implies both the realm of the realised and that of the potential. The four essential, general features of matter are thus space, time, the existent and the potential.

In this connection, it is intriguing to note that for Lenin, as well as for the Marxism-Leninism of the Stalin era, consciousness was not thought to be material. Thus, in Lenin's famous definition, 'the *sole* "property" of matter with whose recognition philosophical materialism is bound up is

10. Lobkowicz 1978, p. 165.
11. Lobkowicz 1978, p. 160.

the property of *being an objective reality*, of existing outside our mind'.[12] In this view, 'Matter is a philosophical category denoting the objective reality which is given to man by his sensations, and which is copied, photographed and reflected by our sensations, while existing independently of them'.[13]

Here, the status of material reality is ascribed only to objective reality, only to what exists outside us and independently of our perception and knowledge of it. In other words, for Lenin and Marxism-Leninism, knowledge and consciousness are not matter. The problem with this approach is, if this is the case, what is the ontological status of knowledge and consciousness? If they are not material, what are they? This all-important question remains unanswered. It does not help to distinguish between the material *base* of consciousness and the *essence* of consciousness. This is the distinction made by Kol'banovsky:

> The material base of thinking and consciousness are the nervous processes that happen in man's brain; but the very essence of understanding and awareness that gives to man the possibility of abstracting from concrete objects and phenomena, the possibility to universalize them, to analyse and synthesize, to discover complex connections of the multiform phenomena of reality ... this essence of thinking and consciousness consists of an ideal reflection of the objective world.[14]

This distinction is a subterfuge that cannot escape the question raised above: what is this 'very essence of understanding and awareness', if it is not material? Neither does it help to maintain that, if material reality exists only outside us, psychic events, being subjective, cannot be material.[15] Here, too, the same question arises as to their ontological status.

The question is why Lenin and Marxism-Leninism denied consciousness materiality, thus sliding into a theoretical cul-de-sac. Kol'banovsky uses a somewhat curious argument: given that 'the conflict of materialism and idealism' is the fundamental struggle in the history of philosophy, if consciousness were material then this struggle would become meaningless

12. Lenin 1972, Chapter 5, Section 2; emphasis in the original.
13. Lenin 1972, Chapter 2, Section 4.
14. Kol'banovsky, quoted in Lobkowicz 1978, p. 183.
15. Lobkowicz 1978, p. 180.

and all philosophy would be needless.[16] However, it is clear that it is precisely the recognition that knowledge and consciousness are material that delivers the decisive blow to idealism.

The reason for denying knowledge the ontological status of materiality resides in the acceptance of the reflection theory. The reasoning seems to be that, if matter is only the objective reality, a reflection of matter in our thoughts cannot be material. However, if one deems knowledge not to be material, one lapses into an idealist position. For Marxism-Leninism, idealism is a philosophical position in which matter, by being the objective material reflected in our knowledge of it, exists before ideas and thus somehow determines them. However, the denial of the primacy of ideas in relation to material reality is not sufficient to eradicate idealism. By denying an ideas materiality, Marxism-Leninism creates a much more idealistic position, the admission of something non-material. It is not sufficient to assert the primacy of matter in relation to ideas, as if ideas were not matter; rather, it is necessary to assert the materiality of ideas.

As we have seen above, modern developments in neuroscience show that knowledge is material. Knowledge is matter knowing itself. This is the only true materialist standpoint. There is no 'vulgar' materialism, here, if by 'vulgar' materialism one means the *full* identification of consciousness with matter. It is one thing to argue that consciousness is material, but quite another to reduce it only to its materiality. Consciousness and knowledge are, indeed, material but their materiality – synaptic changes – is only what makes the emergence of new knowledge possible. Synaptic changes do not explain the specificity of the new knowledge emerging through these changes: what does is this knowledge's dialectical, and thus class determination. To put it another way, synaptic changes cause only an undifferentiated change in our knowledge, which may lead in many different directions. The knowledge actually emerging from this material process is the result of its social, and ultimately class determination.

This theoretical position hinges upon the theorisation of social knowledge and of its dialectical interaction with individual knowledge. This is the task of the next section. To anticipate, by definition, different concrete individuals have different views of reality. However, different concrete individuals also have common interests, something that aggregates them (as abstract individuals) into social groups. Thus, each concrete individual belonging to a social group shares a potentially common view of

16. Lobkowicz 1978, p. 182.

reality, which becomes realised as and through the knowledge of its intellectual representatives. These realised social knowledges are internalised and-given a specific form by each concrete individual and emerge concretely as individual knowledges.

At this point, the process starts again when these individual knowledges aggregate again into social knowledges. Synaptic changes are the material processes that lend materiality to the social process through which the different (individual and social) views of reality constantly emerge, change and disappear. Like value, knowledge is both material and social.[17]

Social knowledge

The key to conceptualising social knowledge is provided by the distinction between concrete and abstract individuals as explained in Section 2 above. Social knowledge is neither the concrete individuals' various different subjective views, nor simply their sum total. As a first approximation, we can say that social knowledge is a *commonly shared subjectivity that can reproduce itself irrespective of which concrete individuals share it*. This is a first definition. This commonly shared subjectivity defines a *knowledge-group*, a specific group of abstract individuals. The individuals sharing the knowledge are abstract individuals, since abstraction is made of their specific way of internalising and reproducing that knowledge. Thus, social knowledge can also be understood as the view of reality from the perspective of knowledge-groups.

The question now is: how can concrete individuals, who produce an individual knowledge which is, by definition, different from any other individual knowledge, produce social knowledge? This is possible because from the first moment of (and throughout) their lives concrete individuals experience a process of internalising social phenomena. Through the concrete individuals' internalisation − a process that is different for each individual since it is a part of her personality − social phenomena are transformed from actually existing social phenomena into potential social phenomena existing in concrete individuals' consciousness and individuality. If a certain social phenomenon is internalised by different individuals, inasmuch as different individuals internalise the same class content, its class content becomes the common element unifying the different conscious

17. A concise rendition of the process of production of individual knowledge can be found in the Appendix.

nesses. Then, when concrete individuals engage in individual phenomena, they transfer to those individual phenomena the potentiality to again actualise social phenomena and thus the class content inherent in those phenomena.

It is this potentiality that becomes realised if individual relations become social relations, in other words, if concrete individuals become abstract individuals (replaceable) on the basis of some socially relevant common features. It is for this reason that, as elements of a concrete individual's knowledge, social phenomena are amenable to being actualised again, possibly in a different form, in a different realm of reality, and with a different class content due to the process of determination, as mentioned above. Knowledge is thus social (and this is a second and more precise definition) when it can reproduce itself irrespective of which concrete individuals share it, in the specific sense that different individuals share and reproduce the class content of that knowledge.

But if all concrete individuals develop different forms of social knowledge, only some expand their individual knowledge into forms of knowledge that represent the interests of social groups. They transform those interests into their own view of reality. They become a social group's intellectual representatives. Their individual knowledge becomes, then, their specific, personal rendition of a social knowledge, the specific form of a manifestation of a generality. The importance of these concrete individuals' uniqueness is that it is suited to interpreting collective interests and transforming them into specific forms of knowledge. There may be many concrete individuals with such capacities. Which one of them becomes an actual representative is a matter of the conjunctural situation. In class-divided societies, only some concrete individuals have the possibility to become intellectual representatives, such that a group emerges whose specific (and often paid) function is that of intellectual representatives. This function often requires a special system of rewards and status, such that they develop vested interests in this specific function.

But intellectual representatives do not think in isolation. On the basis of their social practice and their class collocation, they internalise the knowledge produced by the other members of that group and rework it to produce their own knowledge. This process is common to everybody. But in the case of intellectual representatives, the knowledge produced is, as it were, representative knowledge, the knowledge accepted by other members of that knowledge-group even if each individual has his or her own

29

interpretation of that knowledge. The emergence of representative knowledge is the result of the interaction among all the members of knowledge-groups, including the intellectual representative. There might be more than one intellectual representative for each objectively defined social group. It is a matter of chance, who among the many are potentially capable of becoming intellectual representatives of that group, and who actually do so.

Thus, social knowledge has a realised social content, namely, the representation of the interests of a specific knowledge-group. There is no ideologically neutral knowledge. The production (and reproduction) of social knowledge is, at the same time, the transformation of social interests into a commonly shared view of reality. The formation of social knowledge is also simultaneously an ongoing attempt by each group to impose its own view upon that of other groups through the knowledge developed by intellectual representatives. This means that the knowledge produced by the intellectual representatives of a group can incorporate elements of different social knowledges (representing the interests of other groups) up to the point where the social content of that social knowledge may possibly undergo a radical change. At this point, this social knowledge has become the theoretical expression of a different group or class's interests, and thus these intellectuals become representatives of other groups. There is, therefore, no automatic guarantee that a group develops a knowledge (through its intellectual representatives) that represents that group's interests and needs – in other words, that a class becomes conscious of its real interests.

It follows that for members of a knowledge-group accepting a representative knowledge is at the same time their acceptance of the social, and thus class content of that knowledge, irrespective of differences between the individual representations and manifestations of that representative knowledge and irrespective of whether the members of a knowledge-group become conscious of the economic, political, and ideological interests represented by that knowledge. These individual knowledges are different in their personal forms, but are similar from the point of view of their social content. A first approach has defined social knowledge as a commonly shared subjectivity, or as knowledge whose reproduction is ensured by the principle of substitutability. In a second approach, social knowledge has been defined as knowledge that can reproduce itself through the principle of substitutability, that is, irrespective of which concrete individuals share it, in the specific sense that different individuals share the class content of that knowledge. The third and final definition is that knowledge is social when it can reproduce itself irrespective of which concrete individuals share it, in the specific sense that different individuals share its contradictory class content, as represented by the class content of the representative knowledge, irrespective of the specific way each concrete an individual internalises and reproduces that class content.

Capitalist mass media and new methods of communication like information technology are extremely influential in the shaping of collective consciousness by capital under contemporary capitalism. This is an area of research whose importance is vital and which has been the object of extensive research by other authors. However, the capitalist media are not all-powerful in shaping individual consciousness and in aggregating them into forms of social consciousness. Rather, the power of the media is inversely proportional to labour's ability to produce an alternative conception of reality, both social and natural. This is itself premised upon labour's ability to develop a dialectical, class theory of knowledge-production. And this, in turn, is a necessary precondition for the development of a theory of crises and thus for a successful fight against capitalism.

It follows that, under capitalism, the process of the formation of social knowledge is a specific instance of a wider process, of the struggle between the two fundamental classes. This takes the form of the struggle amongst a myriad of phenomena, both individual and social, for the radical transformation in each of those phenomena of one type of rationality (class content) serving the reproduction of capitalism into another, serving its supersession, and vice versa; for the reduction of social phenomena to individual ones; and for the emergence of individual phenomena into social ones (for example, political parties). The two fundamental classes can be theorised at the highest level of abstraction in terms of the capitalist ownership-relation such that labour is composed of all those who do not own the means of production.

However, due to the two opposite rationalities inherent in the ownership-relation, these two classes' form of manifestation is highly fluid and dynamic; it is the product of all the potential and realised social phenomena (individual beliefs, social consciousnesses, traditions, crystallisations of previous struggles, and so on) whose contradictory social content serves the reproduction of capitalism (in the case of the capitalist class) or else its supersession (in the case of the working class). Radically antagonistic movements (for example, women's, anti-racist, student and ecological struggles) are, indeed, elements of labour as a class, just as much as radically antagonistic elements of blue-collar, industrial workers or highly-skilled labour-

31

ers or even isolated objective or mental producers are, inasmuch as they express an anti-capitalist social content, one based on equality, cooperation and self-management. Classes are born at the level of production (of value and surplus-value), but their terrain of empirical manifestation is the result of their attempt to predominate over each other; it is nothing less than a struggle for the change in the class content of each realised and potential individual and social phenomenon. All these struggles are just as important for the development of class consciousness and for the supersession of capitalism. Only the specific conjuncture will tell which one of them is most decisive, under the given specific historical and social circumstances. But the final supersession of capitalism requires the supersession of the ownership-relation.

Thus, other classes besides capital and labour, groups within classes (like women, foreign workers), or groups cutting across classes (homosexuals, ethnic and racial minorities, regional, religious, nationalist, ecological and so on) are not just epiphenomena of little significance for the reproduction of society or for its supersession. Their specific type of oppression, their resistance against it, and the consciousness that emerges from these processes are ultimately determined by the capitalist ownership-relation, since they have ultimately received their contradictory social content from it, in a mediated way and in a transmuted form.

Feminist literature, for example, has rightly stressed that women have specific interests, because they are subjected to a specific form of oppression by male workers both within and outside the household. Their fight for the abolition of this form of oppression in the here and now is not only sacrosanct, but also one of the conditions for the abolition of capitalism. This is because women's oppression by males is a specific manifestation of the struggle between capital and labour, even though it is not reducible to that struggle, given its own specific form of oppression and resistance. Women's oppression is the outcome of the successful attempt by capital to change the social content of the social relation between male and female workers. Labour is thus internally fragmented by capital and made internally contradictory. The productive worker is only a part of it, and is itself internally fragmented and contradictory. However, capitalism can exist without racism or sexism, but not without the extraction and appropriation of surplus-value. Capital and productive labour are an indissoluble, dialectical, unity. To assert that capital cannot exist without labour, but that labour can exist without capital, is to spread confusion, as the supersession of capital also implies the supersession of labour as shaped by capital.

Similar considerations also hold for those social relations that pre-exist the capitalist system, like racism. Having been immersed in a different (that is, capitalist) social context, they acquire a social content serving the reproduction of the ownership (and thus production) relations – for example, lower wages and worse working and living conditions for ethnic-minority groups – or for its supersession: they become determined in their specific form by that relation. As such, they react upon and modify that relation and become historically specific forms of capitalism's reproduction or of radical change.

Labour's knowledge

Theories of the class determination of knowledge are usually rejected with empirical arguments. It is often pointed out that some workers always behave according to their class collocation, some others do so only at particular historical conjunctures, and others never do so. This could show that there is no class determination of consciousness, that workers' choice of labour's rationality is a matter of chance or of non-structural factors. This is the age-old question of whether there is a necessary relation between class location or position and class consciousness.

The first consideration is that this necessary relation does indeed exist in the case of capital and pro-capitalist consciousness. The capitalists cannot continue to be capitalists if they cease to conform to capital's rationality, that is, the exploitation of labour. For them, and for all those who perform the function of capital, their consciousness must conform to their class collocation.[18] Some individual capitalists might hold, at times, a pro-labour rationality. However, this could never become a social subjectivity of capital. The capitalist class expresses various social subjectivities representing the interests of the different fractions within it. But it cannot express social subjectivities with pro-labour class content, in other words commonly accepted and self-reproducing forms of knowledge representing interests antithetical to those of capital.

It is a different matter for workers. They are exploited whether their individual subjectivities – and, at times, their social subjectivities – conform to the rationality inherent in their class collocation or not. The

18. As pointed out above, some agents of production might hold spurious positions, such that they perform both the function of capital and the function of labour. This has consequences for their class consciousness. See Carchedi 1977; 1987.

defining element of the working class's subjectivity is neither a one-sided emphasis on class struggle, nor a one-sided emphasis on the production (ownership) relation, nor a mechanical subjectivism (class consciousness as a reflection, even if distorted, of the objective existence of class). Workers are far from being by definition passive victims of capitalism or the passive bearers of social relations. Nor do they automatically develop an anti-capitalist class consciousness. As concrete individuals, having internalised the contradictions inherent in the capitalist system, they are potentially able to resist and change it. Since individual and social subjectivities are determined by all other social phenomena and, in the last instance, by the ownership-relation, classes, other social groups and individuals constantly attempt to change the social content of the various social and individual phenomena, including forms of individual and social knowledge, to their own advantage. The outcome of the struggle is not determined. However, the fact that labour can express anti-labour subjectivities is no argument against the determination of subjectivity by the ownership-relation.

Just as for capital, labour's class collocation makes itself known at the level of social consciousness. But it does that in a specific way. The capitalist system exhibits a tendency towards its reproduction or towards its own supersession (including a movement in the direction of self-destruction, of which the threat of nuclear wars or the infarct of our ecological system are possible examples). If an objective movement must be represented at the level of consciousness, the movement towards self-supersession produces at the level of social consciousness the daily (re)production of ideas, theories, political and other practices, along with a plethora of social and individual phenomena, consciously as well as unconsciously aiming at this supersession, as well as by the eruptions at critical historical junctures of conscious, collective attempts to supersede the system.

Just as the system oscillates between movement towards reproduction or else supersession, so does society's consciousness oscillate between the dominance of capital's rationality (expressing the reproducing counter-tendency, which could possibly end in the system's self-destruction) and that of labour's rationality (expressing the superseding tendency).[19] While capital consistently expresses capital's rationality, labour expresses now labour's rationality and then capital's rationality, in one sector and then in another, in one place and then in another. There is always a correspondence between labour's class collocation and labour's class con-

19. The argument for supersession as the tendency has been advanced in Carchedi 2008.

sciousness, but in a contradictory way (even in revolutionary moments, labour's class consciousness contains elements of inimical ideologies) and only cyclically, at different times, in different places, and not always for the working class as a whole. Within capitalism, when capital's rationality prevails within labour, there are always knowledge-groups within labour representing labour's rationality (in their many manifestations).

Conversely, when labour's rationality prevails within labour, there are always knowledge-groups holding pro-capitalist forms of social subjectivity. In short, labour's pro-labour subjectivities are internally contradictory, sectoral, cyclical and tendential. When they disappear as realised social phenomena, they are reduced to potential social phenomena, only to reappear again as realised social phenomena in a different form, in different sectors of labour, in different places and at a different time. The outcome is not only a struggle between capital and labour, but also among different sectors of labour expressing different interpretations and different degrees of the two rationalities. The struggle between capital and labour also manifests itself within labour, such that labour can produce different and contradictory types of class consciousness. This is what the history of capitalism teaches us.

It is thus not true to say that there is no correspondence between labour's objective class collocation (in terms of the ownership-relation) and its anti-capitalist consciousness. This correspondence exists, but rather than a general and constant phenomenon, it is sectoral, cyclical, and tendential. Social consciousness arises in the process of the dialectical determination of all social phenomena, including the ownership-relation (which is ultimately determinant). Social consciousness is not determined by class collocation in spite of all other social phenomena, but because of all phenomena, including class collocation, in their mutual determination. It is in this sense that the following should be understood: 'It is not consciousness that determines life, but life that determines consciousness'.[20]

The question then concerns the relation between changes in social 'life', where social life stands for the whole of individual and social phenomena in their dialectical interrelation , and changes in labour's consciousness. Changes in 'social life' change the potential, contradictory, sectoral, tendential and cyclical manifestation of labour's contradictory forms of consciousnesses, but cannot prefigure their specific form, time of occurrence, and class content.

20. Marx and Engels 1970, pp. 36–7.

It is thus mistaken to conclude from the determination of the super-structure by the economic structure (and primarily by the ownership-rela-tion) that knowledge (one element of the superstructure) is determined only by the economic structure. Knowledge in all its manifestations is ultimately determined by the ownership-relation and thus by the economic structure, but the specific features of each form of knowledge are determined by the whole of society (social life) through the process of dialectical determina-tion. In sum, the age-old antinomy – between economic determinism (the superstructure being just a reflection of the base), and mutual interrelation in which the economic base has no preferred role – fades away.[21]

A certain 'radical' sociology usually associated with Analytical Marx-ism searches for the maximum degree of correspondence between objective factors (for example, class collocation, status, education, income) and class consciousness (for example, ideology and voting behaviour). This type of class analysis defines classes in different ways, for example as occupational categories or in terms of levels of skills. It then chooses an indicator of class consciousness, for example, voting behaviour. Then, it uses statistical procedures to relate class consciousness to objective factors. Finally, it con-cludes that that objective factors account for a certain proportion of those individuals sharing a certain class consciousness. Often, one approach is judged to be better than another if an objective factor accounts for a greater number of people sharing a certain class consciousness. Erik Olin Wright is the prominent sociologist who has worked with this methodology within a Marxist perspective.[22]

There are many reasons why this is unsatisfactory. The first one is that this is a Weberian approach, rather than a Marxist one.[23] Within the Weberian conception, there is a simple interrelation between all vari-ables without any ultimately determining factor (ownership-relation). For want of this factor, the necessarily contradictory nature of the phenomena studied (and of capitalism, in the last analysis) remains unexplained. It can be observed and even measured, but there is no reason to assume that this contradictoriness is the essence of this society. That is the class content of this approach.

21. For a discussion of the theoretical quicksand in which the base and superstructure debate sank in the US Communist Party in Hollywood, see Ceplair 2008.
22. Wright 1989; for a detailed critique, see Carchedi 1989.
23. Weber 1949.

Second, there is another reason why the content of this approach is pro-capital: it is a static approach. Statistical correlations do not explain why the same objective factors determine different forms of class consciousness at different times. It relates statistically two or more sets of data at any given moment (a static relation). Empirical studies of the correlation between the same phenomena can be accomplished at different points in time. But consideration of successive static moments does not make this method a dynamic one. The reason is that it considers only realised (objective and subjective) factors, thus ignoring the potential aspects of reality. But it is precisely that potential that accounts for change. A theory that cannot explain movement and change has an inherently pro-capital class content.

Third, this is an individualistic approach. Class (defined in various ways) is seen, here, as an element affecting individual behaviour. The ability to explain individual phenomena in terms of social ones is not a proof of the ability to explain social phenomena in their contradictory movement and thus explain society's laws of movement and change. While there are always very personal and unique causes accounting for each concrete individual's manifestation of (a mix of) one of the two rationalities, at the level of society, there are always bearers of the two opposite types of rationality, because of the opposite tendencies inherent in the capitalist system.

What methodological individualism cannot account for is how and why social determination in one realm of reality (the necessary and constant aggregation of concrete individuals in two fundamental classes, which necessarily express opposite types of rationality) manifests itself as a number of chance events in another realm of reality, that of concrete individuals and, on the other hand, why chance events in one realm of reality (that of individuals) manifest themselves as social regularities in another realm (that of social classes). As far as the class determination of knowledge is concerned, there is no irreconcilability of social determination and free will.

That is not to say that statistical correlations between realised objective determinants and realised determined social subjectivities are useless. On the contrary, they can be helpful and provide useful information: but only if they are part of a dynamic, dialectical approach which alone can explain determination and thus movement, change and ultimately the class nature of capitalism. Outside this approach, they become tools of a conservative social science.

APPENDIX

Objective and mental labour-processes.

Define
O^T = objective transformations
M^O = means of objective transformations
O^O = objects of objective transformations
L^O = labour-power's capacity to transform objective reality

and
M^T = mental transformations, or transformations of knowledge
K^S = subjective knowledge
K^O = objective knowledge
L^K = labour-power's capacity to transform knowledge

Then,
(1) $O^T = (L^O \; \check{Z} \; M^O, O^O)$
(2) $M^T = (L^K \; \check{Z} \; K^S, K^O)$

where $\check{Z}$ indicates labour-power's transformative action; the parentheses indicate unity in transformation; and M^T is both observation and conception. The outcome of M^T is the new knowledge produced. Thus, relation (1) says that an objective transformation is the transformation of the objects and of the means of objective transformation by labour-power. Similarly, relation (2) says that a mental transformation, whose outcome is new knowledge, is the transformation by labour-power of the knowledge which is an element of the workers' labour-power and of that contained in the objective means of mental transformation.

Transformations are combined in labour, both objective and mental. So, if => indicates determination, so that the element to the left of the arrow is the determinant element and that to the right is the determined one, and if the curly brackets indicate unity in determination:

(3) $OLP = \{O^T => M^T\} = P^O$
(4) $MLP = \{M^T => O^T\} = P^K$

Relation (3) says that an objective labour-process (OLP) is the unity in determination of objective transformations (determinant) and mental transformations (determined) whose outcome is an output in which the objective aspect is determinant relative to the knowledge contained in it (P^O). Relation (4) says that a mental labour-process (MLP) is the unity in determination of mental transformations (determinant) and objective transformations (determined) whose outcome is an output in which the objective aspect is determined by the knowledge contained in it (P^K). Some mental labour-processes, like a concert, do not need a material shell.

If relations (1) and (2) are inserted in relations (3) and (4), we obtain

$$(5)\ OLP = \{O^T => M^T\} = \{(L^O\ \check{Z}\ M^O,\ O^O) => (L^K\ \check{Z}\ K^S,\ K^O\ )\} = P^O$$

$$(6)\ MLP = \{M^T => O^T\} = \{(L^K\ \check{Z}\ K^S,\ K^O\ ) => (L^O\ \check{Z}\ M^O,\ O^O)\} = P^K$$

Relations (5) and (6) become *the most concise representation of the production of individual knowledge both for an objective labour-process* and *for a mental labour-process*.

REFERENCES

Carchedi, Guglielmo 1977, *On the Economic Identification of Social Classes*, London: Routledge and Kegan Paul.
– 1987, *Class Analysis and Social Research*, Oxford: Basil Blackwell.
– 1989, 'Class and Class Analysis', in Erik Olin Wright (ed.), *The debate on Classes*, London: Verso.
– 2008, 'Logic and Dialectics in Social Science, Part I', *Critical Sociology*, 34 (4), pp. 495–523.
- 2010, *Behind the Crisis*, Brill: Leiden.
Ceplair, Larry 2008, 'The Base and Superstructure Debate in the Hollywood Communist Party', *Science and Society*, 72 (3), pp. 319–48.
Marx, Karl 1967a [1867], *Capital*, Volume I, New York: International Publishers.
– 1967b [1894], *Capital*, Volume III, New York: International Publishers.
Marx, Karl and Friedrich Engels 1970 [1845–6] *The German Ideology*, edited

by Chris Arthur, New York: International Publishers.

– 1975, 'The Holy Family', in *Collected Works*, Volume 4, Moscow: Progress Publishers.

Lenin Vladimir, 1972 [1909] Materialism and Empirio-Criticism, in *Collected Works*, Volume 14, Moscow: Progress Publishers.

Lobkowicz, Nicholas 1978, 'Materialism and Matter in Marxism-Leninism', in McMullin (ed.) 1978.

McMullin, Ernan (ed.) 1978, *The Concept of Matter in Modern Philosophy*, London: University of Notre Dame Press.

Woolf, Nancy. J 2006, 'Microtubules in the cerebral cortex: role in memory and consciousness', in Jack Tuszynski (ed.), *The Emerging Physics of Consciousness*, Berlin: Springer, pp. 49–94.

CHRYSALIS AND BUTTERFLY, GHOST AND VAMPIRE

Marx's Capital as the 'Gothic critical political economy of zombie capitalism'

Riccardo Bellofiore

A synthetic balance-sheet

Marx's economic theory has always been a 'contested' theoretical object: a site of interpretative conflicts, and of premature declarations of a supposed death. The centre of the discussion of the Second International, and an element that marked the reflections of the Third International as well, was constituted above all by the second and the third volumes of *Capital*. The theory of value was then prevalently understood as a theory of the determination of 'equilibrium' exchange ratios, while the capitalist dynamic was discussed on the basis of the inevitability, or non-inevitability, of a tendency towards a final 'collapse'.

From the first point of view, that of the determination of prices, it was clear that the problem consisted in holding together the 'exchange-values' of the first volume, proportional to the quantity of labour 'contained' in the commodities, and the 'prices of production' of the third volume, including an average rate of profit. The former allowed Marx to analyse the process of extraction of value and surplus-value as result of capital's exploitation of the working class. The latter took account of the fact that, as free competition and mobility of capital exists in capitalism, the total profit had to be distributed between the various branches of production according to the average rate of profit.

The transformation of exchange-values into prices of production seemed to have been left half complete by Marx. The prosecution of the debate, from Bortkiewicz onwards, showed that the bridge between values and prices was fragile. In the 1960s and 1970s, a few decades after the re-commencement of the discussion with Sweezy's *Theory of Capitalist Development* (1942), it was argued that this bridge does not exist. You could arrive at the prices of production from the 'physical' description of the methods of production and of real wages, without beginning from exchange-values, which were then declared to be redundant. Many read Sraffa's book of 1960, *Production of Commodities by Means of Commodities*, in this way. 'Critical' Marxism of a Sraffian accent could do without deriving value from labour, as it was above all interested in a marriage with left-wing Keynesianism. It was a marriage justly rejected by many shrewd critics, for in this perspective the nucleus of economic theory is reduced to bare and meagre outlines; there could be distributive conflict, but money, accumulation and uncertainty remained outside the fundamental analytic. Classes and politics were 'exogenous'. The theory of value and its claim to provide a complete reconstruction of the capitalist economic organism beginning from the centrality of production was, purely and simply, consigned to the dustbin by economists who wanted to present themselves as respectable.

From the second point of view, that of the dynamic theory of capital, the question began from the judgment given on the reproduction schemes of the second volume. Did these schemes perhaps demonstrate that capital not only created its own demand, but did so to such an extent that the aggregate supply is always equal to demand, so that there could only be 'disproportionality' crises? Tugan Baranovski maintained this, as did Hilferding, but also Lenin and Bukharin. Or instead, should one put the accent on the tendency towards the insufficiency of total demand due to the low consumption of the masses? This was what Kautsky claimed. Rosa Luxemburg then radicalised this position, within an explicit critique of some parts of Marx's reasoning. In her opinion, there would necessarily be, sooner or later, a tendency towards collapse due to a lacking realisation of surplus-value, once the capitalist area had been 'globalised' to the point of cancelling the possibility of an outlet constituted by the net exports to non-capitalist areas. The only alternative to barbarism was socialism.

Others attributed the final collapse to another cause, also deducing it from a reading of Marx: the 'tendential fall of the rate of profit'. Certainly, if the accumulation of capital gives rise, following mechanisation, to an augmentation of the value composition of capital (the relation between constant capital and variable capital) superior to the increase of the rate of surplus-value (the relation between surplus-value and variable capital), the average rate of profit has to fall. This thesis, however, doesn't work: the increase of the productive power of labour, as well as the increase of the intensity of labour that results from the technical and organisational innovations, can give way to a rate of surplus-value that rises more quickly than the value composition of capital.

Equally unconvincing is the argument, which once again can be found in Marx, that technical progress would determine an inevitable fall of the maximum rate of profit, that is, with zero wages and maximum working day. According to these hypotheses, the expulsion of living labour from production would make surplus-value fall (due to the limits of the social working day), while constant capital would continue to grow. If this is the case, it is maintained, sooner or later the effective rate of profit must also fall. One forgets, however, that technical progress can reduce the labour time contained in the elements of constant capital, even when these augment in terms of use-value, and the rate of profit can thus rise even in these circumstances. Also in this case, these conclusions were already clear between the 1940s and the 1970s.

Those who privileged the disproportions or the fall of the rate of profit generally maintained a theory of imperialism that is different from Luxemburg's theory. They concentrated their attention on exports of capital, from the 'centre' to the 'periphery', with capital hunting a higher rate of profit. Once again in the second half of the twentieth century, it became clear that reality had silenced both sides of the polemic, just as the theory of underdevelopment and of unequal exchange failed to find empirical confirmation. The 'periphery' has entered into the 'centre'. Financial capital is concentrated in the most advanced countries. Effective demand is politically managed, and the 'old' capitalism is able to create this demand internally. A unipolar and 'imperial' situation has emerged. It is not, however, a pacific ultra-imperialism, in the Kautskian sense, a notion that has been substantially resuscitated by Hardt and Negri. Rather it is a result, unstable and provisional, of the economic and political conflict between the great economic zones, fated to fragmentation.

The reopening of the debate

The debate that we have inherited, from the Second and Third International up until the early years of the 1960s, denied the most interesting and fundamental elements in Marx's thought: the theory of value, as a theory of exploitation in an essentially monetary economy; and the theory of accumulation, as a process destined to run up periodically against the effects of crisis. The reason consists in the fact that, as has been said, the foundation of Marx's theoretical edifice, the theory of value, was read as a theory of equilibrium prices in which money did not play any determinant role, and capitalist reproduction was constrained within the reference to a

43

scheme of proportional, quantitative, 'balanced' growth. Anarchy or collapse were seen as the only alternatives.

From the end of the 1960s, however, a series of interpretative contributions and some re-readings of neglected lines of research were proposed, which changed the theoretical context and reopened the debate. Among the former were the writings of Lucio Colletti and Claudio Napoleoni; among the latter, the works of Isaak I. Rubin, Heinrich Grossmann or Luxemburg herself. This renewed debate led to the rebirth of the studies that have matured in more recent years, which has enabled us to speak of a more accurate 'philological' re-reading of Marx's writings thanks to the new historical-critical edition of the original manuscripts, the *Marx Engels Gesamtausgabe* (MEGA 2).

There have even been decisive philosophical interpretations, albeit quite different from each other, like those of Hans-Georg Backhaus and Helmut Reichelt, Alfred Schmidt and Chris Arthur, Etienne Balibar and Wal Suchting. In Italy, among the most significant new perspectives have been those of Roberto Finelli and Raffaele Sbardella, Massimiliano Tomba and Roberto Fineschi. The latter is a young and rigorous scholar who, as a part of a recommencement of the publication of the Complete Works of Marx and Engels in Italian, is now organising a critical edition and new translation of *Capital* on the basis of the MEGA 2 for La Città del Sole. This edition will take its place alongside that now 'classical' Italian version of Delio Cantimori, Raniero Panzieri and Maria Luisa Boggeri published by Editori Riuniti. There has also been renewed interest in the problematic relation between Marx and Hegel.

Finally, new understandings of the question of value and of transformation in Marx have been published by economists who ascribe significance to the role of money in Marx. Among the most stimulating and promising are those of Duncan Foley and Gérard Duménil; among the most rigid, fascinated by the dream of re-establishing an orthodox position, there is the reading of authors who adhere to the *Temporal Single System Interpretation*. In Italy, an original development of the first position is present in the studies of Giorgio Gattei and Stefano Perri, while the second is promoted by Luciano Vasapollo.

The following discussion should be seen against the background of these works, to which I cannot refer directly due to limited space. I believe, however, that three risks, very much present in many of the positions I have mentioned, should be avoided. First, we should not believe that the 'philological' rediscovery of Marx allows us to reclaim a pure and uncorrupted Marx, reduced to the neutral status of a classic. Second, we should not be seduced into believing that a finally adequate philosophical perspective will allow us to attain, after a long journey, either to an originary Marx or to a 'ever more true' Marx. Third, we need to acknowledge that there is no theoretical self-sufficiency of Marx. Recently published volumes, though important, have not avoided these temptations, such as a volume edited by Marcello Musto or the *History of Marxisms in Italy* by Cristina Corradi. It is hard to imagine something less Marxian, in my view, than a Marx squeezed between philology and philosophy alone. It is certainly of little interest for us today.

Marx is a critic of political economy who, in the first instance, is a critical political economist. He is an analyst of capital and of its incessant metamorphoses; and thus of class antagonism, here and now. This means that we always have to renew the critique of social and economic theory from the beginning, bringing it up to the level of our own times, because the theory we receive from the sacred texts is not enough. It obliges us to get our hands dirty with the reconstruction of the contemporary capitalist dynamic, in order to make a political and social intervention that cannot be thought of as an application of a presumed immutable truth. If this is the case, then Marx should not simply be interpreted, but also reconstructed, and to a certain extent rewritten, in the terms of our own period. To oppose Marx to the various Marxisms is indeed legitimate, but only if we understand that those various Marxisms have had the merit of attempting to reckon accounts with their own historical periods. In other words, the return to Marx is legitimate only if it means a return to Marx's problems, and to a problematised Marx.

Abstract labour and the monetary circuit

In the course of the 1960s, two positions, in my opinion, established the conditions for a different, richer relation to the Marxian legacy. I am referring to Claudio Napoleoni and Augusto Graziani.

Napoleoni is an author whose thought was marked by many discontinuities, and many times his constant reference to Marx gave rise to problematic results. In some phases, as in the first half of the 1970s, he tried to hold together the qualitative and the quantitative sides of the theory of value, without separating philosophy from political economy. However, the point that rightly traverses all his thought is that deriving value only from labour

45

cannot be taken for granted, or reduced to a postulate or to an axiom, which is what was and is done by practically all the old and new Marxisms (positions which then claim an empirical verification regarding the truth or otherwise of what has been postulated).

This position is not only epistemologically naïve; it also cannot be sustained today. Such a tracing back has to be founded on an argumentation, and the argumentation of Marx is anything but acceptable in the form in which he presented it. The problem, for Napoleoni, refers substantially to the meaning of the category of 'abstract' labour. It is an immediately private labour, which becomes social only after production, in the universal exchange of commodities. However, 'abstract' labour is also wage labour, labour commanded by capital. The two definitions do not contradict each other but are integrated with each other, because exchange is generalised only with capital. In these conditions, it is clear that the 'private' labours that are socialised *ex post* in commodity exchange are nothing but the labours of individual workers unified in a 'collective worker', which is nothing but one capital opposed to the others in competition. When wage labour with its struggles carries the rate of profit beneath a determinate level, and puts in question capitalist command within the labour process and the nature of production, the problem of a political exit is posed.

Graziani demoted the transformation problem, re-reading *Capital* as a work in which the theory of value constitutes the macroeconomic and monetary foundation of the class relation between total capital and the totality of workers. Total capital is split into monetary capital (the banking sector) and productive capital (the firm sector): the former has to give general purchasing power to the latter in order to allow it to acquire the only factor that it does not possess, namely, labour-power. On the basis of this privileged access to bank credit, firms, together with the banks, are able to determine the level and the composition of output, and consequently the quantity and quality of the commodities made available to the wage-workers as subsistence. It is not so much through the struggle over the monetary wage or nominal transfers that the condition of the working class can be improved, but by means of struggle in production and/or political intervention. We are dealing here with a macro-social logic that has priority and autonomy over individual behaviours, and not, therefore, with a microeconomic determination of prices of production. Both Napoleoni and Graziani, explicitly or implicitly, but very clearly, were opposed to the positions that wanted to reduce critical political economy to the sum of

Sraffianism and Keynesianism, or to reduce Marx to an orthodox funda-mentalism regarding the transformation or the tendency to collapse.

In this perspective, it seems to me that we have to revisit together the twin questions emphasised by Napoleoni and Graziani: that of the ex-ploitation of (living) labour in valorisation, and that of the (bank) financing for the capitalist production of commodities for the market, in order to gain more abstract wealth. They are twin questions because, seen correctly, it is a case of two different but complementary ways of viewing valorisation as a process of the constitution of the capitalist totality that occurs over time. Exploitation refers to the circumstance that labour-power, acquired by capital on the labour market at its exchange-value (corresponding to 'necessary labour') is 'used' in the capitalist process of production. This means that the amount of living labour extracted is higher than that of necessary labour.

The 'objectualised' labour that is contained in the commodities, and which has evidently to be realised on the final market of commodi-ties, is expressed in a value that, beyond transferring to the future previous labour in the employed means of production, adds a 'new value', commen-surable to the labour spent in the given period. The monetary nature of capitalism implies that the production of the firm sector is activated thanks to a bank-financing equal to the wage bill.

After this initial finance, production occurs, followed by the sale on the market that allows the advanced liquidity to be recovered (by means of final finance, in the terminology of Graziani), thus closing the monetary circuit. When capital has been given back to the banks, there remains a 'surplus' which is potential capital, reinvested on the basis of the (uncer-tain) expectations of future valorisation, and thus also on the basis of the state of the class relations. They are, evidently, two sides of the same coin: because the 'labour' sequence labour-power/living labour/objectualised labour that has to be 'actualised' on the final market runs in parallel to the 'money' sequence of initial financing/production/final finance.

Re-reading Marx in this way opens a path to a triple, decisive step forward. The first dimension consists in resolving the controversial problem of deriving value from labour, referring, as ultimate and founding reason, to exploitation as 'use' of labour-power – namely, to living labour as the only source of the new value added in the period. The second dimension con-sists in reformulating Marx's theory of distribution in such a way that the distribution of this new value between classes, is, from the macroeconomic

47

point of view, adequately defined by the rate of surplus-value expressed in terms of 'contained' labour. The third dimension is to move forward to a unitary reconstruction of the fragmented Marxist theories of crisis, beyond any vision of a collapse, but centred on the social relations of production, in such a way as to open up to the comprehension of the novelties of the current phase.

Before saying something about these points, it is worth returning to the first book of *Capital*. For the distinctive characteristic of the reasoning of Napoleoni and of Graziani, as well as of what will be said here, is to see the heart (the most fertile, but also the most delicate) of Marx's discourse in the first book.

The Chrysalis and the Butterfly

Marx's thesis is that abstract labour (as activity) and value (as its result) already exist, in a latent form, in production. The transition from the potential to the actual occurs in circulation, in the exchange on the commodity final market. In the cycle of capital, value cannot be assumed to be completely constituted only in production, and even less as created only in circulation: the two sides, both false, on which the discussion has concentrated. Rather, it emerges from the intersection of production and circulation that marks the flux of the capitalist process. This has an intrinsic temporal connotation, and it is cadenced by successive phases within a monetary sequence. The generation of new value in immediate production depends on an advance of money as capital, and it has necessarily as its outcome money and more money.

Capital – value, money, which gives birth to surplus-value, surplus-money – presents itself as a totality closed in itself. It appears as a totality that automatically posits its own presuppositions, in a spiral movement. The surplus-value produced, which is part of the living labour spent in the period, becomes the totality that acquires means of production and labour-power; in this way it is able to give rise to a growth of itself, that is purely quantitative.

It is here that Marx can seem like nothing more than the application of the epistemological and ontological Hegelian circle to capitalist reality. But where the point of contact with the philosopher of Stuttgart is at its maximum, there is also the greatest distance. Value and money do not grow by means of ideal parthenogenesis, but only because, insofar as they are dead labour, they manage to include 'materially' within themselves, and to command within a particular form of the organisation of labour, the alterity that is human labour-power, 'attached' to the workers in flesh and bone. Labour-power, acquired with the wage, becomes a (variable) part of capital. Put in movement, as the living labour of the bearers of labour-power, it produces new value and thus surplus-value, which, once invested, constitutes the origin of all capital.

The totality of capital exists only to the extent to which it constitutes a specific social relation of production, which cannot be taken for granted as reproduced mechanically by the totality itself. Rather, the social relation of production 'opens' the totality of capital and to a certain extent 'breaks' it. It is a relation that is articulated in two moments: first, the buying of labour-power on the labour market; second, the use of labour-power in the capitalist process of labour. Circulation and production, once again. Without the first moment – without, that is, the acquisition of the labouring capacity by means of the money-wage – there is no production: because in capitalism conceived in its 'pure' state, the workers are not slaves or serfs, but free and equal subjects, whose labour-power can only be rented for a determinate time. The second moment – production – gives rise to 'exploitation' if it can be argued not simply that the new value is superior to the value of the labour-power, but only if two further conditions are fulfilled: first, that the new value is reducible without residue to the labour objectified by living labour in this period; and second, that the value of labour-power can be reduced to the hours of labour which are necessary to produce the commodities bought by the workers, corresponding to their subsistence. We thus should not limit ourselves to maintaining a philosophical reference to the theory of value as a theory of alienation, or reduce economic analysis to the conflict of profits and wages in distribution. Marx wouldn't have been interested in such generic philosophical criticism, just as he wouldn't have been content simply to repeat Ricardo's political economy.

We can now understand well how crucial the foundation of the connection that refers value to labour is. Without it, Marx's theory of exploitation dissolves like snow in the sun. Why does value 'expose', or 'exhibit', only labour? Marx responds in the first section of the first book: the commodity is the unity of use-value, a product that has utility, and exchange-value, a quantitative relation between commodities. But behind exchange-value is the value that is 'intrinsic' to the commodity, but which has to be presented in a certain relation with money as general equivalent. The crucial point to understand is that the value in the commodity, before

49

the effective exchange with money, is nothing other than a 'ghost'. Marx expresses himself in these terms literally in the German original, and talks of a 'coagulation', a 'congealed state' of abstract labour, that is, of the 'fluid' of generic activity that has produced the commodity: immediately private labour that has to become social in the exchange of commodities. Stated in other words: abstract labour is the same labour that, endowed with concrete properties, produces use-value, but regarded according to that other side of it that involves producing, beyond something useful, also money. This ghost, Marx tells us, cannot remain in this state, mystical and untouchable. It has to be 'embodied', which occurs when it 'possesses' a particular body, that of the money-commodity that functions as universal equivalent, for example, gold. In this way, value is 'incorporated', or 'incarnated', in money. Thanks to the same movement, the concrete labour that produces the money commodity exhibits the abstract labour that produces the commodity. Value and labour are redeemed from an only latent existence in order to finally attain to effective reality.

Abstract labour is 'immediately private' labour, labour that has to become social on the market through exchange with money. The labour that produces money, on the other hand, is the only 'immediately social' labour. The reasoning is clear. A 'social' labour exists at the level of the system; it is the quantity of total labour effectively set to work. Nothing guarantees, however, that the allocation of this labour in the various sectors is in a quantity adequate to social need, or that labour is performed there according to the average techniques and intensity. This can be verified only *ex post*, at the moment of the monetary validation in final circulation. The situation in pre-capitalist societies is different, as is that in a communist society, where labour, Marx says, is 'immediately socialised': it is a part of a social relation with others within the same process of production, regulated *ex ante*. This is only the case, in its way, in capitalism itself, insofar as in the 'factories' labour is 'immediately socialised' in the technical division of labour. Nonetheless, in these conditions the time of labour spent by the collective workers, organised by one capital in competition with other capitals, is subject to the sanction of the market, in order to check *post factum* its adequacy with respect to the social division of labour.

It is important to understand the very peculiar way in which this relation between labour, commodity and money is constituted. The commodities do not exchange because they are made homogenous by money. On the contrary: they exchange for money because they are already commensurable insofar as they are commodities, before the final exchange, as coagulations of abstract labour. Money is passive: a *'Materiatur'*, or a passive materialisation in an adequate material. The 'exhibition' of the commodity in money is however also an 'expression' of value, a movement from the inner to the outer. The latent element, the ghost, governs this relation. How is this possible? The reason is that, for Marx, the latent value is money *in potentia*: something that is already evident in the money price immediately ascribed to the commodity. Insofar as it is 'potential' money – money as a commodity, that is, produced by labour – value already expresses a quantity of labour. Due to this, value is measurable in time-units according to a certain 'monetary expression of (socially necessary) labour time'.

This chain of deductions constitutes one of the high points, but also the Achilles heel of Marx's work. The reason for this can be given briefly. Marx's theory of value is the only theory of value in which the dimensions of value and money are inseparable. Due to this, the origins of surplus-value must be sought within a monetary sequence. Marx's object of analysis is not equilibrium but the formation, 'outside of equilibrium', of economic quantities. The monetary dimension is so essential as to appear at the foundation of the theoretical construction: in the inquiry of the mode of constitution of the configuration of production and exchange as socially and historically determined processes.

Nowadays the situation is very different. Economic theory is divided between, on the one hand, various theories of value, opposed but united in being non-monetary, and mostly obsessed by the dimension of equilibrium (the contained labour of Ricardo, the scarcity and utility of Walras, and so forth); and, on the other hand, monetary approaches, certainly attentive to disequilibrium, but silent about the nature of value. A problem, however, is that, in Marx, the internal link between value and money is given within a theory of commodity-money, while in capitalism money has to be conceived as sign-money.

It is evident, however, that by eliminating the reference of money to gold, Marx's reasoning becomes aporetic. If the path from value to commodity-money is severed, the only dimension of the acts of labour in production remains their 'private' and 'concrete' dimension; those acts of labour are therefore not homogenous. It is money that puts them in a social relation, making them commensurable. Given that money is without 'value', not being produced by labour, the labour theory of value dissolves. This is the conclusion reached by many of the authors of the approach of

51

the so-called value-form. If instead, like the Sraffists, one begins from a productive configuration given in 'physical' terms, the monetary dimension is added from the outside to an already defined economic core.

Proceeding in this way, the very importance of value is cancelled, insofar as the analysis begins when the process of production is already terminated, and before exchange. The extraction of labour from the labour-power that has given rise to potential new value has already taken place. The uncertain translation of that new value into an actual quantity is equally disregarded. In sum, Marx's problems don't exist anymore. It is not surprising that this Marx is declared to be redundant.

We will consider one possibility for exiting from this dead-end. It is clear that when value incarnates in gold as commodity-money, the gelatinous condensation of labour is 'cocooned' into a 'chrysalis'. The miracle, however, has not yet occurred. The chrysalis must transform itself into a 'butterfly'. The body that the ghost of value has possessed needs to find a way of giving rise to more value. One does not see how this can happen by referring to the sphere of circulation.

The ghost and the vampire

Marx explains valorisation by 'breaking' the closure of the capitalist totality, revealing the impossibility of capital as a self-sufficient Subject. We understand this well if we keep in mind the repeated metaphor, to be taken very seriously, of capital as a 'vampire'. It is a 'dialectics of fear', as Franco Moretti felicitously defined it. The analytical content is cogent.

Advanced capital, and the very means of production insofar as they are capital, are dead labour. But it is a 'living dead', a dead that returns to life, sucking the blood of the workers, and thus reproducing death. It is a mechanical monster, that can produce and reproduce itself only by including **within itself** – 'incorporating' in a second sense – living labour-power, from which it extracts living labour. At this point, it becomes animated and moves frantically, 'as if it were by love possessed'; and then, as the implicit reference to Goethe's *Faust* clarifies, it immediately returns to a state of death, given that the living loses its vital essence in the relation with the dead. In a sense, *Capital* is the (critical) political economy of capitalism as a world of zombies – Zombie Capitalism.

Marx's argumentation is, once again, linear and illuminating. Let us examine it in more detail. It is based on an intellectual experiment, a 'counter-factual comparison', which we could call, following Rubin, a 'method of comparison'. On the labour market, the sale of labour-power occurs according to a sale of equivalents. The labour objectualised in the money wage corresponds to the value of labour-power, to 'necessary labour'. In a first moment, the use of labour-power, living labour, is imagined to be equal to necessary labour. In this case, there is neither surplus, nor gross monetary profit (therefore, no surplus-value). The prices would be 'simple', that is, proportional to the quantity of labour 'contained' in the commodities.

In a second moment, Marx considers the variability of the use of labour-power. Living labour is prolonged beyond necessary labour, maintaining prices fixed at their 'simple' ratio. Then there is the emergence of surplus-value, which is owed to 'exploitation', to the use of labour. The transformation of these simple prices, exchange-values, into prices of production is postponed to a successive theoretical moment, when valorisation is completed, and the problem of the redistribution of the new value between capitals will be posed.

From the point of view of capital, there is no (capitalist, abstract) wealth if labour-power – the only element, except for nature, external to capital itself – isn't compelled to work. In order to put the workers to work, it needs to furnish them with the means of production. There is, on the other hand, a substantial difference between labour-power and means of production. Technology fixes the methods of production, the productive power of labour and the real wage. The quantum of labour that is extracted, however, is not determined by technology; this depends on the social relations and thus, also on the organisation of labour and the technology that capital designs in its image, according to a will and a knowledge external to the workers. While the working day is considered as given, Marx introduces a variability of labour's productive power and of the intensity of labour, and therefore a variability of surplus-value. Marx's reasoning thus cannot be supposed to take a given productive configuration for granted, unless we first ask ourselves about how this given productive configuration is 'constructed' by capital as a social relation.

Few interpreters have really understood Marx's comparison in its authentic terms. Rubin, like Croce before him, and like Sraffa in 1960, makes surplus-value and/or gross profit emerge from a reduction of the wage relative to a hypothetical situation in which the social working day remains the same, and the wage absorbs all the value of the product. The paradox is that Sraffa, in his long preparatory studies for *Production of Commodities by Means of Commodities*, had clearly understood Marx's line of reasoning, which is developed on the basis of an extension of the social working day relative to necessary labour. The problem that he chose, however, consciously, was more Ricardian than Marxian. Due to this, he had to return to reasoning in terms of a minus-wage rather than in terms of surplus-labour. This is the reason for which the Sraffists, the followers of Sraffa who miss this dimension and oppose the propositions of the book of 1960 to Marx's theory of value, are not 'Sraffian'. In other words, just as Marx is not Marxist, so Sraffa is not Sraffist.

The originality, not explicit but evident, of Marx's discourse consists in this insight. Only thanks to its own vampire nature, capital transforms the chrysalis – the embodiment, in money as a commodity, of the ghost of value – into the butterfly: value that gives birth to more value, dead labour that returns to life, and amasses every more dead labour. To use the term 'vampire', however, means not only the inclusion of labour in capital, but also the dependence of capital on labour.

What type of dependence is this? Capital needs, within immediate production, the vivifying 'fluid' of labour as activity. It is a movement that removes value/money from its fixity and gives monstrous life to capital. In order to obtain labour in production, capital must first, on the labour market, acquire labouring capacity. But, as we have already recalled, capital cannot really detach either labour-power or living labour from the workers. Capital exists on the basis of what the philosophers call a real hypostasis – at the same time, a substantification of the abstract, and an inversion of subject and predicate. Labour-power, as a part of capital, and living labour, as the activity originating the whole of capital, are the subject, of which the workers are nothing more than a predicate, or an appendage. Capital has bought labour-power from the workers; it has full rights to use it; it owns it. On the other hand, in a completely transparent sense, labour-power and its use are still, at the same time, of the workers. Due to this, it cannot in fact be taken for granted that the labour obtained in production corresponds to that expected by capital on the labour market.

Capital has to win the class struggle in production. It has to keep a possible antagonism at a distance; to conquer hegemony, cooperation, consent. It does this by controlling the workers, and perverting the nature of their labour. It is impossible, from this perspective, to separate the extraction of absolute and relative surplus-value, and thus not to see the simultaneity of the times of exploitation.

A monetary theory of (surplus-) value

The argumentation of the first three chapters of *Capital* Volume One regards money as essentially a commodity. I would argue, however, that this is not the case, due to the reasoning that unfolds in chapters 6 and 7, in the second and third section. There, we find a very solid argument. Commodities are produced due to the 'use' of labour-power, thanks to the 'exploitation' of living labour during the entire social working day. This is the first meaning of exploitation.

Any excess of new value beyond the value of labour-power must, at this point, be referred back to labour. The labour added during the period that 'creates' new value depends on the capacity of the total capital to subjugate, to subordinate the workers. Without this 'real subsumption of labour to capital' – which is based today not only on the dynamics in production but also on the dynamics in consumption and saving – there is no value and surplus-value. In order to be able to use labour, capital must always reproduce its bearer, the worker. Necessary labour is 'necessary' precisely because labour-power and living labour do not float in the air, but are linked intimately to human beings in a certain social and material context. Surplus-value is thus nothing more than surplus labour, expressed in monetary form. This is the second meaning of exploitation, derived from the first meaning focused on the command on all labour, which emphasises the 'excess', the 'difference' of labour objectualised by the workers beyond the labour necessary for their reproduction. Marx's comparison clarifies why this reasoning, at the level of class, must begin from 'simple' prices proportional to contained labour. Prices that are different from the simple prices cannot do otherwise than redistribute this same quantity of new value, thereby allocating differently the same living labour.

This deduction is not linked too closely to money as commodity. It can be reformulated within an exposition of the capitalist process in sequential terms, of a circuit, in a macro-monetary logic. It is true that bank credit, which allows enterprises to finance the activation of production, is sign-money; it is not, therefore, produced by labour. But the wage bill. is regulated by social conflict that determines the real wage of the working class. Given the techniques, the real wage bill corresponds to a certain quantity of 'contained' labour which is necessary for its production.

To put it another way: given the wage contracted on the labour market, the variable capital anticipated in money, i.e. the bank financing of production, has a precise purchasing-power: the number of workers that

55

firms buy with that amount of money. To that employment there corresponds a very determinate 'value' in Marx's sense, the labour time required in order to produce 'subsistence'. In the course of production – if the capitalists succeed in extracting living labour, and in selling commodities according to their expectations – this labour-power spends a certain amount of 'labour', as socially necessary labour time. At the expected prices, this allows a monetary expression to be given to the new value produced before the final exchange. Even if this ideal mass of money, taken in itself, does not express contained labour, the corresponding value can be easily derived from the objectualisation of labour in the commodities to be sold on the market.

We could therefore define a 'latent' surplus-value, a surplus-value *in potentia*. If the selling of commodities on the market proceeds without obstacles, that surplus-value and surplus labour will become actual. Even more: if, with Luxemburg, one acknowledges that the immediate valorisation process is driven by demand – that is, that capitalist firms engage in production because of the effective demand that they foresee; and if we also assume, with Keynes, that these expectations are realised in the short-term without significant errors; then the rate of potential surplus-value, as it results from production, becomes the actual ratio of surplus-value, as confirmed in exchange. This assumption about short-term expectations does not in fact mean that the long-term expectations about the profitability of investments in fixed capitals, which are highly uncertain, are also realised. Rather, it is exactly the instability of investments that is one of the main reasons for the capitalist crisis, of the fluctuations of aggregate demand, and of involuntary unemployment.

A reading of this type has another advantage. As we hinted before, it can seem that, without commodity-money, labours within production are only concrete and thus incommensurable. It can seem, that is, that social homogeneity is granted by nothing other than the eventual monetary validation on the market. Before the final circulation of the commodities, there would not exist either value or abstract labour, not even as latent qualities: admitted, and not conceded, that one can still speak of a value-labour nexus in an approach of this kind. The exclusive stress on money as universal equivalent in the first section of *Capital* leads to this position, once gold as commodity-money is rejected. That exclusive stress is, however, inevitable: at that stage of the investigation, in fact, production is not yet, and cannot be, the object of the analysis, and money seems to be essential only in post-validating labour.

56

The picture changes from the second section onwards. Advanced money capital constitutes a genuine monetary 'ante-validation' of production, or rather, of the capitalist production of commodities. Bank financing of production – which opens the cycle of capital, allowing firms to buy labour-power as labouring activity *in potentia* – is exactly what reinstates the Marxian sequence 'from the inner to the outer'. The monetary ante-validation is followed by the extraction of living labour, which is extinguished in the objectualised labour contained in the commodity: latent value and ideal money, which is actualised on the final market.

The proposed approach also has important consequences for the theory of distribution. As has been said, bank financing of production means that the totality of capitalist firms, defining in an autonomous way the level and composition of output, also determines the real consumption of the working class. Whatever the system of prices, there exists a rate of surplus-value, expressed in terms of 'exchange-values' or of 'simple' prices, therefore in 'contained' labour, which represents precisely the state of class relations on the basis of living labour and of necessary labour, and which is not modified by the transformation. If the prices of production diverge from simple prices, the quantity of labour 'commanded' (i.e., bought) in exchange by net profits will diverge from total surplus-value (as the surplus labour contained in profit-goods), just as the quantity of labour 'commanded' in exchange by the money wage bill will diverge from the value of the labour-power (as the necessary labour contained in wage-goods). Such divergence does not matter, however, for valorisation as a relation between the two classes, which is a macroeconomic reality. That divergence tells us only this: that the producers of the commodities bought by the wage-earners, and the producers of the commodities bought by the recipients of the net profits, gain money amounts whose translation in terms of commanded labour diverges from the labour that was necessary to produce those commodities. There is, so to speak, a duplication of the rate of surplus-value, in the sense that now one has to consider, beyond the relation between surplus-value and variable capital in terms of contained labour, also the relation between net profits and money wage bill in terms of labour commanded. It is a doubling that contributes to obscure exploitation in production.

The shifting of the accent, from the universal equivalent to initial finance, re-establishes the primacy of the class relation in production (sale of labour-power + its use by capital) over final circulation. In the capitalist totality, immediate production, a contested terrain *par excellence*, is securely located at the centre. The circularity of capital, which 'absorbs' labour within capital, is grounded on a more basic linear path from labour to capital, which can never be exhausted in logical deduction, and even less in a totalising and totalitarian 'closed' logic. The critique of political economy is redefined, because in the twentieth century the objects of critique are no longer only Smith and Ricardo, but also Schumpeter, Keynes, Minsky, partially Stiglitz, and also Sraffa himself. They constitute the central elements of a science that has to be taken up and subverted.

Capitalist dynamic and social crisis

A re-reading of Marx's theory of value of this kind has as one of its central elements living labour as the source of new value, and the scandal of the real hypostasis that is radicalised in the real subsumption of labour to capital. Its worth would be much less, however, if it were not developed into a theory of crisis (outside of a breakdown perspective), able to open up to an analysis of contemporary capitalism in its continuities and discontinuities with the preceding phases.

Once armed with the Marxian theoretical lenses reconstructed in the preceding paragraphs, the capitalist dynamic must be referred primarily to the development of the rate of surplus-value, within a non-mechanistic reading of the 'tendential fall of the rate of profit'. Capitalism is characterised by a recurrent technical revolution of the modalities of production, linked in a twofold way to the intensification of labour and the lengthening of the social working day. That can effectively give way to an augmentation of the composition in value of capital that is more rapid than the augmentation of the rate of surplus-value, and thus induce a decline in the profitability of capital. This is what occurred at the end of the nineteenth century, with the Great Depression. The capitalist reaction, then represented emblematically by the introduction of the assembly line and by the consequent revolution in the organisation of labour, however, inverted the situation. Not only the devaluation of the elements of constant capital became ever more significant, but the productive power and the intensity of labour began to grow in such a way as to push up the rate of potential profit. That was in its turn accelerated by bank credit and by financial innovations. The growth of supply was detached temporarily from the development of effective demand.

The extraction of relative surplus-value always carries with it a fall of the relative wage, and therefore also of the share of the real wage in new

58

value. There follows a reduction of workers' consumption within national income. In the abstract, that could be compensated for by investment demand. But up to what point? The reproduction schemes show that, when the rate of surplus-value changes, the conditions of equilibrium change as well. That means that the growth of the rate of surplus-value due to innovations can determine a disproportionality crisis that, when affecting important branches of production, leads to losses, failures and layoffs, and consequently also to a fall of both investments and consumption demand. All that degenerates into an insufficiency of effective demand in the aggregate, and into an interruption of the chain of payments, which in its turn leads to a financial crisis.

This is what happened at the end of the 1920s, with the explosion of the Great Crash, which was then amplified by the deflation of wages and of debts. In the general uncertainty that thus was established, the inevitable fall of demand, but therefore also of supply and of bank financing of production, coupled with the desire without limits of money as a store of value, entrapped the capitalist economy in a situation of 'poverty in the midst of plenty' and in an equilibrium with involuntary unemployment. We came out of this only thanks to WWII, and then thanks to post-war Keynesianism, which was also a military Keynesianism. The subsequent sustained capitalist development rendered possible the extension of the welfare state.

These were the 'Glorious Thirty Years', as Fourastié calls them, the 'Golden Age' of capital of Glyn, the Fordist Keynesian 'regulation' of Aglietta. Between the middle of the 1960s and the middle of the 1970s, for a series of concomitant causes, that period came to an end. Among the reasons for the crisis, central, even if not exclusive, was the explosion of a class antagonism within the capitalist labour process. It was not so much the distributive conflict over the wage, as the workerists and the Sraffists said in unison. More fundamentally, it was a case of workers putting in question the command over labour in the immediate valorisation process, and of the beginning of an unprecedented challenge regarding 'what' to produce and 'how' to produce it.

In the terms of the Marxist categorisation, the point is simple to understand. We had come out of the crisis of realisation of the 1930s with state interventionism, higher public spending (mostly covered by higher taxes) and also an extension of areas not directly productive of (surplus-) value, but providers of demand. That allowed the rate of surplus-value,

59

which grew rapidly, to be confirmed by a politically governed effective demand. The necessity of a continual deepening and intensification of the exploitation of labour, however, remained crucial, and even became more important, in order for the mechanism to be reproduced without problems. The crisis of demand had been tamed, the fall of the rate of profit was checked, but the totality was based increasingly on a rate of surplus-value that had to assume particular values. Thus, the tendencies of the composition of value and of non-productive deductions from surplus-value were beaten back. That dynamic of the rate of surplus-value necessarily at a certain point was seen to be unsustainable socially, even more so in the presence of a 'full employment' of determinate sections of the world of labour. Keynesianism fell 'on the left', before the neoliberal counterrevolution.

In place of a conclusion

It is on this foundation that we can understand not only the crisis of so-called 'Fordism' but also of 'After-Fordism' (misrepresented by the Post-Fordist literature). Capitalism, after the turn of the early 1980s, has produced a 'centralisation' without 'concentration'. The technical unity of production has often been reduced, the world of labour has been fractured. Even without 'concentration', however, technical, financial and productive command has continued to centralise, with mergers and acquisitions. Firms are connected in 'networks', along transnational lines stratified according to an internal hierarchy. Their corporate governance depends increasingly upon financial 'valorisation': that is, on the management of households' savings by the money managers of institutional funds (among which pension funds have an ever more important role). All of that has occurred while so-called globalisation, and within it the new face assumed by Asia with the rise of China and India, on the one hand, and the affirmation in the US of an unprecedented economic policy, on the other, contributed to produce the infernal whirlpool linked to the triple combination of 'traumatised' worker / 'manic-depressive' saver / 'indebted' consumer, about which I have written elsewhere with Joseph Halevi.

In the last thirty years, an increasingly dangerous symbiosis has emerged. It consists, on the one hand, in an excessive push of structural supply (the result of an evermore aggressive competition on a planetary scale between global players) and, on the other, in a stagnationistic tendency on the side of demand (the poisoned fruit of the monetarist counterrevolution of Thatcher and Reagan in terms of its effects on wage consumption, on the public and particularly social spending, and on private investments). The consequent crisis was for a long time postponed thanks to new (non-monetarist) monetary policies of great activism, that have repeatedly given rise to speculative bubbles in the financial markets or in real estate. The growth of the value of the 'assets' pushed up the internal demand in some countries, allowing the practice of neo-mercantilist policies in others, where growth was driven by net exports.

It is thanks to this genuine 'real subsumption' of labour to finance and to debt, and to the consequent private Keynesianism paradoxically driven by the speculative financial bubbles, that consumption demand has been maintained, wage compression notwithstanding. At the same time, the process trapped the world of labour in insecurity and in fragmentation. It was a process that was not only unstable, but ultimately unsustainable. In fact, it is within this internal connection between so-called 'financialisation' and the causalisation of labour – precisely the two twin arms by means of which capital exited from the 'social' crisis of the 1970s – that we can understand the new systemic crisis of capital 40 years later: that is, within a 'secular' re-reading of Marx's theory of crisis.

One cannot respond to this world with the nostalgia of wage conflictualism or of budget deficits. They do not help us to understand the novelty of the dangerous times in which we live, nor do they allow us to confront it with any real efficacy. We can exit from this situation only by taking up again the instruments of analysis individuated by Marx's theory of value: money as capital, living labour as source of new value. This means that proposing an analysis of class that extends into an intervention of economic policy poses immediately and primarily the question of what and how to produce: a structural redefinition of supply and of demand, which assumes the point of view of labour as central. It is a theme that, to the surprise of many, including a left that flees from labour or reduces it to its redistributive dimension, has returned to currency in last years, thanks once again to the materialisation of a Great Crisis; that is, due to hard social objectivity.

Certainly, this is not a 'fundamentalist' or orthodox perspective. Equally certain, it does not drown the reference to Marx in an indefinite 'critical' Marxism, in which the theory of value vanishes without a trace, class conflict becomes an ideological postulate, and money something that is added to a logical skeleton of commodities that produce commodities.

A Marxism without Marx: without the Marx of *Capital*. Yet perhaps this perspective amounts to a new revisionism? Yes and no. Yes, because it is precisely the lesson of Marx that obliges us to rewrite constantly the critique of political economy: it sets us the task, that is, of a constant 'revision'. Yes, again, because it takes up the problem from Marx, without needing to repeat his solutions faithfully always and everywhere, according to the letter. No, because within the horizon that I suggested, the elements of Marx that remain most alive are those which the revisionists either haven't seen or have always contested: the monetary labour theory of value, accumulation as disequilibrated process, the theory of crisis. No, finally, because the very 'centralisation without concentration' and the 'real subsumption of labour to finance and to debt' have been the factors that have eroded from within the capitalist growth of the so-called 'new' economy, causing it to fall: making more and not less urgent the reunification of the world of labour.

We will only be able to speak of 'socialism' and 'communism' in the twenty-first century if we learn how to 'deconstruct' theoretically, and to transform practically, the capitalism of the twenty-first century. If Marx alone is not enough to achieve this, it is certain that without Marx – without the Marx of value, of money and of crisis – a perspective of this type simply will not be possible.

A SHORT HISTORY OF
MARX'S ECONOMIC CRITIQUE[24]

Michael Heinrich

Marx and Marxism

> Men make their own history, but they do not make it just as they please; they do not make it under circumstances chosen by themselves, but under circumstances directly encountered, given and transmitted from the past. The tradition of all the dead generations weighs like a nightmare on the brain of the living.[25]

These very often quoted sentences from the *Eighteenth Brumaire* also apply to every debate on Marx's work. Of course, this is 'our' debate, but we do this in a certain historical situation, with a background of certain political experiences and theoretical debates, from which specific questions and discussions emerge, ones which looked totally different a few years ago and will look different again a few years later.

The rise of the Social-Democratic workers' movement before 1914, its split into a Communist and a Social-Democratic wing after the First World War, the experience of fascism and of Stalinism, the Cold War following the Second World War, the eruption of May '68, the decay of the new movements and the disappointed hopes of the 1970s, the collapse of the Soviet Union, the globalisation processes of the 1990s, and the subsequent growth in worldwide protest actions, all established totally different political and social relations in which the discussion of Marx's work took place. The problems considered as urgent are different, other certainties are put into question, and different conclusions are drawn.[26]

Not only the historical context in which the debate on Marx's work

---

24. A revised version of Heinrich 2009a.
25. Marx 1979, p. 103.
26. Indeed, there are several histories of Marxism, in which different Marxist thinkers are presented (see, for example, Vranicki 1972; Anderson 1976; Kolakowski 2005; and on economic theory especially, Howard and King 1992), but there is not yet a comprehensive history of the reception of Marx. Important approaches to this can be found in Elbe 2008, Hoff 2009, and in English in Elbe 2013.

took place, but also the work itself to which the debate was linked, changed significantly several times during the twentieth century. Many of Marx's writings central for current debates were not published until decades after his death. Especially important was the first complete edition of Marx and Engels's works (*Marx-Engels-Gesamtausgabe*, *MEGA*) which began in 1927 under the direction of David Riazanov. During the early twentieth century, the three volumes of *Capital* counted as Marx's most important work, outshining all his other writings.

At the beginning of the 1930s, this changed fundamentally. The first publication of the *Economic and Philosophic Manuscripts of 1844* and of the *German Ideology*, dating from 1845, in the *Marx-Engels-Gesamtausgabe*, brought the young 'philosophical' Marx to the fore, and they were immediately used against the dominant interpretation of Marx-as-economist.[27] Fascism and Stalinism ended such discussions. However, the first *MEGA* project was unable to keep going and hence remained unfinished.[28] As a final result of the original *MEGA* series, in 1939–41 the *Grundrisse* – written in 1857–8 – was published for the first time in the Soviet Union, though it was only fully taken into account in the 1960s. On the basis of the *Grundrisse*, not only many methodological questions, but also the broader context of Marx's social and historical considerations, which constituted the background of *Capital*, became clearer. The difference between the young philosophical Marx and the late Marx-as-economist was also discussed in a new light: *Grundrisse* constituted the mediating link between the early and the late Marx.[29]

Marx's texts were only published in their entirety with the new (second) *MEGA*, which was begun in the middle of the 1970s.[30] This not

27. See, for example, Marcuse 1932.
28. Riazanov, a critical and independent mind, was appointed by Lenin as the first director of the Marx-Engels Institute in Moscow. He was dismissed by Stalin in 1931, and later exiled to Saratov, where he was executed in 1938 after a short show-trial. The work on the first *MEGA* project was abandoned in the 1930s, after the publication of 12 volumes.
29. For the current discussion about the *Grundrisse*, see Musto (ed.) 2008.
30. The first volume of the new *MEGA* was published in 1975 by the Institutes for Marxism-Leninism in East Berlin and Moscow. With the end of the GDR and the USSR, the editorial rights were transferred to the *Internationale Marx Engels Stiftung (IMES)* in Amsterdam. The *MEGA* is a critical edition, which means that it consists of all texts and manuscripts in the form in which they were transmitted, whereby all variants as well as the condition, the origin and the transmission of the texts are explained in the publishing apparatus. Each volume of the *MEGA* consists of two sub-volumes, one with the published texts, and a second containing the publishing apparatus. The *MEGA* is divided into four parts: Part 1 comprises all 'works' except *Capital*; Part 2 comprises *Capital* and the preparatory manuscripts; Part 3 contains the letters (also the letters addressed to Marx and Engels); and Part 4 contains extracts. There are 114 volumes planned, 60 have been published until the end of 2013.

only produced a whole series of first editions, such as the complete *Economic Manuscript of 1861–63* (of which only the *Theories of Surplus Value* had previously been published), or Marx's original manuscripts for the second and third volumes of *Capital*.[31] It also meant that well-known texts were now presented without editorial changes, and this not simply as a purely philological sophistication, such changes influenced the understanding of the text. As in the case of the *Economic and Philosophic Manuscripts of 1844*, for example, or the *German Ideology*, earlier editions had always attempted to produce a complete work 'in the spirit of the author', by reordering the text, inserting subtitles, and so on.[32] Hereby a certain interpretative framework was implemented by means of the editorial method used.[33]

In every discussion of Marx, one is confronted with the tradition of 'Marxism'. Here, too, we can say that it 'weighs like a nightmare on the brains of the living'. 'Marxism', however, is an ambiguous cipher. On the one hand, it represents the transformation of Marx's critique into an all-encompassing worldview [*Weltanschauung*], into a 'system' which claims to possess, at least in principle, the fundamental knowledge concerning history and society. This transformation was used to legitimise the policy of the 'Marxist' Social-Democratic Party in Germany before the First World War and, after the War, the Communist Parties' claim to authority. After Lenin's death, Marxism was canonised as 'Marxism-Leninism'. It was largely displayed as a series of formulas to be learned and believed in and as an ideology used to legitimise extremely repressive régimes.

31. The most complete English edition of the works of Marx and Engels are the 50 volumes of the *Marx-Engels Collected Works (MECW)*. However, *MECW* does not contain all texts published in *MEGA*. Not only are excerpts and letters addressed to Marx and Engels omitted, but also Marx's original manuscripts for Volumes II and III of *Capital*.
32. In the *Economic and Philosophic Manuscripts of 1844*, for example, there exists no chapter entitled 'Critique of the Hegelian Dialectic and Philosophy as a Whole' (which we can also find in the *MECW*: see Marx 1975c). This chapter is an editorial compilation of single paragraphs criticising Hegel's philosophy in different contexts in the manuscript. Even more serious editorial interventions can be found in the chapter on Feuerbach in the *German Ideology*. The *MEGA* volume with the *German Ideology* has not yet been published, but there is at least a pre-publication of the so called chapter on Feuerbach which is not at all a "chapter", that clearly shows the differences with the traditional editions (see Marx, Engels and Weydemeyer 2004).
33. On the history of the publishing of Marx's writings, especially those concerning economics, see Hecker 1999; Marxhausen 2006; 2008; and also the special issues 1–3 of the *Beiträge zur Marx Engels Forschung Neue Folge*.

On the other hand, 'Marxism' also consists of an attempt to break up and to fight these dogmatisms and the effects of dominance which flow from it. The twentieth century witnessed various different renovations of Marxism with an emancipatory and anti-authoritarian purpose. But the question must nevertheless be asked: what is it, precisely, that requires renovation? What does 'Marxism' mean? Does it just mean reference to Marx, bowing to his big head? Or do we, indeed, understand Marxism as a 'system', a 'worldview' [*Weltanschauung*], but this time without the dogmatism of 'orthodox' Marxism (whereby what is considered as an expression of dogmatism, changes historically)?

It is widely known that Marx, confronted with the first beginnings of 'Marxism', categorically declared '*Je ne suis pas Marxiste*'.[34] But it was also argued that Marx said this only in relation to early French Marxism, which originated by the end of the 1870s, and that Marx was, on the contrary, not averse to a systematisation of his and Engels's views.[35] Indeed, the circumstances in which this phrase was formulated can be interpreted in different ways. Nonetheless, Marx was no less categorically opposed to the assumption that he had 'established a "socialist system"'.[36] Above all, there are no texts to be found that show directly or indirectly that he wanted to build any kind of -ism. On the contrary, he stressed again and again the demand for recognition of the 'scientific' character of his work,[37] an entitlement, it should be said, which he does not deny to the representatives of classical political economy either.

34. Engels quoted this phrase, expressed by Marx to his son-in-law, Paul Lafargue, several times (see Engels 1990 p. 70; 1992, p. 356; 2001, p. 7). See also Marx's complaint to Engels regarding 'the "Marxistes" and "Anti-Marxistes" having, at their respective socialist congresses at Roanne and St-Étienne, *both* done their damnedest to ruin my stay in France' (Marx 1992a p. 339: emphasis by Marx).
35. See Walther 1982, p. 950.
36. Marx 1989, p. 533.
37. He writes in the preface of *A Contribution to the Critique of Political Economy. Part One* that he examines the 'system of bourgeois economy' (Marx 1987a, p. 261), but not that he wants to set up his own system. Concerning this book, he writes in a letter to Weydemeyer of 1 February 1859: 'I hope to win a scientific victory for our party' (Marx 1983a, p. 377). Marx situates his own work within the progress of the science of economics, with the certain claim of revolutionising this science (see his letter to Kugelmann of 28 December 1862: Marx 1985a, p. 436). And in the preface of the first edition of *Capital* there is no celebration of the founding of any new -ism, but he emphasises clearly: 'I welcome every opinion based on scientific criticism'''(Marx 1976c, p. 93). Marx has only contempt for any 'accommodation' of science: 'But when a man seeks to *accommodate* science to a viewpoint which is derived not from science itself (however erroneous it may be) but from *outside*, from *alien, external interests*, then I call him "*base*"' (Marx 1988–94, Vol. 31, p. 349: emphasis by Marx).

Science and worldview, however, do not just fit together as simply as one would expect from the phrase 'scientific worldview' [*wissenschaftliche Weltanschauung*]. The aim of a worldview is to provide an orientation. Particular events are to be put into context. This context must be made understandable by returning to the permanently valid principles which underlie it. Science seeks to understand relationships and to explain their origin, but science is clear about the fact that its knowledge is provisional and that nothing, not even its own results, is exempt from scientific criticism.

A worldview can only provide this desired security insofar as it claims to have finally discovered the *ultimate* foundations and principles about which there can be no more doubt. At the same time, these fundamental principles represent, in most cases, a mixture of general ideas about the world and the generalisation of a given level of scientific knowledge. As a consequence, they come into conflict with new scientific results as scientific knowledge advances. As a reaction, these fundamental principles are interpreted in such a general way that they do not contradict scientific results but the principles themselves become empty of all concrete content: they lose any meaning. Both can be said about the 'philosophical' foundation of the 'Marxist worldview'. 'Materialism' and 'dialectics' play an important role for Marx precisely not as principles of a worldview, but rather as particular *strategies* of research and presentation [*Darstellung*].[38]

Engels's *Anti-Dühring* played a not unimportant role in the process of the formation of 'Marxism' as a worldview. In the early 1870s, the writings of the Berlin academic Eugen Dühring where considered in parts of the fast-growing ranks of German Social Democracy as the complement and philosophical basis for Marx's analyses. Engels, mainly under pressure from Wilhelm Liebknecht, opposed Dühring's views but, in order to do this, he was obliged to follow him into different fields of knowledge and to present alternative views. This critique – and Engels was clearly aware of its limits – became quickly transformed into the positive foundation of a kind of 'Marxism'.

This process was not only facilitated by a series of problematic formulations and arguments on Engels's part,[39] but also by the existing

38. In Heinrich 2008a, I outline the meanings of 'dialectics' and 'materialism' for Marx beyond any worldview.
39. There are plenty of debates on the question of the theoretical differences between Marx and Engels, whose existence was denied from the outset by Marxism-Leninism: see, amongst others, Mehringer and Mergner 1973; Kittsteiner 1977; Liedman 1986; Arthur 1996; and Steger and Carver 1999.

need, felt by a more and more self-confident working class, to have its 'own' worldview offering an orientation which could be counterposed against the bourgeois worldview. Furthermore, there was the search by the party bureaucrats for simple formulas and explanations useful in everyday propaganda. After Engels's 1895 demise, this 'Marxism' was build into a 'system' mainly by Karl Kautsky. Kautsky, after Engels's death, became the leading theoretician amongst German and international Social Democracy. Lenin's Marxism was fundamentally influenced by Kautsky's views – Lenin only started criticising Kautsky in 1914, when the SPD gave its support to the German war policy.

The development of Marxian thinking

From this emphasis on the differences between Marx's writings and the different forms of Marxism, however, we cannot conclude that we are able to return to an unadulterated, authentic Marx. A whole series of clearly false interpretations can be easily rejected, but we cannot escape from the fact that we are explaining Marx in the context of certain political and social circumstances and that they have a certain influence on our explanations. An authentic, ever-present Marx, waiting to be finally discovered by us – this is pure fiction. But the issue is more than that: what is it in Marx's work that we want to explain? And anyway, to what extent can we consider his work as a unified whole?

For more than forty years, Marx was extremely active both at the political and scientific levels. His themes, his opinions, his theoretical coordinates, and his political reference points, all experienced a whole series of changes and shifts – which is no surprise, in the case of someone like Marx, who was so learned and reflected so much. In the discussion on Marx, the matter of the relationship between continuity and rupture within his intellectual development is an extremely controversial one. Did Marx find his own critical approach early on (somewhere in his *Dissertation* dating from 1840–1 or in the *Contribution to the Critique of Hegel's Philosophy of Law* from 1843), an approach which he simply developed and unfolded during the following years? Or is there a (or several) breaking point in Marx's development, such that we could make the distinction between an 'early' (philosophical) Marx and a 'late' (economics-focused) Marx?

This question has been vehemently debated, especially since Louis Althusser's assertion in *For Marx*[40] of the existence of a sharp 'epistemologi-

40. Althusser 2010.

cal break' between the young and the old Marx, a split that was linked, in the first place, to the *German Ideology*, written in 1845–6.

Those in favour of the thesis of continuity are having a hard time at the moment, because we have clear indications that the *German Ideology* expressed much more than simply a gradual progression in Marx's thinking. In the only text containing an outline of an intellectual autobiography of Marx, the 1859 'Preface' to *A Contribution to the Critique of Political Economy. Part One*, it is said of the *German Ideology* that it was 'in fact to settle accounts with our former philosophical conscience'.[41] This is a radical formula which raises a challenge to those who maintain a far-reaching continuity in Marx's work, since they must then explain the meaning of this 'philosophical conscience', with which Marx 'settled accounts', without there being any break in his theoretical development.

Whilst reading the *German Ideology*, it very quickly becomes clear with whom Marx 'settles accounts': it is with Ludwig Feuerbach, who was still praised to the heavens in the *Economic and Philosophical Manuscripts of 1844* and in the *Holy Family*, published in spring 1845. Marx's 1844 concept of a human 'species being' [*Gattungswesen*] from which humans are alienated under capitalism, was profoundly influenced by Feuerbach's philosophy. In 1845, in the *German Ideology*, we witness a fundamental critique of the philosophy of human essence as well as of the concept of an alienation from this essence. After 1845, Marx no longer spoke of an 'essence of the human being'.[42] Against 'philosophical speculation' the *German Ideology* opposes, to the greatest possible extent, 'real science'.[43]

However, what this science should examine, what its starting point should be, and so on, was only explored at a programmatic level. The critique of the previous 'philosophical conscience' left an empty space, momentarily filled in the *Theses on Feuerbach* and the *German Ideology* with the

41. Marx 1987a, p. 264.
42. I explain the break with the philosophy of the essence – which was, admittedly, only a part of the break with the theoretical field of political economy realised by Marx – in Heinrich 2006, pp. 121–57). There, I demonstrate in detail that Marx's critique in *German Ideology* also aims at the views held previously by Marx himself.
43. In the *German Ideology*, it is expressed as follows: 'Where speculation ends, where real life starts, there consequently begins real, positive science, the expounding of the practical activity, of the practical process of development of men. Empty phrases about consciousness end, and real knowledge has to take their place. When the reality is described, a self-sufficient philosophy [*die selbständige Philosophie*] loses its medium of existence' (Marx and Engels 1976a, p. 37).

vague concept of 'practice'. 'Practice' now means the concrete, the empirical in contrast to the philosopher's abstractions. Nevertheless, until 1857, Marx understood 'practice' not as the cause of explanation, but rather, as the object of explanation.[44] That is why one will search in vain in the *Grundrisse* or in *Capital* for any clear references to the concept of 'practice', which abound in the *Theses on Feuerbach* and the *German Ideology.*

Marx sees 'real science' first of all in the most advanced parts of bourgeois social sciences. He grants bourgeois historians their analysis of classes and of class struggle[45] and he uses Ricardo's political economy in 1847 in his critique of Proudhon, in the *Poverty of Philosophy*. He has the highest praise for Ricardo's analysis of the capitalist mode of production. The only criticism of Ricardo that Marx has at that time is the reproach that Ricardo does not consider the relationship of capital as a historically transient form, but as an everlasting relation of production.[46]

A fundamental critique of bourgeois science, and not simply another usage, begins only in the 1850s, after Marx had emigrated to London. As he explains in the 1859 'Preface', he starts 'again from the very beginning'.[47] The extensive so-called 'London notebooks' emerge, which contain several thousand pages of excerpts and commentaries on economic literature. For Marx, these notebooks remain a major source for all his later economic manuscripts.[48] The early 1850s see the first doubts concerning Ricardo's theory on money and his theory on ground rent. These doubts grew and ultimately led to the fundamental critique of political economy (not only Ricardo's). That manuscript which was much later published as the *Grundrisse* originated in 1857-8. During the work on this manuscript, Marx designed a plan to realise a 'critique of political economy' in six books (capital, landed property, wage-labour, the state, foreign trade, the world market). In the first book, the distinction was to be made between 'capital in general' and the 'competition between many capitals'.

This difference expresses the understanding, which grew in the 1850s, that competition between capitals was not the cause of the laws of the capitalist mode of production (as explained by the bourgeois economists and accepted without criticism by Marx in the late 1840s) but merely the form in

44. See Heinrich 2004.
45. See his letter to Weydemeyer of 5 March 1852: Marx 1983b.
46. See also Marx's letter to Annenkow of 28 December 1846: Marx 1982.
47. Marx 1987a, p. 265.
48. These notebooks will fill more than four *MEGA* volumes; they are included in *MEGA* II/7–11, but as yet only MEGA II/7–9 have been published.

which those laws worked. The fundamental laws of the capitalist mode of production – in contrast with bourgeois economics – had to be described and explained beyond the terms of the competition between capitals. Such an explanation was to be carried out in the section on 'capital in general'.

In the aforementioned 1859 'Preface', he announced his plan for the six books. The 1859 book was to be only the beginning of the *magnum opus*. The continuation can be found in Marx's largest manuscript (*Economic Manuscripts of 1861–63*). It was published in its entirety for the first time in 1976–82 in the new *MEGA*; before that, only the *Theories on Surplus Value* had been published.[49] But here, we see, Marx's original intention met with quantitative as well as conceptual problems. It became clear to Marx that he could not complete the six planned books in a foreseeable period of time. But there were also limitations at the conceptual level, in the separation between 'capital in general' and 'competition': the plan to develop a certain content (expressed in the series of categories from value to profit and rent) at a determined level of abstraction (abstraction from the various capitals) was not feasible in the way it was planned. He had to search for a new structure of presentation without giving up on the old insights.[50]

Marx now decided not to publish a continuation of the 1859 text, but to write a separate work – *Capital* – which would consist of four books (the production process, the circulation process, the total process, and the history of the theory). After 1863, Marx did not again mention the planned six books or 'capital in general'. Instead of the latter, we see 'individual capital' and 'total social capital' being discussed and presented at different levels of abstraction. A draft for the first three volumes of this new concept of *Capital* was written in 1863–5, and the first volume finally published in 1867. The second German edition, with considerable changes, appeared in 1872–3, and further changes were made in 1872–5 in the French translation of the first volume. New outlines for the second and third volumes were developed from 1867 up to the end of the 1870s. Nearly all of those outlines have now been published in the second set of *MEGA*.

Likewise, the various manuscripts on the critique of political

---

49. The whole manuscript can be found in *MECW*, Vols 30–4 (Marx 1988–94).
50. Whether or not 'capital in general' still plays a role in *Capital* is debated in the literature. That it no longer plays a role and why, has been substantiated in Heinrich 1989; and also in Heinrich 2006, pp. 179–95. For a detailed critique of this view, see Moseley 2007. A recent critique by Moseley and my answer to it, can be found at http://monthlyreview.org/features/exchange-with-heinrich-on-crisis-theory

economy, beginning in 1857, do not belong to the same conceptual whole. We can distinguish between two different conceptual projects: a six-book project with the distinction between 'capital in general' and 'competition of many capitals' as its central theoretical concept, and then the four-book plan of *Capital* covering only the first three books of the original project, but with an altered theoretical framework. There exist several drafts for each of these projects.[51]

After 1845, Marx further developed his views, including quite fundamentally those on other subjects which we do not deal with here. Elements of a teleological philosophy of history, which are clearly expressed in the *Economic and Philosophic Manuscripts of 1844*, still remain after 1845, but they are explicitly criticised in the 1870s.[52] Eurocentric points of view which can be found in Marx's articles during the 1850s were likewise increasingly surpassed during the 1870s.[53] Marx's theories on the state and on class also changed substantially after 1845.

Already, then, it should be clear from this short and incomplete sketch of the development of Marx's thinking, that there is no single unified work, one which is continuously perfected. Nor can we assume that there is a simple divide between a younger, philosophical Marx and a later Marx, working on a critique of political economy. Rather, we find in Marx a whole series of attempts, discontinuations, shifts, new concepts and new beginnings. All of Marx's central projects remained unfinished and shifted some central point or other throughout their elaboration.

Because of this, we cannot clearly answer the question as to how far these projects have advanced. The idea that there is an *oeuvre*, written by Marx, that exists as such and should simply be read and understood beyond all preconceived prejudice, is naïve in the extreme but nevertheless commonplace. To speak of 'Marx's *oeuvre*' presupposes a predetermined construction in the mind of the reader. This construction will never be produced independently of the political and social situation in which it is built. These 'circumstances directly encountered, given and transmitted from the past', which define our problems, conflicts and questions, and which were mentioned by Marx in the quote at the beginning of this essay enter into that construction.

51. For more details, see Heinrich 2009b; and, in an extended version, Heinrich 2011.
52. For more on this, see Heinrich 1997.
53. See Anderson 2010; Lindner 2010

But this constructed character does not mean that through refer-ring to the circumstances one can justify any interpretation. Any serious debate about Marx needs to relate in a precise way to his texts. Instead of considering the many Marxian texts as a stone quarry in which one can freely serve oneself, we should, first of all, deal with the constitutive elements and the structure of the work formed by the main categories and then try to base our own attempts at interpretation on the texts themselves.

Marx's *Capital*

In his preface to the first edition, Marx announced that *Capital* was going to consist of the four volumes previously mentioned. He himself could only publish the first volume in 1867. The second and third volumes were published by Engels after Marx's death, in 1885 and 1894 respective-ly. Finally, in 1905–10, Karl Kautsky published the *Theories of Surplus Value*, widely considered to be the fourth volume, on the history of economic theory, which seemingly constituted the completion, after forty years, of Marx's major work.

But things are not that simple. The *Theories of Surplus Value* trace, with many digressions, the history of a single category, but they do not sys-tematically discuss the 'history of theory' Marx announced that the fourth book of *Capital* would comprise. The text of *Theories* is part of the *Economic Manuscript of 1861-63*, which was written before the concept of *Capital* emerged. As PEM showed convincingly,[54] the *Theories of Surplus Value* are an important step on the road to *Capital* in which Marx comes nearer to the solution of a series of objective problems, but this is still a long way from the history of theory, which should be built, as a conceived history, on the basis of the solution of those problems.[55]

There are also problems with Volumes II and III published by En-gels. Although in his prefaces Engels made himself accountable for his edito-rial activity, the extent and the type of his interventions into Marx's texts are not clearly visible to the reader. The volumes published by Engels demon-strate, on the one hand, the unfinished and fragmentary character of those

54. PEM 1975.
55. In this sense, Marx has a lot of trouble in the Theories with, for example, the so-called 'Smithian dogma' (the view that one could completely break down the value of commodi-ties into wages, profit and ground rent, because the elements of constant capital can always be further divided into wages, profit and ground rent) because Marx himself had elucidated the problem of the global process of reproduction in only an incomplete way. The solution of such problems is necessary in order to come to an adequate treatment of older theories.

manuscripts (many contemporaries reproached Engels's lack of editorial activity), but on the other hand, Engels himself mentions in prefaces and letters several material and stylistic changes that he made to the text. This fact, and the long period needed for the publication of the third volume, make it clear that Engels reworked Marx's texts to a considerable extent.

Now the extent of this editing can be studied in detail since the original manuscripts of Marx have been published in the new *MEGA*. Most manuscripts used by Engels for the second volume were published in *MEGA* II/11 in 2008. The main manuscript for the third volume was published at the beginning of the 1990s in *MEGA* II/4.2. A comparison between the original manuscript and Engels's edition shows that many of the changes made by Engels were not only of a stylistic nature. A violent debate on the meaning and importance of those changes subsequently erupted.[56] For students just starting to read Marx, Engels's edition of *Capital* may well suffice. A serious scientific debate, however, should rely on Marx's original manuscripts.

The first volume of *Capital*, published by Marx himself, also shows a certain evolution. The second German edition is very different from the first one, particularly in the first section on the commodity and money.[57] Marx made additional changes for the French translation, especially in the section on accumulation. And finally, as can be seen in Marx's correspondence in the 1880s, he planned a fundamental reworking of the first volume,[58] which he was unable to realise. After Marx's death, Engels published, in 1883 and 1890, the third and fourth editions of the first volume. In these editions, Engels incorporated some of the changes that were made in the French translation, but not all of them. The fourth edition, which

56. See, amongst others, Vollgraf and Jungnickel 2002; Heinrich 1996/7; Krätke 2007; and Elbe 2008a.
57. The first edition presented two different versions (in the main text and in an appendix) of the analysis of the form of value, both with major differences as compared to the text of the second edition. The text of the first edition of *Capital* is neither included in *MECW* nor in the Penguin edition. The text of the appendix was translated in English by M. Roth and W. Suchting and appeared in *Capital & Class* No. 4 of 1978 and as an improved version in Mohun 1994 (see Marx 1994). Important for the understanding of Marx's value-theory is also his manuscript *Ergänzungen und Veränderungen* (written in 1871–2) in which he reworked the first chapter of the first edition. Here we can find (among other points) a kind of self-commentary. This manuscript is only published in *MEGA* II/6, and not translated. In a detailed commentary on the first two chapters of *Capital*, I have shown that none of these four versions unambiguously represents the 'best' one (see Heinrich 2009c).
58. See his letter to Danielson of 13 December 1881: Marx 1992b.

is different from each edition published during Marx's lifetime, is the basis of the commonplace version that appears in *Marx-Engels-Werke* Volume 23 and provides the source of many translations.

Historical development and 'ideal average'

By the late 1840s, Marx had already criticised Ricardo's view that the laws of the capitalist mode of production were eternal when, in fact, those laws had developed over time and would vanish in the future. Even more, this criticism concerns the then-dominant neoclassical theory, which argued that it was concerned with 'economic behaviour' as such – namely, the use of scarce resources for different purposes, which is said to count for each economy.

In contrast, Marx stresses the historical character of the object of his research. The capitalist mode of production is only one of the many modes of production that have evolved in the course of human history. Marx is consistent, from the very start of his research, in making a distinction between 'material content' and 'social form'.[59] Use-values are, in every society, the material content of wealth, but it is only in societies where exchanges occur that use-values can take the form of commodities, and it is only in societies in which the capitalist mode of production prevails that the commodity-form becomes the prevalent social form.

Every production process needs means of production, but it is only under capitalist conditions that the means of production take the form of capital. Marx reproaches bourgeois economists for their confusion of form and content. Since they do not make the distinction between material content (means of production) and social form (capital), bourgeois economists can claim that capitalist production was always present and that the abolition of capitalism would mean the abolition of production itself.

The subject presented by Marx is certainly historical and not transhistorical. That, however, says nothing about the manner in which he presented it. Karl Kautsky wrote in his introduction to the first volume of *Capital*, widely read before the First World War, that Marx's work was essentially an historical analysis of the formation and the development of capitalism.[60] For Lenin, Marx's work was, specifically, an analysis of 'competitive capitalism', which was then being replaced by a new phase of capitalist development. Thus, there was a need to expand Marx's analysis

59. See, for example, Marx 1976c, p. 126.
60. Kautsky 1887.

by examining imperialism and monopoly-capitalism. These historicising views were very common at the time, and are now often used by some of Marx's critics, who argue that Marx's analysis may have been accurate for nineteenth-century capitalism, but given that capitalism has subsequently undergone further developments, his categories have since been rendered obsolete.[61]

However, what Marx actually claims about his presentation is something very different. In his preface to the first edition of *Capital*, Marx writes that he wants to deal with 'the capitalist mode of production'; 'until now', he continues, 'their *locus classicus* has been England. This is the reason why England is used as the main illustration of the theoretical developments I make'.[62] The links with contemporary English capitalism are only an 'illustration' of the 'theoretical development' and it is this with which he is clearly concerned. That it is not about a particular phase of capitalist development is made even clearer in the next paragraph, where Marx writes, 'it is not a question of the higher or lower degree of development of the social antagonisms that spring from the natural laws of capitalist production. It is a question of these laws themselves'.[63] At the end of the manuscript for the third volume, when he looks back on the presentation up to that point, Marx employs a striking expression to indicate the level of abstraction of his research. There it is stated that 'we are only out to present the internal organization of the capitalist mode of production, its *ideal average*, as it were'.[64]

What Marx wants to show in the course of his 'theoretical development' is not an *empirical* average of the capitalist mode of production (what, in his time, were the mere common features of most developed capitalist

---

61. This kind of criticism comes not only from the 'Right' but, time and again, from the 'Left'. A recent example for such a critique from the left can be found in Hardt and Negri 2000: where it is said that Marx's theory of value has become obsolete because in contemporary capitalism 'material' labour no longer prevails over 'immaterial' labour (namely, that which does not produce material products). However, Hardt and Negri have never attempted to prove their claim for the dominance of immaterial labour with empirical research. Furthermore, their criticism of Marx clearly rests on a confusion between abstract labour (producing value) and concrete labour (producing use-value): the difference between 'material' and 'immaterial' labour concerns the use-value aspect; whether labour produces value or not does not depend on the characteristics of the produced use-value but on the social form determination [*gesellschaftliche Formbestimmung*] of labour: whether it is labour producing a commodity sold on the market, or else labour producing something that is not sold.
62. Marx 1976c, p. 90.
63. Marx 1976c, pp. 90–1.
64. Marx 1991, p. 970: my emphasis.

countries), but rather, the 'ideal average' of this mode of production: those elements that belong, necessarily, to a developed capitalism. Following on from this claim, Marx examines the basic properties of the capitalist mode of production, regardless of how strongly or weakly present these were at that time. Marx's presentation is not at all the prisoner of the time in which it was developed; sometimes it was even far ahead of it. The production of relative surplus-value had only happened in a rudimentary way during Marx's lifetime. Its full enforcement came only during the twentieth century. Insofar as Marx was successful in presenting this claimed 'ideal average', his analysis remains relevant today.[65]

The fact that Marx did not present capitalism 'historically', and that he was more concerned with the presentation of developed capitalism, was not an arbitrary decision. In order to understand the formation of capitalism, one must already know what capitalism is, and only then can one observe the development of elements in the historical process. In the 'Introduction' of 1857, Marx summarises this metaphorically by saying, 'the anatomy of man is a key to the anatomy of the ape'.[66] Marx also adopted this view in *Capital*, as is clear already from the table of contents. The historical parts, which describe the formation of capitalist relationships, always follow *after* the theoretical parts.[67]

The supremacy of the capitalist mode of production is not only part of a whole historical development; this mode of production itself has a certain dynamic, whose general properties belong to Marx's analysis of the 'ideal average'. The valorisation of capital, as previously expressed in the general formula of capital, $M - C - M'$, belongs to a dynamic moment, and repeats itself again and again without reaching an end: it is without

---

65. He has not always been able to fulfil this claim, especially in relation to the role of money as a commodity (see Heinrich 2006, p. 233ff.; see also Stützle 2006). Beyond that, Marx's presentation in *Capital* still contains a whole series of ambivalences, even within the theory of value and in its unfinished theoretical parts, such as the framework of his theory on crises. We cannot go further into these ambivalences here (see Heinrich 2006, Part 3 for an extended overview).

66. Marx 1986, p. 42.

67. The part on 'primitive accumulation', which concerns the historical formation of capitalistic production processes in England, is situated at the end of the first volume of *Capital*, which first presented the analysis of the 'production process of capital'. The third volume also deals with the historical development of merchant capital, from pre-capitalistic to capitalistic, and the historical development of pre-capitalistic usury capital into capitalistic credit, *only after analysing* the capitalist mercantile capital and capitalist interest-bearing capital.

limits. There is nowhere, in any way, a *sufficient* degree of valorisation.[68] These basic characteristics of the valorisation of capital create a dynamic; although not initially originating in competition, this dynamic is executed by means of the pressure of competition between single capitals and by the continual class struggle (whether it is recognised as such or not). The essential elements of this dynamic, also historically illustrated by Marx, are the increased production of absolute and relative surplus-value, the accumulation of capital and the capitalist development of the productive forces: these lead again and again to radical changes in society's working and living conditions, to the formation of an 'industrial reserve army' and, finally, to recurring crises associated with widespread social and economic devastation.

Nevertheless, Marx's analysis of the dynamics of the capitalist mode of production is not identical with the real history of capitalist society. Nor does his analysis of the 'ideal average' of the capitalist mode of production coincide with the investigation of a given capitalist society. Such a concrete investigation needs further research. However, the 'theoretical development'[69] produced by Marx in *Capital* constitutes the necessary basis for an understanding of the development of individual capitalist societies in their particular historical contexts.

Critique, fetishism and action to change society

Marx does not simply produce a new description of the capitalist mode of production, a new political economy alongside the one that already existed. His claim, expressed in the subtitle of *Capital*, is a 'critique of political economy'. This means not only a critique of individual economic theories, but a critique of the whole science. Marx not only criticises the conclusions of this science, but he criticises its questions, or, more precisely, the systematic absence of certain questions. Already in the first chapter of *Capital*, he argues that:

> Political economy has indeed analysed value and its magnitude, however incomplete, and has uncovered the content concealed within these forms. But it has never once asked the question why this content has assumed that particular form, that is to say, why labour is expressed in value and why the measurement of labour by its duration is expressed in the magnitude of the

68. See Marx 1976c, pp. 252–3.
69. Marx 1976c, p. 90.

value of the product.[70]

The fact that political economy is not asking this question is not an oversight by individual economists. Rather, it rests more on the fact that they consider the commodity-form of the product of labour as self-evident, and unavoidable. Consequently, they do not consider as a possible object of their research this form *as form*. The social form fuses with the material content. This is not only the case with the commodity, but with more developed forms like money and capital as well.

The fetishism of commodities, money and capital is not simply a false perception by people, but the result of the specific economic mode of constituting society. Under capitalist conditions, the relations between economic actors are always mediated through objects; the social character of these relations can only appear objectively, as properties of objects. Thus, relations in bourgeois society produce fetishism and, in this sense, Marx can describe the economic categories that express these relations as 'objective forms of thought' [*objektive Gedankenformen*].[71] The description of the relations and the critique of the enunciated categories are inseparable.

The critique of the categories is not simply a matter of concern within the science. The fetishism linked to bourgeois relations constitutes a 'religion of everyday life'[72] within which people in bourgeois society operate. It constitutes the background for their spontaneous views of this society.[73]

Marx's analysis of the capitalist mode of production demonstrates the destructive ways in which the production of wealth works (see his description of the fight over the length of the working day or his treatment of the large-scale industries in the first volume of *Capital*). But one does not need Marx's analysis to notice the extremely destructive consequences of capitalist production for humans and nature. However, it is this analysis that demonstrates the *necessary* connection between capitalist production and destruction. This destructive characteristic is inherent in the capitalist mode of production.

It is neither the narrow-mindedness of individual businessmen nor wrong policies by the state, but rather the mode of production itself, whose sole aim is the valorisation of capital by the maximisation of profits through competition between individual capitals, that produces those

70. Marx 1976c, pp. 173–4.
71. Marx 1976c, p. 169.
72. Marx 1991, p. 969.
73. See Heinrich 2012, Chapter 10.

destructive consequences. Humans and nature are only means in the valorisation process, and they are treated accordingly. The workforce is physically and mentally drained and nature is impoverished – and this only in order to increase the profits of the various capitals. Marx summarises thus: 'Capitalist production, therefore, only develops the techniques and the degree of combination of the social process of production by simultaneously undermining the original sources of all wealth – the soil and the worker'.[74] Although the destructive tendencies of capitalist production (which act not only at the level of the production process, but also at the level of consumption) are somewhat mitigated by legal limits on working hours, measures to protect health in the workplace (also dealt with by Marx in *Capital*) and laws to protect the environment, those problems are not eliminated. When we calculate the social and ecological costs of capitalism, it is not as a moral accusation, but as a simple statement of an objective connection: capitalism cannot exist without these consequences.[75]

As his criticism of fetishism showed, capitalist relations of production are not at all the natural forms of social production. Within capitalist relations there are, indeed, many 'objective constraints', but capitalism, in itself, is not that constraint: it can be replaced. It represents a *historical form* of production, which has simultaneously productive as well as destructive impacts, which generates incredible possibilities for the individual and social development of human beings; but, at the same time, these possibilities are geared only towards the narrow goal of maximising profits.

Marx did not expect people to take action against capitalism on moral grounds, but because of the fact that their immediate vital interests are constantly put into question. When people repeatedly resist those relationships, however, they will learn to fight, not only for an immediate improvement in their situation under capitalism, but also, from time to time, to challenge the very existence of capitalism as such.[76] Marx's *Capital* is quite helpful in those struggles. It may well turn out, as a self-confident

74. Marx 1976c, p. 638.
75. In *Capital*, Marx mocks Proudhon's moralising criticisms (see, for example, Marx 1976c, p. 178–9, footnote 2). For Marx, a critique relying on 'justice' is out of the question because the normative foundation of such a critique receives its plausibility from the society which is being criticised. See his critique of Gilbart in Marx 1991, p. 460).
76. In the last part of *Value, Price and Profit*, Marx formulated the expectation that in the long run trade unions would not only fight against the effects of the wage system, but against the wage system as such – not for moral reasons, but because of an insight into the structure of capitalism (see Marx 1985b, pp. 148–9).

Marx once claimed, to be the 'the most terrible missile that has yet been hurled at the heads of the bourgeoisie (landowners included)'.[77]

However, such a movement can no longer rely on historico-philosophical certainties about the necessary end of capitalism or the inevitable formation of a revolutionary subject (views to be found in the young Marx and in the *Communist Manifesto*, and which also continue to play an important role in many Marxist traditions today). If history were genuinely not conceived as predetermined, as a process moving towards a predetermined endpoint, but, on the contrary, as an open-ended process, this would mean that much is possible but that nothing is for sure.

REFERENCES

Beiträge zur Marx Engels Forschung Neue Folge 1997, Sonderband 1: David Borisovic Rjazanov und die erste Hamburg: Argument Verlag.

Beiträge zur Marx Engels Forschung Neue Folge 2000, Sonderband 2: Erfolgreiche Kooperation: Das Frankfurter Institut für Sozialforschung und das Moskauer Marx-Engels-Institut (1924-1928), Hamburg: Argument Verlag.

Beiträge zur Marx Engels Forschung Neue Folge 2001, Sonderband 3: Stalinismus und das Ende der ersten Marx-Engels-Gesamtausgabe (1931-1941), Hamburg: Argument Verlag.

Althusser, Louis 2010 [1965], *For Marx*, London: Verso.

Anderson, Perry, 1976, *Considerations on Western Marxism*, London: New Left Books.

Anderson, Kevin B. 2010, *Marx at the Margins. On Nationalism, Ethnicity, and Non-Western Societies*, Chicago: University of Chicago Press.

Arthur, Christoph J., 1996, 'Engels as Interpreter of Marx's Economics', in *Engels Today. A Centenary Appreciation*, Basingstoke: Macmillan, pp. 173–209.

Elbe, Ingo 2013, 'Between Marx, Marxism, and Marxisms – Ways of Reading Marx's Theory', in: *Viewpoint Magazine*, October 2013, http://viewpointmag.com/2013/10/21/between-marx-marxism-and-marxisms-ways-of-reading-marxs-theory/

Elbe, Ingo 2008, *Marx im Westen. Die neue Marx-Lektüre in der Bundesrepublik seit 1965*, Berlin: Akademie Verlag.

Elbe, Ingo 2008a, 'Die Beharrlichkeit des "Engelsismus". Bemerkungen zum Marx-Engels-Problem', in *Marx Engels Jahrbuch 2007*, Berlin: Akad-

77. Letter to Becker, 17 April 1867: Marx 1987b, p. 358.

emie Verlag.

Engels, Friedrich 1990 [1890], 'Reply to the Editors of the *Sächsische Arbe-iter-Zeitung*' in Marx and Engels Collected Works, Vol. 27, London: Lawrence & Wishart.

– 1992 [1882], 'Engels to Eduard Bernstein. 2 and 3 November' in *Marx and Engels Collected Works*, Vol. 46, London: Lawrence & Wishart.

– 2001 [1890] 'Engels to Conrad Schmidt. 5 August' in *Marx and Engels Collected Works*, Vol. 49, London: Lawrence & Wishart.

Hardt, Michael and Antonio Negri 2000, *Empire*, Cambridge, MA: Harvard University Press.

Hecker, Rolf 1999, 'Die Entstehungs-, Überlieferungs- und Editionsgeschichte der ökonomischen Manuskripte und des *Kapital*', in Elmar Altvater, Rolf Hecker, et al. *Kapital.doc*, Münster: Westfälisches Dampfboot.

Heinrich, Michael 1989, 'Capital in general and the structure of Marx's *Capital*. New insights from Marx's *Economic Manuscript of 1861–63*', *Capital & Class*, 38: 63–79.

– 1996/7, 'Engels' Edition of the Third Volume of Capital and Marx's Original Manuscript', *Science & Society*, 60, 4: 452–66.

– 1997, 'Geschichtsphilosophie bei Marx', in *Geschichtsphilosophie oder das Begreifen der Historizität*, edited by Diethard Behrens, Freiburg: Ça ira.

– 2004, 'Praxis und Fetischismus. Eine Anmerkung zu den Marxschen Thesen über Feuerbach und ihrer Verwendung', in *Gesellschaft als Verkehrung. Perspektiven einer neuen Marx-Lektüre. Festschrift für Helmut Reichelt*, edited by Christine Kirchhoff, Lars Meyer et al., Freiburg: Ça ira.

– 2006, *Die Wissenschaft vom Wert. Die Marxsche Kritik der politischen Ökonomie zwischen wissenschaftlicher Revolution und klassischer Tradition*, Fourth edition, Münster: Westfälisches Dampfboot.

– 2008a, 'Weltanschauung oder Strategie? Über Dialektik, Materialismus und Kritik in der Kritik der politischen Ökonomie', in *Kritik und Materialität*, edited by Alex Demirovic, Münster: Westfälisches Dampfboot

– 2009a, 'Theoriegeschichte der Marxschen Ökonomiekritik', in Peter Bescherer and Karen Schierhorn (eds.), *Hello Marx: Zwischen "Arbeiterfrage" und sozialer Bewegung heute*, Hamburg: VSA Verlag, pp. 15–35

– 2009b, 'Reconstruction or Deconstruction? Methodological Controversies about Value and Capital, and New Insights from the Critical Edition', in *Re-reading Marx. New Perspectives after the Critical Edition*, edited by Riccardo Bellofiore, Roberto Fineschi, et al., Basingstoke: Palgrave Macmillan, pp. 71-98.

– 2009c, *Wie das Marxsche Kapital lesen? Hinweise zur Lektüre und Kommentar zum Anfang des "Kapital", Teil 1*, Stuttgart: Schmetterling Verlag.

– 2011, 'Entstehungs- und Auflösungsgeschichte des Marxschen Kapitals', in Heinrich, Michael and Werner Bonefeld (eds.), *Kapital & Kritik. Nach der "neuen" Marx-Lektüre*, Hamburg: VSA-Verlag, pp. 155–94.

– 2012, *An Introduction to the Three Volumes of Karl Marx's Capital*, New York: Monthly Review Press.

Hoff, Jan 2009, *Marx global. Zur Entwicklung des internationalen Marx-Diskurses seit 1965*, Berlin: Akademie Verlag.

– 2006b, 'Einleitung', in Hoff, Petrioli, Stützle and Wolf (eds.) 2006a.

Howard, Michael Charles and J.E. King 1992, *A History of Marxian Economics*, 2 Vols., Princeton: Princeton University Press.

Kautsky, Karl 1887, *Karl Marx Oekonomische Lehren. Gemeinverständlich dargestellt und erläutert*, Stuttgart: J.H.W. Dietz.

Kittsteiner, Heinz 1977, '"Logisch" und "historisch". Über Differenzen des Marxschen und des Engelsschen Systems der Wissenschaft (Engels' Rezension "Zur Kritik der politischen Ökonomie")', in *Internationale wissenschaftliche Korrespondenz zur Geschichte der deutschen Arbeiterbewegung*, 13, 1: 1–47.

Kolakowski, Leszek 2005 [1977–9], *Main Currents of Marxism*, New York: WW Norton & Co.

Krätke, Michael 2007, 'Das Marx-Engels-Problem. Warum Engels das Marxsche "Kapital" nicht verfälscht hat', in *Marx Engels Jahrbuch 2006*, Berlin: Akademie Verlag.

Liedman, Sven-Eric 1986, *Das Spiel der Gegensätze. Friedrich Engels' Philosophie und die Wissenschaften des 19. Jahrhunderts*, Frankfurt: Campus.

Lindner, Kolja 2010: 'Marx's Eurocentrism. Postcolonial studies and Marx scholarship', *Radical Philosophy*, 161: 27–41.

Marcuse, Herbert 1932: 'Neue Quellen zur Grundlegung des Historischen Materialismus', in *Ideen zu einer kritischen Theorie der Gesellschaft*, Berlin: Suhrkamp 1969.

Marx, Karl 1975a [1840–1], *Difference Between the Democritean and Epicurean Philosophy of Nature*, in *Marx and Engels Collected Works*, Vol. 1, London: Lawrence & Wishart, pp. 25–107.

– 1975b [1843], *A Contribution to the Critique Hegel's Philosophy of Law*, in *Marx and Engels Collected Works*, Vol. 3, London: Lawrence & Wishart, pp. 3–129.

– 1975c [1844], *Economic and Philosophic Manuscripts of 1844*, in *Marx and Engels Collected Works*, Vol. 3, London: Lawrence & Wishart, pp. 229–346.

– 1976a [1845], *Theses on Feuerbach*, in *Marx and Engels Collected Works*, Vol. 5,

London: Lawrence & Wishart, pp. 3–5.

– 1976b [1847], *The Poverty of Philosophy. Answer to the Philosophy of Poverty by M. Proudhon*, in *Marx and Engels Collected Works*, Vol. 6, London: Lawrence & Wishart, pp. 105–212.

– 1976c [1890], *Capital*, Volume I, translated by Ben Fowkes, London: Penguin Classics.

– 1979 [1851], *The Eighteenth Brumaire of Louis Bonaparte*, in *Marx and Engels Collected Works*, Vol. 11, London: Lawrence & Wishart, , pp. 99–197.

– 1982 [1846], 'Marx to Pavel Vasilyevich Annenkov. 28 December', in *Marx and Engels Collected Works*, Vol. 38, London: Lawrence & Wishart.

– 1983a [1859] 'Marx to Joseph Weydemeyer. 1 February', in *Marx and Engels Collected Works*, Vol. 40, London: Lawrence & Wishart

– 1983b [1852] 'Marx to Joseph Weydemeyer. 5 March', in *Marx and Engels Collected Works*, Vol. 39, London: Lawrence & Wishart

– 1983c [1867], *Das Kapital. Erster Band* [1. Auflage], in *Marx-Engels-Gesamtausgabe (MEGA)* II/5, Berlin: Dietz Verlag.

– 1985a [1862], 'Marx to Ludwig Kugelmann. 28 December', in Marx and Engels Collected Works, Vol. 38, London: Lawrence & Wishart

– 1985b [1864], *Value, Price and Profit*, in Marx and Engels Collected Works, Vol. 20, London: Lawrence & Wishart, pp. 101–49.

– 1986 [1857–8], *Economic Manuscripts of 1857–58 [Grundrisse]*, in *Marx and Engels Collected Works*, Vol. 28, London: Lawrence & Wishart.

– 1987a [1859], *A Contribution to the Critique of Political Economy. Part One*, in *Marx and Engels Collected Works*, Vol. 29, London: Lawrence & Wishart, pp. 256–417.

– 1987b [1867], 'Marx to Johann Philipp Becker. 17 April', in *Marx and Engels Collected Works*, Vol. 42, London: Lawrence & Wishart.

– 1987c [1871–2], *Ergänzungen und Veränderungen zum ersten Band des "Kapitals"*, in *Marx-Engels-Gesamtausgabe (MEGA)* II/6, Berlin: Dietz Verlag, pp. 1–54.

– 1988–94 [1861–3], *Economic Manuscripts 1861-63*, in *Marx and Engels Collected Works*, Vols. 30–4, London: Lawrence & Wishart.

– 1989 [1881], *Marginal Notes on Adolph Wagner's 'Lehrbuch der politischen Oekonomie'*, in *Marx and Engels Collected Works*, Vol. 24, London: Lawrence & Wishart, pp. 531–59.

– 1991 [1894], *Capital*, Vol. III, translated by David Fernbach, London: Penguin Classics.

– 1992a [1882] 'Marx to Engels. 30 September' in *Marx and Engels Collected*

Works, Vol. 46, London: Lawrence & Wishart.

– 1992b [1881] 'Marx to Nikolai Danielson. 13 December' in *Marx and Engels Collected Works*, Vol. 46, London: Lawrence & Wishart.

– 1992c [1863–5], *Ökonomische Manuskripte 1863–1867 Teil 2: Das Kapital (Ökonomisches Manuskript 1863-1865). Drittes Buch*, in *Marx-Engels-Gesamtausgabe (MEGA)* II/4.2, Berlin: Dietz Verlag.

– 1994 [1867], *The Value-Form* [*Capital* first edition, appendix] translated by M.Roth and W.Suchting, in Mohun, Simon (ed.), *Debates in Value Theory*, Basingstoke: Macmillan, pp. 9–34.

– 2008 [1868–81], *Manuskripte zum zweiten Buch des 'Kapitals' 1868-1881*, in *Marx-Engels-Gesamtausgabe (MEGA)* II/11, Berlin: Akademie Verlag.

Marx, Karl and Friedrich Engels 1975 [1845], *The Holy Family or Critique of critical Criticism. Against Bruno Bauer and Company*, in *Marx and Engels Collected Works*, Vol. 4, London: Lawrence & Wishart, pp. 5–211.

– 1976a [1845–6]: *The German Ideology*, in *Marx and Engels Collected Works*, Vol. 5, London: Lawrence & Wishart, pp. 19–539.

– 1976b [1848], *Manifesto of the Communist Party*, in *Marx and Engels Collected Works*, Vol. 6, London: Lawrence & Wishart, pp. 477–519.

Marx, Karl, Friedrich Engels, and Joseph Weydemeyer 2004 [1845], 'Die deutsche Ideologie. Artikel, Druckvorlagen, Entwürfe, Reinschriftenfragmente und Notizen zu I. Feuerbach und II. Sankt Bruno' (Vorabpublikation aus MEGA I/5) in *Marx-Engels-Jahrbuch 2003*, Berlin: Akademie Verlag.

Marxhausen, Thomas 2006, 'MEGA – MEGA und kein Ende', *Utopie kreativ* 189/190: 596–617.

– 2008, 'Kapital-Editionen', *Historisch-kritisches Wörterbuch des Marxismus* 7, 1: 136–60.

Mehringer, Hartmut and Gottfried Mergner 1973, *Debatte um Engels*, 2 Vols., Reinbek: rororo

Moseley, Fred 2007, 'Kapital im Allgemeinen und Konkurrenz der vielen Kapitalien in der Theorie von Marx. Die quantitative Dimension', in *Marx Engels Jahrbuch 2006*, Berlin: Akademie Verlag.

Musto, Marcello (ed.) 2008, *Karl Marx's Grundrisse. Foundations of the critique of political economy 150 years later*, New York: Routledge.

PEM (Projektgruppe Entwicklung des Marxschen Systems) 1975, *Der 4. Band des "Kapital"? Kommentar zu den "Theorien über den Mehrwert"*, West-Berlin: VSA.

Steger, Manfred B. and Terrell Carver (eds.) 1999, *Engels after Marx*, Manchester: Manchester University Press.

Stützle, Ingo 2006, 'Die Frage nach der konstitutiven Relevanz der Geldware in Marx' Kritik der politischen Ökonomie', in Hoff, Petrioli, Stützle and Wolf (eds.) 2006a.

Vollgraf, Carl-Erich and Jürgen Jungnickel 2002 [1995], '"Marx in Marx's Words"? On Engels' Edition of the Main Manuscript of Book 3 of *Capital*', *International Journal of Political Economy*, 32, 1: 35–78.

Vranicki, Predrag 1972, *Geschichte des Marxismus*, Frankfurt: Suhrkamp.

Walther, Rudolf 1982, 'Marxismus' in *Geschichtliche Grundbegriffe. Historisches Lexikon zur politisch-sozialen Sprache in Deutschland*, Vol. 3, Stuttgart: Cotta.

HOW MONEY CONSTITUTES VALUE: FROM 'ABSTRACT LABOUR' TO MONEY

Geert Reuten

Introduction

In *Capital* Marx establishes a complex break [*césure*] with the then dominant Ricardian theory of value. The complexity has to do with articulation of his method of immanent critique with an intrinsic epistemological break from the political economy of his day. Central to this break is a rejection of naturalistic 'labour-embodied' notions of value. Nevertheless, the main 20th century reading of Marx's theory of value in *Capital* has been a naturalistic one, although coupled with a non-naturalistic focus on the capitalist mode of exploitation of labour.[78]

In this paper I provide a novel interpretation of Part One of the first volume of *Capital*, that is, its first three chapters. As Marx adopts a systematic-dialectical methodology in this work – into which the above mentioned methodological aspects are integrated – the crucial break from the naturalism is to be traced to the entry point of the work. In this paper, I will argue that Chapter 1 is merely *one moment* of the entry point. The *second* moment of the entry point is Chapter 3 on money. These two moments subsist at the same level of abstraction and thus inseparably belong together.

My paper is restricted to these chapters, however my reading has consequences for the interpretation of all of *Capital*. This paper is historiographic and hence I abstain from presenting my own (value-form theoretical) views. There is thus no question of agreement or disagreement with Marx involved, other than those aspects that emerge from a process of internal critique.

Section 1 sets out the general problematic. Sections 2 and 3 provide further details.

78. The terrain from which Marx sets out is of course the Ricardian theory. In previous texts (esp. Reuten 1989, 1993 and 2000), I suggested that whereas Marx made a fundamental 'break' from Classical Political Economy there are (inevitably) Classical/Ricardian remnants in his work. For a discussion of this issue see Murray's (2000a) critique of Reuten 1993, my reply (Reuten 2000) and Murray's rejoinder (2002). A rereading of a number of German texts of *Capital* (and together with insights from Hegel's work) makes me conclude that there are far fewer such remnants than I previously thought. Along with this paper, Reuten 2004 provides a fuller discussion of these themes.

1. THE MONETARY DIMENSION

1.1. From form and prevalence to systemic existence

The standpoint of Chapter 1 of *Capital* is 'the commodity'. The relatively brief Chapter 2, on the process of exchange, posits the *prevalence* [*Dasein*] of money in practice. Although Chapter 1 already posits *the form* of money, nevertheless money itself – that is, its systemic existence – is derived only in Chapter 3.

Throughout Chapter 3 Marx frequently uses the term *veräußerlichen* in order to indicate 'to sell'. *Veräußerlichen* literally means 'to outer' or 'outering'. The normal German term for selling, however, would be *verkaufen* (a term that he also uses – the difference is lost in the translation, or at least in the English translation). He also uses *entäußeren*, as well as other terms with the same root, especially *Außdruck* (expression; compare the roots *außer*, outer, utter). This homology is lost in the translation, again at least in the English translation.

The term 'outer' makes one of course alert for an 'inner' or for something that is 'immanent'. Moreover, against the background of Marx's familiarity with Hegel's *Logic* the terms are rather severe; they point at 'moments' that can be distinguished but that inseparably belong together. At the end of the first section of Chapter 3 Marx writes:

> Die Preisform schließt die *Veräußerlichkeit* der Waren gegen Geld und die Notwendigkeit dieser *Veräußerung* ein.[79]

The standard English translation is:

> The price-form therefore implies both the exchangeability of commodities for money and the necessity of exchanges.

This translation loses the sense of 'outering' contained in *Veräußerlichkeit* and *Veräußerung*. My preferred translation would be:

> The price-form includes the 'extroversibility'/exchangeability of commodities for money and the necessity of this 'extroversion'/exchange.

79. Marx 1867M/1890, p. 118 – italics added.

1.2. The introversive and the extroversive constituent moments of value

In Marx's view, money is one *constituent* moment of value (he does not use exactly this formulation).[80] The immanent or introversive constituent moment of value is the undifferentiated 'abstract labour' presented in Chapter 1. Its extroversive constituent moment is money, as presented in Chapter 3. However, these two moments *inseparably* belong together. Money is the *necessary* form of expression (*Außdruck*) of value. That is, *value has no existence without money*. This is the end-result of Part One.

Because of the inseparability of the introversive and the extroversive constituent moments of value, monistic phrases like 'labour-values', or conversely, 'value-prices', do not fit Marx's theory and hence are never used in *Capital* I or II.[81]

Another way of saying that value has no existence without money is that value is *without exception* of monetary dimension. In fact, this is already the outcome of Chapter 1. Section 3 of Chapter 1 presents the *formation* of the form of money – or rather, it posits the *form* of extroversion (*Veräußerlichung*) which is the starting point for Chapter 3.[82]

80. 'Moment' is a systematic-dialectical term stemming from Hegel's *Logic*. It refers to essential interconnectedness and mutuality (to such a way that could not be comprehended by a term such as 'aspect'). Marx uses the term sometimes but not frequently. In the following passage he provides an illuminating explanation of the term: 'The relative form of value and the equivalent form are two inseparable moments, which belong to and mutually condition each other; but at the same time, they are mutually exclusive or opposed extremes, i.e., poles of the expression of value' (Marx 1867F/1890, pp. 139-40; cf. Marx 1867M/1890, p. 63). Much more frequently, as indicated, he uses the terms 'inner' and 'outer' (or their equivalents), which have the same connotation of inseparable connection.

81. The term 'value prices', however, is used one time in *Das Kapital III*, Chapter 10 (*MEW* p. 184; English Fernbach translation p. 275; cf. *MEGA II/4.2* p. 250).

82. See also Arthur's excellent discussion (2004, pp. 36-8). He writes: 'to be a commodity involves *all* the determinations of Chapter 1, including those of Section 3 on its *form*, in which it is shown that an adequate expression of the value of commodities requires the existence of money.' See also his discussion in (2005). The notion that value has no existence without money is also key to Murray's analysis (2005), although he arrives at this from an angle different from the one proposed in the current paper. Elson (1979) is an inspiration for the research presented in this paper. 'Marx's examples', she wrote, 'are always couched in money terms, *never* in terms of hours' (139). The same applies for the case of Marx's equations (Reuten 2004). Elson notes that 'values cannot be calculated or observed independently of prices' but she also thought that 'in *Capital* Marx does not highlight the conceptual distinction which he [Marx] makes between an "immanent" or "intrinsic" measure, and an "external" measure, which is the mode of appearance of the "immanent" measure' (p. 136). I assume that she had not seen the German text, because in fact the German text is rather explicit. So she intuitively felt that Marx 'must' highlight the distinction.

Marx introduces the concept of 'value-form' in Chapter 1. After that, the term is only sporadically used. The reason is that in Chapter 3 the concept is concretised into its monetary expression.

1.3. From a simple to an enriched notion of value

Section 1 of Chapter 3 sets out the 'function' of money as 'measure *of* values'. This may make the false impression of there 'being' value entities existing independently of the 'measure' – that is, independently of money. If Marx had started again here from scratch and considered the measurement of a use-value in terms of money, the problem would not have arisen. In fact, he considers *commodities* as introduced in Chapter 1. Near to the opening of Chapter 3 Marx writes:

> Money as a measure of value is the necessary form of appearance of the measure of value which is immanent in commodities, namely labour-time.[83]

Note that the meaning of 'measure' here is not obvious – I return to this later (§3.2).

If my interpretation is accepted we move from a simplified notion of value – that of Chapter 1 – to an enriched one – that of the full Part One – each indicated with one term: 'value'. Evidently we cannot but start Chapter 3 with the simple notion of value inherited from the previous chapters.

Value's monetary *dimension* does not imply that it only exists in monetary shape. Entities in capitalism – e.g., machines – may have value of monetary dimension without being money. Equally, things may be of monetary dimension – e.g., machines as functioning means of production – without having a price: things have a price only when they are offered for sale. Within the circuit of capital $M \rightarrow C_i...P...C_j' \rightarrow M'$, the $C_i...P...C_j'$ is ideally accounted in monetary dimension. This ideality may be exciting (as it should) but it is not surprising. Every businessman, accountant or auditor knows that most of the balance sheet of an enterprise is made up in terms of an ideal monetary dimension (the balance sheet is a static version of the circuit of capital).

83. Marx 1867F/1890, p. 188; cf. Marx 1867M/1890, p. 109.

2. 'VERY ABSTRACT LABOUR' AND ITS DISAPPEARANCE AFTER CHAPTER 1

In Section 1 of Chapter 1 we find Marx's famous presentation of the concept of 'abstract labour':

> If then we disregard the use-value of commodities, only one property remains, that of being products of labour. But even the product of labour has already been transformed in our hands [*bereits in der Hand verwandelt*]. ... the different concrete forms of labour ... are all together reduced to the same kind of labour, human labour in the abstract.Let us now look at the residue of the products of labour. There is nothing left of them but the same spectral objectivity [*gespenstige Gegenständlichkeit*]; they are merely congealed quantities of homogeneous human labour ... As crystals of this social substance ... they are values – commodity values [*Warenwerte*].[...] The common factor in the exchange relation, or in the exchange value of the commodity, is therefore its value. THE PROGRESS OF THE INVESTIGATION WILL LEAD US BACK TO EXCHANGE-VALUE AS THE NECESSARY MODE OF EXPRESSION [*AUSDRUCKSWEISE*], OR FORM OF APPEARANCE, OF VALUE. For the present, however, we must consider the nature of value independently of this form. A use-value, or useful article, therefore, has value only because abstract human labour is objectified [*vergegenständlicht*] or materialized in it. How, then, is the magnitude of this value to be measured? By means of the quantity of the 'value-constituting substance' [*wertbildenden Substanz*], the labour, contained in the article. The quantity of labour itself is measured by its duration; in turn the labour-time is measured on the particular scale of hours, days etc.[84]

Three aspects need to be stressed. First, Marx refers to a transformation [*Verwandlung*] as resulting in a spectral 'objectivity' – I return to this in §3. Second, he indicates that he abstracts from the *necessary* mode of expression of value. Thus, he presents a simplification. Third, this simplified entity (that is, value in abstraction from its necessary form) is measured by labour-time – supposedly, this is 'abstract labour-time'.

84. Marx 1867F/1890: 128-9; 1867M/1890: 52-53, translation modified, emphasis in small caps added.

Let us consider an analogy. When we measure the length of a table with a metre stick, the table's length exists independently of the stick.[85] Note that the table is fully constituted as introversive material or substance *and* extroversive form. However, there is no obvious unique way to measure the length of the *material* of the table. That is, the length of timber and nails. Surely, we can in principle measure the length of two odd pieces of freshly cut timber – in this sense we have things that can be measured – but we cannot add those up in a unique sensible way because of their unequal shapes.

Similarly there is no obvious unique way to measure 'concrete labour', the 'introversive substance' of value. In Section 1 of Chapter 1, therefore, Marx takes recourse to the notion of 'abstract labour' as a *simplified constituent* moment of value.

It is most telling that after the presentation of the simple form of value (the first form presented in Section 3) the term 'abstract labour' disappears! (In fact there are a couple of references back to the simplified notion: two in Section 4, one in Chapter 2, two in Chapter 3 and one in Chapter 6, which is Chapter 8 of the English edition.) There are no occurrences in Volumes II or III. The term 'homogeneous labour' similarly disappears after Chapter 3. Relatedly the term labour as 'substance' disappears after Chapter 3 (to this there are three exceptions in each one of the three volumes; these are references back to the notion presented in Volume I, Chapter 1).

The reason for this disappearance is obviously the conceptual progression of Marx's presentation, that is, his movement beyond – or the supersession of – the Chapter 1 simplification.

In light of the Marxian discourse of the last twenty years this disappearance of the term 'abstract labour' cannot be stressed enough. When in Chapter 1 Marx presents the commodity, he *posits* their being and prevalence [*Dasein*]. At that point he presupposes the money measure that is only grounded in Chapter 3. *Abstract labour foreshadows the money measure.*

Marx's immanent measure of value in Chapter 1 – time of 'abstract labour' – is *very* abstract. It does not provide a measure of value in the sense that we usually adopt the term 'measure'. 'Abstract labour' cannot be measured (in terms of time) with more sense than timber as abstracted from, for example, anything but its length. However, for the timber, this does not provide

---

85. Its length *in metres* does *not* exist independently of the stick (or rather the metric system), but that is not my point here.

the full constitution of a table (merely substance); similarly, for the abstract labour, this does not constitute value (merely substance).

I use the term 'very abstract labour' because in the literature on Marx the term 'abstract labour' has become somewhat worn out: it seems often identified with a *quantitative part of concrete (!) labour*: 1) producing at average conditions of production (hence, it is said, 'necessary'); 2) for the product of which there is demand (hence, it is said, 'necessary'); 3) that contributes to production in a particular sense – 'productive' labour (hence, it is said, 'necessary'). These issues can be announced; however, there is no way of *knowing* them or measuring them prior to the market. Thus, abstract labour has no determinate existence. Abstract labour has a dimension of time but, paradoxically, it cannot be measured unless we *assume* that abstract labour equals concrete labour (thus abstract from abstract labour). Rather, value is fully constituted only when we have money; money in the market measures 'abstract labour' and so determines 'abstract labour' so to speak. However, in reality, at this point of the presentation the term 'abstract labour' is superfluous: we have 'value'.

Marx never uses the phrase 'labour theory of value'. He provides an immanent critique of, as well as a break from, Ricardian notions of value. The notion of 'very abstract labour' indeed implies that Chapter 1 does not present a 'labour theory of value' in any quantifiable sense. From this again derives the conclusion that abstract labour, *a fortiori*, cannot be quantitatively implanted into lower levels of abstraction (and – to repeat – Marx does not do this).

3. MONEY'S MEASURING: IDEAL TRANSUBSTANTIATION

3.1. Idealities.

In this section I expand on the core of Chapter 3: 'money's measuring'. I begin with a long quotation from early on in the chapter, which I take to be programmatic. It shows, first, that the *value* of an entity is a purely ideal form (this denies ontologically real 'embodiment'); second, the measurement in terms of money is an *ideal* act – it is performed through an *imaginary* equalisation with money; third, as a result, the second performance can be established by imaginary money.

The price or MONEY-FORM of commodities is, LIKE THEIR FORM OF VALUE GENERALLY, quite distinct from their palpable and real bodily form; it is therefore a purely IDEAL or imagined [*vorgestellt*] form. Although invisible, the value of iron, linen and corn exists in these very things: it is imagined [*vorgestellt*] through their equality with gold, a relation to gold, even though this only haunts their heads, so to speak. The guardian of the commodities must therefore lend them his tongue, or hang a ticket on them, in order to communicate their prices to the outside world. Since the expression of the value of commodities in gold is purely ideal, we may use purely imaginary or ideal gold to perform this operation ... In its function as measure of value, money therefore serves as merely imaginary or ideal money.[86]

I expand on the first two issues in §3.2 and on the third in §3.3.

3.2. Marx's notion of measurement: 'verwandlen' and standardised measurement.

When Marx refers to money's measurement he refers to an abstract genus. Usually when we think of a measure we think of a standard. However, when Marx says 'money measures value' he means that it establishes *commensuration*, i.e., homogenisation. On the other hand, the 'taking measure' (and ticketing) of the value of a commodity is established in terms of a standard of price. The distinction between this 'measurement in general' and the specific 'taking measure' by way of a particular standard is most important. (Marx's terminology might seem idiosyncratic – in current language, that is. However, in Hegel's *Logic* (both of its versions) we have a similar usage of the term 'measure'. In hindsight, this also sheds light on Marx's usage of 'immanent measure' for the Chapter 1 moment of value.)

As the measure of value it [money] serves to transform [*verwandlen*] the values of all the manifold commodities into prices, into imaginary QUANTITIES OF GOLD {that is, money in general}; as the standard of price it [money] ... measures, on the contrary, QUANTITIES OF GOLD BY A UNIT quantity of gold.[87]

---

86. Marx 1867F/1890, pp.189-90; Marx 1867M/1890, pp. 110-11; translation modified; emphasis in small caps added.
87. Marx, 1867F/1890, p. 192; Marx 1867M/1890, p. 113; translation modified; emphasis in small caps added; phrase in curly brackets added.

Note again (cf. §1.3) that Marx of course embarks from the first Chapter's notion of 'immanent value' – a notion that is now, with the extroversion, transformed into a more concrete concept of value.

The second phrase, about the standard, specifies a unit (a quantum) for the measurement of the quantity in the first phrase. As the standard of price, particular money (named, e.g., euro or dollar) measures quantities of money (a pile of notes or coins) by a unit of price (e.g., one euro or one dollar).

For the first phrase, regarding measure and transformation, I should point at a metaphor used by Marx throughout Part One, namely that of the Catholic ritual of the 'transubstantiation' of bread and wine into the body of Christ. This is one connotation of the German term *Verwandlung*.[88] Compare the direct reference to the priest holding the bread and wine in the quotation from Chapter 1 (§2 above): 'But even the product of labour has already been transformed in our hands [*bereits in der Hand verwandelt*].' (Appropriately, whether the transubstantiation is real or ideal has been a matter of debate within Christianity)

Now reconsider the quotation. For the commodities, *prior* to the measurement of the first phrase, we merely have the 'introversive substance', which is a *purely ideal or imagined* introversive substance (as indicated in the earlier quote, §3.1). The act of measurement by money (that is, prior to the actual exchange) ideally 'transubstantiates' commodities into form-determined entities and *hence* commensurate or homogeneous (see the last quote). This is like a miracle. But just as most Catholics that go to church every week or perhaps every day may not be very attentive any more to the miraculousness of the transformation of bread and wine into the body of Christ, we are, when we mundanely buy our daily bread, usually not very attentive to the miraculous ideal transubstantiation that is performed by the people in the bakery. (You point at half a loaf of bread and ask: 'How much is this?' They reply: 'It is 1.47' – '*Hic est 1.47 euro.*')

Thus money's measurement per-forms the value-homogeneity of commodities. Or: money turns the hopelessly abstract immanent notion of 'abstract labour' into extroversive form, and therewith into a concretum (concretum, that is when the *salto mortale* is completed into the metamorphosis $C \rightarrow M$). Without this 'measurement *überhaupt*', standards of price (or standards of value) make no sense.

Thus value is, in *both* its constituent moments – introversive and

88. See Reuten 1993.

extroversive – imaginary or ideality. Although it is beyond the subject of this paper, I should add that ideality can have real effects.[89]

3.3. Imaginary measurement by imaginary money

I now turn to the third aspect of the 'programmatic' quotation. If we restrict the discussion to money's function as measure of value, Marx goes as far as one could go at all in the commodity-money based monetary regime of his days (1867).[90] If we consider today's (2011) 'pure credit-money' regime, the crucial episode was not the demise of the gold–dollar standard, or the Bretton Woods regime, in the mid 1970s – the latter is the tail. Crucial is the national irredeemability of banknotes and the prevalence of 'money of account' at all: imaginary money (see Marx's treatment of money of account in Section 3 of Chapter 3). Thus the ideal *Verwandlung* is accomplished by ideal, or imaginary, money! (Or – from a perspective of pure credit-money – by nominal money.)

Here we seem to have before us all the ingredients of a weird spectral world.[91] Yet for those possessed by spectres, spectres are real. And since we engage in the ideal transubstantiation every day, it is normality. This, the presentation of a weird normality, is the almost insurmountable problem of Marx's entry point of Part One – and one that he struggled with throughout its many versions.

---

89. See Murray 2000b and 2004 on subsumption.

90. Over the last fifteen years commentators of Marx have much focused on the aspect of the 'commodity money' basis in Marx's theory. This is of course relevant for the current Marxian theory of capitalism, but it is irrelevant for the historical assessment of an author writing in the second half of the nineteenth century. It is obvious that a Marxian theory of pure credit-money can be constructed. See Williams 2002, Realfonzo & Bellofiore 1996, Bellofiore & Realfonzo 1997, Bellofiore 2004 & 2005; see also Reuten & Williams 1989, Chapter 2 and Chapter 8, §4). However, pure credit-money cannot be introduced early on in *Capital*: an implantation of the stuff of *Capital III*, Parts Four and Five early on in *Capital I* would demolish the systematic structure of the work. Hence it would require a complete reconstruction of the work. A related issue is the methodological question of why Marx – given that commodity money basis – postpones a full account of credit money until later in the work. Here I agree with Campbell, who argues that this issue should be assessed from within Marx's method and systematic, especially the gradual movement from relatively simple to complex concepts and accounts. See Campbell 1997, 1998 & 2002. See also Williams 2002.

91. This theme was focussed upon by Jacques Derrida (*Specters of Marx*, 1994). See also Arthur 2001.

CONCLUSIONS

The normality is weird. Much of twentieth century Marxism has refused to read that in Part One of *Capital I*, and instead has interpreted its Chapter 1 in a 'sophisticated' Ricardian vein!

However, value cannot be concretely measured without money – any effort to do so comes down to a Ricardian 'timber–nail tale' of measurement. Of course 'as every child knows', next to nature, labour is the co-source of *materiality* (use-values) – but that is not even worth mentioning, especially not given the mainstream Ricardian discourse of Marx's day for which labour is the source of a 'naturalistic' value. For Marx, that materiality is ideally transubstantiated into the social form of value – something that bears a spectral logic of its own, which is the logic of capital.

In my interpretation of Part One of Marx's *Capital I* the IDEAL *introversive substance of value* – 'abstract labour' – is inseparable from the *ideal extroversive form of value* – money. Money establishes the actual homogeneity of commodities, and is the only one actual ideal measure of value (adopting a particular standard). It is only with the latter moment that 'value' has been fully constituted. Consequently, the term 'abstract labour' disappears in and after Chapter 3. To be sure, 'concrete' labour does *not* disappear ('living labour', as Bellofiore emphasises)[92] because labour in process becomes *explanatory* for value and surplus-value. Of course, any Ricardian identification of labour and value would make the rest of *Capital* a tautology.[93]

The impact of the spectral ideality of value is unfolded in the logic of capital (the further subject of the book). The continuous transubstantiation that is the essence of the expansion of the circuit of capital is haunting the world.

Das Kapital posits (qua intention) the truth of capital: the spectral logic of capital that has taken possession of the world. One might be conscious of the *material* power of capital (as most people are of course), however such consciousness does not imply consciousness of the spectral logic, since that is as 'normal' as the bread and wine transubstantiation for practising Catholics. We participate in it every day. Thus a weird ideality has a real material impact.

92. See Bellofiore 2004; cf. Bellofiore 1999.
93. See Reuten 2004.

REFERENCES

Superscripts indicate first and other relevant editions; the last mentioned year in the bibliography is the edition cited.

Arthur, Christopher J. 2001, 'The spectral ontology of value', *Radical Philosophy*, 107 (May-June); reprinted in Arthur, *The New Dialectic and Marx's 'Capital'*, Leiden/Boston/Köln, Brill: 153-74.
— 2004, 'Money and the form of value', in Bellofiore & Taylor (eds 2004): 35-62.
— 2005, 'Value and money', in Moseley (ed, 2005).
Arthur, Christopher J. & Geert Reuten, eds. 1998, *The Circulation of Capital: Essays on Volume II of Marx's 'Capital'*, London/New York, Macmillan/St.Martin.
Bellofiore, Riccardo 1999, 'The value of labour value; the Italian debate on Marx: 1968-1976', *Rivista di Politica Economica*, 89, No. 4-5: 31-69. Italien version: 'Quanto vale il valore lavoro? La discussione italiana intorno a Marx: 1968-1977', *Rivista di Politica Economica*, 89, Fasc. 4-5: 33-76.
— 2004, 'Marx and the macro-monetary foundation of microeconomics', in Bellofiore & Taylor (eds 2004): 170-210.
— 2005, 'The monetary aspects of the capitalist process in Marx: a re-reading from the point of view of the theory of the monetary circuit', in Moseley (ed, 2005).
Bellofiore, Riccardo & Riccardo Realfonzo 1997, 'Finance and the labour theory of value; toward a macroeconomic theory of distribution from a monetary perspective', *International Journal of Political Economy*, 27/2.
Bellofiore, Riccardo & Nicola Taylor eds. 2004, *The Constitution of Capital; Essays on Volume I of Marx's 'Capital'*, London/New York, Palgrave–Macmillan.
Campbell, Martha 1997, 'Marx's theory of money: a defense', in Moseley & Campbell (eds 1997): 89-120.
— 1998, 'Money in the circulation of capital', in Arthur & Reuten (eds 1998): 129-58.
— 2002, 'The Credit System', in Campbell & Reuten (eds 2002): 212-27.
Campbell, Martha & Geert Reuten eds. 2002, *The Culmination of Capital; Essays on Volume III of Marx's 'Capital'*, London/New York, Palgrave–Macmillan.
Elson, Diane 1979, 'The Value Theory of Labour', in Elson (ed.), *Value – The Representation of Labour in Capitalism*, London, CSE Books.

Marx, Karl 1867[1]M, 1890[4], *Das Kapital, Kritik der politischen Ökonomie, Band I, Der Produktionsprozeß des Kapitals*, MEW 23, Berlin, Dietz Verlag 1973.

— (1867[1]F, 1890[4]), *Capital, A Critique of Political Economy, Volume I*, translation of the 4th German edition by Ben Fowkes (1976[1]), Harmondsworth, Penguin Books, 1976.

Moseley, Fred ed. 2005, *Marx's Theory of Money: Modern Appraisals*, London/New York, Palgrave–Macmillan.

Moseley, Fred & Martha Campbell eds. 1997, *New Investigations of Marx's Method*, Atlantic Highlands (NJ), Humanities Press.

Murray, Patrick 2000a, 'Marx's "truly social" labour theory of value: Part I, Abstract labour in Marxian value theory', *Historical Materialism* 6: 27-66.

— 2000b, 'Marx's "truly social" labor theory of value: abstract labour in Marxian value theory (Part 2)', *Historical Materialism* 7: 99-136.

— 2002, 'Reply to Geert Reuten', *Historical Materialism* 10.1: 155-76.

— 2004, 'The social and material transformation of production by capital: formal and real subsumption in "Capital Volume I"', in Bellofiore & Taylor (eds, 2004): 243-73.

— 2005, 'Money as displaced social form: why value cannot be independent of price', in Moseley (ed, 2005).

Realfonzo, Riccardo & Riccardo Bellofiore 1996, 'Marx and money', *Trimestre* 29/1-2: 189-212.

Reuten, Geert 1988, 'Value as Social Form', in, Michael Williams (ed.), *Value, Social Form and the State*, London, Macmillan: 42-61 [Spanish translation retrievable from http://www.feb.uva.nl/pp/greuten publications 2008]

— 1993, 'The difficult labour of a theory of social value; metaphors and systematic dialectics at the beginning of Marx's *Capital*', in Moseley (ed. 1993): 89-113.

— 1999, 'The source versus measure obstacle in value theory', *Rivista di Politica Economica*, 89/4-5: 87-115 [retrievable from http://www.feb.uva.nl/pp/greuten, publications 1999]. Italien translation: 'Il problema dell'origine e quello della misura nella teoria del valore, *Rivista di Politica Economica*', 89, Fasc. 4-5: 97-128;

— 2000, 'The interconnection of Systematic Dialectics and Historical Materialism', *Historical Materialism* 7: 137-66 [retrievable from http://www.feb.uva.nl/pp/greuten publications 2000]

— 2004, 'Productive force and the degree of intensity of labour', in Bellofiore & Taylor (eds, 2004): 117-45 [retrievable from http://www.feb.uva.nl/pp/greuten publications 2004]

— 2005, 'Money as constituent of value', in Moseley (ed, 2005) [retrievable from http://www.feb.uva.nl/pp/greuten publications 2005]

Reuten, Geert & Michael Williams 1989, *Value-Form and the State; the tendencies of accumulation and the determination of economic policy in capitalist society*, London/New York, Routledge

Williams, Michael 2000, 'Why Marx neither has nor needs a commodity theory of money', *Review of Political Economy* 12/4: 435-51.

WHAT 'CAPITALISM' IS,
WHAT IT MEANS TO BE AGAINST IT,
AND WHAT IT TAKES TO END IT

Frieder Otto Wolf

The certainties of the post-modern moment of history are in full retreat. Instead of a broadly shared scepticism concerning any kind of claim of talking about the 'real thing' we are struggling against, a vague feeling seems to make itself felt in various contexts of social, cultural and political life that this real thing is becoming quite visible again: The intuition seems to come back that it is somehow *capitalism* we have to deal with, in order to open up a real future for ourselves. Almost like in the 1960s, when unrequited love was routinely explained by the dire workings of 'the system'. And, in fact, again real insights are to be gained from inquiring how capitalist exploitation conditions and permeates our unhappy lives.

Yet the confusion accompanying such a generalised feeling, such a *Zeitstimmung* may be enormous, and one fears that it will be strategically disastrous – like economicist simplification or class reductionism, reification of 'the industrial working class' into 'the subject of history'. Such simplifying approaches tend to enclose left wing politics in sectarianism; and, what is probably still more wide-spread, their mere, uncritical opposites, i.e. culturalism, identity politics, reification of the newest 'social movements', tend to preclude the building of the needed alliances with the producing classes.[94] There is, hopefully, still time to share some useful philosophical distinctions which may help the on-going debates to avoid some of those pitfalls.

The present historical reality

We, as human beings, have good reasons for being afraid now. Since

---

94. As it can be seen (again) to some degree in Germany or in Arab countries, an unenlightened anti-capitalism can even be used to feed right wing ideologies and anti-Semitism – with which emancipatory politics or struggles can have no truck. On the theoretical level, this correlates with an anti-capitalist "theory" restricted to criticising the paying of 'interest on capital'.

the end of the last boom and the bursting of the last bubble in 2007 the economic world, as it has resulted from post-cold-war history, our societies seem to be heading towards a great economic depression, comparable to the ones of the 1850s, 1870s and 1930s. The crisis of really existing 'financial capitalism' is certainly no longer limited to the financial system: nation states are stepping in to save banks defaulting, and bigger nation states 'saving' smaller ones with a view again of avoiding the default of the banking system. This crisis has begun to deepen the general economic recession which was already under way.

Public attendance and government action tend to concentrate on this economic crisis which is articulating accumulated problems – bubble economies, over-capacities, under-consumption, surfeit of capital, impending scarcity of materials and energy sources – in the economic field. These diverse processes of crisis are seen as being integrated into one larger crisis, and some political actors have begun to look for a comprehensive solution in a rearticulation of economic processes on a global scale. Such a historical search process – the successful completion of which cannot be taken to be guaranteed in advance – can be expected, judging by historical precedent, to go on for decades. Identifying its structural determinants and key mechanisms will be a decisive help in this search process.

'Capitalism', the 'capitalist mode of production' and 'modern bourgeois societies'

Marx very rarely referred to anything called 'capitalism'.[95] Apparently, he reserved this expression for two occasions only: for a journalistic reference to the present enemy (and state of affairs) the labour movement was confronted with, and for looking back to this present state of affairs from the anticipated point of view of a liberated society.

The central theoretical concept he elaborated in the scientific effort of his critique of political economy should be clearly distinguished from this 'journalistic' or 'historically retrospective' concept: When in the opening phrase of *Das Kapital* Marx refers to the general object of his inquiry he uses the expression of the 'capitalist mode of production' (c-m-p) and puts it in a relation of 'domination' with regard to some 'societies' – as we know from other formulations by Marx, he is here talking about 'mod-

---

95. In the German CD comprising most of Marx's and Engels's works, as published in Marx Engels Werke "Kapitalismus" occurs in less than 20 instances.

ern bourgeois societies': "Within the *societies* dominated by[96] *the*[97] *capitalist mode of production*" [emphasis FOW]. This concept of the *capitalist mode of production* – and not the older Marxian concepts of relations of production (*Produktionsverhältnisse*) and productive forces (*Produktivkräfte*) – constitutes Marx's theoretical articulation of the specific object of inquiry analysed and reconstructed in *Capital*.[98] Marx is not only talking about the cmp. in this general, dialectical (or systematic) way[99], he is also relating it to its specific other – modern bourgeois societies – as well as to its unspecific other – pre-modern societies. The specific relation of domination (*Herrschaftsverhältnis*) the cmp. is exercising within modern societies is absent from pre-modern societies.[100]

This *relation of domination* calls for some more theoretical discussion – as Marx in Capital only starts from it, but never managed to come back to it, articulating how it is bound up within and consequent of the concluding theoretical reconstruction (cf. Krätke 2002 and 2003, Elbe 2008) of the 'superficial manifestation' (*erscheinende Oberfläche*) of the cmp.

I think it would be a confusion to equate this relation of domina

96. The German version formulates „herrscht", which is not restricted to the meaning of ‚domination', but also allows the current English translation by „prevails". For theoretical reasons, however, the ‚harsher' translation referring to ‚domination' should be preferred here.

97. The definite article, missing here in the German version, is present in the Roy translation authorized by Marx.

98. I take the Althusserian elaboration of this concept to be an elementary theoretical discovery of something already present in Marx's construction of *Capital* as being about something as difficult to grasp as an 'ideal average' or a 'general concept'. The attempts to retro-project and to banalize this concept of a mode of capitalist production by adopting a philosophy of history centred on the 'necessary sequence of modes of production' (as in theoretical Stalinism) or by defining a mode of production by the combination of 'Produktivkräfte' and 'Produktionsverhältnisse' have generally hampered our understanding of Marx's theoretical discoveries.

99. In Wolf 2004 and 2006, I have proposed an analysis of this specifically systematic character of Marx's ‚dialectical exposition', with special emphasis on its specific presuppositions and, accordingly, limits. Acknowledging this has the implication of a rather strict usage of the expression 'systematic' in a Marxian context – with the implication, I'd propose, of limiting the expression system to entities susceptible of being systematically articulated in such a way, all other comprehensive entities being referred to as 'constellations' or as 'articulated wholes', referring to the degree of contingency or articulation involved in the case of each entity.

100. For example André Gunder Frank's (1998) impressive reconstruction of global economic history suffers from ignoring this modern specificity.

tion with the role of the infrastructure (*Basis*) determining the super-structure (*Überbau*) – in the last instance.[101] My argument for this is twofold: on the one hand, it would definitely be awkward to neglect the problematic of an articulation of modes of production when talking about the economic basis of any given society, in which it is to be specifically determined if the cmp. is constituting this basis all on its own, and to relegate such elementary material processes as child-rearing or house-keeping to the superstructure of societies; on the other hand, the very idea of an economic infrastructure constituted by the cmp. all on its own, pushes aside the elementary intuition of Rosa Luxemburg, that the accumulation of capital needs some relation to the *other* of capital, in order to function at all.[102]

This domination of the cmp. which is being imposed continuously within the infrastructure of all societies "dominated by the cmp." can be analysed with the help of a distinction Marx himself has developed in his *Grundrisse* – the distinction between a *formal* and a *real subsumption of labour under capital* – which should neither be understood as a simple binary opposition allowing for no intermediate positions, nor as a mere continuum allowing no qualitative leaps. *Real subsumption* would then mean, in such a generalised theoretical perspective, that the specific way of working of such a mode of production distinct from the cmp. is eliminated and replaced by that of the cmp. itself, i.e. by turning its specific object into a commodity and the process producing it into wage labour under capital.

The opposite end of this spectrum of historical forms would then be held by a merely formal subsumption – in the sense of the cmp. making use of the results achieved by its own way of working of the other mode of production under analysis, in order to facilitate or reinforce the accumulation of capital – as in the case of early European plundering of the 'discovered countries'. In both cases we have 'subsumption' – in the sense of a clear distinction between a 'dominant' mode of production and 'subalternate' ones – but we have a qualitative leap between them, which is constituted by the internal transformation of the subalternate ones – with their total integration into the cmp. as their last extreme case.

---

101. Althusser's useful discussion of the 'hour of the last instance' – which never tolls – has mislead some into simply disregarding the processes and struggles of the 'economic bases'.
102. It is to be granted, that Luxemburg is guilty of a *fallacy of misplaced concreteness* by identifying this other to geographical spaces and societies still to be conquered by imperialism – but once liberated from this misunderstanding, her intuition is a forceful help in understanding the unique kind of domination exercised by the c.m.p.

There are, obviously, intermediate cases of such a transformation – i.e. cases in which the transformation is not effecting the dissolution of the subalternate mode of production into the cmp, but reproducing it as a distinct cmp which has been structurally transformed in order to make its complicity with the requirements of the cmp more salient – as in the case of slavery in the 19th and 20th centuries or in the case of the second serfdom in Prussia in the 17th and 18th centuries.

In the *Communist Manifesto* we find Marx and Engels still extremely 'optimistic' about these kinds of transformation processes: Real subsumption under the cmp. is imminent everywhere for them – and, consequently, the dissolution of all pre-capitalists bonds[103], and with this dissolution the transition to a situation of proletarian world-revolution. Later on, Marx seems to have become far more reticent in this respect. It is even plausible, that the large theoretico-historical detour he has undertaken in his last years into the underwoods of grounded property have been occasioned by the recalcitrance of this category of private property to 'dissolve' into capitalist property relations.

Within *Capital*, we can find some clues indicating that this perspective of an imminent real subsumption of all reproduction processes of societies (as well as of all processes of human 'meta bolism' with nature) is not realistic, even within the most advanced modern societies.[104] Looking at the very core of the capital relation – at the offer of labour power as a commodity to be bought on the labour market, with a certain expectation of 'applying' it within a capitalist process of production – we find an often overlooked discrepancy between Marx's theoretical construction of labour power as a commodity (in which the entirety of 'necessary labour' is being defined by the value of commodities to be acquired for the sake of its reproduction, implying a 'production of this commodity exclusively by commodities', and his historical exemplification of the transition to the production of relative surplus value in the struggle for the normal working day, where the wage of the wage earner is not only to

---

103. Even the very slow dissolution of that upper layer of patriarchal gender relations in the 'point d'honneur', which made Ferdinand Lassalle get himself killed for asserting his 'possession of a woman' and which is now still present in our societies in the form of murdering women 'for the sake of honour' or 'out of jealousy', has not been an automatic process, but had to be conquered by long-term struggles of different generations of women's movements.

104. This is the elementary truth which has been elaborated e.g. by Kovel (2002) or by Harribey/Löwy 2003.

pay for the commodities needed for reproducing the labour power of the wage earner, but also for the livelihood of his wife and family.

Comparably, when Marx has written the manuscripts used by Engels to construct the second volume of *Capital*, Marx still thought it possible to neglect the own cycle of 'metamorphoses of labour power', concentrating on the one of capital itself in its accumulation process, and relegating the cycle of labour power – in which household and child-rearing work and their respective historical forms were a key item – to the 'book on wage labour'[105] planned for later on.

Feminist critics have argued – quite pertinently[106], although there has been some undeserved confusion between Marx's lack of explicitness on these issues and the massive Victorian blind spot introduced by Engels into 'Marxist' theorizing of gender relations[107] – that there is no sufficient basis for a materialist analysis of gender relations within Marxist theory. I take it that they have made it clear by their critique that Marx's critique of classical political economy is in fact still very much bound to its specific object – the cmp. which is at once specifically 'gender-blind' superficially, while at the same time using the existing gender structures strategically to its advantage[108] and even transforming it historically in order to strengthen their pro-capitalist complicity[109].

105. Since the 1980s, to my knowledge, only two attempts at reconstructing this unwritten work of Marx have been made: Heinelt (1980) makes a conceptual jump from the specific forms and metamorphoses of the reproduction process of labour-power-as-a-commodity to the more general forms of law and the state, Lebowitz (1992) sidesteps the issue of forms by making an immediate transition to a perspective of class struggle. Instead, I would insist on specifically reconstructing the 'changes of form' implied by the working of this cycle, and on the multiple interfaces they present to issues of gender and of ecology, opening a new window of research on 'household work' or on 'care work' or on 'consumerism'.
106. The classical, although – undeservedly – much reviled, text in German is Claudia von Werlhof's breath-taking piece (1983). Cf. my analysis (2007) of the 'missed rendezvous' between ecofeminism and critical Marxism in the 1980s.
107. Cf. the pioneering analysis of this problematique by Danga Vileisis (cf. her retrospective summary in Vileisis 2008.)
108. By taking in the unpaid work of household members as a source for economizing on variable capital, because of its reductive effect on the value of labour power (cf. Werlhof 1983).
109. Especially by the transformation of family structures in the emergence of the 'wage dependent nuclear family' and the creation of the figure of the 'modern housewife' as a central subject of 'consumerism'.

If we take Marx's theoretical work to be a finite scientific theory[110], however, exploring a specific object of knowledge – the cmp. – and not another one like the kind of domination operative within gender relations, we do not have any difficulty in admitting that there are other such objects to be analysed within historical reproduction processes of the internal structures of societies and their external constellations.

Distinguishing the concepts of 'capitalism' as a comprehensive socio-historical formation (and constellation of such formations) [111] and the cmp as a specific concept referring to a determinate theoretical object would lead us to seeing the possibility of conceiving the dominance of the cmp within modern bourgeois societies as something to be studied specifically – and not just to be read off from Marx's "illustrations" of his general theory in *Capital*. To insist on using the broader notion of 'capitalism', when referring to this complex historical reality, and not just the concept of the c.m.p. alone, is, therefore, not unduly legislating on language, but carefully listening to it.

If 'capitalism' means, in a loose, and yet unmistakeable way, our present state of history, we have to admit its complexity: It is clearly composed by at least four irreducible elements: (1) the cmp, with the way it dominates within given 'modern bourgeois societies', (2) the historical forms of human metabolism <u>with</u> nature, which can be referred to under the concept of capitalist industrialism, (3) modern patriarchal gender relations and (4) modern imperialist international relations, which are, all of them 'dominated' by the cmp in specific ways.[112]

---

110. This implies that we have to reduce ,historical materialism' (cf. Küttler et al. 2004) to a philosophy of history, on the one hand, producing no more, in a positive vein, than a general heuristic and instance of critical reflection for real historical research, while remaining forever inconclusive, if not aporetic, and to a gigantic 'production site', on the other, comprising all historical research being undertaken on this kind of materialist lines.

111. This is also the proper context for the use of the plural of 'capitalisms' (as 'varieties of capitalism – Albert 1991 and Hall/Soskice 2001, cf. the balance sheet of the debate in Lehndorff 2009): There are neither geographical nor historical variants of the cmp. as a general structure, neither 'stages' nor 'models', but there are, of course historical and geographical differences in the way its domination is incorporated by specific socio-historical formations, with an enormous potential of varying in time and space.

112. At this point of our argument it is sufficient to underline that this enumeration has no need of being complete – ideology, culture, law, the state, all these instances also come in to determine what the 'capitalism' were are talking about actually is and can come to be – as well as e.g. what is unearthed by Foucauldian analyses (cf. esp. Foucault 1977 and 2007) of specific techniques of discipline and control.

The others of capital:
What can be learned from the example of ground rent

Our inquiry into the limitations of the systematic exposition of the concept of 'capital in general' has unearthed a limitation based on the existence of the theoretical figure of a 'continuous external basis' (*fortwährende Grundlage*) of capitalist accumulation (cf. Wolf 2004 and 2006). Although this figure has only been used explicitly by Marx in his analysis of ground rent which reveals a specific historical relation of humans to the soil (and more generally to the biosphere inhabited by human ecologies) as its 'continuous external basis' which capitalist accumulation is incapable of reproducing as such, we can also develop this argument to extend to the other 'originary source of wealth' (*Springquelle des Reichtums*) the c.m.p. is so busy in destroying in the long run: i.e. to living human labour, as being reproduced in a gendered process within the historical gender relations of modern patriarchy. As the present crisis has, once again, made explicit, the geographically distinct existence of states as relatively autonomous power structures in a hierarchical order also has to be analysed as such a 'continuous external basis' for the very functioning of the accumulation of capital.

What such an understanding of Marx's critical reconstruction does in fact imply, is a strict distinction between theory and history – i.e. between concepts and theoretical propositions referring to general structures, on the one hand, and empirical descriptions or historical narratives (properly denoted by proper names, not by concepts) on the other as an object of theoretical reconstruction: There certainly is no such thing as a Marxian theory of 'competition capitalism', to be substituted for later phases by a Leninist theory of 'monopoly capitalism', by a critical theory of 'late capitalism.' History has indeed taken place, but not within the systematic theory constructed to explain it, but within concrete 'modern bourgeois societies' and their global constellation, challenging us to find adequate periodizations for this real history – based upon historical research and not upon simple quasi-theoretical short-cuts, as in the stage theories of capitalism.

Using this figure of a continuous external basis we may theoretically reconstruct an extended notion of what is constitutive of "capitalism": When talking about "capitalism" in such a comprehensive, an infact 'shorthand' way, we really refer to the existing constellation of those 'modern bourgeois societies dominated by the cmp' in a given period of time, on a global scale. It is their being dominated by the c.m.p., as well as their being determined by these continuous external bases, i.e., at least[113], by a historical form of personal ownership of bits of the biosphere, (mediated by *personal appropriation of the soil,* [114] in contradistinction to *common property*), as well as by a historical form of gender relations – which I take to be *modern patriarchy* in contradistinction to traditional patriarchy as a form of personal domination or to something like a spontaneous gender polymorphy as a form of liberation[115], and by *modern imperialism* in contradistinction to traditional empires, as well as to a non-hierarchical international order.

It can be argued that two of these four figures have something very important in common – the cmp and patriarchy[116] do constitute, at once, modes of production and modes of domination, whereas the *personal appropriation of the soil* is a mere mode of domination, utterly indifferent to the ways in which production is effectively organised[117], except that it is specifically fixed to the 'piece of the biosphere' which constitutes the object of this domination.[118] This is rather clear in the case of the other modes of production loosely mentioned by Marx – the Asian, the Antique, the Feudal m.p. – where the actual organization of production and the extraction of surplus produce are attributable to different moments and functions of their reproductive arrangements as whole societies.

113. I do not claim to be able to give a complete list of these "external bases" at this stage of the debate.
114. Marx has used the term *Grundherrenschaft* for referring to this elementary relation. This should not be confused with the term of '*Grundherrschaft*' used by some to refer to a historical aspect of feudal domination (cf. Rösener 1989).
115. This is, of course, a very tricky notion. As it stands, it helps to avoid any sexist or biological reductionism, and it may be taken as a hint that relatively 'emancipated sexualities' are not necessarily reserved to 'end-states' of history.
116. The isolated aspect of the mode of domination has been articulated specifically by the concept of 'male domination'. The question of which way in the present constellation there still is a full-fledged patriarchal 'mode of production' underlying modern 'consumerism' is a complicated and open one (cf. Walby 1990 and Fraad et al. 1994).
117. It has therefore been, quite rightfully, used by Samir Amin (1988) as the starting point for his concept of the tributary mode of production overarching a variety of specific ,relations of production' – like slavery, bondsmanship or primitive, pre-capitalist ,wage labour'. I should propose to go a lot further in dissolving the traditional problematic common to Engels, Kautsky, and Stalin (and his ghost-writers, especially Mitin), by distinguishing the *modes of domination* from the *modes of production*.
118. In a broadly similar way modern imperialism is building on the basis of the double-bind of territorial sovereignty over (larger) slices of the biosphere and the statist form of politics which puts hypostatized power resources into the hands of governments.

The c.m.p. introduces a decisive historical innovation by intimately linking domination and production: Almost paradoxically, by the formal liberation of labour[119] the emergence of the c.m.p. brings about, it succeeds in linking the domination of capital over labour to the way capital organises production. Whereas in older modes of production based on some kind of *Grundherrenschaft*, especially those centred on feudal relations of production[120], the action of extorting surplus produce had remained clearly divided from the way actual production took place: The violence of lords and overlords did not contribute in any way to a rational conception, planning or organisation of production – quite the contrary, it tended to disrupt its relatively time proved routines.[121] The despotism exercised by capital over labour within the capitalist production process is, by contrast, an essential factor of its continuous rational reorganization, which in turn constitutes the condition of entry for technology – in the sense of a systematic application of scientific knowledge of production processes – into the development of capitalist production as reproduction of, i.e. accumulation of, capital. Therefore two dimensions which had remained separate in earlier societies, are continuously merged within societies dominated by the c.m.p.: The control exercised by capital over the production process and the (re)organisation of this production process itself.[122]

If we look at the real history of humankind we shall certainly find a lot of significant continuities – from patterns of reproduction preceding

119. The capitalist wage labourer is constituted as a historical figure central to the c.m.p. by his formal liberation from all directly personal forms of domination, which are substituted in this very process by – potentially even harsher forms of indirect domination mediated by the free selling and buying of labour power as a commodity, as "sachlich vermittelte Herrschaft". Whereas slave labour has served as a basis of a deep transformation of agricultural practices, based upon economies of scale, as in the case of the Roman *latifundia*.

120. It would be rewarding with respect to this point to take up the critical analysis and debate on Marx's notions of feudalism and feudality, as e.g. elaborated by Alain Guerreau and Ludolf Kuchenbuch (2012).

121. It is tempting to imagine that this may be traced back to the early forms of patriarchy the echoes of which we can find in the Homeric epics, with their warrior-robbers acting as heads of families and households. But what should we make then of the tenacious loyalty of Penelope as the emblematic 'housewife' or of the no less decided loyalty of Telemachos to his absent father as the 'lord of the manor'?

122. Jacques Bidet's idea (2006) that it is necessary to separate the two poles of ‚organisation' and ‚market' within the analysis and reconstruction of the c.m.p., certainly has the merit of explicitly addressing this problematic. It misses, however, the salient point of the c.m.p. which consists in this continuous merger of both dimensions.

Grundherrenschaft to the reproduced patterns of primary human metabolistic activities stretching from early human history into the 'implicit knowledge' of workers even under the most advanced forms of capitalist production (cf. Wainwright 1994). The systematic point to be observed here lies in the qualitative difference introduced by the continuous capitalist 'improvement'[123] of the production process, by which domination and market exchanges are merged into the one process of the subsumption of the reproduction process of modern bourgeois societies under capital – which as a mere accumulation process of capital remains structurally blind to the requirements of a comprehensive reproduction of the societies submitted to it.

This kind of capitalist reorganisation of societies' production processes which tends to coincide with their being dominated by capital has, certainly, very important repercussions on the way in which this 'continuous external basis' is being reproduced. In the case of agrarian production (which is explicitly discussed by Marx as an exemplary case of the more general primary human metabolistic activities) this retroaction takes the form of an industrialisation, a properly capitalist reorganisation of production giving rise to the kind of differential rent analysed by Ricardo. In the case of the network of activities, institutions, and agencies involved in the process of gendered reproduction (which always is biological as well as cultural, and vice verso) the rise of prostitution[124] and the sex industry[125] may be seen as a comparable development, creating a kind of sexual labour directly exploited by capital, and immediately profitable as such. As in the case of landed property this does not eliminate the existence of a continuing sphere of direct patriarchal domination only indirectly used for

123. Throughout the 16th and 17th centuries, ,improvement' has served as the central catchword for the defenders of the ongoing capitalist transformation of Western European societies, with 'progress' serving the same cause in the 18th and 19th, and 'development' in the later 20th century.

124. The historical rise of prostitution as an affair of the ,free market' is historically linked with the externalization of the doublet mistress (of the household)/concubine (of the lord) out of the internal hierarchy of the greater family household into a situation where the duality of freely chosen marriage based upon love and the commodified services of 'venal women' constitute the libidinal reality of the patriarchal nuclear family. In this transition process the quasi-markets of the courts – with their reinterpretation of the same doublet as *official mistress/occasional cocotte* – seem to have plaid a role of moral and motivational transition (cf. e.g. Choderlos de Laclos's *Liaisons dangereuses*).

125. The sex industry is certainly intimately linked to a process of 'commodification' of an important part of real gender relations, even though it seems to remain on the level of the merely imaginary.

its profit by capital.[126]

Now, what is constitutive of the 'proper materiality and contradictions' of this independent sphere of reproduction of patriarchal gender relations as such? And in which sense do domination and production coincide in it?

The first thing to get clear is that – as Marx himself has made explicit concerning landed property – nothing can be expected in this respect from his theory of the c.m.p. It simply lies outside of its remit. What we do and can know about it comes from the work of feminists who have specifically analysed and reconstructed this field of scientific study as well as of strategic practice.

We may however accept a negative lesson from an understanding of Marxism as finite theory (cf. Althusser 1977): We should be wary of too easy analogies with the c.m.p., when trying to understand the proper process of patriarchal gender relations (and, likewise, of too easy analogies with state domination, e.g. when talking about the 'law of the father' – cf. Lecourt on Lacan, 1982). So the transfer of the category of 'subsistence labour' from classical political economy, as operated by Veronika Bennholdt-Thomsen, Maria Mies, and Claudia von Werlhof (1983), calls for some additional conceptual clarifications: especially for being re-contextualized within specific historical, although long-lasting, and not abstractly anthropological patterns of human reproduction. Likewise, the use of the category of rent for the analysis of structures of exploitations within patriarchal gender relations (cf. Werlhof 1983) deserves some additional amplification for being positively determined (i.e. not only to be grasped as being outside of the logic of capitalist exploitation).

At least at first sight, such transfers are not conducive to an understanding of what is proper to patriarchal gender relations, but rather to an understanding of the ways in which they are being instrumentalised, as it were, 'colonised'[127], by the dominance of the cmp.

Some have tried to explain the strong asymmetries existing in this field by the phenomena of male violence. This however, seems to be considerably besides the point – in a way comparable to anarchist explanations of capitalist dominance by capitalist violent repression, which is real too, from the police intervening against striking workers to private thugs aggressing

---

126. The strength of this analogy seems to have motivated Claudia von Werlhof to an attempt at analysing gender domination in terms of rent extraction which does not convince me.
127. Cf. the subtitle of Bennholdt-Thomsen et al. 1983: "Women - the last colony".

recalcitrant workers, no doubt. But this kind of repression happens at the weak borders of capitalist dominance, not in the fields of its functioning core. Likewise, male violence is certainly an additional supporting factor of patriarchal domination, and it may even become rather central in certain critical or marginal situations of its structural weakness, but it does not explain the very facts of patriarchal domination as such. An approach relying on Girard's (1978) analysis of the fragile, yet decisive transposition of physical into symbolic violence will certainly help to produce more pertinent and more interesting findings on the structures commanding the reproduction of gender relations, but it will not really help to address the key question of such an analysis – the problem of the grounds and reasons for the high degree of 'female complicity'[128] with patriarchal domination structures.

Neither is it of much help in achieving such a specific understanding of patriarchal gender relations as such to try to apply to them a general, non-specific perspective of the division of labour (as used in political philosophy and social theory from Rousseau to Durkheim via Ferguson and the young Marx[129]): No doubt, this division of labour is uneven and gender-hierarchical – but in which form and by which processes is this achieved and continuously reproduced? And how are male and female – and other kinds of – subjects specifically constituted as to demand, to impose, to legitimize, respectively to accept, to practice and to hand on this inequitable distribution of labour?

There seems to be no way around trying to understand the specifics of the 'labours of love' – which are in no way all resolvable into specific kinds of 'work'[130]. And, even more specifically, how assent and acceptance is continuously being generated (or fails to be generated) within relations of love.

Certain aspects of gender relations seem to be determined by the observation that there is "a sex that is not one" – i.e. subalternate to the sex that is one (i.e. the dominating male heterosexual 'law of the father')[131]. It

128. Cf. the complex debate on the double role of victim and agent imposed upon women and taken up by them (retrospective summary of the German debate initiated by Frigga Haug in: Löw 2005).
129. Cf. Kriedte et al. 1977 for a first, still superficial overview.
130. In this respect, e.g. the labours of birth-giving, should certainly not be seen within the perspective of an uneven and inequitable gendered 'division of labour'.
131. The equation of the Phallus with 'oneness' presupposes that the female sex is conceived negatively, as a lack – which is certainly a very debatable assumption with little argument behind it. Cf. Helène Cixou's (1974) impressive counter-punch: Pré-noms de personne.

is, however, not really possible to distribute this 'not one-ness'[132] clearly on gender lines: In so far male sexuality is not phallic, it seems to partake of this not being one, while phallic female sexuality clearly seems to partake of this 'being one'. It should be clearly seen, moreover, that this kind of 'being one' opposed to being 'split' or to being 'multiple', which is a rather simple property of an object, should be distinguished from 'identity' (or even 'self-identity') which are complex relations between a multiplicity of subjective positions. And although it seems evident that the 'perversity' ascribed by Freud to primary human sexual polymorphy, we do not really know what it would mean to open human sexuality for this polymorphy, while maintaining an idea of responsibility and – however remote – self-control.[133]

Which brings us to a last important conclusion of this part of our argument: That the continuing foundations of the c.m.p., landed property and patriarchal gender relations as such, although certainly historical in the sense of having had a beginning within human history and, at least potentially, offering a perspective also of coming to an end within it, do cover a far more important time span than that of their existence under the domination of the c.m.p.. Their beginning seems to date back to the transition towards late palaeolithical societies (often misnamed the 'neolithical revolution') which has brought about structured human societies going beyond spontaneous groupings, alongside with the most elementary forms of domination and exploitation. It is even plausible that the patriarchal revolution, leading to gender relations permeated by the domination of human beings over other human beings, has been the *matrix* of all later forms of human domination.[134] This conclusion seems to refute all attempts to

132. Luce Irigaray's concept is certainly a subtle and a difficult one. Yet I do not doubt that it may be sharpened to just one central point: the unavoidable distinction between a 'logic of identity and distinctness (cf. Frege's 'proper names') and a logic of equality/equivalence and difference (cf. Frege's 'concepts') the confusion of which is especially repressive and destructive in relations between persons, therefore in all gender relations.

133. Starting from the effects of state politics on human subjects I have been carried to postulating a liberating pluralization of human sexualities (Wolf 1983, republished in: Wolf 2012, 202f.), but I still must confess that I do not know what this can or can not mean in terms of actual human sexual practice.

134. Mainly this makes me refrain from following Richard D. Wolff (2006) in seeing the present household economy as merely a continuation of the *oikos*-economy central to the modes of production of antiquity or the middle ages – I simply think forms of the household economy are are going a lot further back, while their development in modern times has not been in continuity with ancient and medieval forms. The other problem, that they are not 'modes of production' in the sense supposed by the idea of a sequence of such modes of production could be sorted out by differentiating our terminology (cf. below). Re-

criticize the concept of subsistence labour by simply pointing to its large extension over times and places – it definitely refers to something co-extensive with the patriarchal form of gender relations which functions at once as a mode of production and as a mode of domination: It certainly cannot be restricted to certain dominant modes of production[135] or to certain lines of 'culture', as it has been mistakenly argued (e.g. by Behr 1983).

We may debate on the need to choose a better 'name' for such a concept[136], but there seems to be no reasonable doubt about the existence of the theoretical object it refers to, although this is to be conceived as being modulated differently in the situations before, during and after the domination of the c.m.p..

These presupposed dimensions limiting the possibilities of self-reproduction of the c.m.p. certainly are not 'modes of production' in the sense of a sequence of historical modes of production following one upon the other. On the other hand they certainly constitute specific and important 'historical forms' organising production as well as domination.[137] We may see them as something even more elementary, more basic, than mere 'modes of production'.

Theoretical reconstruction and historical processes

What my understanding of Marx's critique of political economy as a critical reconstruction of the capitalist mode of production in its general structure does in fact imply, is a strict distinction between theory and history - i.e. between concepts and theoretical propositions referring to general

reading Rudolf Bahro (1977) could produce some very useful insights in this respect.

135. The idea that the notion of distinctive modes of production alone may provide an elegant solution to the difficult task of historical periodization by postulating some simple sequence of historical epochs characterised by the dominance of one such mode of production after the other has certainly not been borne out by real historical research – with the plurality of lines of history in a world-wide perspective and with the impossibility of a deterministic understanding of the transitions between such modes of production having turned out to be the major stumbling blocks.

136. The concept of ,meta-industrial labour' proposed by Ariel Salleh certainly would constitute a major improvement – although I still have some qualms both about the understanding of 'industry' this seems to presuppose (as a technique of capitalist exploitation only, neglecting the possibilities of 'alliance-technologies' reaching beyond 'capitalism'), and about the prefix of 'meta-' which I take to combine something that comes after and something which looks back reflectively, neglecting the continuous presence of this dimension as a 'continuous external basis'.

137. Or, in the case of *Grundherrenschaft*, of combining the existing organization of production with a tributary extortion based upon mere domination.

structures, on the one hand, and empirical descriptions or historical narratives referring to particular processes involving singular entities (properly denoted by proper names, not by concepts) on the other.[138] Marx's critical theory of the cmp is definitely not related to history as an abbreviated recounting of historical events; by consequence there can be no 'stages' of the development of the cmp.

This does not make it a closed system – e.g. additional theoretical mediations (like in Marx's analysis of the corporation based on shares publicly noted at the stock exchange as a socialized version of the capitalist firm) may always be introduced into the theoretical development, or – if there is such a thing – monopoly capital may be introduced as a systematic development of the form of capital. This does not give rise, however, to an internal historicization of the cmp as an object of theoretical reconstruction: There is no ground for defending the stages theory of capitalism, because there certainly is no such thing as a Marxian theory referring to the stage of 'competition capitalism', to be substituted for later stages by a Leninist theory of 'monopoly capitalism', by a Stalinist theory of 'state monopoly capitalism', or by a critical theory of 'late capitalism' (Mandel) and so forth.[139]

History has indeed taken place, but not within the general structure of the cmp as such, but within the concrete 'modern bourgeois societies' and their global constellations,[140] challenging us to find adequate periodisations for this real history. The systematic critical theory constructed by Marx to explain the very structure of the cmp does not generate such periodisations – these have to be based upon historical research into the changing plural constellations of global and national histories and not upon simple short-cuts derived from this general critical theory, as in the stage theories of capitalism[141] or in theories based on theoretical sequences

138. This does in no way imply that the really existing object of such a theoretical construction is itself a-historical: the c.m.p. has emerged in historical time, and it will vanish again in historical time. Once established, it will, however, function on the basis of the real mechanisms reconstructed by theory.

139. This certainly is a major weakness of Hardt and Negri's theoretical arguments in 'Empire' that they remain enthralled by the false evidences of the stage theories of capitalist development – depriving themselves of any real access to the systematic sharpness of Marx's theoretical reconstruction of the c.m.p..

140. Cf. Alexis Petrioli's (2006) careful and differentiated summary and analysis of the debate about the 'logical' vs. the 'historical' in *Capital*.

141. The regulation school has started from such real historico-statistical studies of long-term developments, allowing to profile historical periods in the history of specific socio-historical formations like the USA or France. Only in later debates it has occasionally lapsed into a talk about models like 'fordism' which come dangerously close to a stage theory of

like 'formal' and 'real' subsumption or even 'absolute' and 'relative' surplus value. Furthermore, the cmp as such has introduced a decisive historical innovation[142] by intimately linking domination and production: Almost paradoxically, by its very constitutive liberation of the wage labourer from all personal bonds of domination, substituting them by its unique form of indirect domination mediated by the free sale and buying of labour power as a commodity, it succeeds in structurally linking the primary domination of capital over labour to the way capital organises production.

Again, history is about singularities – which can be pointed to, singled out, and described, or narrated as a sequence in time.[143] Social and historical theory is about explaining what happens in terms of the existence and change of such singularities.[144] That this is not an easy thing with regard to history has been the object of vivid debates – on the idiographic vs. the nomothetic moment in 'historical science' (since the late 19th century in the context of a rather successful philosophical battle against a first version of historical materialism (formulated by the young Werner Sombart and Franz Mehring, and taken up, with some reluctance, by the late Engels, and more enthusiastically by Kautsky) within historiography (cf. Petrioli 2005)[145], as well on the respective places of narrative vs. theory within historical debates on class, race, gender and national identities (in the 'postmodern moment' of social criticism since the 1980s).[146]

The argument we have deployed so far allows for a new move in this debate: It is quite apt decisively to reinforce the distinction already present in Marx between 'dialectical presentation' (= systematic theory, as e.g. in *Capital*

capitalist development.

142. Which has been characteristically neglected by economicist theories which tend to use 'capital' in the unspecific sense of a real stock, saved up or to be invested in something – i.e. neglecting its constitutive relation to wage labour which it has to exploit in order *to be* capital. The otherwise useful analyses of the long term historical developments e.g. produced by A. G. Frank and Barry K. Gills (1992) are vitiated by this kind of economicism which fails to see the quite real incision in the historical process operated by the ascent of the c.m.p. The real point it makes is, however, that there has been history before and besides this domination of the c.m.p..

143. This has been forcefully argued by Deleuze/Guattari (1972 and 1980).

144. Such a richer view of scientific explanation has been advanced and deepened within the debates of Critical realism, as initiated by Roy Bhaskar (1975).

145. This debate has been hampered to an astonishingly small degree by the disregard of the then contemporary revolution in logic and linguistics – i.e. with regard to the (normative, constructive and the descriptive, reconstructive) sciences of 'making sense' in human practices, as they have been operated by Gottlob Frege and Ferdinand de Saussure.

146. In the meantime, a 'materialist turn' seems to be on its way, which would again change the framework of the debate deeply (cf. Alaimo/Hekman 2008).

and its surrounding family of manuscripts) and the 'analysis of a segment of contemporary history' (= critical historiography, as e.g. in Marx's '18th of Brumaire'). As it has often been remarked, these two instantiations of Marx's 'materialist view of history' differ markedly – in their underlying concepts, as well as in their implicit methodology: These tend to be rather abstract, restricted to a given level of argument and meticulously controlled in the first case, while far more inclusive, empirical and flexible in the second case. We can now add to this observation – by stating the elementary reason why this is so: The object of systematic theory is being reconstructed in its (relative and limited) purity as an abstract entity, whereas the study of a concrete segment of the historical process always refers to something which is complex, overdetermined and to be taken as it is empirically/historically given – because it is not the effect of one complex of structural causes only, but the compounded effect of the dominating c.m.p. and the two 'continuing external bases' unavoidably accompanying its domination within modern bourgeois societies.

As it has been shown by analyses of very long-term historical processes in a renewed, non-reductionist materialist perspective (as e.g. by Diamond [2005 a & b], Harris [1979; 2001] or Sperling/Tjaden-Steinhauer [2003])[147] a whole world of differences and contingencies opens up before our eyes, once we begin to look at changing and varying human gender relations or at human ecologies and their specific biospheric conditions in time and space. Eurasian, (sub-sahraran) African, American, and Australian lines and patterns of human development could be differentiated, which were only gradually unified again – to some degree – since the 14th century, by the overriding dynamics of the capitalist transformation of key production processes, reaching their high points in the imperialisms of the late 19th and early 20th centuries, as well in the wave of capitalist globalization that started in the 1980s.

This new, extended awareness does not invalidate the older, still recent awareness: This still recent awareness is embodied in the development of 'culture studies' in the Anglo-Saxon world,[148] and in the 'cultural

147. The extensions operated in these inquiries on more traditional forms – Marxist and non-marxist – of historical materialism by making use of more recent ecological, epidemiological, 'anthropological', and gender research are certainly to be welcomed without any reservation. Criticism and critical wariness should set in, however, wherever these new insights are being instrumentalized for marginalising or excluding the real insights of the Marxist critique of the c.m.p. from serious scientific and political discourse.

148. A current overview can be gained from the Website http://www.culturalstudies.net/index.html..

turn' of the human and social sciences within continental Europe[149]. It is focussed on a real insight viz. that ideologies, the state and its apparatuses, as well as the retro-action of law on societal realities are not just present in the historical, empirical reality of such infrastructures as the cmp, but presupposed by them at decisive points of their workings. As, e.g. like state-made law plays a decisive role in the struggle for the normal working day as a moment of enforcing the production of relative surplus value within the cmp., officialised marriage ('wedlock') in the case of patriarchal gender relations, or the simple protection and sanctioning of property rights as such in the case of landed property. The same applies to their variegated ways of coping with such challenges make for an almost infinite variety of concrete structures of domination and their respective domination processes. The new awareness just makes us realize, how deeply anchored these differences are – reaching down to the most elementary levels of material reproduction – and how unavoidable the resulting complexity of processes and constellations must be.

REFERENCES

Aglietta, Michel, 1976, *Régulation et crises du capitalisme: l'expérience des Etats-Unis*, Paris: Calmann-Lévy.

Alaimo, Stacy and Hekman, Susan, eds. 2008, *Material Feminisms*, Bloomington / Indianapolis: University of Indiana Press.

Albert, Michel 1991, *Capitalisme contre capitalisme*, Paris: Seuil (*Capitalism against Capitalism*, London: Whurr/Wiley 1993).

Amin, Samir, 1988, *L'eurocentrisme: Critique d'une idéologie*, Paris: Anthropos/Economica (*Eurocentrism*, New York: Monthly Review Press 1989).

Althusser, Louis 1969, 'Contradiction and Overdetermination', in Louis Althusser, *For Marx*, London: Verso.

Althusser, Louis 1998, 'Le marxisme comme théorie 'finie'', in Louis Althusser, *La solitude de Machiavel et autres textes*, ed. by Yves Sintomer, Paris: Presses Universitaires de France.

Altvater, Elmar 2005, *Das Ende des Kapitalismus wie wir ihn kennen: Eine radikale Kapitalismuskritik*. Münster: Westfälisches Dampfboot.

Amable, Bruno 2005, *Les cinq Capitalismes. Diversité des systèmes économiques et*

149. Terry Eagleton has succeeded in summarizing much of these developments, although mainly from a British perspective.

sociaux dans la mondialisation, Paris: Seuil.

Arendt, Hannah 2009, *Elements of Totalitarianism*, New York: Schocken Books.

Aronowitz, Stanley, *The Retreat to Postmodern Politics*, <http://www.stanleyaronowitz.org/articles/article_endofpp.pdf >

Arrighi, Giovanni, Hopkins, Terence K., Wallerstein, Immanuel, eds. 1989, *Antisystemic movements*, London: Verso.

Badiou, Alain 1988, *L'être et l'évènement*, Paris: Seuil.

Balibar, Étienne 1974, *Cinq études sur le matérialisme historique*, Paris: Maspéro.

Balibar, Étienne 1994, *Lieux et noms de la vérité*, La Tour d'Aigues: Editions de l'Aube.

Bahro, Rudolf 1977, *Die Alternative. Zur Kritik des real existierenden Sozialismus.* Köln/Frankfurt.

Bahro, Rudolf 1980, *Elemente einer neuen Politik : Zum Verhältnis von Ökologie und Sozialismus*, Berlin: Olle & Wolter.

Bakker, Isabella ed. 1994, *The Strategic Silence. Gender and Economic Policy*, London: Zed Books.

Beer, Ursula 1983, Marx auf die Füße gestellt? Zum theoretischen Entwurf von Claudia v. Werlhof, in: *Prokla 50*, , 22-37.

Benjamin, Jessica 1988, *The Bonds of Love: Psychoanalysis, Feminism and the Problem of Domination*, New York: Pantheon Books.

Bennholdt-Thomsen, Veronika, Mies, Maria, von Werlhof, Claudia 1983, *Frauen, die letzte Kolonie*, Reinbek: Rowohlt.

Bertrand, Hugues 1979, 'Le régime central d'accumulation de l'après-guerre et sa crise', in: *Critiques de l'économie politique*, n°7-8., 114-16

Bhaskar, Roy A. 1997, *A Realist Theory of Science*, London.

Bhaskar, Roy 1979, *The Possibility of Naturalism*, Hassocks: Harvester.

Bidet, Jacques 2006, 'Die metastrukturale Rekonstruktion des Kapital', in Jan Hoff, Alexis Petrioli und Ingo Stützle, F. O. Wolf, eds., *Das Kapital neu lesen. Beiträge zur radikalen Philosophie*, Münster: Westfälisches Dampfboot 146-158.

Bourdieu, Pierre 1997, Die männliche Herrschaft', in Dölling, Irene, Krais, Beate ed., 1997, *Ein alltägliches Spiel. Geschlechterkonstruktion in der sozialen Praxis*, Frankfurt a. M.: Suhrkamp.

Callinicos, Alex 1991, *Against Postmodernism: a Marxist critique*, Cambridge: Polity Press.

Callinicos, Alex 2003, *An Anti-Capitalist Manifesto*, Oxford: Basil Blackwell.

Cixous, Hélène 1970, *Le Troisième Corps*, Paris: Grasset.

Cixous, Hélène 1974, *Prénoms de Personne*, Paris: Grasset.

Cohen, Gerald Allen 1978;, *Karl Marx's Theory of History: A Defense*, Oxford: Clarendon Press.

Debeir, Jean-Claude, Deléage, Jean-Paul, Hémery, Daniel 1991, *In the servitude of power: energy and civilisation through the ages*, Lodon: Zed Books.

Deleuze, Gilles, Guattari, Félix 1972, *Capitalisme et schizophrénie*, vol. 1: *L'anti-oedipe*, Paris: Editions de Minuit vol. 2.: *Mille Plateaux*, Paris: Editions de Minuit.

Diamond, Jared 1998, *Guns, Germs and Steel*, London: Vintage.

Diamond, Jared 2005, *Collapse*, London: Allen Lane.

Dölling, Irene, Krais, Beate ed., 1997, *Ein alltägliches Spiel. Geschlechterkonstruktion in der sozialen Praxis*, Frankfurt a. M.: Suhrkamp.

Donzelot, Jacques 1977, *La police des familles*, Paris: Editions de Minuit.

Dutschke, Rudi 2000, *An den Genossen Professor Lukács*, ed, by F. O. Wolf, in: *Das Argument*, No. 138, 829-858

Elbe, Ingo 2008, *Marx im Westen. Die neue Marx-Lektüre in der Bundesrepublik seit 1965*, Berlin: Akademie-Verlag.

Elster, Jon 1985, *Making Sense of Marx*, Cambridge/Paris: Cambridge University Press.

Foucault, Michel 1975, *Surveiller et punir: la naissance de la prison*, Paris: Gallimard 1975.

Foucault, Michel 2007, *Security, Territory, Population: Lectures at the Collège de France, 1977-78*, Houndmills, Basingstoke: Palgrave/MacMillan.

Fraad, Harriet, Resnick, Stephen, Wolff, Richard 1994, *Bringing It All Back Home: Class, Gender and Power in the Modern Household*, London: Pluto Press.

Frank, A. G. 1998, *Reorient: Global economy in the Asian age*, Berkeley, Calif.: University of California Press.

Frank, A. G., Gills, Barry K. 1992, 'The Five Thousand Year World System: An Interdisciplinary Introduction', in *Humboldt Journal of Social Relations*, Vol. 18, No. 2, Spring 1992, pp. 1-80.

Fraser, Nancy 2008, *Scales of Justice: Reimagining Political Space in a Globalizing World*, New York: Columbia University Press.

Gindin, Sam, Panitch, Leo, Gems and Baubles 2002, 'Empire', *Historical Materialism*, 10, pp. 17-43

Girard, René 1977, *La Violence et le Sacré*. Paris: Grasset.

Girard, René 1987, *Things Hidden since the Foundation of the World: Research undertaken in collaboration with Jean-Michel Oughourlian and G. Lefort*. Stanford: Stanford University Press.

Godelier, Maurice 1984, *L'idéel et le matériel*, Paris: Editions Fayard.

Guerreau, Alain, Kuchenbuch, Ludolf 2012, *Marx und der Feudalismus (1983/2012)*, Heft 1: Zur Entwicklung des Feudalismuskonzepts im Werk von Karl Marx (Philosophische Gespräche 24), Berlin 2012; Heft 2 (Philosophische Gespräche 25), Berlin.

Hall Peter, Soskice, David, eds. 2001, *Varieties of Capitalism. The Institutional Foundations of Comparative Advantage*. Oxford: Oxford University Press.

Hardt, Michael, Negri, Antonio 2000, *Empire*, Cambridge, Mass.: Harvard University Press.

Hardt, Michael, Negri, Antonio 2004, *Multitude: War and Democracy in the Age of Empire*, New York / London: Penguin.

Hardt, Michael, Negri, Antonio 2009, *Common Wealth*, Cambridge, Mass.: Harvard University Press.

Harris, Marvin 2001, *Cultural Materialism: The Struggle for a Science of Culture*, New York: Random House 1979, updated Walnut Creek, CA: Altamira Press.

Harribey, Jean-Marie, Löwy, Michael, eds. 2003, *Capital contre nature*, Paris: Presses Universitaires de France.

Hausen, Karin, ed 1993, *Geschlechterhierarchie und Arbeitsteilung. Zur Geschichte ungleicher Erwerbschancen von Männern und Frauen*, Göttingen: Vandenhoeck & Ruprecht.

Hawkins, Mike 1997, *Social Darwinism in European and American Thought, 1860-1945: Nature as Model and Nature as Threat*. Cambridge: Cambridge University Press.

Heinelt, Hubert 1980, *Arbeiterbewegung und Sozialpolitik*, Hannover: SOAK.

Hoff, Jan 2009, *Marx global: Zur Entwicklung des internationalen Marx-Diskurses seit 1965*, Berlin: Akademie Verlag.

Ders. Petrioli, Alexis, Stützle, Ingo, Wolf, Frieder Otto eds. 2006, *Das Kapital neu lesen*, Münster: Westfälisches Dampfboot.

Holloway, John 2002, *Change the World Without Taking Power: The Meaning of Revolution Today*, London: Pluto Press.

Irigaray, Luce 1974, *Speculum: de l'autre femme*, Paris: Editions du Minuit.

Kovel, Joel 2002, *The Enemy of Nature: The End of Capitalism or the End of the World?*, London: Zed Books.

Krätke, Michael 2002, "Hier bricht der Text ab...". Hat das Kapital einen Schluss?, in: *Beiträge zur Marx Engels-Forschung. Neue Folge*.

Krais, Beate, Engler, Steffani ed., 2004, *Das kulturelle Kapital und die Macht der Klassenstrukturen. Sozialstrukturelle Verschiebungen und Wandlungsprozesse des Habi-*

tus. Weinheim/München: Juventa Verlag.

Kriedte, Peter, Medick, Hans, Schlumbohm, Jürgen 1977, *Industrialisierung vor der Industrialisierung: Gewerbliche Warenproduktion auf dem Land in der Formationsperiode des Kapitalismus*, Göttingen: Vandenhoek & Ruprecht.

Kriedte, Peter 1983, 'Die Proto-Industrialisierung auf dem Prüfstand der historischen Zunft. Antwort auf einige Kritiker, in: Geschichte und Gesellschaft', 9. Jg., H. 1, Literatur und Sozialgeschichte, pp. 87-105

Küttler, Wolfgang, Petrioli, Alexis, Wolf, Frieder Otto 2004, 'historischer Materialismus', in *Historisch-kritisches Wörterbuch des Marxismus*, ed. W. F. Haug, vol. 6/I, Hamburg: Argument, 316-334.

Lebowitz, Michael 1992, *Beyond Capital:* Marx's political economy of the working class, Basingstoke: Macmillan.

Lehndorff, Steffen, ed., 2009, *Abriss, Umbau, Renovierung? Studien zum Wandel des deutschen Kapitalismusmodells*. Hamburg: VSA-Verlag.

Lévi-Strauss, Claude 1962, *La pensée sauvage*, Paris: Plon.

Levine, David 1977, *Family Formation in an Age of Nascent Capitalism*, New York: Academic Press.

Löw, Martina, Frigga Haug, eds. 2005, „Frauen – Opfer oder Täter?", in: Dies. / Mathes, Bettina, eds., *Schlüsseltexte der Geschlechterforschung*, Wiesbaden: VS Verlag für Sozialwissenschaften, 148-157

Löwy, Michael 1993, *On Changing the World. Essays in political philosophy: from Karl Marx to Walter Benjamin*, New Jersey: Humanities Press.

Lukács, Georg 1923, *Geschichte und Klassenbewusstsein*, Berlin: Malik Verlag (*History and Class Consciousness*, London: Merlin Press 1971)

Medick, Hans 1976, „Zur strukturellen Funktion von Haushalt und Familie im Übergang von der traditionellen Agrarwirtschaft zum industriellen Kapitalismus: die proto-industrielle Familienwirtschaft", in: Werner Conze, ed., *Sozialgeschichte der Familie in der Neuzeit Europas*, Stuttgart: Klett, 254-282

Trepp, Anne-Charlott hg. 1998, *Geschlechtergeschichte und allgemeine Geschichte: Herausforderungen und Perspektiven*, Göttingen: Wallstein Verlag.

Mendels, Franklin F. 1972, "Proto-*industrialization: the first phase of the industrialization process*", in *Journal of Economic History*, 32, pp. 241-261

Möller, Carola, Überlegungen zu einem gemeinwesenorientierten Wirtschaften, in: Stiftung Fraueninitiative Köln (ed.) 1997, *Wirtschaften* für das „gemeine Eigene' – Handbuch zum gemeinwesenorientierten *Wirtschaften*. Berlin: Trafo-Verlag, pp. 17-32.

Resnick, Stephen, Wolff, Richard 1987, *Knowledge and Class: A Marxian Critique of Political Economy*, Chicago/London: The University of Chicago

Press.

Roemer, John E. 1986, ed., *Analytical Marxism*, Cambridge, Cambridge University Press.

Rösener, Werner, ed. 1989, *Strukturen der Grundherrschaft im frühen Mittelalter*, Göttingen: Vandenhoeck & Ruprecht.

Salleh, Ariel 1997, *Ecofeminism as Politics*, New York/London:Zed Books/ Palgrave.

Sohn-Rethel, Alfred 1971, *Materialistische Erkenntniskritik und Vergesellschaftung der Arbeit: zwei Aufsätze*, Berlin: Merve-Verlag.

Sperling, Urte, Tjaden-Steinhauer, Margaret, eds. 2004, *Gesellschaft von Tikal bis irgendwo: Europäische Gesellschaft, gesellschaftliche Umbrüche, Ungleich- heiten neben der Spur*. Kassel: Verlag Winfred Junior.

Swyngedouw, E A. 1999, "Marxism and historical-geographical mate- rialism: A spectre is haunting geography", in *Scottish Geographical Journal*, 115(2), pp. 91-102

Vallicella, William F. 2002, "Relations, Monism and the Vindication of Bradley's Regress'", in *Dialectica*, 56 (1), pp. 3–35

Vileisis, Danga 1996, „Engels' Rolle im "unglücklichen Verhältnis" zwischen Marxismus und Feminismus. Geschlechterhierarchie und Herrschaft in den vorkapitalistischen Gesellschaften bei Marx und Engels", in: *Beiträge zur Marx-Engels-Forschung N.F.*, Hamburg: Argument.

Dies 2008, „Geschlechterverhältnisse und gesellschaftliche Reproduktion. Zur marxschen Rezeption von John Millar", in: Lindner, Urs / Nowak, Jörg / Paust-Lassen, Pia, hg., *Philosophieren unter anderen*, Münster: West- fälisches Dampfboot, 106-118

Virno, Paolo 2003, *Gramática de la multitud. Para un análisis de las formas de vida contemporáneas*. Madrid: Traficantes de Sueños 2003 (*A Grammar of the Mul- titude: For an Analysis of Contemporary Forms of Life*, New York: Semiotext(e) 2004)

Vollgraf, Carl-Erich, Jungnickel, Jürgen 1995, „Marx in Marx' Worten? Zu Engels' Edition des Hauptmanuskripts zum dritten Buch des 'Kapitals'", in: Vollgraf, Carl, ed., *MEGA-Studien 1994/2*, Berlin: Dietz 1955, 3-55.

Wainwright, Hilary 1994, *Arguments for a New Left*, Oxford: Basil Blackwell 1994.

Walby, Sylvia 1990, *Theorising Patriarchy*, Oxford: Basil Blackwell.

Wallerstein, Immanuel 1992, "The Collapse of Liberalism", in: *New World Order? Socialist Register*, ed. Ralph Miliband and Leo Panitch, pp. 96-110

Wallerstein, Immanuel 2004, *World-Systems Analysis: An Introduction*. Durham, North Carolina: Duke University Press.

Werlhof, Claudia von 1983, „Frauenarbeit: der blinde Fleck in der Kritik der politischen Ökonomie", in: *Beiträge zur feministischen Theorie und Praxis*, No.1, pp. 18-32.

Wolf, Frieder Otto 2004, "The 'limits of dialectical presentation' as a key category of Marx's theoretical self-reflection", in: *Capitalism, Nature, Socialism*, 15 (3) pp. 79-85

Wolf, Frieder Otto 2006, "Marx' Konzept der ‚Grenzen der dialektischen Darstellung", in: Jan Hoff, Alexis Petrioli und Ingo Stützle, eds., *Das Kapital neu lesen. Beiträge zur radikalen Philosophie*, Münster: Westfälisches Dampfboot.

Wolf, Frieder Otto 2007, "The Missed Rendezvous of Critical Marxism and Ecological Feminism", in: *Capitalism, Nature, Socialism*, 18 (2), pp. 109-125

Wolf, Frieder Otto 2012, *Rückkehr in die Zukunft − Krisen und Alternativen*, Münster.

Wolff, Richard D. 2006, „Die überdeterministische und klassentheoretische Kapital-Lektüre in den USA", in: Jan Hoff, Alexis Petrioli und Ingo Stützle, eds., *Das Kapital neu lesen. Beiträge zur radikalen Philosophie*, Münster: Westfälisches Dampfboot, pp. 128-145.

Wood, Ellen Meiksins 1999, *The Origin of Capitalism: a longer view*, London/New York: Verso.

Wood, Neal 1994, *Foundations of Political Economy : Some Early Tudor Views on State and Society*, Berkeley, Calif.: University of *California* Press.

Wright, Steven 2002, *Storming Heaven. Class composition and struggle in Italian Autonomist Marxism*, London: Pluto Press.

RE-READING CAPITAL

IS MARX A FICHTEAN?

Tom Rockmore

We are still in the process of understanding Marx's position, and thus in assessing his specific contribution. It is always better to read an author through his or her writing, as distinct from writings about him or her. But for various reasons, over many years Marx was mainly read by Marxists, non-Marxists and anti-Marxists alike through *Marxism*. In the Marxist reading of Marx, Hegel plays a key but variable role.

In the West, at least since Engels invented Marxism, Hegel is still routinely regarded as a central influence on Marx. This is not the case in the East, for instance, in China, where Hegel's influence in the formulation of Marx's position is only now starting to be taken seriously. Western Marxism has always insisted on the crucial character of Marx's reaction against Hegel. According to this approach, Marx, in reacting against Hegel, came to grips with and 'left' philosophy. One of its presuppositions is that Marx's relation to philosophy can be adequately depicted through his reaction to Hegel, since, it is claimed, classical German philosophy reached a high point and culmination in the thought of the latter. Hegel, of course, never made this claim, asserted by the Young Hegelians very soon after his passing

Obviously, Hegel remains a centrally important philosophical figure, even if not all aspects of classical Germany philosophy can be addressed through his thought. But if not all of classical German philosophy can be reduced to Hegel's position, then it is important to consider other philosophers to whom Marx reacted in formulating his position. I will be focusing on his relation to Fichte, who is rarely mentioned in the Marxist debate, but who, I will argue, was crucial for the formulation of Marx's position, and hence for assessing his contribution. One of the results of this study will be to indicate that in reacting against Hegel, Marx did not 'leave' philosophy, but in fact made a crucial philosophical contribution.

Feuerbach and the Marxist reading of Marx

If it turns out that Fichte did in fact influence Marx, then it will be necessary to revise the Marxist view of his link to German Marxism, since Engels depicts the relation of Marx to philosophy mainly through Hegel, whom he allegedly rejects, and Feuerbach, who supposedly makes this rejection possible. To state it rather informally, the argument goes something like this: Marx's position arose in reaction to Hegelian idealism. Idealism presents a distorted, hence false, view, based on an inverted conception of the real world as viewed through the lens of bourgeois thought. Marx later freed himself from idealism through Feuerbach. Idealism and materialism are incompatible opposites. Idealism in all its forms is false, but at least one form of materialism is true. Feuerbach provides a decisive materialist critique of Hegel, hence of idealism. Marx follows Feuerbach's lead in 'leaving' idealist claptrap behind for materialism, whose dialectical version provides the only correct approach to contemporary society. To keep this article within reasonable limits of space, let me restate this complex claim as a series of four discrete propositions:

1. Marx's position arose in reaction to Hegelian idealism.
2. Idealism and materialism are incompatible opposites, of which one is true and the other is false.
3. Marx followed Feuerbach's lead, more precisely his decisive critique of Hegelian idealism, in giving up idealism for materialism.
4. In giving up idealism for materialism, Marx moved beyond philosophy.

These assertions are often regarded as true, but each is in fact false. By 'false', I mean inaccurate, tendentious, or misleading. There is a widespread tendency to understand Marx in terms of his roots in Hegelian idealism. Now, Marx's relation to Hegel and Hegelianism should not be denied. He was obviously influenced by Hegel, whom he read as a teenager, whom he criticised in his early writings while still in his mid-twenties, and on whom he continued to rely for key categories used in *Capital*. Though himself a Young, or left-, Hegelian, he was also critical of other Young Hegelians. It is initially plausible – but, on reflection, misleading – to understand Marx's position as arising solely in reaction to Hegelian idealism, if that means it can somehow be adequately accounted for or understood simply in terms of its Hegelian roots. It may well be, as Engels reports, that the origin of Marx's position lies in coming to grips with Hegel's *Philosophy of Right*. But this led Marx well beyond the confines of his understanding of Hegel,

130

towards other economic and political horizons and, within philosophy, towards thinkers he regarded as supplementing or even correcting Hegel.

The second proposition concerns the relation between idealism and materialism. Most observers regard materialism (or realism) and idealism as incompatible, and believe that a simultaneous commitment to both would be self-contradictory. The view that no version of idealism and materialism (or realism) can be combined within a single position is common to objections raised against idealism in different ways by its Marxist and analytic critics. Elsewhere, I have examined 'idealism' in detail in the context of an account of Kantian, hence German, idealism.[150] There are different types of idealism and materialism. It is doubtful that there is a single, shared doctrinal commitment for either idealism or materialism, whose subtypes appear to overlap in terms of family resemblances rather than a shared essence. In a famous paper, G.E. Moore influentially suggested that idealists of all stripes are committed to the denial of the existence of the external world.[151] Yet this is a clear error, since he does not specify any idealist guilty of this mistake and none has ever been identified. Further, the supposed incompatibility between idealism and materialism, though often asserted, is nowhere demonstrated. On a closer look, it appears that, if properly understood and under appropriate conditions, idealism and materialism are compatible.

The relation between these doctrines is long and complex. The philosophical term 'idealist' seems to have been invented by Leibniz. In responding to Bayle, he objects to 'those who, like Epicurus and Hobbes, believe that the soul is material' in adding that in his own position 'whatever of good there is in the hypotheses of Epicurus and Plato, of the great materialists and the great idealists, is combined here'.[152] Leibniz's usage of the term implies idealism and materialism differ, but can be combined, in a single position. He suggests, as Fichte later appears to suggest, a simultaneous commitment to idealism and materialism (or realism).[153]

Marx is often regarded as following Feuerbach's lead in giving up idealism, which he supposedly vanquished, for materialism. Feuerbach, who was an opponent of Hegel, criticises the latter in various texts, notably in terms of the so-called *Principles of the Philosophy of the Future*.[154] But it is not

150. See Rockmore 2007.
151. See Moore.
152. Leibniz 1875–90, Vol. IV, pp. 559–60.
153. See Fichte 1982.
154. See Feuerbach 1986.

the case, as the name of his position clearly suggests, that he vanquishes idealism for extra-philosophical materialism. It is further exaggerated to claim that Feuerbach, who is a minor figure, 'overcomes' Hegel, a true philosophical giant. At most, he can be read as pointing beyond Hegel in other directions. Fourth, even if Marx were a materialist, it would not follow that he had moved beyond philosophy. There are numerous philosophical materialists, beginning with Democritus, Leucippus and Epicurus, the materialists of antiquity, and continuing up to the present. Even if Marx supported Feuerbach against Hegel, it would not follow that he as such moved beyond philosophy.

Schelling and Marxism

The view that Feuerbach played a crucial role in Marx' thinking as Marx moved beyond philosophy is, famously, not formulated by Marx, but rather by Engels, the first Marxist, who pioneered this reading of Marx. Yet it is not well-known that Engels invented Marxism by means of combining ideas drawn from Schelling with his view of Feuerbach.[155155] Engels, who did not have a university degree, was an autodidact, without more than a cursory philosophical background. In inventing Marxism, he was decisively influenced by a short period of study with Schelling in 1841. Another student in the same class was Kierkegaard. In the Munich lectures, held shortly after Hegel's death, Schelling sharply criticised Hegel's position as negative, in advancing his own supposedly positive philosophy, which ultimately became his theory of revelation. Engels and Kierkegaard both later formulated different versions of Schelling's complaint that Hegel was unable to grasp concrete existence. In Marxism, this became the difference between theory and practice, or Praxis. Engels developed Schelling's distinction between negative and positive philosophy in substituting the familiar distinction between materialism and idealism. In Engels's revision of Schelling's critique of Hegel, idealism, which is intrinsically abstract, cannot grasp the real social context. It is grasped only by materialism, which, unlike idealism, is concrete. Marxism, which is only distantly related to Marx's own position, is a philosophical amalgam thrown together by borrowing from different sources, constructing a crude but highly misleading view of the Western philosophical tradition on the basis of a simplistic account of German idealism. The most influential statement of this theory is found in Engels's little book, *Ludwig Feuerbach and the End of Classical German*

155. On the relation of Marxism to Schelling, see Frank 1975.

132

Philosophy.[156] Here and elsewhere, Marxism consists of a misleading, simplistic three-fold claim regarding the relation of Hegel to prior philosophy, the relation of philosophy to philosophical problems, and the relation of Marx to philosophy and philosophical problems. According to this view, philosophy came to a peak and to an end in Hegel.

Hegel, who never made this claim, contradicted it by suggesting that all positions, including his own, belong to the history of philosophy. Kant notoriously suggested that philosophy comes to an end in the critical philosophy. Yet no philosophical theory, position, insight or argument can suffice to bring the philosophical tradition to an end. Earlier theories are either ignored or refuted by later theories, which continually take the discussion beyond any given point. Engels generalised Schelling's view of Hegel's supposedly negative philosophy to philosophy in general. According to Engels, philosophy in general is inadequate to solve, resolve or otherwise dispose of its problems, concerns, or difficulties. His basic insight that reason must be adapted to – or, in another formulation, made congruent with – its object goes back in the early Greek tradition at least to Parmenides. In distinguishing between the way of error, which is straight, and the way of truth, which is circular, he indicates that the cognitive instrument of knowledge must be adapted to its cognitive object, that which it seeks to know. This idea is later restated many times: for instance, in Kant's Copernican revolution, which centers around the claim that one can only know what one in some sense constructs. Engels suggests that philosophy is inadequate to come to grips with its problems, which are, however, real. These problems are resolved only by Marxism, which is situated beyond philosophy. Engels's unsupported blanket-claims rapidly became articles of Marxist faith, with roughly the same status as religious beliefs. Such beliefs need neither argument nor demonstration in order to be accepted, and cannot be refuted through ordinary forms of argument. Engels, who did not demonstrate any single one of his claims, made no pretense of arguing for his interpretations, which remain mere assertions. He did not, for instance, show that philosophy came to an end in Hegel, that it cannot carry out its self-assigned tasks, nor that Marxism can provide an extra-philosophical solution to philosophical problems. It seems doubtful that philosophical questions can be answered 'outside philosophy'.

---

156. See Engels 1941.

Lukács and Hegelian Marxism

In Engels's reading of Marx, Feuerbach enabled the latter to 'leave' philosophy in favour of a scientific perspective situated outside it in order to solve, resolve or overcome its difficulties, problems and concerns. This is tantamount to suggesting that, as Althusser insisted, Marx turned away from an approach based on the actions of one or more individuals, illustrated in German idealism, to instead rely on science, and thus scientific laws. Althusser worked out this interpretation through a so-called *coupure épistémologique* [epistemological break] leading to a 'scientific' theory that, since it is no longer philosophy, does not depend on subjectivity. On the contrary, when we inspect Marx's texts, we see that his position relies on rethinking the conception of the subject that does not leave behind, but rather depends on, German idealism, especially Fichte.

Engels's simplistic, unargued account of the relation of Marx to Hegel and German idealism is literally transformed in Lukács's complex, closely argued account. Simultaneously with Karl Korsch,[157] Lukács invented Hegelian Marxism. Unlike Engels, and unlike most students of Marx, including Korsch, Lukács had a thorough grasp of classical German philosophy. He did early work in Kantian aesthetics before turning to Marxism. His particular form of Hegelian Marxism has two characteristics. First – like Korsch, and like other Hegelian Marxists – he resisted a simplistic, binary reading of the relation of Marx to Hegel, in formulating a richer, multi-dimensional account. Second – unlike Korsch as well as other Hegelian Marxists – Lukács, in emphasising Hegel, also pointed to the importance of Fichte for Marx's position.

Lukács's most significant account of Hegelian Marxism occurred in *History and Class Consciousness*,[158] which appeared in 1923, the same year as Korsch's important study *Marxism and Philosophy*. Lukács, who employed a Marxist reading of Marx with Kantian and neo-Kantian elements, comprehended Marx's theory as a form of commodity-analysis. According to Lukács, only Marxist political economy is capable of comprehending the economic structure of advanced industrial society.

His Kantian argument for this claim consists of two points. First, non-Marxist political economy cannot know its object, that is, the real structure of the social context. So-called bourgeois political economy, which is limited to grasping false appearance, is implicitly irrational. Second, Marx-

157. Korsch 1972..
158. See Lukács 1971.

ian political economy grasps true appearance through the Marxian theory of commodity-analysis, and hence is implicitly rational. It is the only approach that can lead to knowledge of social reality. Marx's theory of commodity-analysis, as Lukács asserted in a dazzling example of Marxist faith, can resolve any and all problems.[159] Lukács's attitude towards Engels was both positive and negative: positive in that he supplied arguments to buttress the latter's simplistic assertions as he restated Marxism on a philosophical basis, but negative in that he sharply criticised Engels's philosophical inadequacies, such as his simplistic treatment of Kant's key conception of the thing-in-itself.[160] Engels simply claimed that philosophy reaches its peak and end in Hegel without being able to resolve its problems. Lukács argued for this claim in identifying a specific flaw in classical German philosophy on the level of the subject, which is allegedly corrected by Marx.

Lukács's argument in favour of Marxism extends Kant's analysis of the uncognizable thing-in-itself throughout classical German philosophy, which is unable to know its object. According to Lukács, Kant advanced an inadequate conception of the subject, whose difficulty culminated in Hegel's appeal to a mythological concept of the absolute, expressing a manifest inability to understand the real historical subject, the proletarian class, or identical subject-object. Lukács adduced three reasons, all well-known in the Hegel literature, for Hegel's supposed failure to provide an adequate conception of the subject. First, the relation of reason to history is merely contingent, since reason is not actually imminent to history. This is a version of the familiar Marxian view that Hegel began from an abstract, theoretical perspective, which never grasps the social and historical context. Second, Hegel supposes that history has an end, which lies in the Prussian state. In this context, Lukács restated the frequent claim that in Hegel's later thought he turned away from the revolutionary ideals of his youth and assumed a reactionary political stance. Third, he complained that in the *Encyclopedia*, in an abstract, contemplative discussion, Hegel separated genesis from history in a merely logical analysis of the transition from logic through nature to spirit. The resultant conception of the absolute only seems to make history. This is a form of the well-known assertion – which Lukács never abandoned, and which formed the basis of his critique of Hegel in *Zur Ontologie des gesellschaftlichen Seins* – that Hegel's philosophy is a panlogism.[161]

159. See Lukács 1971, p. 83..
160. See Lukács 1971, pp. 131–3.
161. See Lukács 1984..

According to Lukács, the interest of the German-idealist tradition consists of pointing through its method towards the way beyond these limits. The correct path lies in a return to the early Marx's discovery of the true historical subject. Through the dialectical method as the true historical method, we identify the real 'we' of the historical process in the proletariat, as the identical subject/object of history. Lukács writes:

> The continuation of that course which at least in method started to point the way beyond these limits, namely the dialectical method as the true historical method, was reserved for the class which was able to discover within itself on the basis of its life-experience the identical subject-object, the subject of 'action' the 'we' of the genesis: namely the proletariat.[162]

The claim for the proletarian standpoint as the solution to the problem emerging from the thing-in-itself is, in fact, a transparent restatement of the Young-Hegelian view that philosophy comes to an end in Hegel's thought. In other words, the theory of the proletariat discovered by Marx and continued by Marxism provides the solution for the problem left unsolved by classical German philosophy. In the final analysis, philosophy does not end in the Hegelian synthesis: rather, it is completed and comes to an end in the Marxian transformation of absolute idealism, seamlessly prolonged in Marxism. We can summarise as follows: according to Lukács, Marx's key move lay in rethinking the subject in his early writings. In this context, Lukács turned his attention towards Fichte. Lukács was critical of the Fichtean concept of activity, whose importance lies in a prototypical solution of the relation of theory and praxis, subjectivity and objectivity. He followed others in maintaining that Fichte failed to understand the true nature of human activity, which he assimilated to mental activity alone.

Fichte's conception of the subject as wholly active and never passive is significant as a contribution to the Kantian problem. Kant made theory dependent on practice, since problems not amenable to theoretical analysis can, nevertheless, be resolved in practice. Fichte went beyond Kant in correctly locating the unity of subject and object in activity. Lukács suggests that, in rethinking the unity of subject and object as activity,[163] Fichte showed that the given can be understood as the product of the identical

162. Lukács 1971, pp. 148–9.
163. Lukács 1971, p. 123.

subject/object, which derives from this unity. The importance of Fichte's view for Lukács becomes clear in his argument that the unity of subject and object, which Fichte allegedly located in mental activity, is, in fact, brought about through the activity of the proletariat.

Fichte and the Marxian conception of the subject

As a co-founder of Hegelian Marxism, Lukács provided a richer, more nuanced account of the relation of Marx to Hegel and classical German idealism than any other observer has before or since. Though his intention was to show that Marx went beyond German idealism in answering Hegel, he correctly points out Fichte's significance for Marx's conception of the subject, thereby undercutting the claim that Marx left philosophy behind. In the wake of Descartes, the problem of the subject has recurred throughout modern philosophy, including German idealism. In reacting against Hegel, the Young Hegelians, including Feuerbach, turned to Fichte in order to formulate an adequate account of subjectivity. Kant had considered the question of what 'man' (sic) is to be the single most important theme. He worked out his view of the subject in the *Critique of Pure Reason* through the transcendental deduction,[164] isolating the conditions of knowledge in general from psychological factors. Though he accounted for types of experience through types of activity, he was unable to formulate a unified theory of the subject. In Kant's wake, Fichte formulated a unified theory of the subject based on its activity. After Hegel, a number of Young Hegelians, including Feuerbach and Marx, turned to Fichte for a model of subjectivity that they then proceeded to develop.[165]

Marx, who was familiar with Fichte's position, maintained an interest in him throughout his career. This interest in Fichte is clear in his early writings, especially in the 1844 Paris *Manuscripts*. In the third *Manuscript*, in the section known as the 'Critique of Hegel's Dialectic and General Philosophy', Marx objected to the views of the subject in Fichte and Hegel. It is, he maintained, as much a mistake to consider human being through self-consciousness as to reduce the object of consciousness to a purely mental creation. Marx utilised Fichtean terminology against Fichte, in writing:

> When real corporal man ... posits [setzt] the positing [das Setzen] is not the subject of this act ... An objective being acts objectively ... It creates and establishes [setzt] only objects ... In the act of

164. *Critique of Pure Reason*, §§ 16–17.
165. See Cornu 1955–70, Vol. II, p. 294.

establishing it does not descend from its 'pure activity' to the creation of objects [In dem Akt des Setzens fällt es also nicht aus seiner
'reinen Tätigkeit' in ein Schaffen des Gegenstandes]; its objective
product simply confirms its objective activity, with its activity as an
objective, natural being.[166]

Here, we see Marx insisting on the objectivity of the external world,
in opposition to Fichte, who was widely but incorrectly understood as believing that reality is wholly a product of thought. Marx further insisted that
if human individuals are not solely created through mental activity, they
also cannot be understood through their mental capacities. It is remarkable how far the view that Marx here insists on – presumably for the most
part against Hegel, and perhaps against Fichte as well – resembles Fichte's
own conception of the human subject. In order to bring out this point, it
is useful to quote the relevant passage at some length. 'Man', Marx writes:

is directly a natural being. As a natural being, and as a living natural being he is, on the one hand, endowed with natural powers and
faculties, which exist in him as tendencies and abilities, as drives.
On the other hand, as a natural, embodied, sentient, objective being, his is a suffering, conditioned and limited being, like animals
and plants. The objects of his drives exist outside himself as objective independent of him, yet they are objects of his needs, essential
objects, which are indispensable to the exercise and confirmation
of his faculties. The fact that man is an embodied, living, real, sen
tient objective being with natural powers, means that he has real,
sensuous objects as the objects of his being, or that he can only
express his being in real sensuous objects ... Man as an objective
sentient being is a suffering being, and since he feels his suffering,

166. Marx 1964, p. 206. See also Marx 1968, p. 577: 'Wenn der wirkliche, leibliche, auf
der festen wohlgerundeten Erde stehende, alle Naturkräfte aus- und einatmende Mensch
seine wirklichen, gegenständlichen Wesenskräfte durch seine Entäußerung als fremde Gegenstände setzt, so ist nicht das Setzen Subjekt; [A*] es ist die Subjektivität gegenständlicher
Wesenskräfte, deren Aktion daher auch eine gegenständliche sein muß. Das gegenständliche Wesen wirkt gegenständlich, und es wurde nicht gegenständlich wirken, wenn nicht das
Gegenständliche in seinen Wesensbestimmung läge. Es schafft, setzt nun Gegenstände, weil
es durch Gegenstände gesetzt ist, weil es von Haus aus Natur ist. In dem Akt des Setzens
fällt es also nicht aus seiner "reinen Tätigkeit" in ein Schaffen des Gegenstandes, sondern
sein gegenständliches Produkt bestätigt nur seine gegenständliche Tätigkeit, seine Tätigkeit
als die Tätigkeit eines gegenständlichen natürlichen Wesens.'.

a passionate being. Passion is man's faculties striving [strebende] to attain their object.[167]

To the best of my knowledge, no other single passage anywhere in Marx's voluminous writings offers a more detailed statement of his understanding of the human individual. This passage is, furthermore, fascinating for the remarkable resemblance between Marx's comprehension of finite human being and Fichte's view. Man is described, in Fichtean language, as 'natural', possessed of 'drives', as 'suffering' because limited, and as 'passionate' due to his awareness of his limitations: this reflects Marx's awareness of Fichte's theory as well as his specific conception of finite human being. Though Marx's overall position differed from Fichte's, he did clearly accept the main lines of Fichte's conception of the human individual as a natural being limited by and only able to realise himself in relation to others through transforming the surrounding social context.

Conclusion: is Marx a Fichtean?

I began by asking a question about the relation of Marx to Fichte. The answer depends on what it means to be a Fichtean. This question was already controversial in Fichte's time. The young Schelling and the young Hegel were Fichteans for a time, though Fichte rapidly rejected Schelling

---

167. Marx 1964 pp. 206–8; see also Marx 1968, p. 578: 'Der Mensch ist unmittelbar Naturwesen. Als Naturwesen und als lebendiges Naturwesen ist er teils mit natürlichen Kräften, mit Lebenskräften ausgerüstet, ein tätiges Naturwesen; diese Kräfte existieren in ihm als Anlagen und Fähigkeiten, als Triebe; teils ist er als natürliches, leibliches, sinnliches, gegenständliches Wesen ein leidendes, bedingtes und beschränktes Wesen, wie es auch das Tier und die Pflanze ist, d.h. die Gegenstände seiner Triebe existieren außer ihm, als von ihm unabhängige Gegenstände; aber diese Gegenstände sind Gegenstände seines Bedürfnisses, zur Betätigung und Bestätigung seiner Wesenskräfte unentbehrliche, wesentliche Gegenstände. Daß der Mensch ein leibliches, naturkräftiges, lebendiges, wirkliches, sinnliches, gegenständliches Wesen ist, heißt, daß er wirkliche, sinnliche Gegenstände zum Gegenstand seines Wesens, seinen Lebensäußerung hat oder daß er nun an wirklichen, sinnlichen Gegenständen sein Leben äußern kann. Gegenständlich, natürlich, sinnlich sein und sowohl Gegenstand, Natur, Sinn außer sich haben oder selbst Gegenstand, Natur, Sinn für ein drittes sein ist identisch.> Der Hunger ist ein natürliches Bedürfnis; er bedarf also einer Natur außer sich, eines Gegenstandes außer sich, um sich zu befriedigen, um sich zu stillen. Der Hunger ist das gestandne Bedürfnis meines Leibes nach einem außer ihm seienden, zu seinen Integrierung und Wesensäußerung unentbehrlichen Gegenstande. Die Sonne ist der Gegenstand der Pflanze, ein ihr unentbehrlicher, ihr Leben bestätigender Gegenstand, wie die Pflanze Gegenstand der Sonne ist, als Äußerung von der lebenserweckenden Kraft der Sonne, von der gegenständlichen Wesenskraft der Sonne.'

as a disciple and Hegel just as rapidly moved beyond this early phase. If to be a Fichtean means to accept the main lines of Fichte's position, then neither Marx nor, arguably, anyone else was ever a Fichtean. Even Fichte was, arguably, never a Fichtean, since he continually altered his position, a position that he was never able to state satisfactorily, in some 16 versions of the *Wissenschaftslehre*. If, on the contrary, to be a Fichtean means to accept one or more central Fichtean ideas, then it seems clear that in an important sense, Marx is a Fichtean, above all with respect to the conception of finite human being as essentially active. At the dawn of modern philosophy, Descartes invented two views of the human subject, the widely-known, 'official' spectator theory, and the little-known, but perhaps more interesting, actor theory, implicit in the famous remark in the *Discourse* about 'trying to be a spectator rather than an actor in all the comedies the world displays'.[168] The so-called spectator theory of subjectivity has long been popular. But in general, the most interesting views of the subject in the wake of Descartes are different forms of the largely undefined actor view, through which various thinkers strived to understand knowledge, morality and the social surroundings through the prism of the activity of finite human beings.

Marx belongs to this ongoing effort, arising in the first instance in the reaction to the wholly theoretical subject in Kant and the apparent lack of a subject in Hegel, a lack that is initially overcome through the Fichtean conception of the subject as always active and never passive, but whose activity is constrained by self-constructed social surroundings. Marx is certainly not Fichte, though in some respects the resemblance runs very deep. In Fichte's wake, Marx participated in a Fichtean effort to rethink the subject as defined by work – or, indeed, labour [*Arbeit*] – in modern industrial society. He understood capitalism, communism and socialism through the self-production of finite human beings – within capitalism, in the form of work through which one meets one's needs of subsistence; and in a future form of society, perhaps unrealistically, situated beyond the limits of human needs, where one develops one's human potentials through what we can call free human activity.

Marx's entire position turns on working out the real conditions of human freedom in modern industrial society on the basis of a theory of human activity. This approach to human beings through human activity was formulated by Fichte in reaction against Kant and then appropriated

168. Descartes 1970, Vol. I, p. 99.

and transformed by Marx in reaction against Hegel.

Marx's position cannot be reduced to his predecessor's, but it does resemble it and obviously depend on it as it adopts and works out an approach to finite human being and all the many forms of society through a conception of human activity. This approach goes back in the Western tradition at least as far as Aristotle, who advanced a theory of life as activity in the *Nicomachean Ethics*. But its proximal version, which influenced the Young Hegelians in the mid-nineteenth century as they rebelled against Hegel, was in Fichte's position. Fichte is, in this respect, the origin of Marx's conception of human being. I conclude that, in this sense, and perhaps others as well, Marx is, indeed, a Fichtean.

REFERENCES

Cornu, Auguste 1955–70, *Karl Marx et Friedrich Engels*, 2 Vols., Paris: Presses universitaires de France.

Descartes, René 1970, *The Philosophical Works of Descartes*, translated by E. Haldane and G.R.T. Ross, 2 Vols., New York: Cambridge University Press.

Engels, Friedrich 1941 [1886], *Ludwig Feuerbach and the End of Classical German Philosophy*, edited by C.P. Dutt, New York: International Publishers.

Feuerbach, Ludwig 1986 [1843], *Principles of the Philosophy of the Future*, Indianapolis: Hackett.

Fichte, Johann Gottlieb 1982 [1897], 'First Introduction to the Science of Knowledge', in *The Science of Knowledge*, edited and translated by Peter Heath and John Lachs, Cambridge: Cambridge University Press: 3–28.

Frank, Manfred 1975 *Der unendliche Mangel an Sein. Schellings Hegelkritik und die Anfänge der Marxschen Dialektik*, Frankfurt: Suhrkamp.

Korsch, Karl 1972 [1923], *Marxism and Philosophy*, London: New Left Books.

Leibniz, Gottfried Wilhelm 1875–90, *Die philosophischen Schriften*, edited by C.I. Gerhardt, Berlin: Weidmann.

Lukács, Georg 1971 [1923], *History and Class Consciousness*, translated by R. Livingstone, Cambridge, MA: MIT Press.

– 1984 [1971], 'Zur Ontologie des gesellschaftlichen Seins', in *Lukács-Werke*, Vol. 14, edited by Frank Benseler, Neuwied: Luchterhand Verlag.

Marx, Karl 1964, *Early Writings*, edited and translated by Tom Bottomore,

New York: Norton.

– 1968, *Marx-Engels-Werke Ergänzungsband*, Berlin: Dietz Verlag.

Moore, George Edward 1958 [1922], 'The Refutation of Idealism' in *Philosophical Studies*, London: Routledge and Kegan Paul

Rockmore, Tom 2007, *Kant and Idealism*, New Haven: Yale University Press

DID MARX HAVE A PRINCIPLE OF DISTRIBUTIVE JUSTICE?

Wei Xiaoping

Are there any principles of distributive justice in Marx?

We can begin by asking what sense it makes to compare the views of distributive justice in Marx, Nozick and Rawls. After all, they lived in different periods separated by more than a century. Yet the distance in time turns out not to be of significance. Contemporary Western capitalism is still capitalism. The transition to what is now often called post-industrial capitalism is still capitalism, which continues to follow the same basic rules. Other difficulties are, perhaps, more significant. First, it needs to be shown that there are principles of distributive justice in Marx. Second, in order to construct a comparison, we will need to identify a common basis shared by Marx, Nozick and Rawls. In addressing these concerns, I will first discuss Marx and only then turn to Nozick and Rawls.

We know that Marx has never discussed the abstract principle of distributive justice. Yet Marx often criticises the distributive injustice of capitalism, in devoting particular attention to its relations of production. For instance, in the Paris *Manuscripts* of 1844, also known as the *Economic and Philosophical Manuscripts*, he formulates a deep philosophical critique of alienated labour, on the basis of which he elaborates a wide-ranging critical analysis of the economic exploitation central to capitalism.

The entire discussion in the Paris *Manuscripts* is based on the presupposition that in so-called national economy, there is a fundamental separation between capital and worker: the national economy sees capital as the reason for using another person's alienated labour, while Marx sees capital primarily as the result of another person's alienated labour.[169] Marx thus conclusively demonstrates that the labour of working men and women is alienated, in that it is appropriated by the capitalist, or the owner of the means of production. He identifies four forms of economic alienation with respect not only to the workers, but also to the capitalists. For the workers, in terms of the activity of labour and the labour-process; and for both workers and capitalists, in terms of the relations between people and a hu-

169. See Marx 1982, p.372.

man being's relationship to her own species-being, a concept which Marx takes from Feuerbach in order to use it for a somewhat different purpose in his own theory.

The central insight in Marx's theory of capitalism concerns the controversial labour-theory of value. To put it in simple terms, this theory shows that the surplus-value created by workers in the normal functioning of the economic process is simply appropriated by the capitalist. This theory enables us to produce a mathematical representation of alienation within capitalism.

Marx's contribution lies in disclosing the secret, basic to capitalism, whereby workers are paid wages that are not equal to – in fact, less than – the price of the labour-power expended in their work. The missing value, which is not paid for by the capitalist, is the profit of capital, that is, the value on top of the price of labour, which is known as surplus-value. According to Marx, the profit following from investment does not derive from general capital, but rather from variable capital. Marx divides general capital – that is, all forms of capital in general – into fixed (or constant) capital, and variable capital. Only the latter is a source of surplus-value, and thus a source of profit.

Now, we can ask ourselves: what are the principles on which Marx bases the labour-theory of value? Marx himself never addresses this question, and it is also not normally discussed by Marxist scholars. The question is raised by the libertarian theorist, Robert Nozick, in dialogue with Marxists who object to his view of so-called 'self-ownership'. According to Nozick, Marx's labour-theory of value is also based on this same principle. Nozick maintains that Marx regards the capitalist's appropriation of surplus-labour as an injustice, since it can be said that it literally belong to the workers. It follows that, for Nozick, Marx's critique of capitalism rests on the same conceptual basis as his own principle of 'self-ownership'.[170]

Perhaps Nozick is correct. Marx was not opposed to this principle; rather, Marx was opposed to the fact that this principle has effectively been violated in the normal functioning of the capitalist productive cycle. As Marx points out, it is only possible for capitalists to appropriate surplus-labour since the workers do not themselves possess the means of production.

It follows seamlessly that since Marx was critical of the separation of the workers from capital, then he should also be concerned with

170. Cohen has discussed this problem in his book *Self-Ownership, Freedom and Equality* (Cohen 1995). He regards Nozick's challenge as a very considerable one. Cohen's answer to this problem is that this principle could lead either to capitalism or to socialism, after it has been clarified.

the process leading to this situation. How does this process arise? Marx's answer in *Capital*, Volume I is that:

> In actual history it is notorious that conquests, enslavement, robbery, murder, briefly force, play the great part. In the tender annals of Political Economy, the idyllic reigns from time immemorial. Right and 'labour' were from all time the sole means of enrichment, the present year of course always excepted. As a matter of fact, the methods of primitive accumulation are anything but idyllic.[171]

Now, if we suppose that the idyllic plays the main part, the question remains as to whether the model of capitalist distribution can be justified?

Although matters have played out as Marx said, across the whole course of history, force has taken a number of forms – if not the idyllic or legal process – playing the main role in the separation-process. Since nowadays, in certain circumstances, the various different separation-processes have been replaced by a universal, peaceful process, can we ask whether the division between individuals and the means of production – that is some individuals have it, whereas most lose control of it – and the resultant exploitation be justified?

This process can, indeed, be observed in the Russian and Eastern-European experience. After the historical transformations in Russia and Eastern Europe, there was a massive reallocation of state-owned property to individuals.[172] This property, which was formerly held publicly, is now held privately, thus replacing public ownership with private ownership. But if, at first, there was no division, or separation, between individuals and the means of production, and the formerly publicly owned property was now equally redistributed among the people, then, theoretically, everyone had a share of property. As a direct consequence, the prerequisite conditions for exploitation, such as the division between people with respect to ownership of the means of production, did not exist.

However, the division, or separation, between the people and the means of production, was inevitable under the current conditions of pri-

171. See Marx 1990, p.620.
172. The historical transformation I mention here was the one happened at the end of 80s last century, in Russian it began with every person has been allocated a share of public property in the form of bond, but as soon as it has happened, the bond has been concentrated in few hands.

vate ownership within a market economy. Compared with the violent processes that have taken place in history, what has today happened is much more like an idyllic process, though in reality it entailed the abuse of political and economic power.

A further problem relating to the division, or separation, between human beings and the means of production is the problem of the original appearance of private ownership. In the *Paris Manuscripts*, Marx maintained that alienated labour is the sources of private property. In this text, he considered private property to be only a thing, not a system.[173] Slightly later, in *The German Ideology*, Marx and Engels analysed the sources of private property on the basis of its original accumulation:

> Private property, insofar as within labour it confronts labour, evolves out of the necessity of accumulation, and is in the beginning still mainly a communal form, but in its further development it approaches more and more the modern form of private property.[174]

In this English version, the German word *privateigentum*[175] has been translated as 'private property': it is thus hard to say whether it points to a thing or a legalised system. Anyhow, the theoretical link between private property and private ownership,[176] and between private ownership and the process which has produced the separation between individuals and the means of production, is still missing even in *Capital*, which begins with the separation of the workers from capital.

From the above paragraph, we can see that Marx largely saw the separation-process as the result of violence. But this could not have been Marx's only view. In fact, Marx was concerned with the natural history of the changing relations of production, from his early writings right up to his last texts.

We could ask two questions, here. Firstly, are there any universal distributive principles behind Marx's critique of capitalism? Secondly, how can we account for the historical process, except in terms of violence? In other words, are there any universal causal principles?

173. The distinction in Marx between private property with private ownership is not always so clear in his early texts. I have two papers dealing with these problems: see Xiaoping 2005; 2006.
174. Marx and Engels 1975, p. 86.
175. Marx and Engels 2004, p. 87
176. By the process from private property to private ownership, I mean the distinction between a person (or a group of people, family, and so on) owning something as the result of some occasional, natural opportunity, and its embodiment in law.

Marx himself never criticised the universal principle of distributive justice. He went no further than to note that it changes into its opposite under capitalism (or any class-based society). It is unjust because exploitation is unjust. In discussing the link between alienation and exploitation, Marx pointed to the relations of production and the system of private ownership.

In the *German Ideology*, Marx, together with Engels, analysed the changes in the relations of production over the course of their historical development. Still later, in the famous 1859 'Preface' to *A Critique of Political Economy*, Marx stressed that the development of the relations of production was based on the forces of production. According to Marx, although the elimination of such conditions is the prerequisite for the elimination of distributive injustice (exploitation), the elimination of such conditions itself depends on a certain level of productive forces.

In this sense, and also considering his Hegelian background, observers usually think that there are only historical dimensions and no universal dimension to Marx's theory of distributive justice. In China, the universal dimension of distributive justice has always been criticised as an abstract and bourgeois point of view.

What I could say is that the universal dimension does not come into conflict with the historical dimension; in other words, in a certain historical period the capitalist model could no longer justify its relations of production, just like the existence of slavery or feudalism in a certain period of history. This is Marx's standpoint.

The above analysis tries to combine the historical dimension with the universal dimension by dealing with the historical process of the changing relationship between persons (from not divided to divided into different classes) and things (property, means of labour). These historical changes are, to some extent, guided by the universal dimension, no matter how far it becomes its opposite in a class society. In fact, my analysis follows in the tracks of Marx himself, if we remember that Marx asked himself these same questions on the relations of capitalism in his 1844 *Manuscripts*.

What I am saying is that, regardless of whether capital's first origins are violent or idyllic, according to Marx's labour-theory of value, its profits cannot be justified. The key problem for Marx is not whether the process that capital comes from can be justified or not, even if it is guided by a universal principle. As soon as social division (the appearance of classes) has taken place, especially in capitalism, the universal principle has as such been turned into its opposite, even if the process of social division could itself be justified.

Are there any principles of distributive justice in Robert Nozick and John Rawls?

Robert Nozick regards capitalism as resting on the protection of private property, deriving from the principle of 'self-ownership'. He believes that capitalists getting profits from the investment of capital could be justified by means of justifying the process by which control of the means of production is divided between capitalists and workers. According to Nozick, if the original process of appropriation of property (or the means of production) is legal, then its result – the derivation of profits from it – can also be justified, since this can be seen as the chain of justice.

My argument is that although the principle of 'self-ownership' could even justify the original process of the separation between individuals and the means of production, or the initial appropriation of the external world for only some individuals, it cannot justify the transformation of property into capital, by which, furthermore, some people can appropriate the labour of others. This can be explained only by the theory of economic games and economic efficiency.

Through Marx's labour-theory of value, the supposed chain of justice is challenged. The rule of the capitalist system has betrayed the principle of 'self-ownership'[177] because the worker's 'self-ownership' (part of her labour) has been taken away by capitalists, just as Nozick sees that Marx's labour-theory of value is inherent in the same principle of 'self-ownership'. Also, as traditional economy sees capital as the reason of exploiting labour, not to mention that it sees inequality as the result of people's 'self-ownership', the latter would definitely lead to the unequal appropriation of the external world,[178] which cannot be justified even by the principle of 'self-ownership', for it is the basic means of people realising their 'self-ownership'.

What concerns Nozick is only the rights of those individuals whose property could be taxed for purposes of redistribution, as he describes in the preface of *Anarchy, State, and Utopia*. He uses the principle of 'self-ownership' to counter the idea of redistribution by the state, regardless of the fact that part of the worker's individual rights have already been taken from

---

177. Here, I use the expression 'self-ownership' not only because Cohen uses it in the same way, but also for the ease of comparison across different theoretical contexts. For traditional Marxism, a similar word would be 'self-interest', but 'self-ownership' is much more abstract.

178. Cohen strongly challenges the principle of "self-ownership" of Nozick with this argument in his book *Self-Ownership, Freedom and Equality* (Cohen 1995).

her. For Nozick, if the process is just, then the unequal distributive outcome is just, no matter what the conditions of social division (classes). He insists on this principle and its results solely: for him, it does not matter whether it functions in the direct conditions or indirect conditions.

It is only at the point of redistribution that the liberal John Rawls differs from Nozick. Rawls does not challenge the principle of 'self-owner-ship'. Rather, he argues the latter is the natural result of inequality. Where he differs from Nozick is that he does not protest the policy of redistribution as an offence against rich people's 'self-ownership' while he does protest serious differences in distributive outcomes, pays attention to redistribution, and seeks to achieve some kind of equality within the terms of social class structure. Moreover, Rawls does not challenge social class structure. What concerns him is only equality of opportunity, although he knows that for those in different economic positions, the first step on their career-paths will never be equal.[179]

As such, as regards 'self-ownership' and social class structure there are no differences between Rawls and Nozick. We can see this clearly from Rawls's principles of justice as fairness:

> First: each person is to have an equal right to the most extensive basic liberty compatible with a similar liberty for others.
> Second: social and economic inequalities are to be arranged so that they are both (a) reasonably expected to be to everyone's advantage, and (b) attached to positions and offices open to all.[180]

What is important for Rawls, apart from equality of opportunity, is equality of liberty. While he is aware of the effects of social class structure, he never questions the relations of production and their rules, nor the existence of private ownership.

Seeing that distributive justice would unavoidably result in serious inequality, especially under the conditions of class difference, he stresses justice as fairness, which not only justifies distributive inequality from the point of economic efficiency and equal opportunity, as well as equal liberty, but also amends the inequality with regard to redistribution. The difference between the distributive justice of liberalism and Rawls's justice as fairness is that both of them accept the basic system and the rules of capitalism,

179. See Rawls 1971, p.78
180. See Rawls 1971, p.60

while the latter justifies its natural results from the stance of the disadvantaged and seeks to readjust it by means of redistribution.

Yet according to liberalism, if the process of the separation between individuals and property is guided by the same principle and based on the same rule, the existence of unequal distribution could be justified. The slight difference between Nozick and Rawls is that the latter not only justifies the whole capitalist system, but also justifies a redistributional readjustment through substituting the principle of justice with the principle of justice as fairness.

What concerns Rawls about class difference is only that the opportunity to acquire cultural knowledge and skills should not depend upon one's class position, so the school system, whether public or private, should be designed to even out class barriers.[181] In fact, the influence of class goes far beyond access to education. It extends throughout daily life, economic life and political life. What Rawls justifies as the principle of difference is the idea that the economic efficiency it brings about could be to the advantage of those who are disadvantaged, which is his way of unifying the principle of difference with the principle of justice as fairness.

From principles to contexts: comparing Marx, Nozick and Rawls

From Marx's point of view, private ownership of the means of production is the cause of capitalist exploitation. This can only be explained through the double relationship between people and people, and people and things. That is to say, an individual can only take control of and enslave others when he owns the means of production, or an individual can only be taken control of and enslaved by other people when he owns nothing.

For Nozick and Rawls, the existence of private ownership is explained by Locke, being based on the principle of 'self-ownership', the rule of equal exchange guaranteed by the free contract. Neither of the two deal with the fact that as soon as social separation has taken place (property centralised in the hands of some and separated from others), even with equal rights in terms of liberty and opportunity, the principle of 'self-ownership' becomes its opposite.

Nozick justifies the process of separation in terms of the chain of justice: that is, if the initial takeover of the property is legal and could be justified, then it follows that using that property to appropriate the labour

181. See Rawls 1971, p.73

of others can also be justified. While Rawls tries to amend the natural weakness and further the stronger tendency of unequal distribution, he argues justice as fairness instead of justice. Therefore, the relation between a person and property, and between one person with another person, no matter whether we are dealing with an employer or an employee, can be justified as long as it is obeys the legal process and the rules by which remuneration is determined.

But liberal theory neglects the fact that Nozick's chain of justice is broken as soon as the separation between individuals and the means of production occurs. Even if unequal distribution can be justified by individuals' differing levels of ability through the principle of 'self-ownership' the same principle cannot justify one person using his property (means of production) to take control of the labour of others, just as Nozick challenges Marx's labour-theory of value, which means Nozick accepts the fact that part of workers' labour has been taken away. If so, and his principle of 'self-ownership' does not apply for the workers, then we see a real contradiction in Nozick's chain of justice. This contradiction could be explained by means of analysis of these two inter-related relations, that is, the relations between people and things and between people and people. The two relations are different; the second represents a variant of the relation interrupted by the separation of individuals from property (the means of production). Yet it is not possible to appeal to the same principle to represent the two different relations.

Liberal theory does not mention the real problem behind the phenomenon of free contracts, which is not only the relation between two persons, since it is also associated to the relation between people and things. On this point, we can distinguish Marx's position from liberalism. Now we can compare the differences between Marx and liberalism by analysing two different relations, beginning with the differences between Nozick and Rawls.

Based on the principle of 'self-ownership' Nozick opposes redistribution of state property. This opposition is exhibited through three ideas:

1. 'Self-ownership' (the extent of one's property).[182]
2. The differences between rich and the poor deriving from this principle.[183]

182. Nozick 1997, p. ix.
183. In relation to Nozick's formula: 'Whatever arises from a just situation by just steps is itself just', see Cohen 1995, p. 12.

3. Governmental redistribution by way of taxation cannot be justified, since it would violate individual rights.[184]

For points 1 and 2, there is no disagreement between Nozick and Rawls. They only disagree on point 3.

4. All social values are to be distributed equally, unless an unequal distribution of these values is to everyone's advantage.[185]

In comparison with Marx, we see that for Nozick and Rawls, the problem of the differences between the rich and poor only concerns the type of distribution. There are no essential differences between them, although Rawls knows that 'those starting out as members of the entrepreneurial class in property-owning democracy, say, have a better prospect than those who begin in the class of unskilled labourers.[186]

But for liberalism, this kind of difference is not so important. At least in theory, someone who starts out among the class of unskilled labourers can leave behind the class of wage-earners in order to become a businessman. But those few people lucky enough to do so cannot change the position of wage-earners as a whole.

According to Marx's labour-theory of value, we can summarise the differences between Marx and liberalism as follows:

1. Products should belong to their producers.
2. Those (capitalists) who take control of the means of production also take control of the labour of others (workers), which results in exploitation and should be regarded as injustice.

Marx's labour theory of value can be understood only in terms of a dual relation.

a. The relation between people and things (means of production) relies on the relation between people (workers must be employed by those who own the means of production).

b. The equal relations between people are distorted by social divi-

184. Nozick 1997, p. ix..
185. See Rawls 1971, p. 62.
186. Rawls 1971, p.78.

sion (those who own the means of production not only dominate the work of others, but also dominate the surplus-labour of others).

According to the distributive theory of liberalism

1. The prerequisite principle is 'self-ownership' (which could also be understood as the idea that products should belong to their producers).
2. Someone's personal profits come from an investment based on owning the means of production, the unequal result of which is not injustice if the process of getting the property does not contradict the universal rules of freedom and equality cited above.

This obscures two relations:

a. The relation between two people when they exchange their own products is different to the relation between capitalists and workers when capitalists employ workers, since the latter is the result of social division.
b. As soon as the social division has happened, the principle of self-ownership and those universal rules that should be obeyed by all people in freedom and equality become their opposite.

Marx uncovered and criticised both points a and b, which, in liberals' eyes, can be justified if the process is legal.

The key problem, here, is not only that with which the early Marx was concerned, namely the separation between capital and workers (Marx goes further than this), but also how to judge surplus-value in general: who produces it, workers (employees) or capitalists (employers)?

We are dealing with a different problem when we think about the relationship between different nations and between workers and capitalists within a nation. If we were to regard the second relationship in the same terms as the first, then we could easily confuse the relationship between workers and capitalists and the relationship between less productive nations and more productive nations. The former is tied to ownership rather than ability or effort, while the latter is instead tied to the productive strength resulting from sciences and technology (ability). The question as to who produces and who controls surplus-value within a given nation is a different question from how this control is distributed across different nations.[187]

The liberals' view of the dual relation between individuals and property and among individuals only appears as a single relationship. If individuals freely enter the labour market and are not forced to do so, the resulting distribution of property can be justified. Nozick and Rawls only disagree with regard to the redistribution of property.

Based on the analysis sketched out above, it is clear that it is difficult to make out the difference between Marx and liberalism with regard to the principle of distributive justice. It is much easier to distinguish differences in the way they look at the real context. According to Marx, the separation between individuals and property is the precondition of alienated labour and distributive injustice (exploitation). That is why Marx wants to change the social structure (relations of production), not the principle itself.

Even for Marx, justice in distribution does not mean equal distribution.

For Marx, only public ownership of the means of production can guarantee distributive justice. Public ownership of the means of production not only transforms surplus-labour from something in the hands of private owners to something in the hands of the state, such that it no longer belongs to individuals but to the whole of society, and also transforms the relationship between employees and employers, who become equals. Since private-owners-as-employers no longer exist under the conditions of public ownership, there are now only managers, and the proletariat-as-employees also no longer exist. Both the managers and workers are, theoretically, the owners of the means of production. They are now in an equal position.

Even so, for Marx there is a distinction between equal rights and equal distribution. In the *Critique of the Gotha Programme*, Marx criticised a confusion between equal rights and equal distribution.

For Marx it is clear that equal rights are still based on the rule of bourgeoisie. He therefore divides communism into two stages, since at first

187. DeMartino 2003 discusses these problems from three points respectively, such as productive justice, appropriate justice and distributive justice.

it is still a form of commercial economy: 'Here obviously the same principle prevails as that which regulates the exchange of commodities, as far as this is the exchange of equal values'.[188]

At this stage, the conditions according to which an individual could use private property to appropriate the surplus-labour of others no longer exist. As such, 'Accordingly, the individual producer receives back from society – after the deductions have been made – exactly what he gives to it. What he has given to it is his individual quantum of labour'.[189]As a result of this condition:

> 'Content and form are changed, because under the altered circumstances no one can give anything except his labour, and because, on the other hand, nothing can pass to the ownership of individuals except individual means of consumption'.[190]

Equal rights still do not mean equal distribution, as he explains,

> 'But, as far as the distribution of the latter among the individual producers is concerned, the same principle prevails as in the exchange of commodity – equivalents: a given amount of labour in
>
> one form is exchanged for an equal amount of labour in another form'.[191]

Therefore, he wrote, 'Hence equal right here is still in principle – bourgeois right'.[192]

Since equal rights are, by their very essence, still a remunerative right based on the principle of justice, and do not mean equal distribution to every single person, we have to take into consideration the difference in abilities (both mental and manual) that people can contribute and also people's different living conditions (for instance, how big their family is), equal distribution according to one's contribution might actually mean an unequal distribution of consumer goods to each person. Therefore, equal

188. Marx 1989, p. 86.
189. Ibid.
190. Ibid.
191. Ibid.
192. Ibid.

rights actually means unequal distribution, even if based on the principle of justice under the condition of public ownership, drawing a connection between a person's effort and the rewards she receives. As such, Marx believes that it remains a bourgeois right.

If distributive justice means differences in distribution, hence unequal distribution, then, according to Marx:

(a) Since after the elimination of private ownership, the conditions of exploitation no longer exist, justice in distribution can be realised.

(b) Nonetheless, justice in distribution still actually means unequal distribution.

Here, equal rights do not mean equal distribution – or, we could say, there are still contradictions between these two. In order to satisfy the latter, we have to change the former, that is, change the principle of distribution, the problem Marx studies with respect to the second period of communism. But even a view of equal rights under the conditions of public ownership has to face up to a difficult problem. If remuneration implies differences in distribution, how then should we deal with the accumulation of differences? Could this difference be transformed into capital? If the answer is yes, then the process of history would repeat itself. If the answer is no, then the differences are limited.

We know how big the differences could be, given modern science and technology. If we tie science and technology with productive ability, then the difference in results might be almost unimaginable. Now, the question is whether the surplus-value created by the use of newly-developed science and technology, as expressed in the resultant relative surplus-value, should be directly tied to public ownership or attributed to the discoverer (even partly) as a reward for her productive ability? This problem is discussed by DeMartino – namely, what he calls 'productive justice'.[193]

But if we limit differences as to prevent their being transformed into capital, then we also restrict the extent to which that surplus-labour can be transformed into a social productive force. This problem played out in reality in the countries of actually-existing socialism. In practice, in order to avoid the transformation of accumulated differences into capital, the principle of distributive remuneration was replaced by equal distribution.

193. See DeMartino 2003.

Yet the neglect of distributive justice would unavoidably cut down the pace of economic development.

When observers discuss the causes of the historical transformations in Eastern Europe and the Soviet Union, or China's transition, they often say that it could not have succeeded because it was established on a pre-capitalist basis, unlike the socialism that Marx talked about, which was supposed to be a post-capitalism. This implies that the historical period of capitalism is necessary for a later progress to socialism. Yet observers seldom think about the difficult problem of distributive justice even under the conditions of public ownership. This is not to mention that when the Eastern Europe and Soviet Union collapsed, they were already quite industrialised and their productive force was more developed than Marx and Engels could possibly have imagined as a basis for the establishment of socialism.

The principle of justice and beyond justice

The tensions between distributive justice and equality are clear, whether under the conditions of private ownership or public ownership. With the former, inequality comes from the separation of objective conditions, inevitably increasing social division; with the latter, it is difficult to keep inequality within certain limits, especially given the role of modern science. Rawls did not say that there are conflicts between the principle of justice and capitalism, but when he says that the coherence of society requires something more than justice, this shows that he has recognised the existence of a contradiction. He said:

> 'Rather a society in which all can achieve their complete good, or in which there are no conflicting demands and the wants of all fit together without coercion into a harmonious plan of activity, is a society in a certain sense beyond justice'.[194]

This suggests that Rawls understands that a harmonious plan of action can only be achieved by somehow going beyond justice in capitalist society, though he never challenges capitalist social structure.

Marx never thought that distributive justice could be achieved under the conditions of the capitalist system. Marx was also not so naïve as to believe that it could be easily achieved after the transformation of the

194. Rawls 1971, p. 281.

157

capitalist social structure into the socialist social structure. Marx saw that the equal rights of distributive justice (the principle of remunerative distribution) would unavoidably result in unequal material allocation, even after the elimination of the separation of workers from the means of production and under the conditions of public ownership. In order to achieve equal distribution, the principle of remunerative distribution should be replaced by distribution according to people's needs. That is the principle beyond remunerative distribution, which belongs to the second stage of communism as Marx suggested in his *Critique of the Gotha Programme*: 'From each according to his abilities, to each according to his needs!'[195]

This principle is already a step beyond the principle of distributive justice (if it is regarded as remunerative distribution), because it gives up on any direct correspondence between a person's effort and his reward, such that his needs are satisfied no matter how much she has done.

Marx saw that a precondition for the transformation of distribution from a matter of 'each according to his effort' to 'each according to his needs' is that a high level of productive forces has already been reached. It is clear, for Marx, that the principles applying to the two stages of communism are different. If we say that its first stage is still based on the principle of justice, then its second stage is based on a principle beyond justice.[196] Marx does not discuss this problem from the point of distributive justice. Rather, he uses the concept of right, that is, 'To avoid all these defects, right would have to be unequal rather than equal'.[197]

What is the difference between the principle of distributive justice and the principle of equal rights? Both express the same idea as concerns the rule governing distribution, which is complicated as it deals with the relationship between individuals and other individuals, and individuals with things. If the rule were equal, then the results of the rule would be inconsistent, even under the changed social structure (public ownership). Therefore, the rule itself should be beyond equal rights, now replaced with the unequal, or, we should say, ending the connection between what one has done with what one owns. This is the way to solve the contradiction caused by the rule even under the changed social structure. Otherwise, the changed social structure could be undermined by the same rule or principle.

With this in mind, we can understand that even for Marx, the

195. Marx 1989, p. 87.
196. DeMartino 2003 regards it as two principles.
197. Marx 1989, p. 87.

principle of equality does not mean equal distribution. In order to achieve equal distribution for different people, the principle of distributive justice should be something beyond equal rights. Therefore, what Marx proposes for the second stage of communism is not equal distribution, but distribution according to people's needs.

The contradiction of equal rights leading to the result of distribution with real inequalities is recognised by both Marx and Rawls. But they react to the same problem in different ways. Besides their different attitudes towards the relations of production, they also differ in their way of looking at history. Rawls believes that differences in distribution and readjustments in distribution can exist simultaneously. He looks for coherence based on capitalism as well as certain kinds of distributional equality through the principle of going beyond justice in a society based on class. For Marx, the transformation of the principle of distribution based on reward to distribution based on needs is historical, the one following the other.

Problems in theory, actual practice and probable prospect

Based on the above analysis, the way that Marx solves the contradiction between the principle of just distribution and its results – a separation between individuals and the means of production, which turns this principle into its opposite – comes by means of changing the social structure through replacing private ownership by public ownership. Yet Marx does not think that it is only through this change that society can achieve distributive justice. After the transformation of private ownership to public ownership, the tension between just distribution and equal distribution still exists, for the principle of justice leads to distributive differences, even under the conditions of public ownership. But these differences will not be as large as under the conditions of private ownership. But in order to achieve equal distribution, the principle governing remuneration must go beyond justice, since, for Marx, it is not enough to attribute equal rights by means of distribution according to contribution.

In practice, in the countries of actually-existing socialism – the Soviet Union, Eastern Europe and China before its reform process – under conditions of public ownership with a centrally planned economy, the principle of distribution according to contribution was replaced by egalitarian distribution. This is neither exactly the same as distributive justice nor distribution according to people's needs.

After the replacement of private ownership with public ownership, just distribution still has to tolerate differences in levels of remuneration, which raises the problem: how can accumulated labour (the accumulated difference in income) be transformed into social productivity without being turned into private property (means of production)? This problem, which cannot be avoided, is not discussed by Marx. In fact, instead of just distribution, there is egalitarian distribution.

Egalitarian distribution is not beyond – but also does not follow – the principle of just distribution, according to which, no matter what and how much you have done, income is always or almost always the same. The aim of China's economic reform is to enhance just distribution by combining different levels of ability and effort with differences of income. Its result is that the accumulated differences in income, which under market conditions derive either from differences in ability and effort or from competition resulting in winners and losers, can be transformed into private property. This difference can further become means of production, leading to the appropriation of the surplus-labour of others in the form of investment income, which in turn enlarges distributive differences, as has happened in China in recent years.

Now, the problem is whether investment income, the perfectly legal result of just distribution according to contribution, can be justified by the same principle. I think that the answer is no: the same principle becomes its opposite, if we adopt the stance of employed wage-earners. The model of a market economy with private ownership is necessary only for its economic efficiency (Rawls) or economic motivation (Nozick). One must ask: if the principle of just distribution is acceptable, can its natural result of investment income (we could call it exploitation) also be justified?

We know that not only in history but also today, the first 'pots of gold' are usually not only derived from differences in accumulated income, since violence and other factors have often played an important role. Today, all kinds of corruption and the abuse of political and economic power play an important role. But logically, the process of just distribution could legally lead to its opposite.

If we call the difference that comes from investment income the social-structure difference, then under such conditions, all we can do to limit this social division is to carry out redistribution by means of taxation.

To some extent, the system of redistribution, without regard to what a person does but rather with regard to what a person needs – such as basic medical treatment, basic education, and so on – is beyond but not indifferent to just distribution, which is different from egalitarian distribution and also from what Marx expects in the second stage of communism. In this way, Marx's idea of the transformation of distribution from a matter of a person's effort to one concerned with people's needs is replaced in today's China by a system of distribution based on a combination of ability, effort, investment and needs.

In this sense, we could say that the present-day situation in China is closer to the situation that Rawls expresses in his theory than that of Marx, if we consider this situation as a mixture of public ownership with private ownership guided by a market mechanism.

But the role of redistribution is a limited one, for it cannot change the trends of the division between rich and poor, and it cannot prevent advantages in economic power from changing into political power, unavoidably affecting the rate of redistribution. Furthermore, it cannot change the conflicts caused by social divisions.

Even taking into account Nozick and Rawls's approaches, all kinds of fetishism and alienation remain unavoidable, because they are inherent in the motivation, competition, and rules of the market economy. However, with Marx's approach, the process of the liberation of humanity has two steps: first comes justice in distribution rewarding according to effort, and second comes a distribution beyond justice that rewards according to needs. Only in the second stage can people's activity be free of material motivations, reaching the objective of fully expressing and fully developing oneself, and arriving at social community instead of social division. That is the deeper difference between Marx and Nozick and Rawls.

REFERENCES

Cohen, Gerald 1995, *Self-Ownership, Freedom and Equality*, Cambridge: Cambridge University Press.
DeMartino, George 2003, 'Realizing Class Justice', *Rethinking Marxism*, 15, 1.
Marx, Karl 1982, *Ökonomisch-philosophische Manuskripte*, in *Marx-Engels-Gesamtausgabe*, I/2, Berlin: Dietz Verlag.
– 1989, 'Critique of the Gotha Programme' in *Marx and Engels Collected Works*, Vol. 24, Moscow: Progress Publishers.
– 1990, *Das Kapital*, in *Marx-Engels-Ggesamtausgabe*, II/9, Berlin: Dietz Verlag.

Marx, Karl and Friedrich Engels 1975, *The German Ideology*, in Marx *and Engels Collected Works*, Vol. 5, Moscow: Progress Publishers.

– 2004, *Marx-Engels Jahrbuch*, Berlin: Akademie Verlag.

Nozick, Robert 1997 [1974], *Anarchy, State,and Utopia*, Oxford: Blackwell.

Rawls, John 1971, *A Theory of Justice*, Cambridge, MA: Harvard University Press.

Xiaoping, Wei 2005 'Externalization, Alienation and their Relation with Private Property: the Problem of Understanding the Two Concepts does not Come from Translation – Studies of the Theoretical Problems behind the Concept in MEGA2', *Philosophical Trends*, 8.

– 2006, 'Alienated Labor with Private Property and Division of Labour with Private Ownership: the Different Problem', *Social Sciences*, 2.

ELEMENTS OF AN ESSAY ON HUMAN CHANGE

Joost Kircz

A preliminary remark

The following essay is an attempt to analyse the relationship between Marxism, Science and Technology.[198] This is an important and unfortunately often overlooked issue in many debates such as those on ecology. The problem can be understood as follows:

a. All human activity is social, hence also the directions of academic research (in all fields), as well as the application of known technologies, are heavily determined by the socio-economical context. Some scientific activities and techniques fit a certain policy or ideology, and are therefore encouraged. An economy based on carbon fuel will put a lot of effort in Research and Development (R&D) to maximise the exploitation of such fuels. The invention and deployment of the atomic bomb by the American government changed the original aloofness by the Kremlin into an all-out effort to meet the power challenge, and resulted in the dream of cheap energy for millions. Though, originally, nuclear energy came (in both west and east) as a by-product of the military nuclear efforts geared at methods that maximise the production of weapon grade fission materials.[199] The notion of the socio-economical context is the field of the sociology of science and technology (S&T) studies. The key question here is: to what extent science and technology can be seen as tools that can be applied at will in the hands of the societal powers? A club can be used to crack a coconut as well as the skull of a prisoner.[200]

b. The idea that technology is a given, like a club, leads to over-optimistic ideas of the capability to apply a given application or approach in another environment. The best example is again the USSR where catching

198. This essay is an extended version of a presentation given at the International Institute for Research and Education in Amsterdam. It goes without saying that this essay is an attempt to frame the issue and certainly not yet a worked out treatise.
199. Holloway 1994.
200. Stanley Kubrick's A Space Odyssey (1968), starts with the invention of the club. But he overlooks the fact that only humans can throw overarm contrary to chimps as Wilson (1999) explains.

163

up with the capitalist West, based on the same underlying technical premises, became an obsession. In left circles it was not anathema to wonder if nuclear energy (the way we know it) would be safe under workers' control. Technological utopianism is part of all emancipatory movements. This is well described by Paul Josephson in his brilliant study on technological utopianism on the road to Stalinism and the policy of Stalinist states.[201]

c. R&D developments have their own dynamics. Success creates success and if we have a breakthrough in a particular field, we see immediately a bandwagon effect. Hence, such a breakthrough will define a field for considerable time, until new obstacles or new concepts emerge. This means that we face certain autonomy, in the development of successful R&D, which can result in a considerable internal inertia and blind alternative avenues.

d. Because S&T is a human endeavour, and because conscious human political action needs to be in concordance with the historical situation, political action is a craft in itself. The unique contribution of Marx and Engels to human emancipation is that they tried to break away from utopianism and conscientiously analysed the dynamics of their phase of capitalism in order to come to the fore with a theory that was able to understand their present day socio-economical situation in its historical context as well as advance a consequential theory of the means for emancipatory change, by defining classes as agents of change. It is no wonder that Marx and Engels were fascinated by the rapid and extremely productive development of nineteenth century R&D. They spend enormous efforts to try and master the latest developments: Not only in order to understand their phase of capitalism, but also to learn how to develop a rational theory about societal emancipation. In that sense they are children of their time and strong believers in enlightenment thinking; that knowing enables change and mastery of a situation.

e. This attitude faded over the years. Over time most political thinkers became totally ignorant of the content and dynamics of S&T. This led to the already mentioned notion that technology is something that can be applied to the goals of whomever owns it. But ignorance can also lead to the idea of the supposedly intrinsic wickedness of a particular technology. This ignorance of what is actually at stake in new deployments give way to romantic hopes such as the global village as a result of Internet, or to using the fruits of novel science as proof for already existing ideas, or, conversely,

201. Josephson 2010.

as an attack to rock solid beliefs. So it happens that quantum mechanics with its so-called indeterminacy principle was attacked head-on by Stalinist ideologues and is still embraced by all kinds of holistic philosophies. A great example is the Bolshevik of the first hour: Aleksander Aleksandrovich Malinovskii (1873-1928) aka, Bogdanov. Bogdanov became an important competitor of Lenin in the pre-revolutionary period. His most important argument was that in order to change society, delegitimation of the existing power structure, which was a key issue for Lenin, was not enough; a cultural proletarian "counter" culture has to be developed in order to make the change from revolution to a new society possible. To that order he designed an all compassing system named Tektology that tried to include all sciences. Tektology can be understood as a forerunner of a general system theory and a functionalist all-encompassing theory. In a certain sense it can also be seen as a precursor of twentieth-century structuralism. Here, we see an attempt to use the most modern scientific ideas as seeds for an all-embracing social theory for action. His sociology of knowledge is an important attempt to analyse the role of the social context in phrasing phenomena. His strong emphasis on labour as a source of knowledge that has to be organised and his insistence that in the science of the future, which encompasses all parts of human knowledge, the opposition between intellectual and manual labour has been overcome is still important.[202]

In conclusion, the problem at stake is to understand to what extent socialist theory and praxis can be treated as a "science". That means that we firstly have to understand what a "science" is, as not all human intellectual endeavours mimic the paradigmatic model of the hypothetico-deductive model of natural science. The idea that socialism is a science and that the methods of socialism are scientific, introduces a false discourse as if we can prove the validity of socialist theory by a kind of fixed gold standard, as actually Karl Popper tried in his attack on Marxism. [203]

Not the name but the intrinsic dynamics of socialist theory must make it a rational emancipatory theory based on life and society as we know it.

Below I try to set out some notions needed for a more encompassing work.

202. See Sochor 1988 for a balanced view, much better than Lacourt's bizarre suggestion that Bogdanovism acted as a precursor for Stalinist so-called proletarian science, in Lecourt 1977, appendix. Bogdanov, Mirror of the Soviet Intelligentsia, pp. 137-62. For a recent short overview of his more philosophical thinking, see: Gare 2000.
203. Popper 1945.

Stagnation and Development

The term "scientific socialism" has a negative connotation due to the usages of this term in the Stalinist tradition for a system of mental rules that claim to cover all human experiences, investigations and advancements.[204]

The Stalinist codification is called Dialectical Materialism, aka Diamat; an unclear term as it tries to weld two notions of a completely different kind. Dialectics is seen as the mutual determination of antagonisms while materialism is seen as a transcending of the nineteenth century notion of indestructible matter by a notion of absolute and fundamental laws of matter outside of human existence. Friedrich Engels used the term in his studies of natural and biological sciences and used it to indicate that also in nature all activities were mutually interacting processes.[205]

Though, from the Nineteen-sixties onwards, the philosophers of the co-called socialist states became considerably less dogmatic and in many cases grappled with the intricacies of the problems, it remains a belief system. The Marxists-Leninist theory of science of "the socialist states" is an all encompassing *Weltanschauung* (worldview) that not only understands all knowledge in its historical context, but is also a calibration system for new developments. The method became primary and all new developments were analysed within this all-embracing worldview, therewith proving the superiority of the system; so that even the possibility of surprises in any field of knowledge was pre-empted.[206]

Already here we see a semantic problem in the notion of matter and materialism, as this notion changes over time and presently matter can be, scientifically, not better defined than stuff. This notion of really existing things (outside humankind) of which our sensations are the image or copy, is then mixed with a formalisation of the so-called three laws of dialectics (the unity of oppositions, transition of quantity into quality, and the negation of the negation), into a rigid so-called dialectical method, in contradiction to the: a) so-called "metaphysical" method in which objects are treated in isolation and not in their mutually interactions; b) Machism (named after the important late nineteenth century physicist and philosopher Ernst Mach) in which our sensory sensations are the sole basis of knowing; or c) mechanistic materialism in which material interactions are

204. See e.g., Hörz 1976, Lenin 1908.
205. Kircz 1998.
206. Hörz et al. 1980.

the source of everything.

Historical materialism, as an approach to analyse the present as a result of historical processes, in opposition to Hegelian dialectics based on the "idea" and a teleological notion of the state, is, in Diamat, mechanically joined with the material substrate of human life and environment. The issue is NOT that human life is based in matter and that material interactions of all sorts define our existence. The issue at stake is if we are able to impose one method on all fields of knowledge? The whole idea of a superior overarching omnipotent view is already a dangerous idealistic or religious idea, a kind of God that exists outside of humankind itself.

An important task, still to be done, is a worked out analysis of the confusion between the term materialism and realism. Both philosophical currents of that name, take the existence of a real world outside human understanding, or better humankind as such, as starting point. In a simplified way we can state that diamat is realism endowed with the three dialectical "laws" for all aspects of reality, be it natural sciences, history or sociology and politics.

As a result of this dialectical materialism, the revolutionary left turned away from the issue of scientific socialism as a heuristic concept for a rational emancipatory theory. Sometimes a more, sometimes a less, adequate critique is published but these did not provide a full answer to the essential underlying problem of methodology. For decades the main thrust of serious socialists in the discussion was a forceful attack on the ossified and self-destructive Stalinist catechism. Therewith leaving out more fundamental issues of knowledge and understanding beyond the sociological framework.

This lack of a fundamental understanding of the vast problem area of how we actually have to define, analyse and henceforward develop a revolutionary praxis, remains a fundamental obstacle in the development of contemporary, revolutionary theory and its applicability in relation to natural sciences, biology and medicine and vice versa.

The notion that we cannot simply transplant methods from field A to field B, that is to say, we cannot transplant lock, stock and barrel the intellectual tradition form, say, geography to political science, is as obviously true as it is challenging: Obvious, because serious intellectual investigations in a particular field are always framed within the boundaries of its context and historical development; and challenging, because the human intellectual pursuit comprises a wholeness, though within a certain socio-historical context. Field A and field B are both expressions of human intellectual labour and hence must have some common ground, though we simply don't know yet what that is. The endless discussions on Snow's *Two Cultures*, for example, are no more than a confirmation that investigations in different realms of human understanding have different histories and different structures.[207] In a way, a competition exists between fields that allow well-defined or even axiomatic ways of system building, such as physics and mathematics, and fields, mainly in the humanities, that simply try to understand the dynamics, development and appreciation of human endeavour. It is remarkable that people like Karl Popper are still popular in the social sciences and hardly play a role in the hard sciences. This is not because all hard sciences adhere to the Popperian dogma but because currents in the social sciences believe that their methodologies are on par with, for example, those of physics. Something they believe is compulsory to be serious. They claim to be a "science" in the sense of a lookalike of e.g. physics and not just a science as a field of study. As a result, the arrogance of the hard sciences is supported and even enhanced by the belief that they represent "true" knowledge because their results are reproducible and their theories explaining this reproducibility are so successful in their – limited– field.

On the other hand, we see the large field of social studies of science whose merit lies in proving that social context, discourse and rhetoric are part and parcel of the human pursuit of understanding the world. Interestingly, there is also in this field a great desire to prove that their methods adhere to the Popperian dogmas of applicability and falsifiability.

Next to the serious sociological studies on the way research is conducted, we see, on one hand, the cottage industry of debunking the natural sciences, and on the other hand, the intellectually overlapping cottage industry of using the results of physics and mathematics – outside their context – in order to underwrite an immense panorama of religious, semi-religious or new age (though, often based on very old age ideas) *Weltanschauungen*. Most popular in this respect are fundamentally complicated notions such as relativity, quantum uncertainty, randomness versus deterministic chaos and the second law of thermodynamics.

The triviality of such endeavours is exemplified by the fact that in all serious investigations the boundary conditions are explicitly mentioned or, in any event, known and hence methods and technologies are always applied or valid within that limited context. Usage outside their limits is

207. Snow 1959.

168

only a useful exercise for experimenting and as a metaphorical tool.

The dangerous part is illustrated by the deeply ingrained notion that we have a split, between nature and humankind. In this tradition everything in human development is purely a social construct based on a pre-given *tabula rasa*, called nature.

An early start of the notion of the intricate wholeness of nature and humankind was made by Vladimir Vernadsky in his book *Biosphere* of 1926 [208] and is independently reinvented by James Lovelock in his Gaia hypothesis of 1979.[209]

Humankind, and therefore human thinking, is part of nature. In physics terms, we can say humans are combined, non-linear, interacting complex systems; but such a definition is more semantically correct than practical operationally.

Human in nature

The whole enterprise is simple. We want to understand the world in order to change it to improve the well-being of humankind. It is a fully human centred endeavour.

Having said that, my argument follows from the following fundamental observations: 1) that the world is a whole, 2) that humankind is part and parcel of nature; and that, 3) on one hand, nature creates humankind; while on the other hand, humankind is a driving force in shaping nature. But we are not driving a company leased car, which can be traded in, or can use the fruits and animals around us as we wish, as Genesis (1:28-29) states. [210]

Our goal as Marxists—and here we come immediately to one of the main tenets of Marxism—is that we say that we want to start with an understanding of the situation and dynamics of the world and thence want to apply this understanding in such a way that, from a humanistic standpoint (and this is the second prime feature of Marxism) we improve the living conditions of humankind (and ipso facto for all living creatures) in concordance with the natural constraints, so that in the long run the changes we consciously make do not backfire on us. So, the hope expressed by Bukharin and Preobrazhensky that "Concurrently with the disappearance of man's tyranny over man, the tyranny of nature over man will likewise vanish" doesn't mean paradise but means a social structure that un-

208. Vernadsky 1926. On Vernadsky, see: Bailes 1990.
209. Lovelock 1979
210. Kircz 1994 and Kircz 1998.

derstands nature's and a fortiori human's constraints.[211] That is something completely different from a consciousness of so-called natural necessity, the basis of the economic deterministic current in Marxism.

A third feature of Marxism is that, contrary to modest thinkers who understand that the challenge is of an exceptional scale and hence revert cowardly to a higher being for understanding totality, our founders, as good labourious children of the Nineteenth century, state that the only conscious agent for change is humankind itself; hence, stop interpreting and start moving.

So, this last Marxist mission statement in which Marx parts from Feuerbach, leaves us with quite a bit of homework.

Sensing and interpreting

The first issue is to understand the relationship between phenomena and their interpretation within a consistent theory. The second issue is that, as we develop theories, in as many fields as we can discern, the notion of a unifying theory is always looming around the corner, though we have no idea on what level of abstraction it will be reached. The programme of the introduction of an almighty (human made?) god, solves everything beyond comprehension. The big bang theory suggests a primordial unity that is broken into opposing parts. On the other end of the scale the Vienna School's logical positivist programme aimed at unification by a human-made well-formed linguistic approach of naming objects, though based on human observation statements. The differences are enormous.

On the more practical level, in most disciplines we hardly have even a *temporal* set of basic notions and rules. Definitions of objects of investigation change constantly with the progress of knowledge. We stand in the middle of a turbulent stream of observations, interpretations, theory-making, applications and expert guesses and wade towards a goal which is not even well understood: *A better world*.

Marxism, as understood by its founders and some of their heirs, is a conscious enterprise in which we try to understand the mutual metabolism of humankind and nature, void of ungrounded hopes for a better humanity based on abstract notions of perceived intrinsic goodness of humankind. Here we see immediately the difference with utopian currents. The Marxist goal of a better world is grounded in knowledge of the understanding of Nature's behaviour and in particular the conscious human

211. Bukharin and Preobrazhensky 1919, p. 77.

aspect therein; that is to say, human society. I say "Nature's behaviour", because that phenomenological experience is what we try to cast into a theory which helps us to extrapolate from the present to the future. In the dialectic between induction and deduction we start with concrete observations and through hypothetico-deductive reasoning attempt to reach explanatory and forecasting theories, which remain popular as long as they can be applied, even if we understand their limited applicability.

Human-centric

The human observes objects and experiences phenomena, names them and tries to systematise the behaviour of these objects. The mind then suggests notions and from patterns rules and tries to reformulate this in a *symbolic* language. In that process we transcend the physical reality and create a mental model. In the case that this model is fit for calculations we talk of a form of computer program (code) or mathematics; a well-defined, strictly rule-based, system of thinking.

The whole reason for doing this is because we experience regularities and irregularities and have the firm impression that nature is a complex, intertwined system of rules and objects, which we try to approximate with formal mental models.

At this place it might be useful to note that the type of formalities is not yet defined. Nothing demands that we have to adhere to forms of simple, first-order logic and Aristotelian syllogisms and not, e.g. forms of modal logic, which are still rarely applied. It is the other way around. We attack the unknown by prompting it by models – as simple as possible – in order to test to what extent these models are sufficient for certain goals.

This whole enterprise is purely human-centric, including the suggestion (or intuition?) that nature is based on an aesthetically-pleasant framework – from Kepler's Harmony of Spheres for the planetary system via Dirac's aesthetics of well-formed formulae to Weinberg's dream of a theory of everything.[212]

Nature gave rise to humankind, but by conscious human suicide, by a meteoric impact, volcanic explosions or by disturbing the huge solid methane slabs on the bottom of the oceans, nature will change her course and will carry on undisturbed, as you cannot speak of a disturbance without defining a "natural" state or trajectory.[213]

212. McAllister 1996. Weinberg 1992.
213. See also Grundmann 1991.

One thing is clear: humankind is not the "natural" state of nature, in the sense of the biosphere, and certainly not a stage or the end of a teleological route to eternity (whatever that means) but just a phase in a particular setting.[214]

If we talk about the destruction of nature, we only talk about the demolition of the present-day human habitat, including all that comprises it, like the flowers in the fields, the singing birds in the sky and the herring in the North Sea.

On language

In our understanding, what distinguishes humankind from animals, the complex language faculty, can be set aside as a prime feature. Not because non-linguistic communication is impossible, not because we hardly know to what extent animals have consciousness or communicate with each other, which they do, but because our language faculty, together with our memory, is a tool that enables us to name objects which do not exist as such in pure, phenomenological low-level sensory experiences. Human communicative thinking is able to develop theory; that is to say, transmittable understanding and fantasies that can last forever.

It is tempting to spend the next several pages on a discussion of semantics and semiology, because it is by naming an object or a thought that we tear it apart from its environment, let it be born like a child that leaves the mother's womb, and give it the freedom to develop. The essential issue in naming something is the negation of the totality of what we experience. In experiments and experiences we are able to name tangible objects, such as a table, or abstract notions, such as infinity or labour power, and set them apart as elements in a dynamic theory of how parts of our world develop. As Roy Harris clearly states, there is a wide gap between the interplay of symbols which we can define and fix forever, such as those in mathematics, and those in language which represent a much richer and complex resource. In building a theory we transcend the actual.

Harris's integrationist alternative to fixed codes construes communication as a continuum of creative activities in which participants strive to integrate particular circumstances.

The fixed code which science aims for must somehow be able to override all linguistic diversity because its definitions are based on universal truths that brook no denial.

214. See, e.g., the works of Stephen Gould.

His conclusion is: "*at long last, [that] the limits of science are the limits of language. And that is* <u>*toto caelo*</u> *different from believing that the limits of language are the limits of science.*"[215]

This is an important statement which clearly stresses the tension between the understanding of our world in linguistic terms and the ordering of these terms in linguistic theory and the multitude of possible scientific models or theories that demand new ways of linguistic expression. We now arrive at the vexing issue of models, metaphors and analogies.

On metaphors

The crucial issue in education, in conveying knowledge, is in establishing a link between the level of understanding, within the social context of the student, and the material to be conveyed. In Vygotskyian terms this is known as the zone of proximal development or in Leninist-Trotskyist terms a *Transitional Programme* approach.[216] Explaining a new idea or a notion demands the use of a known idea or understanding which can act as a conveyor belt to the new concept. It is beyond the scope of this essay to dwell on the vast literature on metaphors and metonyms, but in relation to our subject, we have to realise that naming and explaining depend heavily on taking examples or metaphors at face value or as vehicles for understanding a transcended meaning or new concept. In science we regularly see the use of metaphors to explain a new idea.

A beautiful example is the breakthrough in understanding the atom. In the early Twentieth century Niels Bohr came up with the metaphor of the atom as kind of planetary system with a positive nucleus at its centre and negative electrons circling around it. This mental model, though scientifically completely obsolete, still serves in endless popular science narratives. The interesting fact is that people must understand and accept the planetary system before they can be exposed to and understand Bohr's model of the atom.

Political rhetoric is littered with sloppy analogies, metaphors and examples, such as the use of the words war, attack, best, etc. This style is disastrous, in particular if works of our founding fathers are promoted lock, stock and barrel to catechisms, as is the case with Lenin's polemic against Bogdanov and empirio-criticism, and Engels' *Anti-During* or his *Dialectics of Nature* notebooks.[217] Interestingly Bogdanov put great emphasis on what he

215. For Roy Harris see: http://www.royharrisonline.com/index.html
216. Vygotsky 1978, p. 84.
217. Lenin 1908, Engels 1882.

calls substitution in the process of phrasing knowledge in the language of the social hegemonic superstructure.

The Dialectical Materialist ideology of Stalinism is a prime example of taking creative reasoning out of its socio-historical context and recasting it in eternal truisms. Words, definitions, examples and metaphors out of context lose their teeth and are reduced to formalisms, that is to say, estranged, alienated and sterile mantras. [218]

What is a science?

Science is a term that came into fashion around mid-nineteenth century; before that time it was called philosophy or natural philosophy. It became, due to the success of the natural sciences and in particular the applied part of those, the Holy Grail for all studies in human understanding. A science is understood as a set of notions and rules that model phenomena. Phenomena, for a long time, could be equated with observables: a technical term in physics for those objects that can be directly or indirectly observed. The important issue here is that observation in most cases is indirect. Many features we do not see or experience at all, but express them in phenomena that we encounter, indirectly, with our senses. The notion that sun burns, vision, astronomical so-called gamma ray burst as well as UMTS wave bands for the next generation mobile telephones are all expressions of the same notion of light particles or waves – named photons – is a good example. Many phenomena are packed into one essence, the photon, which in itself is ontologically a fundamental notion and is a measure of energy, where energy is ontologically something which expresses itself in photons but not in photons alone.

A scientific theory is a consistent model with a very important single feature, namely that it allows us to expand its reach from known phenomena to not yet known. In other words, it allows for verifiable predictions. I like to follow Russo and take one of his important examples to highlight the issue.[219]

---

218. For surveys on the discussions on modern science in the (early) SU see in particular Joravky 1991 and Graham 1987. Certainly in the early days after the revolution the epistemological issues were taken seriously before the bizarre ossified diamat became a state religion. An old anti-communist, but interesting, reference is the overview work of the Soviet Dialectical Materialist doctrine by the Vatican Jesuit scholar Gustav Wetter 1964.
219. Russo 2004.

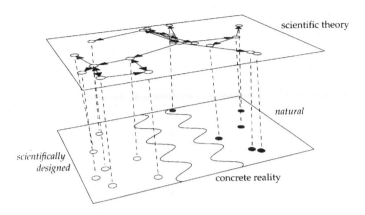

FIGURE 1.1. The role of scientific technology. Dark-shaded circles on the concrete (lower) plane represent objects from nature or prescientific technology. Their counterparts on the theoretical (upper) plane are linked via logical deductions (arrows) to many other constructs, which may or may not have a concrete counterpart. Some of these theoretical constructs give rise, via correspondence rules (dashed lines), to new concrete objects (lightly shaded circles on the lower plane).
Lucio Russo: The forgotten revolution, p.19.

It is clear that we can have a series of scientific theories that all serve their goal within a limited social and historical context. As long as the predictions made by the theory fulfil the needs of its practitioners we see no problem. But new phenomena and new outlooks continually emerge and therewith the desire to reach a consistent patchwork of interlinked theories or preferably a theory that encompasses as much of the phenomena and predictions as possible.

From a pragmatic point of view, an all-encompassing theory is not really needed. As long as a patchwork of theories suffices for all practical purposes, many people can live with that. But the essence of science, as an art of understanding, is that our ontological framework demands the integration of all those various parts because we take the world as a whole and hence all practical "local" theories ultimately have to fit into a comprehensive understanding. By local, I mean theories that fulfil all practical purposes within a certain realm at a certain historical time in a certain social setting. At present we read a lot about so-called string theory as one attempt to overcome the essential ontological differences between two, as far as we know, "true" theories, General Relativity Theory and Quantum Mechanics. But be aware of the fact that ontologically they are at odds to each other. In GRT space, time and energy are coupled notions, in QM wehave a clear so-called "canvas" of independent time and space coordinates on which the theatre of physics is playing. The mathematical trick to add more and more so-called dimensions reach a level in which everything is diluted into a creamy hot soup that curdles into different realms by cooling (so-called symmetry breaking). A beautiful mathematical construct that avoids the age old quest of what the notion time and space actually is, by stipulating that these notions only come to the fore, later in the development of nature.[220]

Historicity of ideas

Marxism is a current of thought that tries to understand the actual as a consequential result of social forces of the past in such a way that continuing developments as well as ruptures are understood and their internal tensions are seen as driving forces for change. This means that Marxism develops her own vocabulary just as any other "science" and that this vocabulary uses words and builds on existing notions, though often by changing the content of the terms. This is a completely normal procedure in every science, where words receive a new connotation every time we make a further step in understanding. Every socio-historical context has its own frame of reference and hence ideas and words are coined within that context. It is precisely for that reason that Marx and Engels used a lot of words in defining their fundamental notions in clear terms as notions that pertain to a particular historical context: modern capitalism.

As an example it is interesting to take the theory of vision, as given by Russo's study on Hellenistic science. In Hellenistic natural philosophy there were various doctrines of sight based on the idea that an *opis* (visual ray) was something actually emitted from the eye.

Herophilus of Chalcedon, a contemporary of Euclid (300 years before our dating system) paid particular attention to the eye. His was the first description of the retina, which he named *arachnoides* ("like a spider web"), and of three other membranes...[221]

This knowledge, and the knowledge of the function of sensory nerves, could have suggested the existence of a discrete set of photoreceptors. To construct a mathematical model of vision, then, it is natural to consider a discrete set of "visual rays", one for each sensory element of the retina, and that is exactly what Euclid does. The resulting theory can explain quantitatively the resolving power of the human eye.

220. For a good readable critique on String theory, see: Smolin 2007.
221. Russo 2004, p. 144.

For Euclid the sharpness with which an object is perceived depends on the number of visual rays.[222]

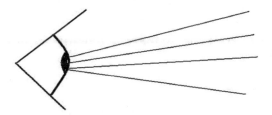

This theory of vision is a good example of the transformation of experimental knowledge into a consistent theory. In the course of time we changed our mind and now have a theory of light which is of a completely different nature and which struggles with the antagonistic interpretation of the well-known enigma of particle-wave duality.

However, in many day-to-day experiences the idea that light is emanating from the eye is still an accepted way of speaking. You still steal a glance or cast covetous eyes upon another person.

J.J.Grandville (Jean Isidore Gerard)
Le Magasin pittoresque Vol.11 1843: Phantasy

In the same way Marxism develops unique ontological categories for its way of analysing the dynamics of world history. The principle, and in my opinion most important, notion is that of Labour Power.[223]

Human labour is that force that enables us to consciously create ideas and subsequently tools and social structures, this according to the famous bees metaphor in Capital volume 1. This human mental and physical

222. Russo 2004, p.149.
223. By the way, this also appears in Lukacs' thinking, though he needs a few thousand pages in his *Zur Ontologie des gesellschaftlichen Seins* to say so. Lukacs 1984.

ability to create new objects shapes its own social structure and therewith also the nonhuman environment, the eco-structure of the planet. In other words, as soon as humankind invented the steam engine and developed the basic notions of energy, free energy and entropy, thermodynamics as a theory started to fill our mind. At the same time, the steam engine became the forerunner of the combustion engine and an economy based on fossil fuels. The ecological effects of that are nowadays again cast in terms of thermodynamic models. Our understanding of the ecological effects of global warming as a result of human labour are grounded in human made mental-labour concepts based on the steam engine.

Two remarks can be made here: Firstly, this ontological notion of labour power is fundamental because it is the creative driving force across human history as a result of our biological propensities, such as the need for procreation and food.[224]

Secondly, it is important to realise that inventions (looking glass, steam engine, space craft, iPod) must not to be mistaken for discoveries (steam and ice are both water, sperm is necessary for a pregnancy). Discoveries are made within a certain socio-historical context that enables it and remain part of our world independent of subsequent changes of the societal context.

This means that mental constructions such as an analytical theory are certainly socio-historical determined; but discoveries are socio-historical determined in another way. Theories come and go, but inventions become part of material life that drives human ingenuity.

This is already exemplified above with Euclid's idea of visual rays. The looking glass, once invented becomes transhistorical. It simply is here and remains. It is a human invention void of any natural evolutionary development, contrary to Therapsids, who died out in the Triassic-Jurassic extinction event. If these creatures had been able to invent the looking glass, it would be still available. It goes without saying that the actual invention or finds and its successes strongly depend on the social-historical context, as history of science and technology studies prove. However, the theory describing its working is changing. That means that products of creative labour, though differently described and rated in different periods are gifts forever. We cannot get rid of the wheel, nor of the nuclear reactor, we can only decide not to use them in well-defined circumstances. However, we

224. See for a forceful attack on genetic predestination and an analysis of the relationships between sex, reproduction and economics: Eldrege 2004.

can lose the knowledge required to make or use inventions as is frequently proven in cases of extreme neglect (the Greek knowledge of building aqueducts during the breakdown of the Roman empire) or destruction (the knowledge of conquered civilisations).

The next level of ontological categories in Marxism beyond labour power includes socio-historical notions such as capitalist labour, class, profit and the like. These are analytical notions, products of human mental labour power necessary to name and understand modern capitalism, its dynamics and its overthrow.[225]

And as the founding fathers of socialism clearly state, these notions cease to have the same content, are transcended, after the abolition of capitalism and the withering away of the capitalist state. This important aspect is the basis of all discussions about cultural revolutions, previous to, during, and after revolutions. Since the already mentioned Lenin-Bogdanov controversy it became an essential element in the discussion about transitional societies and the policy to advance emancipation by changing morals and culture.

Marxism as a science

Rivers of ink have been spilled in discussing a proper definition and methods to compare investigative crafts (sciences) and theories.

Within the zoo of sciences and theories, we can simply state that Marxism is a human endeavour aimed at understanding social phenomena in order to consciously change them. This is not very different from, say, chemistry where the aim is to understand chemical substances and reactions in order to apply them for the well-being of the owner of this knowledge. In Marxism, the owner of its knowledge is the world proletariat and its allies. The underlying fundamental difference between chemistry and Marxism is that humans cannot change the laws of biology and chemistry but only make use of them, as far as they understand them. Whilst in the case of social relationships and societal formations, we are dealing with human-made structures and, hence, we can change these laws. For that reason, all attempts to cast human relations in metaphors of human-made structures are void, though they can play a role as heuristic vehicles. In the

225. This means that the form labour power takes in the productive process will change. Under hegemonic capitalist production it gives rise to the two entangled classes of the proletariat and the capitalist (a 'unity of opposites' in Leninist terns): those who can only sell their labour power on the market; and those who own the means of production. Different forms of exploitation occur under different production relations.

eighteenth century we have seen La Mettrie with his *L'Home Machine*, in since the late 1980's we saw enthusiastic currents defending the supposed modularity of the mind, based on the modularity of computer, input, processor, memory, and output devices. This hype was followed suit with making the (selfish?) genes the cornerstone of all human activities. Presently, this is overtaken by the notion of the neurological plasticity of the human brain. What's next?[226]

In all these cases as well as the cases that Marx, and in particular Engels, investigated, we can learn a lot from it and can try and apply it to a certain extent as metaphors and models for understanding social behaviour. But again, they remain heuristic models. So, we also have to address Marxist heuristics and analyse the key notions in Marxist theory.

We can change social relations if we have a sufficient knowledge of human nature, that is to say that what makes humans as a result of both our biological substrate and our social being. The biological limits of humankind have to be taken into account. We are accursed: we cannot fly, and we also age, feel pain and can suffer illness and brain damage. [227]

In order to act politically we need knowledge on various levels. The surface level of interhuman societal interactions is the playing field of sociology and deals with human behaviour and power plays. However, this level is based on material humans and a material environment. This bedrock provides limits to the capabilities of changing society. Humans will never become angels, saints or animals. After all only the human species is capable of large scale murdering and torturing its fellow humans in a pre-set, conscious, and deliberate way. Humans are a special brand in the animal kingdom.

This notion brings us to the pressing issue: to what extent do the lower levels of life, namely the physico-chemical substrates we are made of, determine the higher surface level of social interactions? And, conversely, how does the social environment alter our body, e.g. by millennia of using tools?[228]

With the emergence of modern science this tension is hotly debated. Are humans machines with a free soul, or are we dealing with a compli-

226. For an excellent critique of this use of modern biology see: Rose and Rose 2012.
227. See, e.g. Sebastian Timpanaro, *On Materialism* 1975, but also the important discussion on the role of the media as extension of human activity started by McLuhan in 1964 and recently eloquently updated by Lanier 2010 and Carr 2010, in their concerns of the usage of Internet.
228. See, e.g. the interesting study of Wilson 1998 on the co-evolution of Hand and Brain.

cated structure where bodily feelings like pain, anger, happiness or well-being are the expressions of the tensions between living matter and thinking (grey) matter, whatever that might be? In a traditional Marxist sense the thinking matter transcends the non-thinking living matter by becoming an antagonist entity as it not only negates mechanical, non-thinking matter, but is also able to exploit it and use it for self-invented, thoughtful, goals. This transcending into living from nonliving matter is still an object of investigations. For millennia we have seen people who tried to overcome their biological substrate by denying their body, as we see with fakirs, Catholic monks, and many other obsessed people.

On the other end of the scale we see a growing tendency to reduce the human as a direct mono-linear extension of its genetic or neurological scaffolding. Interestingly, in both these tendencies we see on the one hand the old, idealistic tradition of denial of the biological substrate of thinking matter and on the other hand the primitive materialist reflex of grounding everything in a linear development from so-called primitive structures to complicated structures. In both extremes, the actual social human body is denied. We safely can forget these currents as they don't solve the problem of the difference between non-living matter and dead matter. As the first is the fertile precondition to life, whereas the latter is the end of the story of life and a return to non-living matter. The religious proposition that in this cyclical development, in the construction of life, a soul is created that escapes again to other worlds in the agony of dead is not part of the discussions in this essay. [229]

It goes without saying that life is more complicated. The primitive contradiction between life and death cannot be sustained in view of modern biology in which the whole notion of life (in the sense of non-thinking life) is under review. Even if we take DNA molecules as the ultimate buil ding blocks of life, then still the creation of those very DNA molecules and the enormous variety of creative power from DNA chips, like viruses, to mammals are still open for research. The hegemonic idea that complicated life is a hierarchical crowning of an evolution from lesser structures does not exclude the notion that new forms of life can result from break-away parts of complicated DNA, as some researchers consider viruses to be.

229. Near-death or out-of-body experiences can be measured as neurological brain activity, even after cardiac arrest.

Dialectics and non-linearity

Many of our mental models or pictures, be they scientific or otherwise, are based on modelling. But modelling is based on well-defined notions and is, like all knowledge, historically contingent. In particular in more technical fields, models serve a most important aid to understanding. It took quite a while before the heliocentric model of our planetary system became a societal accepted truism. However, if we confront regular people with all the arguments against this picture, most of them will drop the idea immediately.[230]

As discussed above, the planetary atomic model is now common sense and still in use in fields like chemistry and pharmacology where atoms and molecules are pictured as different sized balls and chemical binding is represented by sticks. The ball and stick model allows for the most beautiful simulations of chemical reactions and modelling. However, the physicists know that particles are just one kind of representation of matter and in essence we deal with fields, that is to say waves and not balls.[231]

Interestingly, as already said, many a social scientist tries to mimic natural sciences in declaring the same type of modelling and methodologies. The hypothetic-deductive method, which is our current view of performing decent investigations, in no way demands mimicking natural science methods but allows for using them as examples or metaphors. This can be very successful, but does not relieve us from the task of understanding the ontological difference of the input of those "methods on loan". The most bizarre examples of this practise are found in self-declared "sciences", such as marketing science, communication science, religious science, and management science. Here, the almost allegoric use of well-defined notions from the natural sciences are used as rhetorical devices for sloppy reasoning and false metaphors.[232]

230. Why is it not storming if the globe races with 30 km/second around the sun? See: Easlea 1980 p. 33.
231. In many important discussions among socialist physicists (and certainly not only in the USSR) the mutually excluding pictures of elementary entities as waves or particles have been equated with a "dialectical" opposition. To what extend is a wave antagonistic to a particle, I don't know? It depends on your definitions of antagonism. Whilst in quantum field theory both these notions are sublimated, though leaving out the issue of what exactly local and spread out phenomena are. Also here we struggle in understanding the incompatibility of otherwise excellent notions such as place and time. It goes without saying that elevating this nagging issue to a post-structuralist language game obscures matters only more.
232. Terms such as: a quantum jump/leap for a big step forward or change. Whilst a quantum jump is the measure of the tiniest amount of energy. Or chaotic behaviour and bifurcations as examples for unknown behaviour. Whilst chaos theory is stickily deterministic. The

The main problem and the main mistake made by believers of an ideology, such as Diamat, is that in the right social setting, the ultimate truth will be revealed. All human knowledge is socio-historically contingent. It is clear that historically our knowledge is exploding, and it is hopeful, even beautiful, that many chapters in this knowledge get increasingly integrated in a comprehensive book of knowledge. But contrary to this advance of knowledge, the human story cannot be equated with the book of nature. In that book we play our role as agent, not as scribe.

Also the idea that we eventually will reach an all-encompassing theory needs further exploration. It is telling that in modern physics and not in sociology the idea that laws are contingent comes to the fore. It now becomes clear that physical laws, which are human-made constructions based on named observations and relationships between them, hold within well-defined pockets of our knowledge. They are good For All Practical Purposes (FAPP), to use a term of the famous John Bell, after whom the Bell Inequalities in quantum mechanics are named. Self-assembly as one of the features of life can have many forms and rules.[233]

The tantalising feature of natural science is that based on well-defined and well-formed notions of non-living matter we turn out to be able to understand natural activities as well as create totally new contraptions which will never arise from any evolutionary path. The fact that the watch is a unique human-made object, which has a manufacturer, does not mean that the unique feature of an independent thinking bag of proteins, bones and water (the human body) needs a creator. In a sense the human is more mundane, evolutionary speaking, than a watch or an iPod.

The successful application of natural science methods to medicine and other human-related crafts force us to think deeper on the vexing issue of the differences between neurological knowledge, psycho-pharmaceuticals and the understanding of human thinking and mental functioning. In this discussion more than in all other fields we face the problem of determinism. The scientific tradition of humankind is one of analysis, of tearing apart wholeness in those parts which we can, with our knowledge, understand as more or less independent parts. That way we reach the idea of fundamental building blocks that on the way back reconstruct the original whole. The successfulness of these methods is daily proven, this in contrast to more "eastern" ideas of wholeness that certainly serve comprehension

real issue here is not randomness but the level of calculatability and predictability.
233. For a good introduction on so-called emerging properties, see: Laughlin 2005.

but not operational understanding. Zen and religion certainly play a role in fostering human modesty, but not in solving the material contradictions created by modern S&T in capitalist society.

Marxism as guidance for R&D?

All theory is a social construction. The question is to what extent does a particular, socially constructed, theory become a practically useful tool in developing and emancipating humankind. In the philosophy of science much time is spent on the issue of comparing theories. In general the consensus is that a theory that is able to incorporate another one, which means saves all phenomena, and even is able to explain all features of an older theory, as well as explaining new phenomena, is a superior theory and more "true".

Two remarks have to be made. First, theories that describe certain fields in greatest detail can still be at odds with theories that do the same in an adjacent or even the same field. The prime example is the dichotomy between General Relativity Theory and Quantum Mechanics, as mentioned above. Both theories are true as hell, that is to say as far as we understand, based in this terrestrial world. However, both theories are ontologically completely at odds with each other. The present-day discussions on unification of both in a so-called quantum gravity theory is basically close to the discussions between Newton and Leibnitz about the absoluteness of space.

It is certainly a matter of a philosophical taste, or even political outlook, what line of reasoning is preferred. The old communist David Bohm who, in his old days befriended Krishnamurthy, and hence is now an icon of new age philosophies, had his alternative approach of quantum mechanics firmly rooted in a materialist worldview that did not accept chance as a primitive notion. Interestingly, it is now well accepted that the reasons that his ideas were almost universally denied were more of a social-political nature than a scientific one. Today both ways, traditional QM and the Bohm's causal interpretation (now also named Bohmian Mechanics), can reach the same result. In other words they are more or less on par in describing the phenomena.[234]

Standard philosophy of science requests a test in forecasting a measurable effect that one theory can predict and explain whilst the other cannot. The question is if such an experiment *cruxis* really solves this prob-

234. See: Cushing 1994. On the fascinating life of David Bohm, see: Peat 1997.

lem. Such a call for an experiment *cruxis* is a primitive hope for a final answer and a uni-linear development of knowledge. In reality, every theory is, can, and will be falsified. Newtonian mechanics is wrong but we all use it everywhere; QM, which is proved correct in modern electronics, is wrong because it cannot deal with gravity, and GRT, which is proved correct in every car using a GPS, is wrong because it cannot deal with quantum behaviour. All three are human made social constructs that use a particular semantics as well as syntax, and all three serve us well. The interesting point is what standpoint makes one theory fashionable. A strong driving force is applicability, which results in new products on a market (in the world of scientific research funding this is called: Valorisation of Knowledge). But, for instance, in the field of astrophysics it is much more the ontological questions of the beginning of life and the universe that drives the interest, rather than any practical usage. Funnily enough this research endeavour is called fundamental, which is a clear linguistic allusion towards a religious notion of prime movers from which all the rest emerges.

Advanced capitalism demands advanced answers based on contemporary knowledge

One of the most astonishing features of modern Marxism is its complete reduction to social theory as if the notion that everything is a social construction relieves us from an understanding of the ideas and theories on which present day society has been built. Just open any book on management, economics, psychology or any other social science, and you see that it is fully exploiting, metaphorically or directly, methods and theories that sprout from natural science. Statistics, chaos theory, catastrophe theory, thermodynamics, classical mechanics, frivolous incursions in quantum mechanics or even relativity theory.

Something very strange is going on here. On the one hand it is, correctly, said that the social circumstances enable the developments of certain theories and product lines. Society, or better the market, is ready for it and R&D programmes are tuned towards perceived success. On the other hand the intrinsic dynamics of the underlying theories are just taken for granted. Again, the difference between the historicity of theory and the trans-historicity of products must be sharply distinguished.

Another aspect is of course the post-modern claims that deny the fact that all these transient theories do indeed describe part of reality correctly within the limits of their reach. The material rooting of language, and language games, in reality is simply denied.

A good example is the outcry for sustainable energy, a notion the large capitalist industrialists certainly accept as a profitable challenge. Everybody is aware of the energy crisis and the consequences of the human pollution of the environment. However, without a deep knowledge of the intricacies of the various energy forms and production, sustainability is a hollow phrase. Solar energy captured by solar cells is only a solution if, and only if, the intrinsic pollution of the manufacturing of solar cells is understood, otherwise we will see a repetition of the downfall of the Atoms for Peace programme of the 1950's, or the present crisis in hydro-power stations in natural rivers, to name two examples. The answer is not only a reduction of energy consumption (go and tell that to the Chinese and Indian workers), but a massive R&D effort into energy research. A project, which will take many decennia and will have a long time to market. In no way will such a research endeavour see a "knowledge validation" that gives a ready return on investment. Such an understanding demands the call for a long term, non-capitalist, planning, which is at odds with the present hit-and-run economic models.[235]

Countering modern capitalist methods from crowd control to chaos theoretical calculations at the stock market demand an immanent critique, just as capitalist production as such, because it became part and parcel of it.

The same way capitalism is harvesting and pruning all new ideas, methods and techniques modern science and mathematics produce, socialists have to master them and assess their usability for whom and for what. Again this brings us back to the Lenin-Bogdanov controversy about the capability of the proletariat to transcend capitalism, whilst contrary to the bourgeois revolution, the proletariat is not able to build already its own structures within the dying old culture. Following Lenin amassing all knowledge is needed to shape a new proletarian culture, and this cannot come to fruition by starting a new culture now.

Marx and Engels spent enormous time in enthusiastically reading about the latest developments in biology, geology, chemistry, etc., etc. Their notes are now coming into print in the new MEGA2 publications. It is not

---

235. An immediate, quick, answer is a political answer: the only societal source of excess money is presently the direct (Afghanistan, Libya, keeping up the own military forces at home) and indirect (aid, training of troops, etc. for friendly countries) military expenditures, because this subsidized sector of capital destruction is the pure antagonist of a sustainable energy industry.

only for historical reasons, but much more for methodological reasons to appreciate this, though, the books they read and the conclusions or hopes they obtained from their content are now out-dated.

Criticising Engels for his notebooks on Dialectics of Nature, is as unproductive as arguing against any other example that fuelled theoretical thinking, because now partly out-dated science was the metaphor and stimulant for Marx and Engels to shape their theory of mutually interacting and excluding agents. The essence of the issue is that Engels toyed with the rapid and fascinating developments in, e.g., chemistry to get a better understanding of interacting and mutually determining systems. In other words, abstract dialectics could be seen in the metaphorical mirror of chemistry.

The issue is not interesting to prove if nature is or is not dialectical, according to human-made models (Hegelian or not), but to develop creative thinking in which the concepts or mutually interrelated and mutually determining dynamic systems can be worked out further, among other sources by looking at successful theories in the natural sciences, biology (once evolution theory, now also neurology), etc. That does not mean that these, often incompatible, theories are to be taken for granted, but by learning and exploiting their methodological powers we can make progress. The same is true for mathematics. A critique of first order logical reasoning, though still the hegemonic primitive way of thinking for most people, is politically useful. But advanced model logic theories, now already make deep inroads in modern ethics of all sorts. [236]

The relatively new mathematics of non-linear mechanics (that is the field of mutually determining systems such as gravity theory and weather forecasting) can fuel the discussion on notions such as the difference between anti-poles, antagonisms, contradictions, negations and other forms of closely related consequences of naming in context and dynamic developments in practise.

In other words in understanding the world in order to change it, we need a full-fledged programme of how modern bourgeois thinking understands that same world and to what extent the most advanced thinking in that camp is developing and using modern science and biology as metaphors and mental scaffolding.

---

236. Modal logics are those logics, presently part of bachelor programmes, that deal with 'it ought to be that' (deontic), 'it is known that' (epistemic), 'it is believed that' (doxastic) or ' it will be case that' (temporal).

It is outside the scope of this essay to dwell further about such attempts in the early Soviet Union, before all odds were put on centralised developments of heavy industry. Or, to take a more contemporaneous hot potato that the disastrous intrinsic dangerous design of to-days nuclear reactors is equated with the idea that – in principle – the burning of nuclear fuel will always be more dirty and dangerous than other energy sources.

REFERENCES

Bailes, Kendall E. 1990, *Science and Russian Culture in an age of revolutions. V.I. Vernadsky and his scientific school, 1863-1945.* Bloomington: Indiana University Press.

Bukharin, Nikolai and Yevgeni Preobrazhensky 1966 (1919) . *The ABC of Communism,*
Ann Arbor MI: The University of Michigan Press.

Carr, Nicholas 2010, *The Shallows. What the internet is doing to our brains,* New York NY: W.W. Norton.

Cushing, James T. 1994, *Quantum Mechanics. Historical contingency and the Copenhagen hegemony,* Chicago: University of Chicago Press.

Eldredge, Niles 2004, *Why do we do it. Rethinking sex and the selfish gene,* New York NY: W.W. Norton & Company.

Easlea, Brian 1980, *Liberation and the aims of science,* Edinburgh: Scottish Academic Press.

Engels, Friedrich 1985 (1882) *Dialektik der Natur (1873-1882).* In: MEGA Erste Abteiling Band 26, Berlin: Dietz Verlag. For a English working copy see:

Engels, Friedrich 1987 (1882) *Dialectics of Nature.* In: *The Collected Works of Karl Marx and Frederick Engels,* Volume 25, p. 313. New York: International Publishers, London: Lawrence & Wishart Ltd., Moscow: Progress Publishers.

Gare, Arran 2000, Aleksandr Bogdanov's History, Sociology and Philosophy of Science. *Stud. Hist. Phil. Sci.* Vol 31, no2: 231-248.

Graham, Loren R. 1987, *Science, Philosophy, and Human Behavior in the Soviet Union.* New York NY: Colombia University Press.

Grundmann, Reiner 1991, *Marxism and Ecology,* Oxford: Clarendon Press.

Hörtz, Herbert 1976. *Marxistische Philosophie und naturwissenschaften,* Berlin: Akademie-Verlag.

Hörtz H. Pöltz, H.-D, Parthey, H., Röseberg, U. Wessel, K.-F (Autorenkolletiv) 1980, *Philosophische Probleme der Physik,* Berlin: Deutscher Verlag der Wissenschaften. An English language translation has been published by Minneapolis, Marxist Educational Press, Vol. 7, Studies in Marxism, 1980.

Holloway, David 1994, *Stalin and the Bomb.* New Haven: Yale University Press

Joravsky, David 1961, *Soviet Marxism and natural science 1917-1932.* New York NY: Colombia University Press.

Josephson, Paul R. 2010, *Would Trotsky wear a Bluetooth. Technological utopianism under Socialism 1917-1989,* Baltimore: The Johns Hopkins Univ. Press.

Kircz, Joost 1994, *Materialism and the "Makability of the World".* International Institute for Research and Education, Working Paper 32. Amsterdam: IIRE.

http://archive.iire.org/makability.pdf

Kircz, Joost 1998, Engels and Natural Science: A starting Point, *Science and Society,* 62:62-78.

Lanier, Jaron 2010, *You are not a gadget. A manifesto.* London: Allen Lane.

Laughlin, Robert B. *2005, A Different Universe: Reinventing Physics from the Bottom Down* , Cambridge MA: Basic Books.

Lecourt, Dominique, 1977, *Proletarian Science? The case of Lysenko.* London: NLB.

Lenin, Vladimir I. 1908/1920 . *Materialism and Empirio -criticsm.* In: Lenin Collected Works, Progress Publishers, 1972, Moscow, Volume 14, pages 17-362.

Lovelock, James 2000 [1979], *Gaia, a new look at life on earth.* Oxford UK, Oxford University Press

Lukacs, Georg.1984 *Prolegomena zur Ontologie des gesellschaftlichen Seins* /; hrsg. von Frank Benseler Werke / Georg Lukács ; Bd. 13-14. Darmstadt Luchterhand.

McAllister, James W. 1996, *Beauty and revolution in science.* Ithaca NY: Cornell University Press.

McLuhan, Marshall, 1964, *Understanding media: The extension of man,* New York NY: McGraw-Hill.

Peat, F. David 1997, *Infinite Potential. The life and times of David Bohm.* Reading MA: Helix Books, Addison-Wesley Publ. Co. Inc.

Popper, Karl *1945, The Open Society and Its Enemies. Part 2 Hegel and Marx.* London: Routledge.

Rose, Hilary and Steven Rose 2012, *Genes, Cells and Brains. The promethean promises of the new biology*, London:Verso.

Russo, Lucio 2004, *The Forgotten Revolution. How science was born in 300 BC and why it had to be reborn.* Berlin: Springer Verlag.

Snow, C.P. 1996 [1959], *The Two Cultures*, Cambridge UK: Cambridge University Press

Smolin, Lee 2007, *The trouble with physics. The rise of String Theory, the Fall; of a Science and What Comes Next.* Boston MA: Mariner Books .

Timpanaro, Sebastano 1975, *On materialism*, London: NLB.

Vernadsky, Vladimir.I. 1998 [1926], *The Biosphere, Complete annotated edition.* New York NY: Coperincus-Springer Verlag.

Vygotsky, L.S. 1978 [1935], *Mind in society. The development of higher psychological processes.* Cambridge MA: Harvard University Press.

Sochor, Zenovia A. 1988, *Revolution and culture. The Bogdanov-Lenin Controversy.* Ithaca NY: Cornell University Press.

Weinberg, Steven 1992, *Dreams of a final theory.* New York NY: Pantheon Books

Wetter, Gustav A. 1964, *Dialectical Materialism. A historical and Systematic Survey of Philosophy in the Soviet Union.* London: Routledge and Kegan Paul.

Wilson, Frank R. 1999 (1998), *The Hand. How its use shapes the brain, language, and human culture.* New York NY: Vintage Books.

MARXISM AND
INTERNATIONAL POLITICS

TOWARDS A CRITICAL POLITICAL ECONOMY OF EUROPEAN GOVERNANCE

Jan Drahokoupil, Bastiaan van Apeldoorn, Laura Horn

Preface[237]

Now more than ever, critical political economy perspectives are fundamental to understanding the social power relations underlying processes of European integration and governance. We are witnessing a process of neoliberalism in crisis on a global scale.[238] In the period after the text below had been written, the crisis of the Eurozone has intensified, far-reaching austerity programmes have been agreed upon at the European and national level, and the democratic character of the EU has been further undermined through the technocratic and increasingly authoritarian nature of these processes.[239] Most perspectives on European political economy, however, obscure the asymmetrical power relations inherent in the process of European market integration, and hence are not capable of capturing how the current developments are rooted in fundamental contradictions of capitalism itself.[240] In our call for a critical political economy perspective, we lay the grounds for an analysis that can contribute not only to understanding these developments, but also to formulating sustained critique and articulating alternatives for social struggles against austerity.

Introduction

European governance in its current form is in sustained crisis, both politically as well as with regard to its core project, the Internal Market. While European member states were quick to announce national bank bail-outs and rescue packages, EU financial regulators have only slowly

---

237. This text is a revised version of the Introduction to an edited volume on neoliberal governance in the European Union. See for more detail Jan Drahokoupil, Bastiaan van Apeldoorn and Laura Horn (2008) 'Introduction: Towards a Critical Political Economy of European Integration' in Bastiaan van Apeldoorn, Jan Drahokoupil and Laura Horn (eds) (2008) *Contradictions and Limits of Neoliberal European Governance: From Lisbon to Lisbon* (Basingstoke: Palgrave Macmillan)

238. Overbeek and Van Apeldoorn 2012; Van Apeldoorn 2014.

239. Oberndorfer 2012.

240. Bruff and Horn 2012.

come to a cautious consensus on how to proceed. Re-regulation of banking and investment industries has initially been mainly taking place on the national level. In 2008, the Irish rejected the so-called Lisbon reform treaty, that is, the treaty that after long and arduous negotiations was designed as a substitute for – and containing almost identical institutional reforms as – the European Constitution that had been voted down three years before by the French and the Dutch in the referendums of May and June 2005. After a second referendum on the Lisbon Treaty in October 2009 the Treaty finally came into force, but none the less it is clear that the political conflict surrounding the Lisbon Treaty is another slap in the face of Europe's political elite and has brought the European Union (EU) into a new deep crisis, not long after it barely recovered from the set-back of the Constitutional project being deemed to lack the necessary popular legitimacy. The sombre mood now reigning in Europe's capitals stands in stark contrast with the prevailing mood around the turn of the century. Then, with a prospective 'big bang' enlargement of 10 Member States and the Euro having been introduced in 1999, Europe's political leaders were optimistically trying to drive the integration project forward, starting the 'constitutional process' and proclaiming the goal to turn the European economy into the most competitive by 2010 at their Lisbon summit of March 2000. As the European Commission's new 10 year strategy for 'reviving the European economy' has just been published, how to make sense of the current state of the project of European integration: which key developments and shifts have taken place in the past decade or so, and where are they taking us?

At the level of the global political economy, we must perhaps start by observing how the events of 9/11 created a window of opportunity for the US neoconservative project to extend the imperial turn in US foreign policy, which, although not necessarily reversing neoliberal globalization, has created new tensions and rivalries within the capitalist heartland.[241] These developments are arguably further undermining the legitimacy of global neoliberal governance, a legitimacy, which had already been called into question by social forces both within the core and in the periphery in the years before. Next to the geopolitical ramifications, which as yet remain unclear but are bound to be important given the historical linkage (or arguably subordination) of the European project to US hegemony, 9/11 also sparked a world-wide recession after the boom of the 1990s. This recession deeply affected the European political economy that had just more or less

241. Van der Pijl 2006.

recovered from the last downturn in the early 1990s – even if unemployment levels in most Member States had remained high. As the European Union (EU) had just entered the final phase of Economic and Monetary Union (EMU), the deflationary effects of the Stability and Growth Pact really started to make themselves felt, engendering a protracted political battle over the issue. Europe was now divided over both the Iraq war (and foreign policy generally) as well as over what was at the core of its socio-economic governance regime.

Adding to the crisis of confidence was the subsequent anti-climax of the accession of ten new Member States, mostly from the former Eastern bloc. The long-awaited enlargement was in fact greeted with little enthusiasm on either side of the former Iron Curtain. Indeed, whereas in the West the popular complaint arose that the 'new Europeans' were only costing 'us' a lot of money and also threatened to take 'our' jobs, at least in part of the 'new Europe' disappointment has been growing over what the integration into the European and global capitalist market has offered in the end. Although there has been economic development, inequalities have also been growing dramatically and clearly new forms of social exclusion have arisen. Indeed, with respect to the new Member States the EU is far from living up to its promise of social cohesion, as the incorporation of Central and Eastern Europe has arguably rather turned it into a new periphery for the benefit of West-European capital.[242]

The completion of the 'big bang' enlargement reinforced the need for the EU to finally get its act together regarding institutional reform and deal with business left unfinished at the Treaties of Amsterdam and Nice. The Convention presided by former French President Giscard D'Estaing then stepped up the ambitions by proposing to replace all the existing treaties with a new one – containing a number of important institutional innovations such as an EU president, a foreign minister, more qualified majority voting, but also a commitment to undistorted competition – and to call it a Constitution. Although it was ratified by a large majority of Member States in the end, most notably with a huge popular fiat in Spain, the European Constitution proved highly unpopular in several key Member States including not just the usual suspect of the UK, but also France and Germany (although the government of the latter avoided the real test of a referendum). The Constitution then met its premature end with the referenda in France and in the Netherlands. Apparently, for at least part of Europe's

242. Bohle 2002; Holman 1992, pp. 3-22.

population, the treaty which had been designed without any significant involvement of those populations but which did seek to interpolate them as *European* citizens was definitely one bridge too far. At least since the early days of the European Coal and Steel Community, until the relaunching of the integration project with the Single European Act and the Treaty of Maastricht, the process of European integration has always been primarily an elite project. This is also the one thing that analysts from all rival theoretical camps – that is, both neo-functionalists and later supranationalists such as Haas, Stone Sweet and Sandholtz [243] and (liberal) intergovermentalists like Moravcsik [244] as well as various critical theorists including Van der Pijl, Holman, Van Apeldoorn, Bieler and Morton – have hitherto agreed upon.[245] Now, as Liesbet Hooghe and Gary Marks argue, we are – even if in geographically uneven and far from mature manner– witnessing a politicization of the integration process from below.[246] This is not to say that now European integration is no longer an elite project in the sense that it is now the masses rather than the elites who are in the driving seats, but 'the masses' have at least have acted as a temporary brake, and Europe's political and economic elites are now dealing with the consequences. What this politicization from below expresses, above all, is a growing alienation and scepticism vis-à-vis the European integration project.[247] Whether or not we may see this as part of a more general unfolding legitimacy crisis of European governance, we are indeed observing growing signs of contestation of and resistance to the policy output of the EU. Witness for instance, next to the popular rejection of the Constitution, the transnational battle over and against the Services Directive.

A central point of departure for us is that the above developments, in particular the massive popular mobilization in two founding Member States against what would have at least symbolically been a major step forward (that is, the Constitution), point to the (potential) political limits of the European integration project in terms of its ability to sustain sufficient levels of mass legitimacy. In contrast to some other recent approaches[248] the central argument underlying our analysis is that we can only come to a

243. Haas 1968; Stone Sweet and Sandholtz (eds.) 1998.
244. Moravcsik 1998.
245. Van der Pijl 1984; Holman 1992, pp. 3-22; Van Apeldoorn 2002; Bieler and Morton (eds.) 2001.
246. Hooghe and Marks 2007a.
247. Hooghe and Marks (eds.) 2007b.
248. Hooghe and Marks 2007a.

full understanding of these political limits and their implications for future European governance, if we analyze not just the changing institutional *form* but above all the socio-economic *content* or underlying social purpose of the integration process.[249] Examining the nature and limits of the European project in this way also necessitates that we do not stop at analyzing the structures underlying the current configuration of social forces, but also give due attention to the agency of those social forces, including the agency of resistance.

At least since the end of the 1980s the European integration process has witnessed a thorough neoliberalization. This process did not take place without struggle, and was far from fully structurally determined – indeed, it has to be understood as a *political* project (more on this below). Into the 1990s it became clear that, with the internal market project safely steered away from its alternative, neo-mercantilist and social-democratic interpretations,[250] and the 'disciplinary neoliberalism' of EMU being implemented through the Maastricht criteria,[251] European governance had above all become a supranational form of neoliberal governance; that is, the social purpose of the integration process, has become fundamentally intertwined with a transnational process of neoliberal restructuring. Arguably, the zenith of neoliberal European governance as a transnational hegemonic project was reached with the Lisbon Agenda, which has become the core of current European socio-economic governance. This neoliberal governance regime is therefore currently called into question, even if we may yet be far from any real transformation of the integration project's social purpose. It is in this context that we aim to analyze the nature, contradictions and the limits of neoliberal governance in the EU. As such we build upon, yet at the same time seek to go beyond previous critical scholarship on European integration, such as collected in the edited volumes of Bieler and Morton[252] and Cafruny and Ryner[253]. Our analysis goes beyond this literature in as much as we analyse from a critical political economy perspective developments and shifts in the political economy of European

249. Van Apeldoorn 2002; See Van Apeldoorn et al 2003 for a critique of the mainstream approaches that focus either mainly on institutional form or explain the content from a pluralist model that simply ignores the fundamental power asymmetries inherent in capitalist social relations.
250. Van Apeldoorn 2002.
251. Gill 1998, pp. 5–26.
252. Bieler and Morton (eds) 2001.
253. Cafruny and Ryner (eds) 2003.

governance which have taken place since the early 2000s and that we deem critical to an understanding of the current 'state-of-the-Union'. These developments, already briefly sketched above, *inter alia* refer to the changing geopolitical and geo-economic context; the Lisbon agenda as a new mode of neoliberal governance; the Eastward expansion of the EU; the subsequent deepening marketization; but also to the ensuing rising contestation and mobilization against (aspects of) the European project, such as those manifested in the national resistance against the Constitution as well as several instances of (trans)national resistance. As indicated, in capturing these developments and how they are related to broader processes of transnational capitalist restructuring, we adopt a critical political economy perspective, which we outline below in the next section.

Towards a Critical Political Economy of European Integration.

The critical political economy perspective that we propose is by no means a concept amalgamating a broad variety of critical approaches into a well-defined research programme. While we draw upon a neo-Gramscian perception of the socio-economic configuration of the European Union (EU), we do not intend to offer a *synthesis* of various strands of (broadly) historical materialist work. Rather, by analyzing actual manifestations of neoliberal restructuring and concomitant contradictions and social struggle emanating from them, we seek to offer a critical research perspective defined by a commitment to a set of ontological, epistemological and methodological positions and the understanding of recent transformations of capitalism and capitalist societies. As Van Apeldoorn et al put it, 'critical political economy recognizes the power relations, special interests, and arbitrariness contained in market forces and civil societal relations [...], and seeks to relate these to state power.'[254]

We draw to some extent on the transnational historical materialist perspective, and related critique on mainstream European integration theories as formulated by Bastiaan van Apeldoorn, Henk Overbeek and Magnus Ryner,[255] as well as on work by several other contributors of this volume.[256] At the same time, we also stress what we see as core themes in need of further attention, both on the theoretical as well as the empirical

254. Van Apeldoorn et al 2003, p. 20.
255. Van Apeldoorn et al 2003.
256. Bieler and Morton (eds.) 2001; Bieler et al (eds) 2006.

level. Since we focus on presenting cutting edge research on recent developments, rather than on theory development per se, we introduce the key concepts and assumptions that are employed in the empirical analyses. Through a discussion of these key concepts of critical political economy we will seek to show how this perspective can further our understanding of the fundamentally asymmetrical power structures in the EU. Building upon a critique of 'mainstream' integration theories, we particularly point towards the transnational nature and inherent contradictions of capitalist restructuring in the EU.

A critical political economy perspective takes as an important point of departure the distinction between problem-solving and critical theory.[257] Rather than perceiving of social structures as a natural state of affairs, they need to be understood in the context of historically contingent, contradictory and open-ended social relations of production. While the social relations of production indeed stand at the centre of the analysis of the social origins of power in capitalist societies, the role of ideology, ideas and identities is crucial in the (trans)formation of social formations.[258] From a 'critical realist' perspective - which may be taken as the meta-theoretical grounding of the critical political economy we advance here - we stress the dialectical interplay of structure and agency over time in which agency is never pre-social but always operating within the bounds of given social structures while the latter are at the same time dependent upon (individual, collective, strategic or less strategic) human agency for their reproduction or transformation.[259] Next to this relational conception of structure and agency, another important 'critical realist' meta-theoretical starting point is the notion that (social) reality is stratified and that therefore we need research strategies that are able to probe at the deeper levels of non-observable yet real structures that account for what we observe empirically.[260] Such an ontological depth is indispensable for realizing the emancipatory potential of critical political economy, as it enables us to separate the necessary from the contingent and uncover the underlying structures and power relations that constrain human freedom but can very well be transformed by (collective) human agency.

257. See Cox 1981, pp. 126-55
258. Van Apeldoorn 2004a, p. 152; Van Apeldoorn et al 2003, p. 36.
259. Bhaskar 1979; Archer 1995; see Buch-Hansen 2006 for an application of this perspective to EU studies
260. See Sayer 1992 for the methodological implications of this.

Towards a Critical Understanding of the politics in the European Union

Although we do not seek to contribute to an already older debate on the 'nature of the beast',[261] that is whether the EU is merely an international organization in the intergovermentalist tradition or whether it in fact represents a novel form of political authority that has for instance been dubbed a 'post-Hobbesian order'[262] (Schmitter 1991) and even a 'postmodern state',[263] we do maintain that the state, which in an era of multilevel governance[264] includes institutional structures of the EU, remains the quintessential arena of contemporary politics, the institutional ensemble through which capitalist class rule needs to be effectuated, legitimated, and conflicts arising from its contradictions mediated. In capitalist economies, and those of the EU are no exception to this, the state is and remains also indispensable to provide, as Van Apeldoorn and Horn argue,[265] the institutional preconditions for markets to arise, develop and be reproduced. The question of course remains whether in the case of the EU the state is still merely or even primarily national, whether it also supranational or, as Etienne Balibar once suggested, it is in fact 'is *neither national nor supranational,* and this ambiguity does not slacken but deepen over time'.[266] Without pretending to be able to present a theory of the 'European state', we suggest below that Balibar was indeed right and that a fuller understanding of this may lay in a better understanding of 'the transnational'[267] and what Jessop has theorized in terms of 'multi-scalar' governance.[268]

In order to come to an understanding of the EU-European statehood as a multilevel polity we first need to come to a more abstract conceptualization of 'the state'. A conventional distinction would identify three competing explanatory logics for understanding 'the state'. These notorious "three Is" include (1) social interests or domestic coalitions, (2) institutions and the state, and (3) dominant ideas. Particular accounts usually construct explanatory frameworks by combining individual theories. In fact, there is considerable convergence in the "actually-employed" explanatory logics

261. Risse 1996, pp. 53-80.
262. Schmitter 1991.
263. Caporaso 1996, pp. 29-51.
264. Hooghe and Marks, 2001.
265. Van Apeldoorn and Horn 2007, pp. 211-35.
266. Balibar 1991, p. 16.
267. Van Apeldoorn 2004a.
268. Jessop 2007.

— as opposed to self-proclaimed theoretical assumptions — among various Weberian, neo-classical, and Marxist or neo-Gramscian perspectives.[269] By discussing individual "competing" explanations, we develop a conceptual framework that the authors of this volume draw on. Our understanding of the state and of policy-making relies in particular on strategic-relational state theory as developed above all by Bob Jessop.[270] Developed outside of (critical) international political economy, this (neo-)Gramscian approach provides a refined conceptual apparatus, which is not only compatible with the concepts employed within the Amsterdam International Political Economy project,[271] but also allows us to combine "the three Is" into a coherent understanding of the state in transnational political economy. We develop such a conceptualization by discussing major alternative 'theories of the state'.

Social Forces, Hegemony and the State

Focusing on distributional consequences of policies around which interests mobilize, *interest-based or coalition approaches* assume that politicians exchange policies for political support.[272] At the same time, dominant social groups are able to exert influence on politicians and bureaucrats through various channels, including provision of material support, fraud, corruption, clientelistic relations, and other personal ties. The state is thus understood as an arena through which social struggle is waged. In effect, state strategy is likely to reflect interests and preferences of the dominant coalition. There are traditionally two ways to investigate the influence of social interests. First, the deductive approach, such as that of rational-choice institutionalism, starts from identifying groups that are likely to be favoured by a particular policy.[273] Yet, this is problematic as there is no guarantee that political beneficiaries are a cause, rather than a consequence of policy reform. Second, the inductive approach, such as that of pluralism, instrumental Marxism or the radical tradition in American political science, would analyze particular channels of influence through which coalitions of social actors exert influence.[274] This approach, too, is not without problems.

269. These approaches do not correspond to the stylized distinction among ideational, interest-based, and institution-oriented explanations. For instance, both rational choice theory and instrumental Marxism employ the interest group logic.
270. Jessop 1990; Jessop 2002; Jessop 2007; see Drahokoupil 2007
271. Van Apeldoorn 2004b.
272. Friedan and Rogowski 1996; Miliband 1969; Domhoff 1996.
273. Friedan and Rogowski 1996.
274. Miliband 1969; Domhoff 1996; Thacker 2000.

Policies can represent social interests in the absence of direct influence. Social structure can operate as a constraint on government action through the 'law of anticipated consequences'.[275] What is more, the structural power may make governments 'wish to what the dominants actors wish'.[276] Thus, we understand the state as a *social relation* that reflects the changing balance of forces in a determinate conjuncture.[277] The mechanisms that "condense" or "reflect" such a balance include not only direct influence or relational power, but also indirect pressures and constraints, or structural power. *Institutionalist and state-centric theories* emphasize that the state elite — the executive branch in particular — enjoys considerable autonomy of societal interests in designing and implementing policies and in organizing political support for them.[278] Others argue that, while social interests may play an important role in the period of institutional reproduction, they are less likely to be important for explaining change. Particularly during times of economic crisis, state actors are argued to likely enjoy considerable autonomy of social interest, and their strategy is likely to construct, rather than reflect, interests and coalitions.

The question of the autonomy of state managers — or 'the state' — has been a victim of heavy straw-man making. In fact, however, both Weberian institutionalism and structural Marxism emphasize autonomy of state managers from societal pressures. The Weberian idea of "corporate coherence," especially as "embedded" by Evans,[279] and the Poulantzasian notion of 'classwide rationality' are very similar and refer to the same feature of the bureaucratic, as in Weber, or the capitalist, as in Poulantzas, state: that is, the separation of the political from the economic. This does provide the managers considerable autonomy. Yet, the seeming contradiction between this formulation and understanding the state as a social relation can be resolved by insisting on considering state managers as social forces, or as another social interest. We insist, though, that the very institutional position that gives them autonomy — i.e., that of within the *capitalist state* that is structurally separated and thus dependent on 'the economy' and on seeking social legitimacy (to varying degrees) — structures their interests and provides them important incentives to ally with other social forces. Most notably, since state actors are dependent, both economically and po-

275. Haggard 1990.
276. Strange 1988; Nye 1990.
277. Haggard 1990.
278. Evans et al 1985.
279. Evans 1995.

litically, on (capitalist) economy, they are structurally dependent on those who control the production process — the respective growth segments in particular. Thus, the (capitalist) state has an inherent form-determined bias that makes it more open to capitalist influences and more likely to be mobilized for capitalist policies. It is also important to note that state personnel can be by no means considered socially isolated: these spheres — often misleadingly separated as 'state' on the one hand, and 'society', on the other hand — are interlinked or embedded through flows of information, people, money, social ties, and common social aspirations and identifications.

Institutionalist theories, and the strategic-relational approach alike, claim that institutions are constitutive of interests. Moreover, they provide advantages to some groups in pursuing their political goals while imposing constraints on others. The state as terrain of social struggle is considerably uneven, which has independent influence on the balance of forces in society. Institutions will also shape the degree of autonomy from other forces the state managers enjoy. State autonomy thus cannot be assumed, but must be investigated and explained. The degree and nature of state autonomy thus can be understood as a part of institutional mediation of the balance of forces in society. This can be summarized characterizing the state as a *form-determined* social relation.[280] An analysis of public policy thus starts from identifying the "unequal structure of representation" that links particular policy instance to the balance of forces in a given conjuncture.[281] Finally, *ideational perspectives* emphasize the importance of ideas in constituting interests and determining ranges of (imaginable) policy options and goals.[282] They insist on the importance of experts, professional analysts, and international organizations producing and disseminating ideas. While neo-Gramscian and relational perspectives also insist on discursive constitution of reality, they point out that ideas do not float in an endless universe of meaning, but are seen as produced by human agency in the context of social

---

280. Jessop 1990.
281. Mahon 1977; Institutionalists have claimed that state autonomy and capacity is dependent upon organizational resources available to state managers, on the coherence of state apparatus in particular (e.g. Haggard, 1990). We argue, along with Jessop (1990), that the coherence of the state apparatus is an emergent phenomenon to be explained. To achieve such coherence, state managers must articulate the complex, incoherent, and often contradictory ensemble of state institutions by developing a "state project," which may give some operational unity to the state as an apparatus. As lack of coherence and unity of interest within a state apparatus is a norm, there may be competing state projects attempting to impose contradictory institutional unities.
282. Campbell 1998, pp. 377-409; Blyth 2002.

power relations, and as such are also linked with strategic action of social (class) actors.[283] Ideas or knowledge are shaped within these power relations.

Ideas are essential for constituting political coalitions. They constitute or define interests of social groups. At the same time, they may also seek to legitimate these interests vis-à-vis other social groups. Thus, ideational practice is an important element of constituting social leadership. Gramsci has identified various forms of leadership or dominance that can help to secure a social order and function as mechanisms of social integration. These include a rule by force, fraud, and corruption.[284] Hegemony is a form of social leadership of rule based on a combination of consent and coercion, with the former being the primary mechanism and the latter 'always looming in the background'.[285] Strategically, hegemony is contingent upon developing a 'hegemonic project',[286] or what the Amsterdam Project calls 'comprehensive concepts of control'.[287]

This involves the mobilization of support behind a concrete, national-popular program of action which asserts a general interest in the pursuit of objectives that explicitly or implicitly advance the long-term interests of the hegemonic class (fraction) and which also privileges particular 'economic-corporate' interests compatible with this programme. Conversely, those particular interests that are inconsistent with the project are deemed immoral and/or irrational and, in so far as they are still pursued by groups outside the consensus, they are also liable to sanction.[288] Thus, hegemony includes not only presenting the interests of the hegemonic group as general interest, but also incorporating other (opposing) interests into the hegemonic worldview and thus transcending narrow self-interest of the leading group. In this way, various discourses are articulated into a single hegemonic discourse and some of the social antagonisms are neutralized.[289] The related notion of power bloc refers to a relatively stable coalition of forces that is brought together by a hegemonic project. Its unity depends on self-sacrifice of immediate interest of, at least, some of its members and on members' commitment to a common world outlook.[290] However stable,

283. Van Apeldoorn 2002, p. 19.
284. Gramsci 1971, p. 80.
285. Gramsci 1971, pp. 169-70.
286. Jessop 1983, and 1990.
287. Van der Pijl 1998; Van Apeldoorn 2004b.
288. Jessop 1990, p. 208.
289. Laclau and Mouffe 1984.
290. Jessop 1990.

a power bloc is not a static coalition but rather a dynamic process of coalition building that brings together various actors through promoting the hegemonic project in particular places and times.

Ideas, to be effective, have to articulate other (material) elements of social practice. Hegemonic projects, to be successful, need to be organically related to material and ideational constraints and opportunities of the conjuncture. Hegemony does not work as an imposition or negotiation of a consensus. It is a relational moment forging a field of force that shapes social relations in a way that exerts pressures and set limits on achievable social forms. This field of force, or historic bloc,[291] not only shapes production of ideas and the way of thinking, but also makes some ideas and projects more 'comprehensive' and appealing than others.[292] In the field of economic policy, to become hegemonic a political project must articulate a feasible 'accumulation strategy'. A (successful) accumulation strategy is constitutive of growth dynamics. At the same time, it must articulate structural precondition for such dynamics to emerge. Jessop summarizes the links between the hegemonic project and accumulation strategy as follows:

> The collective interests of capital are not reducible to the various interests that individual capitals happen to have in common. Far from these collective interests comprising the lowest common denominator of shared interests in the reproduction of the general external conditions of the circuit of capital (such as money and law), they are not wholly pre-given and must be articulated in, and through, specific accumulation strategies which establish a *contingent* community of interest among particular capitals.[293]

State actors and the state as a site of social struggles have a major role in formulating and implementing hegemonic projects and accumulation strategies and thus in reshaping the balance of interests in society. The state cannot only enjoy considerable autonomy from social interests, but it is also a site where collectively binding decisions are made. Neo-Gramscian approaches have emphasized the role of 'organic intellectuals'[294] and 'cadres',[295] located both within and beyond the state apparatus, in formu-

291. Gramsci 1971, p. 366.
292. Williams 1977; Roseberry 1994; Kalb 1997; Smith 2004, pp. 99-120.
293. Jessop 1990, p. 159.
294. Van Apeldoorn 2002.
295. Van der Pijl 1998.

lating hegemonic projects, shaping social interests and reworking the 'common sense'. Both intellectuals and state actors constitute autonomous social groups. Yet the structural imperative to respect material constraints in formulating strategies, *inter alia*, links them to other social (class) forces.

In sum, state strategies are produced by social forces within the state in the context of a social struggle for hegemony. Ideas, institutions (most notably, state form), and the relations of production are constitutive of social forces and mediate their relative power and ability to influence state strategies. The notion of the hegemonic project, or comprehensive concepts of control, denotes a temporary synthesis between the perspective generated by an ascendant trend in the economy and the capacity of a set of social forces operating in the context of the state (or a number of states) to translate this perspective into a general (comprehensive) programme for society as a whole. This programme, however, does not merely reflect an economic dynamic: it is rather its constitutive element.[296] Such projects thus integrate the reproductive needs of social formations: 'This makes 'hegemony' even less of a magical trick, even though deception and fraud may be part of what the population at large is being told about these reproductive and security needs'.[297]

Beyond methodological nationalism: towards a scalar political economy of transnational processes

By focusing on 'the transnational' the Amsterdam Project of transnational historical materialism contributed to a wide range of voices criticizing deeply entrenched methodological nationalism of mainstream social sciences, in particular international political economy.[298] We insist that it is impossible to distinguish between 'the local' and 'the global' — or internal and external factors — in the real world. On the level of concrete-complex, global is local and local is also global. 'The local turns out not only to be influenced by the transnational but to be a specific site of the materialization of transnational processes. That is to say, the local is not only transnational, but also, there is no transnational that does not have specific and particular local enactments'.[299] In turn, the external is always also internal. Thus, the transnational actors are not external to states as often understood by

296. Van der Pijl 1984; Jessop 1990.
297. Van der Pijl 2004, p. 184.
298. Van Apeldoorn 2004a.
299. Glick Schiller 2006, p. 9.

neo-realist international relations, rather these 'actors by definition operate simultaneously inside different 'national states' rather than 'confronting' those states from the outside'.[300] Yet, the concepts of global-domestic/local and internal-external cannot be avoided; instead, a different meaning should be forged for them. We approach this problem from the strategic-relational perspective in the same way as the structure/agency dichotomy that we already discussed above. From the strategic-relational perspective, neither structure/agency, nor local/global (nor internal/external) exist in themselves; instead, they constitute through their relational interaction. Thus, structure/agency and the internal/external should be understood relationally to the object of analysis both in space and time. The analysis should thus focus on dialectical interplay of structure/agency or internal/external factors in real contexts of social and political interaction. In a similar way to the agency/structure dilemma, the local/internal can be brought into the global/external and the global/external can be brought into local/internal. The former corresponds to uploading and cooptation of locally produced practices and discourses, the latter to different theories of translation, mediation, and internalization of global influences. Yet, in order to give a proper meaning to local/global, internal/external on the level of concrete-complex, it is needed to go further so that the distinctions will dissolve. Thus, the global/local distinction should be dissolved into locally enacted global environment and globally constituted local action.[301] Along these lines, the national case studies in this volume study developments on the national level as domestic articulation of transnational processes. At the same time, they underscore the importance of the national scale in producing particular outcomes.

Social Forces, Hegemonic Projects and the State in the EU

Applying our critical political economy more explicitly to the European arena, we understand neoliberal European governance as a political project (which may or may not be hegemonic), which here we define as an integrated set of 'initiatives and propositions that, as pragmatic responses to concrete national and European problems, conceptually and strategically further the process of socio-economic, societal and institutional restructuring'[302]. Within Europe it is no longer the national states that exclusively provide the regulatory framework that allows the capitalist market

300. Van Apeldoorn 2004, p. 146.
301. Drahokoupil 2007.
302. Bieling and Steinhilber 2002, p. 41.

economy to function – rather, increasingly, a key role here is played by the EU and by the process of European integration. In analyzing this role we adopt a transnational perspective as outlined above in which the institutional intergovernmental and supranational governance structures of the European multilevel polity are seen as embedded within a transnational political economy and a transnational civil society.[303] Such a political project reflects the agency of a dominant set of transnational social and political forces. Concretely, a political project is articulated ideologically through the discursive and political practices of a multitude of (transnational) associations, lobby groups, think tanks, private forums and planning groups, as well as so-called 'expert groups', experts who are far from autonomous (in as much as such a thing exists) but are often directly linked to concrete (transnational) social forces. Through the transnational networks constituted by these actors[304] certain interests are brought to the fore and come to underpin the EU's policy discourse and shape the content of the regulatory framework it seeks to put in place.

From this perspective, then, the European Commission, although indeed an important supranational public actor, whose role as policy-entrepreneur is also underlined by several of the studies collected in this volume, must not be interpreted as an autonomous actor in the way some 'supranationalist' accounts of European integration tend to do.[305] Rather, the Commission can arguably be viewed as a key public actor within the EU as a 'multilevel state formation',[306] and as such embedded in a particular configuration of transnational social forces, and a concomitant (potentially hegemonic) construction and articulation of interests. In capitalist societies generally, it is of course capitalist interests that are privileged through these processes. In the current European Union as a system of asymmetric socio-economic governance establishing a 'free space for capital'[307] it is in particular those interests bound up with the most transnationally mobile fractions of capital that are privileged.[308] At the same time this emphasis on the structural primacy of transnational capital must not be taken to imply that political projects, notwithstanding their presentation as coherent

303. Van Apeldoorn et al 2003.
304. Van Apeldoorn et al 2003.
305. Stone Sweet and Sandholtz (eds) 1998, pp. 1-26.
306. Jessop 2002a, p. 205; Caporaso 1996, pp. 29-51.
307. Van der Pijl 2006, p. 32.
308. See Van Apeldoorn 2002.

programmes, are free from contradictions and therefore uncontested. As indicated, hegemony in a Gramscian sense is in fact never complete, and subordinate groups and classes may always struggle to redefine the terms of the dominant discourse and transform underlying social practices.

Contesting the Neoliberal Project: What role and prospect for resistance?

A central focus of our critical political economy perspective is the emphasis on the social struggle underlying the political project of neoliberal European Integration. Rejecting pluralist notions of agency on the European level,[309] we argue that in order to analyse the potential for contestation of and resistance to socio-economic restructuring, the position and agency of subaltern classes in European governance have to be seen from a perspective that acknowledges the fundamental power asymmetries in the EU. Most critical political economy studies of European integration processes have so far focused on the role of transnational capital (fractions) and the emergence, consolidation and reproduction of hegemonic discourses and 'concepts of control'. This volume seeks to contribute to an understanding of how, on the one hand, these hegemonic discourses are actually maintained and disseminated with the support of subaltern classes. At the same time, as for instance the chapter by Bieler points out, it is crucial to look at the agency of subaltern classes in order to be able to conceptualize resistance to and contestation of neoliberal restructuring. Here, we follow Cox in emphasizing the emancipatory potential of a critical political economy perspective.[310] As Drainville has argued, 'as a political reality, neoliberalism is *both* a broad strategy of restructuring *and* a succession of negotiated settlements, of concessions to the rigidities and dynamics of structures, as well as the political possibilities of the moment'.[311] This understanding of neoliberalism opens up political space for subaltern classes to contest and challenge neoliberal governance, and engenders a research perspective that takes into account the agency of resistance.

309. See Van Apeldoorn et al 2003, pp. 27-8.
310. Cox 1981, pp. 126–55.
311. Drainville 1994, pp. 105-32.

REFERENCES

Archer, Margaret 1995, *Realist Social Theory: The Morphogenetic Approach*, Cambridge: Cambridge University Press.

Balibar, Etienne 1991, 'Es Gibt Keinen Staat in Europa: Racism and Politics in Europe Today', *New Left Review* 186.

Bhaskar, Roy 1979, *The Possibility of Naturalism. A Philosophical Critique of the Contemporary Human Sciences*, Brighton: Harvester Press.

Bieler, Adrian and Adam Morton (eds.) 2001, *Social Forces in the Making of the New Europe*, Basingstoke: Palgrave.

Bieler, Adrian, Werner Bonefeld and Peter Burnham (eds.) 2006, *Global Restructuring, State, Capital and Labour: Contesting Neogramscian Perspectives*, Basingstoke: Palgrave Macmillan.

Bieling, Hans-Jurgen and Jochen Steinhilber 2002, 'Finanzmarktintegration und Corporate Governance in der Europäischen Union', *Zeitschrift für Internationale Beziehungen*, 9, 1: 39-74.

Blyth, Mark 2002, *Great transformations: Economic ideas and institutional change in the twentieth century*, Cambridge: Cambridge University Press.

Bode, Ries 1979, 'De Nederlandse bourgeoisie tussen de twee wereldoorlogen', *Cahiers voor de Politieke en Sociale Wetenschappen*, 2, 4: 9-50.

Bohle, Dorothee 2002, *Europas neue Peripherie: Polens Transformation und transnationale Integration*, Westfaelisches Dampfboot: Münster.

Buch-Hansen, Hubert 2006, 'Beyond rationalism and constructivism: towards a critical realist intervention in EU studies', *Paper presented at the ESA Critical Political Economy Workshop in Amsterdam*, August-September 2006.

Bruff, Ian and Laura Horn 2012, 'Varieties of capitalism in crisis', *Competition and Change*, 16, 3: 161–168.

Cafruny, Alan and Magnus Ryner (eds.) 2003, *A Ruined Fortress?*, Lanham: Rowman & Littlefield.

Campbell, John 1998, 'Institutional analysis and the role of ideas in political economy', *Theory and Society*, 27(3): 377-409.

Caporaso, James 1996, 'The European Union and Forms of State: Westphalian, Regulatory or Post-Modern?' *Journal of Common Market Studies*, 34, 1: 29-51.

Cox, Robert 1981, 'Social Forces, States and World Orders', *Millennium: Journal of International Studies*, 10, 2: 126–55

Domhoff, William 1996, *State autonomy or class dominance? Case studies on policy making in America*, New York: Aldine de Gruyter.

Drahokoupil Jan 2007, *The rise of the competition state in Central and Eastern Europe: The politics of foreign direct investment*, Unpublished PhD dissertation, Central European University, Budapest.

Drainville, Andre 1994, 'International political economy in the age of open Marxism', *Review of International Political Economy*, *1*, 1: 105-32.

Evans, Peter 1995, *Embedded autonomy: States and industrial transformation*, Princeton: Princeton University Press.

Evans, Peter, Dietrich Rueschemeyer and Theda Skocpol (eds.) 1985. *Bringing the state back in*, Cambridge and New York: Cambridge University Press.

Frieden, Jeffry and Roger Rogowski 1996, 'The impact of the international economy on national policies: An analytical overview', in *Internationalization and domestic politics* edited by Robert Keohane and Helen Milner, Cambridge and New York: Cambridge University Press.

Gill, Stephen 1998, 'European Governance and New Constitutionalism: Economic and Monetary Union and Alternatives to Disciplinary Neoliberalism in Europe' *New Political Economy*, 3, 1: 5-26.

Glick Schiller, Nina 2006, 'What can transnational studies offer the analysis of localized conflict and protest?', *Focaal - European Journal of Anthropology*, *47:* 3-17.

Gramsci, Antonio 1971, *Selections from the Prison Notebooks of Antonio Gramsci* edited by Qunitin Hoare and Geoffrey Nowell Smith, London: Lawrence and Wishart.

Haas, Ernst 1968 [1958, with 1968 preface), *The Uniting of Europe. Political, Social and Economic Forces, 1950-1957*, Stanford: Stanford University Press.

Haggard, Stephan 1990, *Pathways from the periphery: The politics of growth in the newly industrializing countries*, Ithaca and London: Cornell University Press.

Hooghe, Liesbet and Gary Marks 2001, *Multi-Level Governance and European Integration*, Lanham: Rowman & Littlefield

Hooghe, Liesbet and Gary Marks 2007a, 'A Postfunctional Theory of European Integration: From Permissive Consensus to Constraining Dissensus', *British Journal of Political Science*, 39, 1: 1-23

Hooghe, Liesbet and Gary Marks (eds.) 2007b, *Understanding Euroscepticism*, Special Issue of 'Acta Politica', 42, 2/3.

Holman, Otto 1992, 'Transnational Class Strategy and the New Europe', *International Journal of Political Economy* 22, 1, 3-22.

Jessop, Bob 1983, 'Accumulation strategies, state forms, and hegemonic projects' *Kapitalistate*, 10, 11: 89-111.

Jessop, Bob 1990, *State theory: Putting the capitalist state in its place*, University Park: Pennsylvania State University Press.

Jessop, Bob 2002, *The Future of the Capitalist State*, Cambridge: Polity Press.

Jessop, Bob 2007, *State Power*, Cambridge: Polity Press.

Kalb, Don 1997, *Expanding class: power and everyday politics in industrial communities, The Netherlands, 1850-1950*, Durham: Duke University Press.

Laclau, Ernesto and Chantal Mouffe 1985, *Hegemony and Socialist Strategy*, London: Verso.

Mahon, Rianne 1977, 'Canadian public policy: The unequal structure of representation', in Leo Panitch (ed.) *The Canadian state: Political economy and political power*, Toronto, Buffalo and London: University of Toronto Press.

Miliband, Ralph 1969, *The state in capitalist society*, London: Quartet Books.

Moravcsik, Andrew 1998, *The Choice for Europe: Social Purpose and State Power from Messina to Maastricht*, Ithaca: Cornell University Press.

Nölke, Andreas 2003, 'The Relevance of Transnational Policy Networks: Some Examples from the European Commission and the Bretton Woods Institutions' *Journal of International Relations and Development*, 6, 3: 267-98.

Nye, Joseph 1990, *Bound to lead: The changing nature of American power*, New York: Basic Books.

Oberndorfer, Lukas, 2012, 'Hegemoniekrise in Europa—Auf dem Weg zu einem autoritä̈ren Wettbewerbsetatismus?', in Forschungsgruppe Staatsprojekt Europa (eds) *Die EU in der Krise* (Muenster: Westfaelisches Dampfboot): 50–72.

Overbeek, Henk and Bastiaan van Apeldoorn (eds) (2012) *Neoliberalism in Crisis*, Basingstoke: Palgrave.

Poulantzas, Nicos 1978, *State, power, socialism*, London: New Left Books.

Risse-Kappen, Thomas 1996, 'Exploring the Nature of the Beast: International Relations Theory and Comparative Policy Analysis Meet the European Union', *Journal of Common Market Studies*, 34, 1: 53-80.

Roseberry, William 1994, 'Hegemony and the language of contention', in Gilbert Joseph and Daniel Nugent (eds.), *Everyday forms of state formation: Revolution and the negotiation of rule in modern Mexico*, Durham: Duke University Press.

Sayer, Andrew 1992, *Method in Social Science: A Realistic Approach*, London: Routledge.

Smith, Gavin 2004, 'Hegemony: Critical interpretations in anthropology and beyond', *Focaal - European Journal of Anthropology*, 43: 99-120.

Stone Sweet, Alec and Wayne Sandholtz (eds.) 1998, 'Integration, supranational governance and the institutionalization of the European polity', in Wayne Sandholtz and Alec Stone Sweet (eds.) *European Integration and Supranational Governance*, Oxford: Oxford University Press.

Strange, Susan 1988, *States and markets*, London: Pinter.

Thacker, Strom 2000, *Big business, the State, and free trade: Constructing coalitions in Mexico*. Cambridge, UK and New York: Cambridge University Press.

Van Apeldoorn, Bastiaan 2002, *Transnational capitalism and the struggle over European integration*, London and New York: Routledge.

Van Apeldoorn, Bastiaan, Henk Overbeek and Magnus Ryner 2003, 'Theories of European Integration: A Critique', in Alun Cafruny and Magnus Ryner (eds.) *A Ruined Fortress?*, Lanham: Rowman & Littlefield.

Van Apeldoorn, Bastiaan 2004a, 'Theorizing the transnational: A historical materialist approach', *Journal of International Relations and Development*, 7, 2: 142-76.

van Apeldoorn, Bastiaan 2004b, 'Transnational historical materialism: The Amsterdam International Political Economy Project', *Journal of International Relations and Development*, 7, 2: 110-2.

Van Apeldoorn, Bastiaan, 2014, 'The European capitalist class and the crisis of its hegemonic project' Socialist Register 2014, 189-206.

Van Apeldoorn, Bastiaan and Laura Horn 2007, 'The Marketisation of Corporate Control: A Critical Political Economy Perspective' *New Political Economy*, 12, 2: 211-35.

Van der Pijl, Kees, 1984, *The Making of an Atlantic Ruling Class.* London: Verso.

Van der Pijl, Kees 2004, 'Two faces of the transnational cadre under neoliberalism', *Journal of* International Relations and Development, 7, 2: 177-207.

Van der Pijl,Kees 2006, Global Rivalries: From the Cold War to Iraq, London: Pluto.

Williams, Raymond 1977, Marxism and literature. Oxford: Oxford University Press

AGAINST RECONCILIATION: THINKING THE PARTISANS IN YUGOSLAVIA[312]

Gal Kirn

Introduction

After the so-called 'democratic revolutions' at the end of the 1980s in the East, the postsocialist era has begun. The collapse of socialism brought the destruction of the socialist welfare state and among other things intensified historical revisionism, where the central target was the recent communist past.[313] Democratic forces, especially those that leaned towards the right political spectre, put on the anticommunist cloak underlined by the discourse of universal human rights and launched a nationalistic project. The nation-building process demanded a new interpretation of history, reinventing national myths and a glorious past. However, the most basic operation that has been at work in official post-Yugoslav ideologies is the rehabilitation of fascism in the name of reconciliation. Reconciliation with past atrocities and traumas has become necessary in order to live together in one National community. Re-visioning the national memory needed to deal with two important historical events in the Yugoslav history: recent wars in the 1990s and the Second World War.

This essay focuses on the specificity of post-socialist ideology in the post-Yugoslav context, where one of the most important signifiers of nationalist ideologies has become 'national reconciliation'. It has major consequences in legitimizing the ethnic divisions in ex-Yugoslavia, its imagined past and future. The most symptomatic case, which we will examine closely, is the management of monuments, which is fashionably labelled the politics of memory. Politics of memory is internally linked to the reconciliation discourse, which had different goals, but first and foremost, it legitimized

---

312. This lecture is a revised version of my article 'Remembering or thinking the partisan movement?' (2009).

313. We should not overlook that in Yugoslavia, neoliberal agenda started due to the implementation of IMF conditions already in the late 1970s. From this follows a very simple conclusion: the 'transition' did not start with the rise of new nationalistic communities in the 1990s, but at least some 15 years earlier. On the analysis of detrimental effects of IMF on Yugoslavia, see Samary (1988), Magaš (1993) and Woodward (1995).

the ethnic divisions in ex-Yugoslavia, its imagined past and future. Other political effects of post-Yugoslav politics of memory are: relativisation of historical facts, universalisation of victims and equalisation of partisans and local fascists/collaborators in WWII. This is done in the name of reconciliation, but even then, we cannot escape the major political effect: the rehabilitation of the fascist collaborators (eg. Serbian Chetniks, Croatian Ustashas, Slovenian Home Guard) that tacitly legitimizes the brutal aggression in the wars of 1990s, where those defeated in the Second World War became the historical victors of the new national communities.

My main target of attack will be the 'reconciliation discourse'. I examine this question in three parts: in the first we I analyse closely the transformation in the landscape of monuments in the Croatian context using Žiži's film *Damnatio Memoriae* (2001) in order to show the formation of Croatian nationalism. Following this, I will outline a critique of the specific reconciliation ideology in the Slovenian context. Apart from the analysis of memorial sites I will conclude with a different historical interpretation of the WWII period. Overall, I argue that the Partisan movement was the only revolutionary event with strong consequences in 'twentieth century' Yugoslavia. To re-affirm the emancipatory past does not mean to melancholically dwell in good old times, but on the opposite attempts to rethink and organize emancipatory politics in the post-Yugoslav context today.

Damnatio Memoriae:
A Defense of the Aesthetic Effect a la Žiži

Bogdan Žiži made the documentary, *Damnatio Memoriae*, on the fate of antifascist monuments, which was screened on Croatian public television in 2001. Apart from some minor comments, it did not really succeed in enhancing public discussion on this important issue. The film's voiceover starts with the proposition that a monument is a "sign of the past and a witness to the future". According to Žiži monuments must be shown respect. *Damnatio Memoriae* shows the monstrous fate of monuments in Croatia, the dynamics and the scope of the politics of retaliations for the antifascist past. The Croatian war of independence fostered extremist nationalism and Catholicism, which materialized most genuinely in grassroots activities of monument destruction. These actions had at least one common denominator: their goal was to eliminate traces of the antifascist struggle in Croatia. A new history was being written.

In the early 1990s there were two prevalent methods of destroying monuments. The first solution could be called conversion of old monuments: they were simply given new form and content. The monument remained on the same place, but the red stars of the former monuments would be replaced by Catholic crosses, while the antifascist slogans and eulogies to the National Liberation Struggle would be replaced by the Croatian checkerboard coat-of-arms and inscriptions dedicated to the Croatian nation. New memorials had been often inaugurated before the former president Tuðman visited to towns or specific memorial places that used to contain antifascist or communist monuments. The other method of getting even with the past was a direct action of destruction. Unknown perpetrators would simply blow up monuments or deface them and write Ustasha – extreme nationalist – slogans on them. Virtually no antifascist monument anywhere in Croatia was spared, barring large parts of Istria. It would be wrong to claim that these actions were directed 'from above' as part of some hidden agenda of the then regime. The documentary leads to the conclusion that the destruction and the purge were systematic; we could call it a 'cleansing regime'. This entailed the process of eradicating the foreign element, the false, un-Croatian element, which was concerning the constitution of the socialist Yugoslavia and the Partisan movement. The struggle for the new Croatian identity, for the constitution of a Croatian nation state included a very specific ideological 'interpellation'. Every member of the new state owed dual allegiance on the one side to the Roman Catholic Church and on the other to the Croatian nation. In other words every true citizen of Croatia was a catholic and Croatian.[314] This dual nature of Croatian-ness, which directly related to the ethnic identity taken from Old (pre-war) Yugoslavia, was also mirrored in the changed image of the landscape itself; the changes of the names of monuments and streets point to the impact of the conflict in the symbolic realm. The fact that the authorities were not indifferent to such actions became plainly evident from decisions of the (most) independent state institutions, the courts, which did not do much to persecute the perpetrators, have even defended them.

As important as Žiži's film is in terms of its informative and historical value, the political message it sends is a little awkward, if not downright art for art's sake. In his analysis of the phenomenon, Žiži puts the destroyers of monuments on trial. His verdict consists of two propositions: the first

---

314. In other parts of Yugoslavia the ethnically cleansed areas would presuppose identical double bind: Orthodox Serbian, Bosnian Muslim, Slovenian Catholic, Albanian Muslim, etc.

and general thesis supports the point that destruction is a morally intolerable act. Monuments must be respected, since they are to bear witness for the future. The second and more problematic thesis can be summed up thus: it is true that many of the antifascist monuments were ideological (communist) and moreover had no aesthetic value, but, despite the deluge of ideological monuments, a number of internationally recognizable monuments were made. They became works of art. By resorting to the argument of aesthetic value, Žiži may have thought that he had managed to sidestep the (antifascist) ideology of the League of Communists of Yugoslavia. The works of art had become wholly autonomous and ideology-free. Aesthetically significant works – such as Vojin Bakić sculptures – should be viewed strictly from the artistic angle and without the involvement of ideology. The fact of their destruction testifies to the barbarism and ignorance of the perpetrators. Although Žiži makes a general plea for the protection of all monuments, he obviously deems some among them privileged. This thesis is in contradiction with the first thesis. One of the hidden presuppositions, quite incomprehensible, is that ideological monuments do not deserve 'protection'. Where the filmmaker was faced with a serious problem and where thinking about the connections between ideology, politics, and art ought to have been introduced, he renounced them. By kicking ideology out through the door, Žiži's argumentation left a window open for another kind of ideology to sneak in: aesthetic ideology. Žiži intervenes in reality through the aesthetic discourse which allows him to avoid getting his hands dirty with ideology. To paraphrase Marx, he pulled his head out of the swamp with his hands for a moment, not knowing that his feet were deep in ideological mire. The unspoken assumption that ideology-free thinking and remembrance are only possible through works of art is of course an ideological assumption. What lies behind it is a naïve idea of the authenticity and purity of the artistic position, floating in the air and divorced from any connections with social reality.

It is true that certain works of art produce truth, bring new ways of seeing and doing in the world [315]. This is definitely true of Bakić monuments/spatial interventions. But this bears no relation either to the communist policies of erecting monuments after the Second World War or to the fascist policy at work in the 1990s. The fact that some of the monuments were real works of art does not make them any more worthy of protection. We should not introduce an artistic measurement for monuments.

315. On the relationship between aesthetic and politics see Rancière (2004).

218

By showing up the vandalism and the barbarism of the perpetrators, the filmmaker does no more than pass moral judgment, without taking a step further, toward thinking about this form of politics. He never even gives a name to these politics. The fascist politics of destruction made no distinction between aesthetic and non-aesthetic monuments. Why and where from the idea of a fascist sensitivity to modernist art? The thesis can be made even more radical: it is not only about fascism not making any differences. Because of its particularist position, fascism had to settle the score with the universalist dimension of the Partisan movement. On the one hand, it broke with the antifascist political message, which was that the national liberation struggle was based on international antifascist solidarity, and on the other, with its universalist artistic tradition. The acuity and the message of the documentary film thus end up hanging in mid-air, in its attempt to transfer the thought behind the policy of destruction and the fight against it into the field of aesthetic discourse. We can reduce the author's work to a self-referential formula: what I do is art (a documentary film), in which I defend art (non-ideological monuments = artworks) through art (aesthetic discourse).

The Slovenian Reconciliation is Forgetting the Revolution and the Antifascist Struggle

What happened to the Partisan heritage and monuments in the 1990s in Slovenia? There was no open policy of large-scale purging in Slovenia, thanks to the activities of the Partisan Veteran's Association and to a strong antifascist tradition. This does not mean, however, that Slovenia was immune to subtle techniques, which were launched by right-wing ideologies. Nationalists launched a huge assault on the Ideological State Apparatuses and the Slovenian independence could not be questioned in any way. Among other things, the debate on recent history has led to the introduction of the passive victims discourse and to a hunt for the criminalsof the former 'totalitarian regime'. The end goal of this debate was thereharbilitation of the Home Guard [316] and consequently, national reconciliation.

316. The Home Guard, or in Slovenian *Domobranci*, collaborated with the German occupation forces and fought against the Partisans in Slovenia. Before Domobranci, the White Guard collaborated with Italian occupation forces, which capitulated in 1943. A civil war occurred everywhere in Yugoslavia during the Second World War: collaborationist regime of Croatian state NDH (Ustasha) and the representative of the old Yugoslavia Draža Mihajlović (Chetniks) fought against partisan forces and terrorized civilian populations. It is noteworthy that the Allies supported Chetniks as representatives of the old Kingdom of Yugoslavia late in 1943, and recognized partisans as the sole antifascist force only on Teheran conference in December of 1943. For the imperialist dimension of the Second World War see Gluckstein (2012).

The first to fly the flag of the Home Guard and anticommunism was the Catholic Church, which has the political support of the rightwing political parties. In their quest for the 'truth' they scored a major point when new monuments were erected. In addition to Partisan monuments we now also have memorials to the Home Guard killed during and after the war. History had to be made more objective, and the victims commemorated.

We can look closer at some differences between the Home Guard and Partisan monuments. The differences lie in the (non)inclusion of history and in the manner of presenting the victims. Partisan monuments bear active, antifascist slogans referring to the historical circumstances of the occupation and the war. Not so the Home Guard memorials: they are shrouded in silence. The most popular slogans found on them are: 'Mother, homeland, God', 'Forgive' or 'Victims of revolutionary violence'. This neutral or conservative inscription on memorials performs a very ideological function: it represents 'Home Guard' members not as active protagonists, but as victims in need of commemoration. This, however, poses at least two problems: one is the positive interpretation of the Home Guard as passive, innocent victims, and the other, the absence of an integral historical context on the Home Guard memorials. The self-appointed interpreters of their contents are bishops (through "masses") and the new historians (exhibitions, films, books), who are actively affirming for a different reading of history.

War monuments are structured like mainstream political discourse. The Partisan side "passively" defends certain aspects of the *National Liberation Struggle*, while the Home Guard side actively persecutes the postwar terror of a part of the National Liberation Struggle. Although the two camps are on opposite banks, they share a common goal in the debate – reconciliation. This is where the monuments come in, playing the crucial role of wrapping the debate in a cloak of dignity and respect for the dead. It is in the national interest to appease the passions and to write a more objective truth, rather than to maintain the division between 'us' and 'them'. However, reconciliation does not have the same meaning for both sides. While both agree that the postwar killings and collaboration with the enemy were problematic, reconciliation nonetheless means a neutralization of how novel the Partisan movement was in Yugoslavia. At worst, reconciliation is no less than the rehabilitation of fascism and the Home Guard. In one fell swoop this rehabilitation puts the Home Guard and the Partisan movement on the same footing and condemns the totalitarian regime that was established after the war. The Home Guard comes out of this apparent equation as the moral winner that had nothing to do with the criminal postwar and totalitarian regime. Reconciliation is possible when we become ashamed of our communist past and come to approve of fascism. From a more Partisan standpoint. On the other hand, reconciliation means acknowledging the postwar killings and praising a certain aspect of the politics of the National Liberation Struggle. It is a defense of the National Liberation Struggle as the core of the Slovenian nationhood, as though the war had only been about national independence. In this way a twofold result is produced: a reduced historical inclusion of the National Liberation Struggle in the history of the Slovenian national struggle and a condemnation of everything that comes after the Second World War until the end of the 1980s. The discourse on reconciliation thus completely relativizes the debate about the Yugoslavian event and attempts to erase all revolutionary traces of the National Liberation Struggle.

As a matter of fact, a single revolutionary trace remains, and the advocates of the 'new truth' have structured the debate around it. This trace is also the chief trauma of the debate: the postwar killings. The debate is displaced from what happened during the war to what happened after the war, or, to revolutionary 'totalitarian terror'. Despite the incorrectness of this displacement, one truth was, paradoxically, stated. The postwar killings were indeed a part of the revolutionary terror, but there was no totalitarian regime at that time and not even later. As is widely acknowledged in the history of political ideas, revolution cannot be equated with totalitarianism.[317] If revolution is the destruction of the old Order and if revolution happens in the conditions of war, one cannot avoid the violence. That said we do not want to excuse postwar killings of collaborationist. We should condemn theses excesses and repression of the Communist Party after the war, but at the same time not attempt to eliminate and criminalize revolutionary events. It would be much more productive to ask ourselves how to find ways to protect revolutions in the light of their excesses; which are the most effective mechanisms to prevent this excess? The defenders of the Home Guard, historical revisionists pose the question of terror in a completely different light. The category of terror is moral in nature, not political; accordingly, they reach two moral conclusions. They formulate their conclusions by counting the bodies and condemning all criminals. When justice has been done, reconciliation will be possible and revolution

317. We do not have to refer only to a revolutionary thought for that claim, also Hannah Arendt wrote on the distinction between revolution and totalitarianism in her work (1966).

eliminated. The problem of the Partisan supporters is that they passively accept the guilt and the moralizing discourse of reconciliation. Instead of presenting a broader defense of the transformational effects of the antifascist struggle, the Partisan side has backed down into defending merely the national aspect of the National Liberation Struggle.

How to Think the Partisan Struggle?

We do not need to pinpoint the Home Guard's guilt or moral responsibility for their crimes during the Second World War. We previously outlined the way the Home Guard defenders displaced the debate into the realm of morality and transhistoricity by removing the historical context of the antifascist struggle. In no way can the Home Guard's fascist domination and their support for old Yugoslavia and the occupation regimes be equated with the revolutionary Peoples' Liberation Struggle. The Partisans were recognised as part of the broad coalition of antifascist forces from 1943 onwards. The Home Guard collaborated with the fascist and Nazi occupation forces, and this predates the post-war executions[318].

How to understand the novelty of partisan antifascist struggle and defend their cause vis-à-vis collaboration? We will try to present our case with the help of Alain Badiou's insights in the prologue to his *Metapolitics* (2005). Starting from a different historical conjuncture, Badiou poses the question of what made people join the French Resistance. Two tendencies predominate in the context of the revisionist discussions in France. One proclaims that wartime France was Pétainist, where collaborators at worst knowingly collaborated with the occupiers, or, in the more moderate interpretation, collaboration was a matter of pragmatism. It was better to wait and not resist. The other tendency is antifascist and declares France to have been 'resistant.' It thinks the political decision through two considerations which, according to Badiou, do not suffice for thinking politics. One trend (Sartre) sees joining the Resistance in terms of a personal decision, that is, a moral choice and a matter of an individual's conscience. This is a case of a 'subjectivity of opinion', as Badiou says. The other, communist interpretation reduces joining the Resistance to an objective fact. It reads the situation by sociologically analyzing the social groups, and retroactively

---

318. There were certainly different ways of dealing with fascists at the end of the war. The post-war killings were consequences of personal revenge, revolutionary terror with war tribunals that rapidly liquidated fascists. After the Second World War many fascist collaborators that fled to Austria were sent back to Yugoslavia by British forces. Some of them were released, some imprisoned, while the majority of them killed.

instates class as the decisive moment for joining the Resistance. According to Badiou, choice cannot be thought either as a collective imperative or as a personal decision related to moral opinion, external to the situation itself. In Badiou's words: "… this resistance, proceeding by logic, is not an opinion. Rather it is a logical rupture with dominant and circulating opinions … (T)he Resistance was neither a class phenomenon nor an ethical phenomenon."[319] In short, resistance is a rupture with the existing situation: "When all is said and done, all resistance is a rupture in thought, through the declaration of what the situation is, and the foundation of a practical possibility opened up through this declaration."[320] Thinking in the circumstances of WWII meant risking, risking thought and opening the bounds of possibility toward the *Real*, the impossible. To think meant inevitably joining the Resistance. Those who did not think remained tied to that situation, a situation that blocked any risk-taking. Badiou sums this up axiomatically that not to think is not *to risk risking*. Positing politics as thought, which for Badiou is material and has material effects, gives us a different means for understanding the issue of the antifascist struggle itself.[321]

Apart from this equation between politics and thought, we should evaluate the additional complexity of the Yugoslavian 'Peoples' Liberation Struggle'. To be clear, both resistances, French and Yugoslav, had universal dimensions and were part of the same international struggle against fascism, but at the same time they had different political consequences. It is not that Yugoslavian Liberation Struggle is morally superior from the French Resistance, but it produced a major rupture with pre-war Yugoslavia. It produced the new, socialist Yugoslavia, whereas the French Re-

319. Badiou 2005: p. 5-6.
320. Badiou 2005: p. 8.
321. I share an important contribution to understanding politics by Badiou, most notably his thesis on the correlation between thought and politics can to large extent explain that many young people joined the Partisans, although not all of them were members of the Communist Party; they did, however, think the situation both from the national and the revolutionary perspectives. Also, many Slovene and Croatian partisans were fighting against Italian fascism from the early 1920s onwards, some partisans were participating in the Spanish revolution as part of the International brigades, some were active in student and workers' uprisings in the 1930s. Not everything can be boiled down to a momentous decision, which is only thought-decision during WWII, but can be also regarded in terms of a continuous organizational and thought work of the communist and socialist Left in pre-war Yugoslavia. It is true that partisan struggle in WWII meant a deep rupture with the former Kingdom of Yugoslavia, one can add that it can be seen as an intensive encounter of the Communist party and the masses that cannot be reduced to the work of any particular group, of any teleology, but also not without its pre-war organisation.

sistance was disbanded and disarmed after the war; it did not produce lasting consequences in terms of new political forms, or in other words, it did not transform the social relations of pre-war France. It remained a nation-state in the core capitalist system. On the other hand, the Yugoslav Partisan struggle comprised, in addition to national liberation, a social revolution, which was a definitive rupture with the old Yugoslavia. The 'Peoples' Liberation Struggle' was not merely resistance, but a revolutionary event, which transformed social and national relations of pre-war Yugoslavia. It also started a cultural revolution, where immense creativity and novelty was effectuated by the entrance of masses into the sphere of culture. During the war, partisans liberated large portions of Yugoslav territory, where they built up new political forms, such as the people's councils of antifascist struggle, which organized cultural events (theatre, graphics, poetry), educational infrastructure, political meetings to mobilize masses and basic conditions for economy. Participation of the masses in the struggle and culture for the building of new world was of major importance by the Liberation Struggle and by new revolutionary government AVNOJ in 1943. The Yugoslav struggle had long-term consequences and cannot be grasped without understanding the dynamics of the class contradictions of the old Yugoslavia. New Yugoslavia was an event with three dimensions: the international antifascist struggle had a universal dimension, which was at the core of new Yugoslavia;[322] a social revolution, which entailed the introduction of new class relations and a transition to communism, socialist Yugoslavia;[323] and a cultural revolution, which meant the break up with the bourgeois cannons and art autonomy and the entrance of masses to the sphere of culture.[324] It is important to note that national liberations took place for the first time in history in all the nations and nationalities of Yugoslavia. All nations were recognized,[325] while the Serbian bourgeoisie lost the hegemony it had had in the old Yugoslavia. The antinationalistic stance became one of the official guidelines of the League of Communists of Yugoslavia until the mid–1980s. The path towards communism was less

322. Yugoslavia was not a nation and did not have one national language, see Buden 2003.
323. Kirn 2009 and Pupovac 2006.
324. Komelj, 2009.
325. The issue of Kosovo Albanians was unresolved also in the new Yugoslavia. The idea of a Socialist Balkan Federation, which would eliminate the substance of 'Southern Slavs' (Yugoslavia), was suppressed by both Stalin and Churchill; in this way the burning question of the division of Albanians among several countries was avoided, a question that remains open to this day. For more on the idea of this federation see Samary (1988).

successful, although an important contribution to the organization of the socialist society was attempted (*self-management*) and Yugoslavia's role in the non-aligned movement should not be overlooked or, as in contemporary politics of memory, eliminated and forgotten.[326]

Conclusion

From the 1990s onwards the post-Yugoslav context underwent a veritable revision in the ideological state apparatuses with degrading political effects. The field of official and everyday discourse has become imbued with liberalism, nationalism and reconciliation. The most insistent nationalistic tendency appeared in the revision of history, school curricula were changed or are still being changed.[327] One of the most exemplary illustrations of historical revisionism is undoubtedly the dramatic change in the landscape of monuments. The post-Yugoslav politics of memory answered to the challenge of Yugoslavia in many ways: ranging from the repression of everything that is Yugoslav, destruction politics to the reconciliation and commemoration of fascism. Against the internationalist Yugoslav community it launched ethnically segregated communities. A bloody break-up of territories was the consequence of the coalition of liberal (technocrats) and nationalist ideologies (cultural intelligentsia, reformed communists) and not a natural consequence of a totalitarian regime. It was an anti-totalitarian dissident ideological offensive that significantly contributed to the break-up of Yugoslavia. In order for a successful launch of the myth that 'it is impossible to live together with other nations in the same community', post-Yugoslav politics of memory needed to erase anything that was deemed 'Yugoslav'. This meant rehabilitating fascism and legitimising ethnic cleansing. The fight to affirm the antifascist and emancipatory past is then connected to the condemnation of fascists' destruction of monuments. This analysis attempted to show that the return to the topic of memory ought not to be grounded on moralistic, but on political grounds, if we are to allow ourselves a position that goes beyond preservation of (aesthetical) heritage. To rethink Yugoslavia in an open and emancipatory way is also to measure the radical difference of the constitution of revolutionary Yugoslavia and its bloody destruction and its current post-Yugoslav

326. I wrote about this in 'From partisan primacy of politics to postfordist tendency in Yugoslav self-management' (forthcoming):
327. We have not touched on the case of Bosnia, where the recent war and nationalistic effects are still most present. Also, one cannot really anticipate, how the reconciliation in Kosovo will take place.

unfolding of ethnical communities and neoliberal recuperation. To stress the revolutionary nature of the partisan struggle means to politicize and intervene in the national-moralistic discourse of reconciliation. Only on the ground of past emancipatory politics can we understand the dissolution of Yugoslavia and current restorations, and also get some insight into future emancipatory politics. If we need to remain in the field of memorials and need to erect a monument, it should activate thought, that is, it should become a "thinking monument", a monument that evokes the struggles of the past and present.

REFERENCES

Arendt, Hannah 1966, *Origins of Totalitarianism*. New York: Harcourt Brace.

Badiou, Alain 2005, *Metapolitics*. London: Verso.

Buden, Boris 2003, 'Još o komunistikim krvolocima, ili zašto smo se ono rastali' [Again on the communist slaughterers or why we broke up]. Belgrade: *Prelom*. Vol. 3. No. 5.

Gluckstein, Donny 2012, *A People's History of the Second World War: Resistance Versus Empire*. London: Pluto Press.

Kirn, Gal 2009, 'Remembering or thinking the partisan movement' in *Museum on the street*, edited by Zdenka Badovinac and Bojana Piškur. Ljubljana: Museum of Modern Art.

Kirn, Gal 2010, 'From partisan primacy of politics to postfordist tendency in Yugoslav self-management' in *Postfordism and its discontents*, edited by Gal Kirn. Maastricht/Ljubljana: Jan van Eyck Academie and Peace Institute.

Komelj, Miklavž 2009, *Kako misliti partizansko umetnost?* [How to think partisan art?]. Ljubljana: založba cf.*/

Magaš, Branka 1993, *The destruction of Yugoslavia*. London: Verso.

Pupovac, Ozren 2006, 'Projekt Jugoslavija: dialektika revolucije' [Project Yugoslavia: dialectics of revolution]. Ljubljana: *Agregat*. Vol.4. No. 9/10. 2006.

Rancière, Jacques 2004, *Politics of Aesthetics. The distribution of the sensible*. New York : Continuum.

Samary, Catherine 1988, *Le marché contre l'autogestion: l'expérience yougoslave*. Paris: Publisud, Montreuil.

Woodward, Susan 1995, *Balkan Tragedy*. Washington DC: The Brookings institution.

Žižek, Slavoj 2001, *Did somebody say totalitarianism?: Five interventions in the (mis) use of a notation.* London: Verso.

Žiži, Bodgan 2001, *Damnatio Memoraie.* [Documentary film.] Zagreb: Gama studio and Zagreb film.

'THE LAST DAY OF OPPRESSION, AND THE FIRST DAY OF THE SAME':

Popular Forces Regroup against Rafael Correa in Ecuador

Jeffery R. Webber

Luis Macas has long been a proponent of the simultaneous struggle against colonial racism endured by indigenous peoples and the exploitation of popular classes under capitalism. When, in mid-July 2010, I sat
in Quito with this ex-President of the National Confederation of the Indigenous in Ecuador (CONAIE), and former presidential candidate for the
Pachakutik Plurinational Unity Movement – New Country (MURP-NP),
we began our exchange with his reflections on the government of Rafael
Correa. 'From my point of view', Macas began,

> 'this is neither a socialist nor even a left-wing government. This is
> a populist government, whose objective is to challenge the model
> on a few points, through a series of modest reforms, so that the
> model as a whole can continue advancing. Fundamental changes,
> radical changes in this country, are not going to come about with
> this government'.[328]

Correa first scraped his way into the presidency in the second-
round of elections in 2006. This was a political contest scheduled at a time
when the prestige of the indigenous movement – by far the most important
popular force in Ecuador for several decades – had still to recover from the
acute setback it suffered as a consequence of the movement's participation
in the ill-fated government of Lucio Gutiérrez.[329]

---

328. Personal interview, Quito, 14 July, 2010.

329. Gutiérrez, of the Patriotic Society Party (PSP), had run his 2002 electoral campaign on
an anti-neoliberal platform but immediately capitulated to the neoliberal policy prescriptions
of the International Monetary Fund once in office. CONAIE supported the party's election
and even provided ministers for the government's first cabinet, although within seven months
the rapidly intensifying rupture between the indigenous movement and the now evidently
neoliberal Gutiérrez had been formally played out with the resignation of these ministers.

The wildly popular process of a Constituent Assembly in 2007 and 2008 offered up an extended honeymoon for Correa and large cross-sections of society. A new, progressive Constitution received the approval of 64 percent of voters in a referendum in September 2008, and Correa was re-elected – this time in the first round – with 52 percent of the popular vote in April, 2009. Things began to sour soon after, however, when Correa's failure to break with the quotidian banalities of the neoliberal economics he had inherited was difficult to reconcile with the President's romantic and ostentatious slogans of 'twenty-first century socialism' and a 'Citizen's Revolution'. Indeed, the President would strain to align his practical commitment to aggressively reorienting the Ecuadorian economy toward the extraction of minerals by multinational corporations with his preferred rhetorical schemas for the next several years.

> 'The weakness of the Left in this country', Macas lamented, 'is that in these crucial and difficult times we have not been able to respond. The priority, from my point of view, is to reclaim our agenda, and rearticulate the social and popular movement in this country. Because the objective of this government is precisely to disarticulate this entire process of struggle'.

Disorientation to Regroupment

If it is still early days, Macas' desires seem at least to have become visible on the horizon after the First Gathering of Social Movements for Democracy and Life was held in Quito on August 9, 2011. Roughly 400 delegates from various sectors of the indigenous, peasant, labour, feminist, LGBT, Afro-Ecuadorian, and environmental movements, joined forces that day with the majority of left-wing parties in the country. CONAIE, the Ecuadorian Confederation of United Class-Struggle Workers Organisations (CEDOCUT), and the National Teachers' Union of Ecuador (UNE) together constituted the core of the social forces involved, while the broad political Left was represented by Pachakutik, the Democratic Popular Movement (MPD), Montecristi Lives, Participation, and a dissident fraction of the Socialist Party.

'We are bringing together the truly organised social movements', according to Delfín Tenesaca, President of ECUARUNARI (the Andean highland indigenous organisation), including 'teachers, workers, youth, stdents, barrio organisations, domestic workers, artists, and the indigenous

230

and peasant organisations from around the country whose activists have been fighting for their entire lives'.[330]

Increasingly, social movements and the political Left are calling into question the deepening and extension of the extractivist development model into mining, the absence of agrarian reform in spite of government promises to the contrary, intensifying attacks on public sector unions, the concentration of authority in the executive power, the absence of participatory democracy, and the criminalisation of resistance under Correa's watch.[331] One representative voice of the building frustration, Humberto Cholango, President of CONAIE, commented on the purpose of the meeting: 'The objective of this gathering was to begin to organise ourselves, to generate ideas, to coordinate, in order to build a front of unity between all organised and social sectors'.[332]

The underlying concerns, anxieties, and disaffection of those gathered were reflected in the themes taken up by each of the six break-away sessions organised for the beginning of the conference – democracy; the labour movement; economic alternatives; women, equality, diversity and feminist resistance; natural resources (land, water, mangroves, fishing, mining and oil); and perspectives on unity. Each session deliberated in isolation and then reported back to the assembly as a whole.

Democracy, Gender, and Diversity

The group on democracy focused on the criminalisation of social protest and popular struggle under the Correa government, and stressed how these repressive dynamics were necessarily linked to 'the implementation of an economic model that strengthens and centralises the state at the service of emergent Ecuadorian bourgeois interests and those of transnational corporations'.[333] Meanwhile, the labour session concluded that Correa was a 'traitor to the project of change of the Ecuadorian people and an enemy of workers'. They vowed to 'reject and to fight the anti-popular and anti-worker policies of the Correa regime'.

The report back on women, diversity, and feminism emphasised the necessity of recovering women's historic struggles in the country across multiple realms – as women workers, peasants, indigenous, and youth.

330. Personal interview, Quito, 14 July, 2010.
331. Ospina Peralta 2011.
332. Personal Interview, Quito, 9 August, 2011.
333. I digitally recorded and transcribed the report-backs of each group.

Women were recognised as 'exploited, oppressed and discriminated against by capitalism, and by the patriarchal system in its entirety'.

Women's right to dignified jobs and recognition for their reproductive work in domestic sphere were pushed forward in the room as key demands. At the same time, space was preserved in this discussion for the 'right to integral health – sexual rights, reproductive rights and the self-determination of our peoples'. Gender equality in all the spaces of the state, political parties, universities and within the popular social movements themselves featured centrally in the group's resolutions.

Natural Resources Struggles

A pernicious disjuncture apparent in all the Andean regimes pledging commitment to 'twenty-first century socialism', between official expressions of the sacred preservation of *Pachamama* and Mother Nature and destructive ecological ramifications of accelerating capitalist extraction, is perhaps most striking in contemporary Ecuador.

The utter continuity of capitalist extractivism under Correa dominated the discussion of natural resources and resistance. This session declared Correa, 'an enemy of the Ecuadorian people', not least because of the 'persecution and criminalisation of social struggle', in extractive resource sectors. They also launched a critique of the way in which Correa's government 'hypocritically talks about the rights of nature and Sumak Kawsay while acting against nature and pushing forward an aggressive and devastating model of development'.

With regard to mining, the natural resource cluster urged a total rejection of open-pit mining in Ecuador, and reasserted that consent be acquired by the government from any affected community before any mining concessions of any type are granted. The struggle around mining, they argued, has to be part of a common struggle for a popular economy based in solidarity.

A fundamental part of the struggle around natural resources, the group concluded, ought to be permanent mobilisation for the nationalisation of oil and the mining sector and the establishment of social control over these sectors. Any exploitation of resources under this schema would be for the benefit of workers and effected communities. Transnational oil companies would be forced to leave protected environmental areas of the country.

Resolutions on water likewise stipulated total opposition to hydro-electrical projects, protection of lakes, rivers and valleys, and the revoca-

232

tion of private water concessions that have already been allotted to these ends. Connections were drawn between the struggle around water and the ecological question, as well as the indispensability of establishing food sovereignty.

Tackling a parallel theme of particular importance for coastal communities, the natural resource session called for the prohibition of industrial fishing and respect for artisanal, small-scale community fishing, as part of an integral effort to protect fragile ecosystems and the rights of nature.

Global Economic Crisis and Socialist Alternatives

A mix of analytical assessment, theorizing alternatives, and formulating strategic proposals characterised the dialogue on economic alternatives. Conclusions revolved around the continually mutating global crisis of capitalism since 2008, and the situation of Ecuador within this panorama. While the crisis originated in the core of the world capitalist system, the group pointed out, its costs were being displaced upon both the popular classes of the core and peripheral countries such as Ecuador. 'We need to radically oppose the notion that this crisis of capitalism will be paid for by workers', they counselled. The political economy of the government of Correa was characterised as 'pro-capitalist, pro-imperialist and extractivist to its core', with petty 'handouts and clientelism' being utilised to ensure 'the submission of the people and to avoid a social uprising'.

The only conceivable escape route from this baleful economic situation, is to abandon 'the basis of oil, the extractivist basis of the economy, and not merely to redistribute this wealth but to re-appropriate it entirely, because the people are its only true owner'. Success is impossible if one country goes it alone in a sea of capitalism. 'These measures', the assembly was reminded, 'have to be made within a project of regional integration, within a framework of actions at the regional level that will permit us to change the model together with our brothers and sisters, the peoples of Latin America – to construct a society based in the equality of work, the elimination of social classes, a society based in Sumak Kawsay (*bien vivir, living well*) and socialism'.

Building Left-Indigenous Unity from the Ground Up

In order to bring to fruition the struggles around labour, gender and diversity, natural resources, and democracy, the participants in the as-

233

sembly recognised that the popular movement needs a level of unity that has thus far proved elusive. The break-away group that addressed this issue welcomed the fact that their session had included 'representatives and leaders from distinct political and social organisations from across the entire country', and noted that the construction of unity across these sectors 'is the best possible response that we could have in the current moment, in which the government is trying to silence the voices of organised social movements'.

In order for the authentic construction of such unity, it was argued that more horizontal relations between various social and political sectors need to be cultivated. The resistance to Correa requires 'closer engagement with the rank and file of the social organisations, because this unity cannot simply be designed from the leadership downward; rather, it must come from the struggle and organised action of organisations, collectives, from the basis of the grassroots that make up the fundamental force capable of transformation'.

After the assembly closed down, I caught up with Humberto Cholango to collect his impressions. 'Today we have determined to struggle for agrarian revolution, to defend working-class sectors, to fight against the criminalisation of social protest, and to defend the territories and land of the indigenous peoples and nationalities', he told me.[334]

Social Movement-State Relations in Context

The social movement gathering in August 2011 can only be understood against a complex backdrop of social movement-state relations over the last number of years. In April 2005, a mass explosion of resentment and agitation in the streets of the capital, against the corruption and betrayal embodied in the administration of then-President Gutiérrez, successfully forced that disgraced figure from power.

The protests were characterised politically by a largely urban middle-class sentiment – anti-party, anti-neoliberal, and anti-corruption, but lacking a coherent political project of its own.[335] Rather than signifying a deep rearticulation of popular sector power or organisational capacity – indeed, the indigenous movement was almost completely absent from the scene – the April 2005 revolt instead encapsulated a relatively spontaneous expression of disdain for the political elite and inchoate rage against the

334. Personal Interview, Quito, 9 August, 2011.
335. Ramírez Gallegos 2010, pp. 28-32.

ongoing imposition of neoliberal economic restructuring in the country.

This was the vacuum into which Correa's newly constructed 'political movement', *Alianza País* (Country Alliance, AP), positioned itself during the 2006 presidential campaign. His main right-wing contender, the multimillionaire banana magnate, Álvaro Noboa, received more votes than Correa in the first round, but was sufficiently hated by the popular sectors that a second-round rally for the AP circumvented his rise to the presidency.

The marketing team of AP pitched Correa as a heterodox outsider, an anti-neoliberal economist who – as a consequence of missionary work as a youngster – spoke Kichwa and was familiar with the needs and aspirations of the country's indigenous, peasant, and urban popular sectors.

The 2007-2008 Constituent Assembly process solidified the President's early popularity, as the country polarised around a hard-right camp represented by Noboa, and a progressive poll led by Correa. Within the Constituent Assembly, as a result of this wider societal divarication, a 'mega-bloc' of the Left emerged around Correa, which included Pachakutik, the MPD, and the Democratic Left (ID), although always under the hegemonic guidance of Correa and the AP.[336]

The Constitution of 2008

As noted, the new constitution that materialised from the assembly was popularly approved through a referendum, and the depth with which its commitments to social, political and economic change resonated with Ecuadorians was expressed in Correa's majority victory in the first round of presidential elections in 2009.

'The new constitution opened the door for a series of profound changes', argues Alberto Acosta, a former Minister of Energy and Mines in Correa's first administration and the President of the Constituent Assembly in 2007 and 2008. 'Its statutes guarantee the construction of a plurinational state. This means the incorporation for the first time of marginalised groups, like indigenous peoples and nationalities and Afro-Ecuadorians. The constitution mandates respect for their unique ways of life and community organizing, and a new way of structuring the state in general'.

Likewise, the new constitution includes probably the most progressive environmental commitments of any constitution in the world. The text ensures, for example, an allegiance 'to 'living well', or Sumak Kawsay,

336. Ibid., pp. 38-39.

in Quichua', Acosta explains, 'which is an entirely distinct way of under-standing development'. A part of this new understanding is reflected in the fact that the 'Constitution guarantees the rights of nature. Nature is a subject with rights in the Constitution. Ecuador's Constitution is the only one in the world with this characteristic'.[337]

The Shifting Political Winds of Rafael Correa

In keeping with the spirit of the Constitution, the 2009 electoral campaign featured Correa's promise of the 'radicalisation of the Citizen's Revolution'.[338] It quickly became apparent, however, that there would be a gaping chasm between the contents of the paper Constitution and the lived reality of the country under Correa's rule. Shortly after the 2009 elec-tions, Correa shifted decisively to the Right, presenting 'infantile Leftism, environmentalism and indigenism' as the preeminent threats to economic modernisation and progress, particularly as regards the President's plans to shift the extractive focus of the economy from oil to mining.[339]

Correa allowed the disintegration of the 'mega-bloc' of parlia-mentary Left forces that had held together loosely during the Constituent Assembly, as the MPD and Pachakutik abandoned the coalition in the face of the rightward drift of the AP. Key business federations that had been hostile to the first Correa administration notably altered their discourse and practical orientation toward the government in the post-2009 conjunc-ture, presumably as a reward for the government's newly invigorated com-mitment to neoliberal continuity.[340] Correa, now openly 'allied with tradi-tional, right-wing businessmen', the Uruguayan sociologist Raúl Zibechi points out, 'reserves his most poisonous darts for the Left'.[341]

'Correa entered the presidency in 2006 with the support of all the social movements – indigenous, environmentalists, human rights move-ments', according to Marlon Santi, former President of CONAIE.[342]

> 'But all of the social and political programs being introduced by this government have nothing to do with the program of his party,

337. Personal interview, Quito, 8 July, 2010.
338. Unda 2011, p. 138.
339. Ramírez Gallegos 2010, p. 41.
340. Unda 2011, p. 138.
341. Zibechi 2011.
342. Personal interview, Quito, 5 July, 2010.

Alianza País, or a Citizens' Revolution. The programs the government is introducing are based on other foundations, foundations that do not respect the collective ideas and demands of the grass-roots that supported him'.

Indigenous peoples in particular are completely excluded from the decision-making circles of the Correa government. 'There's an important popular saying around our independence', Santi explains, 'the last day of oppression, and the first day of the same'.

Expanding Fault Lines of Capitalist Modernisation.

By the end of 2009, the government was in open conflict with the indigenous movement. Mobilisations fought proposed water legislation that would have effectively privatised lakes and rivers in the interests of hydro-electrical development and the water needs of multinational mining corporations, at the expense of peasant and indigenous communities. Teachers unions and university professors, meanwhile, were locked in a confrontation with the government over a new law ostensibly about regulating higher education, but actually designed to weaken union power.

Throughout 2010, a series of conflicts continued to convulse the country. Indigenous movements agitated against mining projects, while public sector workers engaged in defensive battles to defend their most basic of labour rights. Indeed, according to sociologist Mario Unda, the essence of 2010 can be captured in the phrase, 'a project of capitalist modernisation confronting social movements'.[343]

A high point in the indigenous struggle that year took place on June 5. Ecuador was hosting a presidential summit of The Bolivarian Alliance for the Peoples of Our America (ALBA) in the majority-Quichua, Andean city of Otavalo. Despite the fact that the gathering was ostensibly called to discuss themes of indigenous and Afro-Latin American peoples within the ALBA countries, the principal indigenous organisation of Ecuador, CONAIE, was not on the guest list.

The indigenous movement consequently organised a march of three thousand people through the city, and symbolically installed a parallel Plurinational Parliament in the streets and plazas.[344] Police repressed the march and serious charges of terrorism and sabotage were laid against key

343. Unda 2011, p. 138.
344. Zibechi 2010.

237

indigenous leaders, including Marlon Santi of CONAIE. 'When the presidents of the countries involved in the ALBA were meeting here in Ecuador, in Otavolo, they talked about indigenous rights', Santi explained to me:

> · 'But the main representatives of the indigenous movement in the country, that is to say CONAIE, was never invited to the meeting. And we wanted to have a voice in ALBA. We wanted to say to the governments of ALBA that without the indigenous peoples of Latin America ALBA can't exist. We will not be excluded any longer. And for saying this in protests outside the ALBA meeting we have been given this new name of terrorists and saboteurs. We're supposedly against the nation. But we believe the truth will rise to the surface about these claims'.[345]

State Repression and Defamation

'I believe that these types of accusations are tremendously shameful for the country', said Acosta, now a leading Left-critic of Correa, referring to the regime's rhetorical demonisation and juridical persecution of indigenous activists. He continued:

> 'They have no basis in justice or a democratic judicial system. Even during the period of neoliberal governments, when social movements and the indigenous movement were massively involved in protests, there were never accusations of terrorism. This is an issue that is putting the Citizen's Revolution itself at risk. It would appear that there are forces that are configuring themselves in a type of counter-revolution without citizenship'.

At the time of writing, approximately 200 activists are facing charges of terrorism and sabotage with the possibility of lengthy prison terms.[346] For Luis Macas, the motivation for targeting the indigenous movement with such repression is clear enough. 'It's not that the government wants simply to get rid of the Indians, or that it is racism for racism's sake. The objective is to liquidate the indigenous movement in this country, to dismantle and destroy this movement'. The rationale grows out of the fact that 'the indigenous movement is the principal social and political actor in the country

345. Personal interview, Quito, 5 July, 2010.
346. Ospina Peralta 2011.

that has struggled against the economic model, against neoliberalism'. From Macas' perspective, 'Correa wants to have a green light to do as he pleases. And his project of development is rooted in the exploitation of natural resources. We in the indigenous movement have an emphatically different conceptualisation of Mother Nature and are saying no'.

The conflicts over mining are likely to intensify further in coming months and years. Closed-door negotiations with multinational corporations seeking to secure large-scale mining projects were due to be completed in July of this year, but have not yet come to fruition. While the details remain secret, it is estimated that $US 3.5 billion in foreign direct investment will flood the mining sector from 2012 forward.[347] If past patterns are repeated, Canadian imperial mining capital is likely to play a defining role.[348]

'For us, it's very clear', Tenesaca said, 'all of a sudden, a bureaucrat or technocrat appears from the government and tells' indigenous communities, "let us enter these territories because we have to exploit this mine'. When you resist, you are sanctioned, receive death threats and all the rest. This has happened throughout the country. Anyone who opposes this, anyone who resists, is considered a terrorist'.[349] President Correa is 'clashing with indigenous communities', the *Financial Times* reports. 'Once he claimed to champion their rights. Now his government accuses them of terrorism and sabotage'.[350]

Images and Realities of Political Economy

The extreme Right in Ecuador have objected to Correa's increases in public spending, anti-poverty cash transfer programs, the introduction of modest banking regulations, targeted tariffs on specific import items, and geopolitical ties with Brazil, Venezuela, Argentina, Cuba, and Bolivia, at the expense of closer diplomatic relations with the United States.[351]

Coupled with the President's propensity to employ radical sophistry at every turn, and his studied cultivation of a progressive political

347. EIU 2011, p. 13.
348. Gordon 2010, pp. 216-219.
349. Personal interview, Quito, 10 August, 2011.
350. Rathbone 2011.
351. Most dramatically, Correa expelled the US ambassador over the contents of released Wikileaks in April, 2011. The Correa administration has also secured multiple-billion dollar loans from China in recent months as part of an apparent attempt to adapt older geopolitical relations to an increasingly multipolar world. At the same time, the US remains Ecuador's leading trading partner, and an important source of remittances.

identity abroad, the Ecuadorian government is often misperceived as having broken much more thoroughly with the neoliberal model that it inherited than is actually the case. Indeed, the rhetoric of revolutionary change figures so prominently in Correa's discourse precisely because he relies on this mythology to mask some bitter truths.

Early this century, Ecuador enjoyed fairly strong economic growth, as a product of a regional boom for most of South America's commodity exporters. For Ecuador, what mattered most was the high price of oil, its biggest export commodity. Gross domestic product (GDP) grew at roughly three percent in 2002 and 2003, spiked to almost nine percent in 2004, and tapered to six, five, and two percent in 2005, 2006 and 2007 respectively. In 2008 GDP climbed again to seven percent, before plunging to almost 0 percent in 2009 with the onset of the global crisis.[352] Preliminary figures show an almost four percent rate of growth in 2010, with an outlook of roughly three percent for 2011.[353]

Social democratic analysts sympathetic to the Correa regime often stress how this respectable rate of economic growth has allowed for expansionary public spending under Correa. Increases in health and education spending, as well as the priming of pre-existing, targeted cash-transfer programs toward the poorest sectors of society are often flagged in such commentary, as are reductions in poverty rate under Correa's command.[354]

Looked at comparatively, however, the figures for Ecuador do not seem to be the stuff even of post-neoliberalism, nevermind twenty-first century socialism. In the realm of social spending as a proportion of total public spending, for example, Ecuador is situated in the bottom echelons of regional Latin American trends.

On average, social spending in the region rose from 12.2 percent of GDP in 1990-1991 to 18 percent in 2007-2008, whereas Ecuador's fell from 7.4 to 6.4 percent over the same period. A casual perusal of Table I indicates that Ecuador has a much poorer record in this regard than, say, Argentina or Chile, at best Centre-Left regimes during most of the 2000s.[355] Ecuador compares poorly even to Colombia under Álvaro Uribe, or Mexico under Felipe Calderón, whereas Correa's claims to be moving

352. The contraction in GDP in 2006 and 2007 is partially related to the declining rate of production of private oil companies in the country over these years. See Weisbrot and Sandoval 2009, pp. 5-6.
353. ECLAC 2011, p. 67.
354. See for example, Weisbrot and Sandoval 2009.
355. McNally 2011, pp. 8-9.

toward socialism of any type are simply laughable when social spending figures in Ecuador are juxtaposed with the record of the region's leaders in this area, Uruguay and Cuba.

Table I: Public Social Spending as a Percentage of GDP

Country	1990-91	1997-98	2000-01	2007-08
Ecuador	7.4	5.1	4.9	6.4
Argentina	11.3	10.6	11.0	11.8
Chile	12.0	13.2	15.1	13.2
Colombia	5.9	12.8	11.1	12.6
Mexico	6.5	8.8	9.7	12.1
Uruguay	16.8	20.5	21.6	21.8
Cuba	27.6	21.6	23.7	37.4

Source: Derived from ECLAC (2011) *Social Panorama of Latin America 2010*. Santiago, Chile: United Nations Economic Commission for Latin America and the Caribbean, p. 240.

Similarly, the record on poverty reduction is underwhelming for a self-proclaimed socialist government. As Table II indicates, while urban poverty fell from 49 to 40.2 percent in Ecuador between 2002 and 2009, it is less impressive when one considers superior outcomes in Kirchner's Argentina, Lula's Brazil, García's Peru, or Calderón's Mexico.[356]

Table II: Percentage of Population below the Poverty Line in Urban Areas

Country	2002	2008*	2009
Ecuador	49.0	39.0	40.2
Argentina	45.4	21.0	11.3
Brazil	34.4	22.8	22.1
Peru**	42.0	23.5	21.1
Mexico	38.9	32.2	29.2

Source: Derived from ECLAC (2011) *Social Panorama of Latin America 2010*. Santiago, Chile: United Nations Economic Commission for Latin America and the Caribbean, pp. 224-25.
* The Argentine figure for this column comes from 2006.
** Figures from the Institute of Statistics and Informatics (INEI) of Peru.

356. I chose to look at urban poverty rates because no comparable figures on total national poverty rates are available for Ecuador for the relevant years in this dataset, apart from 2008 and 2009 when national poverty rates were 42.7 and 42.2 percent and rural poverty rates 50.2 and 46.3 percent respectively.

As the global economic slump dips more deeply, repeatedly defying sunny recovery forecasts, international financial institutions and economic pundits have been forced to revise downward their outlooks for world growth for 2011 and 2012. As far as Ecuador is concerned, this could mean a drop in oil revenues as international prices fall, and a further decline in remittances sent home from Ecuadorians living abroad, particularly in Spain and the US, where the economies are suffocating under the grip of austerity measures.

One of the most incisive analysts of the crisis on a world-scale explains what he means by the term 'global slump', and the reasons why we should not expect it to go away quickly: 'Rather than describing a single crisis, the term is meant to capture a whole period of interconnected crises – the bursting of a real estate bubble; a wave of bank collapses; a series of sovereign debt crises; relapse into recession – that goes on for years without a sustained economic recovery. That, I submit, is what confronts us for many, many years to come'.[357]

Revolutionary Visions of Resistance

In light of these realities, the contradictions of Correa's development model are likely to accentuate, conflicts to assume a more acute form, and state repression and ideological defamation of popular movements to become consequently more extreme. This will be combined, no doubt, with parallel tactics aimed at social-movement cooptation, including an extension of clientelist and targeted petty handouts in the lead up to the 2013 elections.

The indigenous movement is preparing for such eventualities. Severino Sharupi, an activist in the Shuar indigenous nation, and youth coordinator for CONAIE, advised me that CONAIE has identified three strategic priorities – first, to rebuild and reinforce the rank and file capacities of CONAIE itself; second, to reorganise and strengthen ties between all of CONAIE's wider array of allies within the indigenous movement; and, third, to build new organisational structures of resistance at the national level between all sectors of the popular movement.

From CONAIE we can offer support to the broader movement, drawing from our experiences', he said,

357. McNally 2011, pp. 8-9.

'We want to move beyond thinking merely of this government, because governments are transitory. They are merely pieces in the game that capitalism uses for its own ends. Our job is longer term, a process of political and ideological formation of the popular sectors – of the indigenous sector, of all popular sectors'.[358]

Delfín Tenesaca, of ECUARUNARI, echoed Sharupi's sentiments, particularly the understanding that change will not come from the benevolence of leaders on high, but rather through the self-organisation and self-activity of popular classes struggling from below:

'We are going to fight back, and fight back with a clear position, not one tied exclusively to 2013, when the next elections will occur. The government will be running for re-election, and there will appear a new leadership layer, the new saviours of the world, saviours of the country, saviours of the poor, and all the rest. Confronted with this scenario, our objective will be to save ourselves, beginning now with a fight against extractivism, neoliberalism, clientelism, and a legal system that is attacking our leaderships in an effort to shut us up. We will defend ourselves in the face of this'.

REFERENCES

ECLAC 2011, *Economic Survey of Latin America and the Caribbean 2010-2011*, Santiago, Chile: United Nations Economic Commission for Latin America and the Caribbean, (March).

EIU 2011, *Ecuador: Country Report*, London: Economist Intelligence Unit (September).

Gordon, Todd 2010, *Imperialist Canada*, Winnipeg: Arbeiter Ring Publishers.

McNally, David 2011, *Global Slump: The Economics and Politics of Crisis and Resistance*, Oakland: PM Press.

Ospina Peralta, Pablo 2011, 'La unidad de las izquierdas', *La Linea del Fuego*, 8 September.

Ramírez Gallegos, Franklin 2010, 'Fragmentación, reflujo y desconcierto: Movimientos sociales y cambio político en el Ecuador (2000-2010)', *OSAL*, 28 (November): 17-47.

358. Personal interview, Quito, 10 August, 2011.

Rathbone, John Paul 2011, 'Bolivia and Ecuador Feel Political Heat', *Financial Times*, 6 September.

Unda, Mario 2011, 'Ecuador 2010: El año 4 de la Revolución Ciudadana', *OSAL*, 29 (May): 137-149.

Weisbrot, Mark and Luis Sandoval (2009), *Update on the Ecuadorian Economy*, Washington, D.C.: Center for Economic and Policy Research.

Zibechi, Raúl 2011, 'Ecuador: The Construction of a New Model of Domination', *Upside Down World*, 5 August.

Zibechi, Raúl 2010, 'Bolivia and Ecuador: The State against the Indigenous People', *Americas Program*, 19 July.

HISTORICISING
HISTORICAL MATERIALISM

RECONSIDERING
BOURGEOIS REVOLUTION

Bertel Nygaard

The French Revolution of 1789-99, the English Revolution of the 1640s, the European revolutions of 1848-49 and similar historical developments used to be categorized as *bourgeois* revolutions, that is, as the results of modern, capitalist social forces opposing absolutist monarchy and remnants of feudal or aristocratic social orders. But from the 1960s on, however, so-called 'revisionist' interpretations gained dominance in scholarly studies, heavily criticizing such social interpretations of revolutions in general, and the quite strongly positioned tradition of Marxist interpretations in particular.[359] This 'revisionism' comprised a broad variety of approaches, from traditional empiricist analyses of high politics to discourse analysis. Its relative unity was constituted by a common stand against Marxism. By the bicentenary of the French Revolution in 1989, accompanied by the disintegration of the bureaucratic regimes of Eastern Europe, it was obvious that the result was a marginalization of Marxist perspectives on class struggle and the transition to capitalism in such revolutions.

Within historiography at large, this process was part of a general turn away from a broad tradition of social history, in which Marxism held a prominent position, in favour of both more narrowly confined political or cultural history and post-modernist notions of discourse largely independent of social determination. At a very general level, the success of such outlooks may be interpreted as a reflection of the decline in the general credibility of a victorious socialist revolution, that is, of a radically different and better future beyond the capitalist present. The re-opening of history towards a radically different and better future requires a restatement of our understanding of the past, not only because our present social condi

---

359. The amount of literature in this field is overwhelming. Recent important writings considering this field in relation to contemporary Marxism include Haynes and Wolfreys 2007; Heller 2006; Davidson 2012; Nygaard 2007a. Other titles of interest to such discussions will follow in the references below. Much of the following historiographical synthesis is studied in more detail in my PhD dissertation (in Danish), Nygaard 2007c.

tions are a *product* of history, but also because the *understanding* of present and future from which we act is inevitably linked to an understanding of the past. This makes the critical reconsideration of important historical developments an urgent task beyond the narrow spheres of specialists and beyond any reverence for traditional dogma.

The question of how to interpret the question of 'bourgeois revolution' is particularly crucial in this regard. In what may be termed its most 'classic' versions, the category 'bourgeois revolution' implies a capitalist bourgeoisie conquering the old feudal state from the aristocracy and reconstructing it for new capitalist purposes. In other words, it offers a specific combined understanding of such crucial questions as the historical transition to capitalism and the roles of class struggle, states and social revolutions in such transition and thus also a model of past revolutionary change on which prospects of future revolutionary change may be, and have been, constructed. By comparison, revisionism has contributed to the widespread naturalization and eternalization of the capitalist present, that is, a decline in the sense of the historically delimited character of the capitalism mode of production, as well as the weakening of confidence in the power of collective social agents in reshaping state and society along progressive lines, whether in the past or in the future.

Such considerations do not call for a mere defence of traditional understandings of Marxism and the category of 'bourgeois revolution' against 'revisionism'. Rather, they may explain the scholarly as well as political need to re-open the debate on bourgeois revolution. This article purports to do so by first pointing out significant tensions in traditional uses of the category 'bourgeois revolution' through an outline of main points in its conceptual development, then suggesting a revised model for reconstructing the important issues involved in 'bourgeois revolution' while attempting to avoid the difficulties of earlier uses. The main focus will be the French Revolution and its historiography, but I will also consider the historiography of other countries as well as more general studies.

Revisionism

The first generation of French Revolution revisionists, led by British and American scholars, challenged the interpretation of the Revolution as a vehicle for capitalist development by pointing to empirical difficulties. Thus, in the early 1960's British historian Alfred Cobban denied the existence of any clear economic demarcation between nobility and bourgeoisie in pre-revolutionary France: both groups were in fact attempting to introduce modern business methods into agriculture. The revolutionary movements of the peasants should be seen accordingly as an anti-capitalist reaction against these bourgeois-noble endeavours, not as part and parcel of a 'bourgeois' revolution against the nobility.[360] In addition, the 'bourgeois' spokesmen of the revolution were not an advancing industrial or commercial bourgeoisie, but generally a class of declining *officiers*, lawyers etc.[361] North American historian George Taylor sharpened the latter point by insisting that the categories 'noble' and 'bourgeois' were purely juridical and designated to clear distinction in forms of property.[362] Also, revisionists pointed to the disastrous consequences of the Revolution for immediate capitalist growth in France.[363] Thus, a capitalist bourgeoisie could neither be located among the immediate causes of the Revolution, nor in its results. In the late 1960's, French historians Denis Richet and François Furet suggested instead that the French Revolution was really a struggle about political privileges among fractions of the cultural and political elite, not a clash of great class interests.[364]

A decade later, François Furet's *Penser la révolution française* added more theoretically innovative elements to these initial currents of revisionism by initiating a tradition of discourse analysis of the Revolution. His approach was founded in a severe polemic against the Marxist interpretation, especially that of Albert Soboul, then professor of the history of the French Revolution at Sorbonne. According to Furet, Soboul's interpretation was an eclectic mixture of Jacobinism and dogmatic Marxism, framing the Revolution more or less as a social and political precursor of the October Revolution of 1917. In Furet's view, the political development of the Revolution was determined by discursive dynamics rather than social forces. The Terror of 1793-94 should thus not be explained as the product of external circumstances such as war or in terms of class struggle. Instead, it was the result of the democratic discourse of sovereignty of the 'people' inaugurated in 1789.[365] This interpretation allowed Furet to point out similarities between the French and Russian Revolutions attuned to the theories of totalitarianism fashionable among the 'new philosophers' in France

360. Cobban 1964, pp. 52-3, 168.
361. Cobban 1964, p. 67.
362. Taylor 1967, pp. 487, 489.
363. Compare, for example, Doyle 1978, p. 365.
364. Richet 1969, p. 14; Furet and Richet 1973, p. 101.
365. Furet 1989, p. 287.

during the late 1970s: Both 1789 and 1917, he claimed, had inaugurated totalitarian terror through language. Fortunately, however, this discourse of pure democracy, counterpoising society and the state, was now ended in France: The liberal concern for individual rights and the conservative concern for a strong, patriarchal political state securing social cohesion had now been united, he claimed, thus closing century-long rifts in French society.[366] In other words, by finally 'ending' the French Revolution, Furet was also attempting to end world history in the sense that would make Fukuyama famous a bit more than a decade later, that is, by rejecting any progressive development beyond capitalist democracy.[367]

Marxist traditions

The strong direct political implications of revisionism made it natural for many Marxist historians like Soboul to simply reject such criticism as expressions of cold-warrior mentality. In some senses, this could certainly be justified. Yet, revisionist scholarship also pointed to both empirical and theoretical shortcomings in a way that could certainly not be reduced to mere right-wing propaganda. Even though Soboul's detailed analyses of classes were rather complex, he did tend to conceive the overall character of the French Revolution in somewhat schematic and teleological terms as 'the arrival of modern bourgeois capitalist society in the history of France'.[368] He insisted that the 'bourgeoisie constituted the most important class within the Third Estate: it directed the course of the Revolution and benefited from it'.[369]

This overall view of the Revolution also provided an important part of the general framework of his great achievement as a historian: His studies of the *sans-culottes* (the lower urban classes), their mentality and their key role in the democratic and social radicalization of the Revolution. From the subjective point of view, he claimed, the sans-culottes were both anti-feudal and anti-capitalist. But contrary to their intentions, they 'contributed to the progress of history by lending decisive help to the bourgeois revolution'.[370] They furnished the revolutionary bourgeoisie with forces sufficient to combat the remnants of feudalism in the French social formation, but their own aspirations were incompatible with the ob-

366. Furet 1989.
367. See Nygaard 2007b; Rancière 1992, pp. 3, 5-37; Kouvelakis 2003, pp. 338-40.
368. Soboul 1975, p. 3.
369. Soboul 1975, p. 44.
370. Soboul 1972, p. 376.

jective need for bourgeois, or capitalist, society. In other words, the political and social developments of the French Revolution were basically determined by the historically inevitable result of a succession of social stages as seen within the history of a single country. While social classes were able to radicalize this development through intensified class struggle, they were unable to challenge the succession from feudalism to capitalism.

For all the remarkable complexity of Soboul's analysis, which cannot be fully presented here, this did reveal a certain reification of historical evolution: It did not specify the circumstances determining the pro-capitalist consequences of the actions of the anti-capitalist lower classes, beyond referring to the necessary rise of the bourgeoisie and industrial capitalism or, even more abstractly, to 'history itself'.[371]

Soboul's interpretation of the French Revolution was no isolated instance. The main features of this interpretation were so widely accepted that the bourgeois-democratic French Revolution was considered a normative standard against which the peculiarities of other countries could be judged. This became particularly clear in the reconsiderations of German history in light of the Nazi victory in 1933. Among some Marxists, as well as many other commentators, German history was reinterpreted as the result of a *lack* of a proper bourgeois-democratic revolution of the French type. According to such analyses, this lack of a proper bourgeois revolution had caused remnants of Prussian aristocratic forms of rule to survive and pave the way for Nazism. In 1945, Alexander Abusch, a leading German Communist in exile, later to attain important political positions in the GDR, wrote the history of modern Germany as a giant detour, 'the history of a people forced into political backwardness'.[372] During the 1960's and 1970's, a host of Western academic scholars inspired by modernization theories, some also by Marxian and Weberian elements, proceeded to more sophisticated social explanations of the lack of strong democratic traditions in Germany as the result of the lack of a bourgeois revolution.[373] Often such historians of Germany assumed that the Germans provided the only notable exception to the rule of a proper bourgeois revolution in each single country. However, with the increasing number of national peculiarities noted as the consequences of lacking bourgeois revolution, this seemed rather less so. An oft-quoted Marxist example was Perry Anderson's ac-

371. Soboul 1958, p. 1031.
372. Abusch 1946, p. 257.
373. Wehler 1975; Dahrendorf 1966; Hamerow 1972.

count from the 1960's that the continuity of aristocratic, reactionary influence in Britain and the remarkably non-revolutionary nature of the British Labour movement should basically be explained by the fact that England had experienced 'the first, most mediated and least pure bourgeois revolution of any major European country'.[374]

As critics pointed out, such notions of 'lacking bourgeois revolution' in one country after another were based on inherently problematic assumptions of an immediate homology and contemporaneity within the bourgeois revolution of mode of production (capitalism), social class (bourgeoisie), political ideology (liberalism), progressive historical function (democracy).[375] Historical development was never so straightforward. As both Soboul and, as we shall see, numerous other Marxists had been perfectly aware, democratic rights did not emerge directly result of the struggle of bourgeoisie against the feudal aristocracy. Rather, it was a concession won through the struggles of the lower classes against bourgeois and aristocratic aspirations to a monopoly of social and political power. Also, bourgeois liberalism was never inherently democratic, but only legitimized itself in democratic terms when allied with radical movements or when democratic rights had become a generalized conquest through most of the Western world.

Thus, assumptions about the role of bourgeois revolution in 'normal' historical development were certainly nothing peculiarly Marxist. Nor was there anything inherently 'un-Marxist' in criticizing such assumptions. On the contrary, they could, and should, be criticized from within Marxist traditions. Yet, assumptions about 'history itself' and of 'normal' development did reflect a strong tendency within the dominant versions of Marxism, regarding bourgeois revolution as a historically necessary social and political expression of the transition to capitalism within the development of each single country. The underlying assumption of a fixed succession of social stages proceeding by necessity within each social formation – that is, the theoretical tradition of 'stagism' – became a central part of the construction from the 1880s onwards of Marxism as a systematic, universal outlook capable of rivalling bourgeois science.[376] Likewise, among Marxists in the early 1900s it was a central element in the Menshevik view that Russia would have to proceed through a long capitalist development, rather than hurrying towards proletarian revolution, but also in

374. Anderson 1964, p. 17.
375. Blackbourn and Eley 1984.
376. See Löwy 1981; Anderson 1976a, p. 6; Nygaard 2009.

Lenin's view around 1905 that the proletarian element within the Russian revolution would radicalize its democratic and anti-feudal orientation without, however, questioning the basic bourgeois-democratic character of the revolution.[377] In the Communist International of the 1930s, the latter view was invoked to defend the Marxist orthodoxy of the popular frontist turn towards national history, announced by George Dimitrov as a means of defending the 'revolutionary traditions of the peoples', including the establishment of bourgeois democracy, against the attempts by fascists to monopolize such historiography.[378] This popular front outlook was also crucial in the formation of an entire generation of important Marxist academic historians, including not only Soboul, but also E.J. Hobsbawm, E.P. Thompson, Christopher Hill and others.[379]

Alternative Marxist traditions

Yet, there were other elements of analysis and other interpretations within Marxism, excluded or marginalised by such dominant developments. In his most extensive attempt to grapple with the history of the French Revolution, Marx's notebooks of 1843-44, the French Revolution was conceived not primarily in socio-economic class terms but as the foremost example of *political* emancipation, that is, the separation of the social sphere from the political sphere. This implied the emergence of what Marx termed 'the state as such', that is, the pure state, recognizing each social individual as a citizen (*citoyen*), a public social being. The other side to the same process was the emergence of the privatized social, or economic, sphere of human lives, the sphere of *bourgeois* existence.[380] While acknowledging this as the most basic result of the French Revolution, Marx also criticized the formal-abstract character of this duality of state and society: Far from actually representing universality, the state and its personnel reflected the internal contradictions of bourgeois (or civil) society and thus represent a range of particular interests. Because of its separation from the real socio-historical conditions of existence of human being, the modern state, by claiming to represent true universality, in fact provided itself with an ideological legitimization of the existing social order.[381]

377. See, for example, Lenin 1905, pp. 48-52.
378. *Protokoll* 1974, p. 369.
379. Kaye 1984; Dworkin 1997; Mazauric 2004.
380. Marx 1843a, p. 233; Marx 1843b, p. 361.
381. Marx 1843s, pp. 233 and passim

While this was, of course, only the broadest outlines of an historical analysis of the French Revolution, it was based on the insistence that analysis should begin from the concrete and historically specific character of the object, not transhistorical schematism.[382] This point was basic to both Marx and Engels and may help explain the paucity of schematic formula in their writings, not to mention the deep ambiguity of the few texts that might seem to contain such formula: *The German Ideology*, the 1859 *Preface* and the 1848 *Manifesto*.

A similar point also holds when considering the discussions of the problem of bourgeois revolution as contemporary strategy, rather than just history, in the writings of Marx and Engels. They did point to 'bourgeois revolution' as the aim for Germany in 1848, but this was far from any 'pure' bourgeois revolution.[383] Rather, it was closely intertwined with the strategy of proletarian revolution and tended to be conceived at an international level, not confined to the development the individual state or social formation. And when their contemporary Russian followers during the 1870's and 1880's attempted to universalise 'bourgeois revolution' as a strategic recipe applicable to every single national development, they replied to the effect that the different concrete circumstances in which Russian society faced modern industrial capitalism would lead to a radically different historical development than the one seen previously in the West. Thus, instead of a purely 'bourgeois' stage Marx and Engels advocated a strategy of international anti-capitalist alliance between the industrialized working classes of Western Europe and the Russian peasant communities.[384]

This international frame of reference was developed further during the early 1900-debates on the Russian Revolution, notably in Trotsky's conceptions of uneven and combined development and the strategy of permanent revolution.[385] Against stagist conceptions of the inevitably bourgeois character of the revolution in Russia, Trotsky repeatedly emphasized that because the high level of industrial development on a global scale would necessarily have repercussions in Russia, even the backward country would not have to proceed through a pure stage of bourgeois revolution, before

382. Cf. Nygaard 2007a.
383. Cf. Draper 1977; Draper 1978.
384. Engels 1875, p. 565; Marx and Engels 1882, p. 297; Marx 1877, pp. 111f; Marx 1881, pp. 384-406.
385. I have studied such debates within a somewhat different conceptual framework in Nygaard 2013.

constructing a socialist order, as long as the revolutionary movement of the backward country proceeded in conjunction with Western developments.

This perspective prompted Trotsky as early as 1906 to stress more immediate features of the specific social formations susceptible to strategically oriented analysis: 'Between the productive forces of a country and the political strength of its classes there cut across at any given moment various social and political factors of a national and international character, and these displace and even sometimes completely alter the political expression of economic relations.'[386] Consequently, it could not be taken for granted that an essentially bourgeois revolution must occur in every country.[387]

Furthermore, this different strategic analysis was closely intertwined with different analyses of the past. Unlike Lenin's interpretation, Trotsky's analysis of Russian capitalism did not stress processes of 'primitive accumulation' in the agrarian sector similar to Marx's account of English precedents. Instead, he focused on the development of manufacturing and industrial sectors since Peter the Great as a result of international relations, specifically the competition between the Russian state and Western states based upon capitalist systems: 'It was not the village craftsman, nor even the rich merchant, but the state itself which finally came face to face with the necessity of creating a large-scale industry.'[388]

At the same time, though, he urged some reconsideration of the transformative role of the lower classes even in previous revolutions: 'Within the framework of the bourgeois revolution at the end of the eighteenth century, the objective task of which was to establish the domination of capital, the dictatorship of the *sansculottes* was found to be possible.'[389]

Thus, in stressing the *possibilities* of a *sans-culotte*-victory – if only a temporary one – even in the unfavourable situation of 18th century France, he differed significantly from the typical Marxist focus on negatively defined, 'objective' demarcations and limits of such victories. In these senses, the analytical suggestions in the writings of Trotsky represented a road followed briefly during the Russian revolution itself, but generally not taken by later historians of 'bourgeois revolutions'.[390]

386. Trotsky 1906, p. 65.
387. Trotsky 1906, p. 67, compare p. 119.
388. Trotsky 1907-9, p. 30.
389. Trotsky 1906, p. 67.
390. Two partial, but notable, exceptions to this are Guérin 1946; James 1980.

Marxist challenges and responses

Partly as a reflection of such continual tensions within Marxism, partly as part of critical reflections arising from the revisionism controversies, some Marxists began challenging the concept 'bourgeois revolution'. In broad terms, we may outline three main types of criticism, pointing to different alternatives.

The first type of criticism derived from the mid-1960's debate on the 'peculiarities of the English' between Perry Anderson and E.P. Thompson as well as the challenges put to the notions of a German *Sonderweg* by British Marxists Geoff Eley and David Blackbourn in the early 1980's.[391] Discussing Anderson's view of the peculiarities of the English as a result of the English Revolution being 'the first, most mediated and least pure bourgeois revolution of any major European country', E.P. Thompson objected 'to a model which concentrates attention upon one dramatic episode – *the* Revolution – to which all that goes before and after must be related; and which insists upon an ideal type of this Revolution against which all others may be judged.'[392]

In thus questioning normative models of the revolution as part of the 'correct' historical trajectory of individual social formations, these debates also contributed to a clarification of the relationship between the revolution as an event and long-term developmental tendencies. While Anderson's ideal type revolution was clearly a rapid rupture with the past, Thompson stressed the long-term implications by viewing the Rose Wars, the Tudors, the Wars of Religion during the 16th and 17th centuries and the impending revolution in 1832 altogether as 'pieces of that great arch which in fact, in the epochal sense, make up the bourgeois revolution'.[393] Somewhat similar views had been stated previously by Victor Kiernan and Jürgen Kuscynski and have later been echoed in the historiography of Germany by scholars in the GDR as well as Eley and Blackbourn.[394]

Thus, all of these analyses shifted the focus of interest from *the* bourgeois revolution in each country towards a view of the great political transitions accompanying the transition to capitalism as more gradual processes shaped by punctual ruptures. But such analyses tended to remain within the framework of one single country or, at most proceeded to a

---

391. Anderson 1964; Thompson 1980; Blackbourn and Eley 1984.
392. Anderson 1964, p. 17; Thompson 1980, p. 47.
393. Thompson 1980, p. 47, compare pp. 86, 78.
394. See Dworkin 1997, pp. 34ff; Bleiber 1977.

comparison between the trajectories of two or three individual countries.

The second type of criticism was based on Robert Brenner's analysis of the distinct historical origins of capitalism in specific early-modern class relations in English agriculture, against traditional assumptions about the century-long emergence of capitalism among the bourgeoisie (which, in this case, is meant literally as: city-dweller).[395] In 1989, Brenner himself explicitly rejected the historical necessity of bourgeois revolution for capitalism. Not only was the orthodox model of bourgeois revolution as necessary in the emergence of capitalism historically untrue, since capitalism had originated in agricultural production, not in urban trade, the assumptions about historical necessity in this model were also logically inconsistent, since it presented urban capitalist development as both cause and effect of the bourgeois revolution. Finally, this model was theoretically suspect, reducing political and social struggle to mere epiphenomena expressing an underlying economic content regarded as universally valid throughout history, thus ignoring the specificity of the capitalist separation of the economic and the political.[396] To replace the category 'bourgeois revolution' Brenner's supporters called for studies of 'the developing structural relationships between class and state in each social context'.[397] Thus, George Comninel argued in 1987 that the French Revolution was a political event, an 'intra-class struggle' within an essentially pre-capitalist continuum in which questions of political privilege had been closely tied to questions of surplus extraction.[398] Summing up this interpretation, Benno Teschke has stated that 'while the English Revolution was not bourgeois, it was capitalist, and while the French Revolution was bourgeois, it was not capitalist'.[399]

The insistence on a precise sense of capitalism as well as on the historical specificity of capitalism and its particular laws of development in the Brenner school is certainly valuable. Nonetheless, this school has tended to ignore questions of totality in several important fields. Thus, while formally recognizing the influence of state building inter-state relations, trade and competition as *preconditions* of the transition to capitalism, it has tended to regard such preconditions as mechanically separate from the true *causes* of capitalism. This has been done in order to present capitalism as formed

---

395. Aston 1985.
396. Brenner 1989, pp. 280, 285.
397. Comninel 1987, p. 205.
398. Comninel 1987, p. 200.
399. Teschke 2005, p. 12.

exclusively by specific class relations in one country, England, as opposed to all other countries (the prime example of which is, tellingly, most often France). The result of this has not only been what one of critic of this school, Perry Anderson, termed a conception of 'capitalism in one country', but a predetermined separation of national trajectories even more pertinent than in Soboul's case.[400] As a consequence of this, the Brenner school has tended to regard the English point of interception of capitalism as something completely separate from its dissemination to the rest of the world, making its analyses a lot less relevant to studies of transitions to capitalism in all other countries than England. Yet, while such inclinations towards mechanical separation are objectionable, especially when repeated as dogmatically as some adherents of the school do, their basic insistence on precise and historically concrete categories of investigation is certainly important.

Conversely, a third type of criticism proceeded precisely from notions of totality and functional interrelation. One of the prime examples is Immanuel Wallerstein's analyses of the modern capitalist world system existing since around 1500 as a functional, international totality based mainly on trade relations. On this basis, Wallerstein interpreted the two most 'classic' bourgeois revolutions, the English Civil War and the French Revolution not as social class conflicts, but as political struggles within the elite.[401] Thus, for Wallerstein as well as for Comninel, the Revolution was primarily a political event, but Wallerstein saw this within an essentially capitalist, not feudal, continuum. Furthermore, while the English Civil War had contributed to a strengthening of the state, the main function of the French Revolution within the world system had been the 'normality of change', the assertion of the 'people' as conceptual orientation points for modern politics and the beginning of 'anti-systemic movements', in other words: cultural, discursive and anti-capitalist social movements rather than any social struggle for capitalism.

While providing important elements for reinterpreting the meaning of the French Revolution in particular, this alternative to bourgeois revolution tended to rule out any dialectic of agency and social dynamism within the development of the totality. This left history in the rather un

400. Anderson 1993, p. 17.
401. Wallerstein 1974, pp. 282, 209f; Wallerstein 1980, p. 33; Wallerstein 1989, p. p. 100. The first volume did, however, employ the term a few times to characterize the Dutch Revolt and the French Revolution: Wallerstein 1974, pp. 208, 296.

convincing position of having been created not by the social interactions of human beings, but by the apparently self-sufficient rise and decline of the world system. Despite the nuance of analysis, Wallerstein's basic framework tended to reify historical development to a degree that most Marxists, including Soboul, would reject immediately.

In view of the difficulties haunting the traditional Marxist accounts as well as the advantages and drawbacks of the three main alternatives just outlined, some Marxists insisted on the validity of a redeployed category of 'bourgeois revolution', mainly in order to stress a differentiated unity of class struggle, political development of the transition to capitalism. Around 1990, Alex Callinicos, Colin Mooers and others argued that revolutions should be judged as bourgeois from their pro-capitalist results, not the social character of their agents.[402] In retrospect, this has been termed the 'consequentialist' version of the bourgeois revolution thesis. Mooers provided the most expanded defence of the category 'bourgeois revolution', tracing the long-term development of bourgeois states in, respectively, France, Germany and England, and the role of revolutions in such developments. His interpretation distinguished between patterns shaped by revolutions from below and patterns shaped by revolutions from above, relating each of them to different phases in the development of the world market. Thus, this restatement of 'bourgeois revolution' integrated several of the Marxist criticism of the category, while showing its usefulness as a total interpretative framework attempting to overcome the limitations of traditional Marxism and the Brenner School as well as the functionalism of Wallerstein.

A different recent use of 'bourgeois revolution' as interpretative category was developed simultaneously by the German historian Heide Gerstenberger. Criticizing assumptions of the universal validity of social categories found in traditional Marxism, non-Marxist modernization theory and Wallerstein's approach, she defined 'bourgeois revolution' as 'the structural transformations which revolutionised societies of the *Ancien Régime* into bourgeois societies, leaving it to concrete analysis to spell out how much of this revolutionary change occurred at any date'. According to her, 'bourgeois revolution' should simply mean the genesis of the modern duality of purely political state and bourgeois society.[403] Thus, Gerstenberger

---

402. Callinicos 1989, pp. 124-7; Mooers 1991, p. 176; Katz 1989, pp. 152-162.
403. Gerstenberger 1992, p. 195. Compare Gerstenberger 1990, p. 11. Gerstenbergers main study has been published in English as Gerstenberger 2007.

restated 'bourgeois revolution' in the sense of bourgeois transition.

Finally, Perry Anderson sketched a theoretical reconstruction of the concept of bourgeois revolution in a short essay written in 1976, but unpublished until 1992, seemingly conceived as part of an introduction to the unpublished third volume of his remarkable analysis of the formation of modern capitalist states.[404] Noting the accumulation of national peculiarities resulting from the mappings of national revolutions (and thus implicitly criticising his earlier interpretation of British peculiarities) he proposed instead to start from 'the formal structures and limits of any possible "bourgeois revolution"'.[405] This enabled him to explain by the very nature of bourgeois revolutions why none of them could be 'pure'. First of all, they were interrelated, meaning that their 'order was constitutive of their structure'.[406] Thus, for example, the structure of 1848 revolutions were partly constituted by the results of the 1789 French Revolution, whose structure was itself partly determined by the English Revolution of the 1640s and so on. Furthermore, each of the bourgeois revolutions was over-determined 'from above' because of the many compromises of the early bourgeoisie with existing feudal structures; 'from below' because of the involvement of the lower classes; 'from within', since the capitalists proper had to align itself with the bourgeoisie in a broader sense; and 'from without', since capitalism emerged in tandem with the growth of nation states, resulting in numerous wars and conflicts with other states as part of each national transition to capitalism. Finally, the development of capital from dominantly mercantile and agrarian to industrial resulted in a temporal shift from revolutions from below, in which the bourgeoisie allied with the lower classes, to revolutions from above, that is, compromises with the existing state apparatuses.[407]

Thus, even while emphasizing the complex interrelatedness of bourgeois revolutions, this sketch reproduced a basic organizing principle of Anderson's two published volumes: a distinction between abstract theory and the analysis of each national trajectory as the basic unit of analysis, a sort of container of social struggles, conceiving interrelatedness primarily as encounters between states, that is, not as transnational social processes. Also, perhaps more paradoxical in view of the two published volumes,

404. Anderson 1974a, and 1974b.
405. Anderson 1976b, p. 109.
406. Anderson 1976b, p. 116.
407. Anderson 1976b, pp. 111-118.

Anderson's conception of the interrelatedness of great bourgeois revolutions perhaps tended towards overdrawing not only the international effects of such early events as the Dutch Revolutions of the sixteenth century or the English Revolution of 1640-60 but also the extent of immediate linkage between these specific great revolutionary moments.

These different attempts at reconstruction clearly solved some important problems inherent in earlier uses of the concept. Yet, despite the openness of especially the latter defences of 'bourgeois revolution' to elements of criticism, several of these writings tended to reproduce problematic assumptions inherited either from traditional Marxist historiography of the Soboul type or the newer traditions of the Brenner school. The next, and final, part of this article shall attempt to confront these problems briefly in an attempt at reconstructing the category 'bourgeois revolution'. This reconstruction will take the form of hypotheses stated in a general and abstract way, but aiming towards concrete historical studies.

Reconstructing bourgeois revolution

Four main interrelated axes may be distinguished in reconstructing in the problem of bourgeois revolution.

The first axis is the *relation between external and internal aspects*. As I mentioned above, the traditional Marxist historiography of Soboul tended to presume a succession of main stages of social development within each single country. The Brenner school criticized this assumption, yet proceeded to one-to-one comparisons of single country trajectories in order to categorize early modern England simply as 'capitalist', and France during the same period simply as 'feudalist', disregarding not only important relations between the two countries, but also elements of uneven and combined development rising from such interaction. And even writers critical of this aspect of the Brenner tradition, including Mooers, often tended to shape their concrete analyses similarly as national, intra-societal genealogies for comparison. Thus, despite frequent acknowledgments of the significance of international relations, Marxists have frequently reproduced what is often termed 'methodological nationalism', resulting in presentations of the international totality as an exogenous, even reified, factor, rather than an integrated aspect of a whole. In view of the historically limited validity of the nation state as a framework of reference, in pre-capitalist societies as well as world market competition and colonial exploitation, Marxists should develop a much more flexible view of the dialectic of part and totality in this field. One crucial starting point, among others, could be the marginalized methodological internationalism found in Trotsky's view of the particular social formation as 'an original combination of the basic features of the world process.'[408] This perspective allows for a consideration of the relative specificity of a concrete social formation not only compared with other social formations or with an alleged 'normal' development, but as part of a diverse totality. Though the exact methodological consequences of this will of course be relative to the concrete object under study as well as the concrete aims in studying it, it is at least clear that such a perspective points towards studies of social, political and cultural transfer and international conflicts in the relations between different social formations, regions etc., thus transcending the view of national trajectories as relatively closed units.

The second axis is the *relation between modern state building and transition to capitalism*. Again, a crucial problem in the approach of traditional Marxism has been the relation between the specific English context of the transition to capitalism as studied by Marx and the development of capitalism on a world scale. Assumptions about capitalism as the immediate offspring of a certain level of the development of the productive forces, interpreted simply as technological and economic progress, have sometimes surfaced in historiography, but have never been substantiated seriously. Global explanations of the rise of capitalism as a result of expanded trade relations, from Max Weber and Henri Pirenne to Paul Sweezy and Immanuel Wallerstein, have rightly been criticized for actually obscuring the origins of capitalism by presuming its main results to be present before its very beginning. Conversely, explanations starting from specific relations of production have found it hard to move beyond Marx's original focus on England. Lenin's analysis of Russian capitalism, written in the late 1890's, tended to look for similar stages of development in Russia. Maurice Dobb's rich and classic study of the historical development of capitalism half a century later similarly tended to regard the English development under study as somehow representative of the transition to capitalism as such.[409] The Brenner school, on the other hand, emphasized the absolute specificity of the origin of capitalism in English property relations, leaving the transition to capitalism in the rest of the world to be analyzed as the result of an initial competitive advance on the part of the English.[410] Thus, in

408. Trotsky 1930, p. 147. See the discussion of this statement in Rosenberg 2006.
409. Lenin 1899; Dobb 1963; Hilton 1978.
410. This contrast is particularly clear in Wood 2004.

effect, the Brenner school not only summarily agreed with their 'commercializationist' adversaries when discussing transitions to capitalism in most of the world. Despite its allegiance to concrete historical studies of 'each social context', it also virtually dismissed all particular endogenous social relations shaping the particular developments of capitalism outside its restricted point of origin.

In order to escape the unsatisfactory one-sidedness of such conceptions of world capitalism as either having no real origin, or being the mere derivation of an exclusively English origin, or being a reproduction of 'many capitalist Englands' with this or that essential 'deviation' from the 'correct' pattern of development, Marxists should work towards a conceptualization of the transition to capitalism as a global process consisting of multiple transitions at the national or regional level. This does not necessarily exclude a Brennerian acknowledgment of the world-historical origins of capitalist relations of production in very particular circumstances. It does, however, indicate the need for an international contextualization of this point of origin. Similarly, such a reconceptualization should imply new vantage points in concrete studies of not only how and where capitalism as such originated, but how it developed and spread, without succumbing to merely repeating the old question-begging conceptions of the 'rise' of capitalism as deriving spontaneously from the growth of the productive forces, or of 'history itself'.

In such an analysis, the category 'bourgeois revolution' (or some similar term) may be useful in reintegrating a crucial moment often insufficiently theorized in Marxist approaches to the transition to capitalism: How the strong 'political' mediation of pre-capitalist exploitation necessarily determined and shaped the development of capitalism, and how the privatized and purely 'economic' mechanisms of exploitation in the capitalist mode of production were yet preconditioned by the existence of a capitalist state form providing, in a complex and uneven way, the general means of reproduction under the guise of an illusory community. A reconstructed category of 'bourgeois revolution' could start from this sense of a revolutionary separation of state and society not only as a functional precondition of the development of capitalism, but in many cases even as the initiator of capitalism within a particular social formation in order to enrich that social formation by attempting to meet world market demands. This methodological possibility was already hinted at in Trotsky's analysis of Russian capitalism, as we saw above.

The third axis in the reconstruction of 'bourgeois revolution' is *the relation between the revolution as process and the revolution as moment*. This reflects a duality inherent in conventional uses of the category: On the one hand, revolutions have been identified as particular moments of rupture in history in which collective social agency caused significant change: 1640-1660 in England, 1789-1799 or 1789-1815 in France, 1917 in Russia. On the other hand, the revolutionary character of such ruptures consisted not only in the revolutionary moments themselves, but also in the deep-seated structural change with which they were intimately bound: separation of state and society, transition from feudalism to capitalism and so on. For the sake of conceptual clarity, the latter aspect could be termed bourgeois *transition* rather than revolution, in view of the fact that deep-seated structural change can neither be immediately identified with particular events, say, the storming of the Bastille or the proclamation of the third estate as the nation in 1789, nor be expected to be completed within the terms of a few months or years.

Starting from this consideration, it is clear that one weakness of the traditional Marxist historiography of bourgeois revolutions has been its search for points of immediate identification of a particular moment and a broader social process, viewing France in 1789-1799 as an instance of the essence of 'bourgeois revolution'. On the other hand, it is equally clear that if the revolution as event is regarded as virtually isolated from the long-term transition, it deprives the revolutionary moment of its revolutionary content.

Consequently, while a reconstructed category of 'bourgeois revolution' should acknowledge the difference between revolution as moment and revolution as process, it should comprise both within a total analysis and not reduce the category to either long-term transition or short-term moment. Our methodological apparatus should be capable of highlighting internal relations between the totality and the specific object: the *process* as reflected in the specific *moment* and in its causes. Thus the French Revolution of 1789-99 was *itself* bourgeois in so far as it was related to this general process.

Far from implying a simple subsumption of the particular event under a preconceived, reified notion of totality, this calls for a flexible and differentiated conceptualization of the moment itself. Thus, 'bourgeois revolution' is contained within this theoretical complex as an *aspect of rupture*, a constituent among others, within the real historical events. Coexisting with this aspect of rupture, the concrete historical events will also reveal elements of continuity. This implies that the concept of 'bourgeois revolution' contains guiding threads for concrete studies of the French Revolution, not that this historical event might be *reduced* to a mere example of a bourgeois revolution, nor that this specific revolution should necessarily be seen as the archetype of such revolutions. The French Revolution is not an individual instance of some universal essence by the name of 'bourgeois revolution'. It may be seen, rather, as an integral part of a complex of determinations, one of which has been termed 'bourgeois revolution'. In other words, the French revolution was more than *a* bourgeois revolution, but much less than *the* bourgeois revolution.

The final axis of reconstruction to be discussed here is *the relation between revolution and reform* in the bourgeois transition. Traditional uses of the category 'bourgeois revolution' have proceeded from a comparative contrast between revolutionary trajectories (that of France as compared to Britain, Germany or others, for example) and non-revolutionary trajectories marked by reform from above (say, those of Germany against France and Britain). The category 'revolution from above' has been used by many Marxists, echoing Engels's reflections on post-1848 developments, especially in Germany, to emphasize the deep-seated nature of the changes involved in carrying out the 'tasks' of the bourgeois revolution without intervention from below. While such traditional interpretations have been useful in highlighting contrasts between differences in social and political structures resulting from such divergent paths, they have also contributed to overdrawing such contrasts to the point of caricature, say, by ignoring authoritarianism in the French trajectory in order to explain the specific Nazi rule in Germany as the result of an national authoritarian tradition stemming from a lack of bourgeois revolution.

Such overdrawn contrasts should be rebalanced by acknowledging the international preconditions and results, even of what would immediately seem to be purely 'national' revolutions. Deep-seated structural reforms may often be studied as parasitic reflections of revolutionary results, as the Prussian reform era of the early 1800s reflected the constitutional accomplishments of the French Revolution. In other words, national bourgeois transitions, whether concentrated in one revolutionary moment or spread across a long process of smaller battles and reforms, were parts of the international bourgeois transition in which the great revolutionary moments constituted qualitative leaps. In many concrete cases, the will to introduce reforms on the part of the governing class in one particular social formation reflects the fear of revolution urged on by the example of successful revolutions elsewhere. And even within the revolutionary process itself we may find a dialectical relation of revolution and reform, most successful revolutions having developed not directly from revolutionary aspirations, but through demands for partial reform, whether demands for political representation, alleviation of poverty or an end to war. This was obvious even in the Russian revolutions, in which consciously revolutionary forces did exist, but even more in the processes leading up to 1789, in other words, before the shaping of the modern concept and idea of making revolution.

Conclusions

By reflecting on important chapters in the history of the category 'bourgeois revolution' in historiography we have thus arrived at elements of reconstruction of the concept aiming at further historical studies. Such a reconstructed category of 'bourgeois revolution' should situate the study of particular historical developments within a consideration of the international process of bourgeois transition as a totality, characterized by the formation of the duality of state and society as part of the uneven and combined global transition to capitalism. This transition should be conceived as existing through its internal relation with individual revolutionary moments marked by social agency. This implies a double-sided, non-reductive relation: Particular revolutionary moments could be categorized as 'bourgeois' insofar as their consequences relate to this international bourgeois transition, but such individual revolutions were always shaped and/or triggered by immediate circumstances that did not spring directly from this process of transition. Thus, on the one hand, 'bourgeois revolution' should be taken to encompass much more than that with which it is conventionally associated, but on the other hand, its validity should be regarded as concerning only some aspects of the particular causes, agents and event of each revolution. This should allow us not only to develop more nuanced understandings of revolutionary change in the past, but also to work towards a richer understanding of social change in the present and future.

REFERENCES

Abusch, Alexander 1946, *Der Irrweg einer Nation*, Berlin: Aufbau-Verlag.

Anderson, Perry 1964, 'Origins of the Present Crisis', in Anderson 1992.

Anderson, Perry 1974a, *Passages from Antiquity to Feudalism*, London: NLB.

Anderson, Perry 1974b, *Lineages of the Absolutist State*, London: NLB.

Anderson, Perry 1976a, *Considerations on Western Marxism*, London: New Left Books.

Anderson, Perry 1976b, 'The Notion of Bourgeois Revolution', in Anderson 1992.

Anderson, Perry 1992, *English Questions*, London: Verso.

Anderson, Perry 1993, 'Maurice Thomson's War', *The London Review of Books* 1993, November.

Aston, T.H. et al. (eds.) 1985, *The Brenner Debate: Agrarian Class Structure and Economic Development in Pre-Industrial Europe*, Cambridge: Cambridge University Press.

Blackbourn, David and Geoff Eley 1984, *The Pecularities of German History*, Oxford: Oxford University Press.

Bleiber, Helmut et al. (eds.) 1977, *Bourgeoisie und bürgerliche Umwälzung in Deutschland 1789-1871*, Berlin: Akademie-Verlag.

Bonefeld, Werner et al. (eds.) 1992, *Open Marxism, Volume I: Dialectics and History*, London: Pluto.

Brenner, Robert 1989, 'Bourgeois Revolution and Transition to Capitalism', in Meier 1989.

Callinicos, Alex 1989, 'Bourgeois Revolutions and Historical Materialism', *International Socialism*, 43: 113-171.

Cobban, Alfred 1964, *The Social Interpretation of the French Revolution*, Cambridge: At the University Press.

Comninel, George 1987, *Rethinking the French Revolution: Marxism and the Revisionist Challenge*, London: Verso .

Dahrendorf, Ralf 1966, *Gesellschaft und Demokratie in Deutschland*, München: R. Piper.

Davidson, Neil 2012, *How Revolutionary were the Bourgeois Revolutions?*, Chicago: Haymarket.

Dobb, Maurice 1963 [1946], *Studies in the Development of Capitalism*, London: Routledge and Kegan Paul.

Doyle, William 1978, *The Old European Order, 1660-1800*, Oxford: Oxford University Press.

Draper, Hal 1977, *State and Bureaucracy: Karl Marx's Theory of Revolution I*, New York: Monthly Review Press.

Draper, Hal 1978, *The Politics of Social Classes: Karl Marx's Theory of Revolution II*, New York: Monthly Review Press.

Dworkin, Dennis 1997, *Cultural Marxism in Postwar Britain: History, the New Left and the Origins of Cultural Studies*, Durham: Duke University Press.

Engels, Friedrich 1875, 'Flüchtlingslitteratur. V. Soziales aus Rußland', Marx and Engels 1965-74, vol. 18.

Furet, François and Denis Richet 1973 [1965], *La révolution française*, Paris: Pluriel.

Furet, François 1989, *Penser la Révolution française*, Paris: Gallimard.

Gerstenberger, Heide 1990, *Die subjektlose Gewalt: Theorie der Entstehung bürgerlicher Staatsgewalt*, Münster: Dampfboot .

Gerstenberger, Heide 1992, 'The Bourgeois State Form Revisited', in Bonefeld 1992.

Gerstenberger, Heide 2007, *Impersonal Power: History and Theory of the Bourgeois State*, Leiden: Brill.

Guérin, Daniel 1946, *La lutte de classes sous la Première République. Bourgeois et 'bras nus' 1793-1797*. 2 Vols. Paris: Gallimard.

Hamerow, Theodore S. 1972, *Restoration, Revolution, Reaction: Economics and Politics in Germany, 1815-1871*, Princeton: Princeton University Press.

Haynes, Mike and Jim Wolfreys (eds.) 2007, *History and Revolution: Refuting Revisionism*, London: Verso.

Heller, Henry 2006, *The Bourgeois Revolution in France, 1789-1815*, New York: Berghahn.

Hilton, Rodney (ed.) 1978, *The Transition from Feudalism to Capitalism*, London: Verso.

James, C. L. R. 1980 [1938], *The Black Jacobins*, London: Allison & Busby.

Katz, Claudio J. 1989, *From Feudalism to Capitalism: Marxian Theories of Class Struggle and Social Change*, New York: Greenwood Press.

Kaye, Harvey J. 1984, *The British Marxist Historians*, Oxford: Polity Press

Kouvelakis, Stathis 2003, *Philosophy and Revolution: From Kant to Marx*, London: Verso.

Lenin, V.I 1899, 'The Development of Capitalism in Russia' (1899), in Lenin 1961-70, vol. 3.

Lenin, V.I. 1905, 'Two Tactics of Social Democracy in the Democratic Revolution' (1905), in Lenin 1961-70, vol. 9.

Lenin, V.I. 1961-70, *Lenin Collected Works*, 45 vols., Moscow: Progress.

Löwy, Michael 1981, *The Politics of Combined and Uneven Development: The Theory of Permanent Revolution*, London: Verso.

Marx, Karl 1843a, „Kritik des Hegelschen Staatsrechts', in Marx and Engels 1965-74, vol. 1

Marx, Karl 1843b, in Marx and Engels 1965-74, vol. 1

Marx, Karl 1877, '[Brief an die Redaktion der 'Otetschestwennyje Sapiski'] in Marx and Engels 1965-74, vol. 19.

Marx, Karl 1881, [Drafts of letter to Vera Sasulich], in Marx and Engels 1965-74, vol. 19.

Marx, Karl and Friedrich Engels 1882, '[Vorrede zur zweiten russischen Ausgabe des 'Manifests der kommunistischen Partei']' in Marx and Engels 1965-74 vol. 19

Marx, Karl and Friedrich Engels, *Marx Engels Werke*, Berlin: Dietz 1965-74

Mazauric, Claude 2004, *Un historien en son temps. Albert Soboul (1914-1982)*, Narosse: Éditions d'Albret.

Meier, A.L. et al. (eds.) 1989, *The First Modern Society: Essays in English History in Honour of Lawrence Stone*, Cambridge: The Past and Present Society.

Mooers, Colin 1991, *The Making of Bourgeois Europe*, London: Verso.

Nygaard, Bertel 2007a, 'The Meanings of 'Bourgeois Revolution': Conceptualizing the French Revolution', *Science and Society*, 71, 2: 146-72.

Nygaard, Bertel 2007b, 'Revolutions and World History: A Long View', in *Revolutions: reframed – Revisited – Revised*, edited by Agata Stopinska et al., Frankfurt am Main: Peter Lang.

Nygaard, Bertel 2007c, *Borgerlig revolution. Et begreb undersøgt gennem politisk teori og historieskrivning* (unpublished PhD thesis, Aarhus University)

Nygaard, Bertel 2009, 'Constructing Marxism: Karl Kautsky and the French Revolution', *History of European Ideas*, 35: 450-64.

Nygaard, Bertel 2013, 'French Revolution and Communist Future. Historical Time and Agency in European Labour Movements at the End of the First World War', in *Zero Hours: Conceptual Insecurities and New Beginnings in the Interwar Period*, edited by Hagen Schulz-Forberg, Bruxelles: P.I.E. Peter Lang.

Protokoll des VII. Weltkongresses des kommunistischen Internationale, Moskau 25. Juli-20 August 1935 1974, Erlangen: Karl Liebknecht Verlag.

Rancière, Jacques 1992, *On the Shores of Politics*, London: Verso.

Richet, Denis 1969, 'Autour des origines idéologiques lointaines de la Révolution française: Élites et despotisme', *Annales. Économies – sociétés – civilisations*, 24, 1: 1-23.

Rosenberg, Justin 2006, 'Why Is There No International Historical Sociology?', *European Journal of International Relations*, 12, 3: 303-40.

Soboul, Albert 1958, *Les Sans-culottes parisiens en l'an II: Mouvement populaire et gouvernement révolutionnaire 2 juin 1793 – 9 thermidor an II*, Paris: Librairie Clavreuil.

Soboul, Albert 1972, *Précis d'histoire de la Révolution française*, Paris: Éditions sociales.

Soboul, Albert 1975, *The French Revolution 1787-1799: From the Storming of the Bastille to Napoleon*, New York: Vintage Books.

Taylor, George V. 1967, 'Noncapitalist Wealth and the Origins of the French Revolution', *American Historical Review* 72, 2: 469-96.

Teschke, Benno 2005, 'Bourgeois Revolution, State Formation and the Absence of the International', *Historical Materialism*, 13, 2: 3-26.

Thompson, E.P. 1980, *The Poverty of Theory and other Essays*; London: Merlin.

Trotsky, Leon 1906, 'Results and Prospects' in Trotsky 1969.

Trotsky, Leon 1907-9, '1905' in Trotsky 1973.

Trotsky, Leon 1930, 'Introduction to the German Edition' in Trotsky 1969.

Trotsky, Leon 1969, *The Permanent Revolution & Results and Prospects*, New York: Pathfinder Press.

Trotsky, Leon 1973, *1905*, Harmondsworth: Penguin.

Wallerstein, Immanuel 1974, *The Modern World-System. Capitalist Agriculture and the Origins of the European World-Economy in the Sixteenth Century*, New York: Academic Press.

Wallerstein, Immanuel 1980, *The Modern World-System II: Mercantilism and the Consolidation of the European World-Economy, 1600-1750*, New York: Academic Press.

Wallerstein, Immanuel 1989, *The Modern World-System III: The Second Era of Great Expansion of the Capitalist World Economy, 1720-1840s*, San Diego: Academic Press.

Wehler, Hans-Ulrich 1975, *Das deutsche Kaiserreich 1871-1918*, Göttingen: Vandenhoeck & Ruprecht.

Wood, Ellen Meiksins 2004, *The Origin of Capitalism*, London: Verso.

CONCEPTUALISING THE WORLD WORKING CLASS [411]

Marcel van der Linden

The "working class" concept, which originated in 19th-century Europe, has been questioned more and more in the past decades. This criticism comes partly from scholars who are interested in Asia, Africa and Latin America. They point out that the borderlines between "free" wage labour, self-employment and unfree labour are not clear-cut and that the opposition between urban and rural labour should not be made absolute.[412] Jan Breman has already defended this view since the 1970s in his studies of contemporary Gujarat. In addition, Nandini Gooptu has demonstrated in her research of the urban poor in Uttar Pradesh that it is plausible that this view is also true of the early twentieth century.[413] Criticism has also been expressed in part by historians of the early modern North Atlantic region. Peter Linebaugh and Marcus Rediker made a fragmentary picture of how a multiform proletariat of "hewers of wood and drawers of water" developed, with various sites of struggle: "the commons, the plantation, the ship, and the factory." They made it seem likely that slaves and maroons from Africa, indentured labourers from Europe, native Americans, and "free" wage earners and artisans constituted a complex but also socially and culturally interconnected amorphous multitude. A multitude, which was also regarded as one whole (a "many-headed Hydra") by those in power, Linebaugh and Rediker referred to the 1791 rebellion of Haitian slaves as "the first successful workers' revolt in modern history." They suggested that this revolution contributed to the segmentation of that rebellious "multitude" afterwards: "What was left behind was national and partial: the *English* working class, the *black* Haitian, the *Irish* diaspora."[414] The narrow nineteenth-century concept of the proletariat we find in Marx and others

411. This article is a revised version of chapter 2 of my book Workers of the World. Essays toward a Global Labor History (Leiden and Boston: Brill, 2008).
412. V.L. Allen (1972) was one of the first to initiate this discussion, pp. 169-189. See also Bergquist (1986), especially chapters 1 and 6.
413. Breman (1974), (1985), (1993), (1996). Gooptu, 2001.
414. Linebaugh and Rediker, 2000, p. 327, p. 319, p. 286.

was a result of this segmentation.

The question I will address in the following pages is what a new concept of the working class might look like that would take into account the insights offered by Breman, Gooptu, Linebaugh and Rediker, and others. In order to find an answer to this question, I will start off with a constructive critique of Marx's concept of the working class. I use Marx as a starting point for two reasons: he is still an important source of inspiration for scholars around the world and in spite of several weaknesses his analysis is still the best we have.

The Complexity of Labour Power Commodification

The opening sentences of Marx's Capital are famous: "The wealth of societies in which the capitalist mode of production prevails appears as an 'immense collection of commodities'; the individual commodity appears as its elementary form. Our investigation therefore begins with the analysis of the commodity."[415] Marx regarded the capitalist mode of production as the consequence of the commodification of (i) labour power, (ii) means of production and raw materials, and (iii) labour products. The first element is crucial in this context. Marx made the assumption that labour power can be commodified in only one way that is "truly" capitalist, namely via free wage labour, in which the worker "as a free individual can dispose of his labour-power as his own commodity" and "has no other commodity for sale."[416] He emphasized that "labour-power can appear on the market as a commodity only if, and so far as, its possessor, the individual whose labour-power it is, offers it for sale or sells it as a commodity." [417]

The narrow concept of the working class is based on this idea. If only the labour power of free wage labourers is commodified, the "real" working class in capitalism can only consist of such workers. Marx's hypothesis has, as far as I know, never been supported by proper reasoning. It probably appeared self-evident for a long time, because it seemed to correspond to the process by which a proletariat was formed in the North Atlantic region. Nevertheless, Marx's hypothesis is based on two dubious assumptions, namely that labour power should be offered for sale by the person who is the *carrier* and *possessor* of this labour power and that the person who sells the

415. Marx 1976, p. 125.
416. *Ibid.*, p. 272.
417. *Ibid.*, p. 271.

labour power offers it *exclusively*.[418] Why should that be so? Why can the labour power not be sold by someone other than the carrier? Why can the person who offers (his or her own, or someone else's) labour power for sale not sell it conditionally, together with means of production? And why can a slave not perform hired labour for a third party to the benefit of his owner? If we only look at the distinction between a "carrier" and an "possessor" of labour power as such, we can already distinguish four types of labour commodification, namely *autonomous* commodification, in which the carrier of labour power is also its possessor and *heteronomous* commodification, in which the carrier of labour power is not its possessor; in both cases, the carrier's labour power can be offered by the carrier him- or herself or by another person (Table 1).

Table 1: Some Forms of Labour Commodification

	Autonomous (the carrier is the possessor)	Heteronomous (the carrier is not the possessor)
The carrier sells his or her own labour power	Free wage labour (Marx) Sharecropping Labour by self-employed artisans	Wage labour by slaves
The carrier does not sell his or her own labour power	Subcontracted wage labour	Labour by chattel slaves Wage labour by children

It seems to be a reasonable assumption that labour commodification has many forms of which the free wage labourer is only one example.[419] I will explore these multiple forms below both by pointing at the transitional forms between Marx' subaltern classes, and also by uncovering

418. The term "selling" is not really appropriate in the case of wage labour, because it is always a temporary sale, and usually we would not refer to such a transaction as "selling," but as "hiring out." This seems a futile difference but the theoretical implications can be great. See Oppenheimer 1912, pp. 119-122; Eldred and Hanlon, 1981, pp. 24-60, p. 44: Lundkvist 1985, pp. 15-46, pp. 16-18; Burkhardt 1995, pp. 121-137, pp. 125-127; Ruben 1995, pp. 167-183; and Kuczynski 2013, pp. 305-318.

419. John Hicks already came to the conclusion that there are several forms of labour power commodification: "Either the labourer may be sold outright, which is slavery; or his services only may be hired, which is wage-payment." Hicks 1969, p. 123. A first elaboration of this view can be found in Rohwer 1991, pp. 171-185.

some false implicit assumptions. I hope this deconstruction will prepare the ground for a new conceptualization.

Gradual transitions.

In addition to capitalists and landlords, the Marxian tradition distinguishes five subaltern classes or semi-classes in capitalism in addition: the free wage labourers, who only own their own labour power and sell this; the petite bourgeoisie, consisting of small commodity producers and distributors; the self-employed, who own their labour power and means of production and sell their labour products or services (the "self-employing labourer is his own wage labourer, his own means of production appear to him as capital. As his own capitalist he employs himself as his own wage labourer"[420]); the slaves, who neither own their labour power nor their tools and *are* sold (in slavery "the worker is nothing but a living labour-machine, which therefore has a value for others, or rather is a value."[421]); and the lumpenproletarians, who are not sold and do not sell anything. The last group usually remains outside the analysis and is mainly used as a residual category.

The class struggle is waged mainly between capitalists, landlords and wage earners. The other classes are historically less important; they "decay and finally disappear in the face of modern industry."[422]

Slavery is "an anomaly opposite the bourgeois system itself", which is "possible at individual points within the bourgeois system of production", but "only because it does not exist at other points."[423]

Self-employed workers are "anomalies" which exist in "small family-based agriculture (in connection with cottage industry)."[424]

The petite bourgeoisie, "the small tradespeople, shopkeepers, and *rentiers*, the handicraftsmen and peasants — all these sink gradually into the proletariat."[425]

The lumpenproletariat is the "'dangerous class', the social scum, that passively rotting mass thrown off by the lowest layers of old society,"[426]

420. Marx 1988, p. 111.
421. Marx 1973, p. 465.
422. Marx 1973, p. 77.
423. Marx 1973, p. 464.
424. Marx, 1968, p. 414.
425. Marx 1973, p. 75.
426. Marx 1973, p. 77. On Marx's conceptualization of small commodity producers see also the appendix in Jaeger 1982, pp. 297-314.

which includes "vagabonds, criminals, prostitutes".[427]

According to this Marxian scheme, there is a gap between the free wage labourers and the other subaltern groups. But does this scheme at all match historical reality? Do Marx's free wage labourers really exist? I would argue that there is an almost endless variety of producers in capitalism and that the intermediate forms between the different categories are vague and fluid.

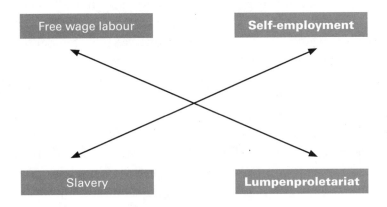

It is perhaps useful to look more closely at some of these intermediate forms; between wage labour and slavery; between wage labour and self-employment; between slavery and self-employment; and between wage labour, slavery and self-employment on the one hand, and the lumpenproletariat on the other.

Intermediate forms between wage labour and slaver

There are various labour relations in which the wage earner is physi-

427. Marx 1976. Compare *The Class Struggles in France, 1848-1850*: "a mass sharply differentiated from the industrial proletariat, a recruiting ground for thieves and criminals of all kinds, living on the crumbs of society, people without a definite trade, vagabonds, *gens sans feu et sans aveu*." Marx and Engels, *Selected Works*, vol. I (Moscow, 1951), p. 142. See also Hayes 1988, pp. 445-465. Different views on the position of prostitutes in the class system can be found in Marx' writings. When he discusses the relative surplus population in *Capital*, he regards prostitutes as an important part of the "actual lumpenproletariat" (*Capital*, I, p. 797) Elsewhere, especially in the *Theories of Surplus Value*, Marx says that prostitutes, if they work for a brothel keeper, perform unproductive wage labour, like actors or musicians, and thus are, by implication, part of the proletariat. (*Marx-Engels Werke* [MEW], vol. 26/1, p. 136, p. 157) This shows once again how the ways in which social class is defined is full of false considerations, which often remain implicit, precisely because they are their moralistic and characteristic of their time. This is probably what Resnick and Wolff refer to as the "discursive device" inspired by "an urgent polemical intent". Resnick and Wolff 1987, pp. 161-162.

cally forced to do his or her work, whereas the wages are paid or have to be handed over to a third person. Child labour, in which case the parents or guardians of the child receive the wages, is a good example. Young Japanese girls who were hired out as *geishas* in exchange for a sum of money were an example of this.[428]

Many instances are known of slaves who performed wage labour for their masters. In Buenos Aires at the end of the eighteenth century, for example, this phenomenon was so common that many slave owners were completely dependent on the wages of their slaves. The notarial accounts of the time suggest that "in long labor contracts, wages, minus estimated living expenses, were commonly paid directly to slave owners by employers of hired slave labor."[429] It is perhaps useful to distinguish three varieties:

The slave owner compels the slave to do wage labour for another employer and collects all or part of the wages. Often, "the slave-owners and slave employers arranged the rate of hire over the slave's head", but "the situation of a slave actively seeking and negotiating his or her own hire" occurred as well.[430]

The slave owner pays his or her slaves in cash for an extra effort, either by means of "bonuses, either as gifts or as incentives", or as a "payment made for extra work in task systems or for working overtime."[431]

The slave works voluntarily for his wages, for an employer or for a fellow slave. The Blue Mountain estate in Jamaica in the late eighteenth century is an example of the latter case: "The slaves paid each other wages. Sunday work on the provision grounds, for example, could earn 1s.8d per day plus breakfast".[432] Of course, especially this last variety considerably blurs the distinction between a wage earner and a slave.

Conversely, wage labourers are often less free than the classical view suggests. Employers have often restricted their employees' freedom to leave in case of labour scarcity. An employee can be tied to an employer in many ways:

Debt bondage is a method that occurred on all continents, from the Scottish coal mines in the eighteenth century to contemporary agriculture in Latin America and South Asia.[433]

428. Ramseyer 1991, pp. 89-116, here 101.
429. Johnson 1997, pp. 265-280, here 273.
430. Bolland 1995, pp. 123-147, 128.
431. *Ibid.*, p. 127.
432. Turner 1995, pp. 33-47, here 39.
433. Ashton 1928, pp. 307-334, here 308.

Indentured labour is of course closely related to debt bondage. The Indian, Javanese and Chinese coolies who were employed in South Africa, Latin America of other parts of Asia are a well-known example of this.[434]

The mobility of workers could also be limited by means of certificates of leave. Without these means of identification, workers could not be hired by any employer. It was a characteristic feature of this practice that the employer took possession of the certificate at the start of the employment and gave it back to the worker only when he or she had, in the employer's view, satisfied all his or her obligations.[435]

Physical compulsion was another option for employers. Sometimes employers went as far as locking up their wage-earning employees to prevent them from being "tempted" by their business rivals. In the Japanese textile industry of the 1920s, female workers were locked up in dormitories for that reason. Sometimes, they were not allowed to leave the premises for more than four months. [436]

Social security provisions and other special benefits offered a less aggressive way of binding employees. Around about 1900, Argentinian companies, for example, created mutual aid and friendly societies which were run by the company and designed to make the workers dependent on the firm.[437] Garden plots which were provided by the company could have the same effect, because they made a supplement to the wages possible, either because the home-made vegetables, poultry, etc. reduced the living expenses, or because this garden produce was bought up by the employer.[438]

Finally, the connections between an employer and an employee outside the immediate employment relationship could have a binding effect. (I will expand on this below.)

Intermediate forms between wage labour and self-employment.

In the classical view, the labourer only disposes of his or her own labour power, but not of other means of production. There were many exceptions to this rule.

One example is the labourer who takes his or her own tools to the

434. See the review in Potts 1990.
435. See the example of Cuban cigar makers in the 1850s in Casanovas 1998, p. 60.
436. Orchard 1930, p. 343.
437. Thompson 1992, pp. 160-176, here 161.
438. The buying up of produce by the employer occurred according to Parpart 1983, p. 42, in the copper mines of Northern Rhodesia in the 1930s.

workshop, as was and still is common in many places. Already in the 1880s, the German economist August Sartorius von Waltershausen observed in the United States that "Unlike their European counterparts, American factory workers commonly own their own tools. [...] Tools often constitute a sizable proportion of a worker's wealth."[439]

A second possibility is that workers have to borrow their means of production from the employer. In that case, they pay a deposit and are formally independent. The rickshaw pullers in Changsha, Hunan Province, China, around 1918 are an example of this. Their rickshaws were the property of "garages" (*che-zhan*) and had to be hired every day. The garage owner paid the rickshaw tax and the puller had to make a deposit of ten Mexican (silver) dollars. "Each cart had a number and was assigned to a certain puller who was always responsible for it. If the rickshaw was broken and laid up for repairs, the daily rent still had to be paid."[440] The puller's income consisted of the difference between his earnings and his payments to the garage owner.

It also happened that an employee was allowed to keep part of his labour product (output) and sell it independently. Silver miners in Pachuca (Mexico) in the mid-eighteenth century received a sum of money (wages) for a specified basic amount of silver ore and everything they produced in excess of that was divided in two parts: "from his half, the pickman gave a certain proportion to the porters, timber-men and to the other mine workers who had helped him."[441] We know that similar arrangements existed in agriculture, in Java and in many other places.[442]

Intermediate forms between slavery and self-employment.

The case of Simon Gray, a slave from the south of the United States, who served as the chief boatman of the Natchez lumber company from 1845 until 1862, shows how complicated capitalist reality could be. Gray's crews usually numbered between ten and twenty men and were made up of both African-American slaves and white rivermen. "Some of the slaves were the property of the company, while others, like Gray himself, were hired from their owners by the firm. The white crewmen, on the other hand, were employed by the Negro, who kept their records, paid their ex-

439. von Waltershausen1998, p. 216.
440. McDonald, Jr. 1978, p. 147. Nowadays, a very similar arrangement still exists in the case of *jeepney* drivers and taxi drivers in Manila. See Pinches 1987, pp. 103-136, here 118.
441. Avila 1985, pp. 47-67, here 57.
442. See for instance Hart 1986, pp. 180-182; Hüsken 1979, pp. 140-151.

penses, lent them money, and sometimes paid their wages. Consequently, they looked upon Gray as their employer." Gray and his men were often away from home for two to three weeks. During these trips, Gray performed a great many managerial tasks. "In addition to making deliveries he also solicited orders for the mill, quoted prices, extended credit to customers, and collected money owed to the lumber company."[443] Thus, this case shows a slave who functioned as a manager, free wage labourers who were employed by a slave, and other slaves who had to obey this employer. Not all of the slaves were owned by the Natchez Co., but some, including Gray, were hired from other slave owners. This situation is, no doubt, unusual from a historical point of view. In another situation, slaves worked as sharecroppers. In Jamaica in the late eighteenth century, the situation sometimes occurred "that the 'better sort' of slaves had established grounds and were using the 'poorer sort' to work them in return for the share of the produce."[444]

Intermediate forms between wage labour/slavery/self-employment and lumpenproletariat

The transition from the three main forms (slavery etc.) to the "non-class" of the lumpenproletariat is also gradual. V.L. Allen claimed that "In societies in which bare subsistence is the norm for a high proportion of all the working class, and where men, women, and children are compelled to seek alternative means of subsistence, as distinct from their traditional ones, the *lumpenproletariat* is barely distinguishable from much of the rest of the working class."[445]

"Respectable" workers who were destitute also felt compelled to steal. Organized looting of food by workers was "a nation-wide phenomenon" in the United States by 1932. [446] Such looting reappeared in Italy in the early 1970s.[447]

Scavenging also occurred frequently in hard times and could even become customary law. Louis Adamic noted in 1935 that "[e]ver since anyone in the Pennsylvania anthracite field can remember, it has been customary for miners and their families to go with sacks or pails to the culm dumps

443. Moore 1962, pp. 472-84; reprinted in: Newton and Lewis (eds), 1978, pp. 157-67, here 158-59.
444. Turner 1995, pp. 33-47, here 34.
445. Allen 1972, p. 188.
446. Bernstein 1960, p. 422.
447. Collonges and Randal 1976, Ch. 4.

surrounding their bleak towns and pick coal from among the rock and slate thrown out in the breaking and cleaning processes at the big collieries. The pickers usually were the poorer families."[448]

Theft, embezzlement and pilfering have traditionally been "normal" activities for some groups of workers. It is common among dockers in many countries to steal part of a shipment, but in factories and offices, such thefts by lower employees also occur frequently.[449]

Implicit assumptions

The classical view does not only make sharp distinctions between phenomena that are no fixed entities in reality, but it also makes implicit assumptions that need to be scrutinized. A number of these assumptions arise from the idea that workers exchange their labour power with an employer for money and then buy food products with that money. By consuming these goods, they reproduce their labour power, which they can then sell again to the employer. Thus, on the level of circulation, there is a cyclical process, which is shown in the following diagram:

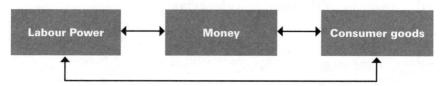

This concept of circulation is an abstraction of many elements and suggests a complex, isolated process. In the first place, it suggests that the consumption of the wages earned by the employee does not require labour. The purchase of consumer goods and the effort to make them suitable for consumption (for instance selling and preparing food, or hiring and cleaning a living space) are not taken into account. Feminists however have pointed out for decades that wage labour cannot exist without subsistence labour.[450] Sporadically, there are employees who reproduce their labour power without subsistence labour, but these are people with a very high income:

448. Adamic 1935, p. 46. A description of concurrent developments in Upper Silesia appears in: Machtan 1982, pp. 141-155.
449. Ditton 1977, pp. 39-71. Case studies include: Mars 1974, pp. 209-228 Grüttner 1982, pp. 54-79; d'Sena 1989, pp. 130-147; Randall 1990, pp. 193-219; Green 1992, pp. 100-114; Smyth and Grijns 1997, pp. 13-22, here 21. Freund reveals the possibility of a smooth transition to theft as a collective act in 1982, pp. 68-86.
450. The literature on this theme is so enormous that I will limit myself to the mention of one representative work: Walby 1986.

The real proletarian fully reproducing himself through the wage for his labour is at the most the Yupi (Young Urban Professional), who as an upwardly mobile executive of a multinational firm buys a sandwich for lunch and meets his Yupi wife (perhaps a stock-broker or university professor) in the evening in a restaurant for dinner, while a domestic servant cleans the rented apartment. The normal wage labourer however is reproduced by a housewife or actively participates in subsistence production.[451]

In most cases, subsistence labour is done by one or more women in the household, the wife or wives and sometimes the daughters of the *paterfamilias*. It is also possible that the wage earner himself employs one or more wage earners who do the domestic work. Many white working-class families in South Africa in the early twentieth century, for instance, had a black domestic servant, who, among other things, was responsible for "the making of fires, cleaning stoves, sweeping, washing dishes, preparing morning and afternoon tea, keeping the yard clean, and doing such routine garden work as weeding and watering."[452]

Secondly, the diagram seems to suggest that the relationship between employer and employee is limited to the exchange of money for labour power. Possible ties between both parties outside the circulation process are not taken into consideration. But, of course, these ties can exist. The employer can bind the employee economically, for instance by providing accommodation owned by the company or by making it obligatory for the employee to buy consumer goods that the employer offers for sale with the income earned as wages (the so-called truck system).[453] But the relationship between the employer and the employee need not be economic, for instance if both are related or belong to the same religious community. Instances of company housing and other similar forms of material bonds can be found especially, but certainly not exclusively, in large companies, for example the United Fruit Company, which housed its *campesinos* in Central America on the plantations, or the steel firm Krupp in Germany.[454] Non-economic bonds are probably relatively more common in small companies.

451. Evers 198), pp. 353-366, here 360.
452. Van Onselen 1982, pp. 30-31.
453. On the truck system see for example: Hilton 1960.
454. Studies on company housing include: Aggarwal 1952; Tipple 1981, pp. 65-85; Melling 1981, pp. 255-301; Honhart 1990, pp. 3-21; Crinson 1997, pp. 341-359;

Thirdly, the cyclical diagram suggests that an employee has only one employer and that he or she is only involved in one labour relation at a time. This phenomenon did indeed occur frequently and is common among artisans and skilled labourers, but this is not the case for a large part of the world population dependent on wages, neither in the past, nor at present. People with several jobs are quite common in Asia, Africa, and Latin America. The same was true for Europe in the decades before the rise of the welfare state. It is again true for contemporary Russia, where at least around 15 to 20 percent of the employed population had supplementary employment in the mid-1990s.[455] It is of course also perfectly possible that the employee has different kinds of income. André Gunder Frank has rightly spoken of "fluidity in owner-worker relations." He gives the example of "a single worker who is simultaneously (i) owner of his own land and house, (ii) sharecropper on another's land (sometimes for half, sometimes for a third of the crop), (iii) tenant on a third person's land, (iv) wage labourer during harvest time on one of these lands, and (v) independent trader of his own home-made commodities."[456] The relative importance of the different sources of income can change repeatedly in the course of time, as Adam Smith already knew.[457]

Fourthly, the circulation model focuses on the relationship between one employee and his or her employer. But it is perfectly possible that labourers are employed *as a group* by an employer. Sometimes this is done by means of a subcontractor who recruits workers in the surrounding area and subsequently hands them over to an employer. In the Shanghai textile industry of the early twentieth century, for example, there was the *pao-kung* system in which the subcontractor "hired" girls from neighbouring villages for three years from their parents and then "hired them out" to British and Japanese cotton mills in the city during that period.[458] In another arrangement, the subcontractor supervises the workers recruited by him and is thus working for his client as well. This was, for example, the case in many Indian and Chinese coal mines.[459] It could also happen that a group of labourers hired

---

455. Hussey 1997, pp. 217-235; Klopov 1998, pp. 64-87.
456. Frank 1969, pp. 271-272.
457. "In years of plenty, servants frequently leave their masters, and trust their subsistence to what they can make by their own industry. [...] In years of scarcity, the difficulty and uncertainty of subsistence make all such people eager to return to service." Smith 1991, p. 74.
458. Chesneaux 1968, p. 57.
459. Simeon 1995, pp. 25-26; Wright 1981, pp. 656-678.

themselves out to an employer without the mediation of a subcontractor, as in the case of harvest workers operating in the European part of Russia in the nineteenth century, who were organized in *artels* ("cooperatives").[460]

Fifthly and finally, according to the model, the cycle is broken when a labourer does no longer offer his labour power for sale and stops working. This suggests that strikes are a form of collective action that is associated especially with free wage labourers and also that this is the only possible form of action. But if we look at the ways in which protest is expressed and pressure is exerted by the different groups of subaltern workers (i.e. the slaves, the self-employed, the lumpenproletarians, and the "free" wage labourers), these appear to overlap considerably. In the past, all kinds of subaltern workers went on strike. The sharecropping silver miners in Chihuahua, for instance, protested as early as the 1730s against the termination of their work contacts by the owners of the mine by entrenching themselves in the nearby hills. "There they built a makeshift stone parapet, unfurled a banner proclaiming their defiance, and vowed to storm the villa of San Felipe, kill San Juan y Santa Cruz, and burn his house to the ground. For the next several weeks they refused to budge from their mountain redoubt, where they passed time by composing and singing songs of protest."[461] The miners returned only after mediation by a priest sent by the bishop. Slaves regularly went on strike too. On plantations in the British Caribbean in the early nineteenth century, for example, there were one-sided walkouts.

"The rebellions in Demerara in 1829 and Jamaica in 1831 both began as versions of the modern work strike, coupled with other acts of defiance, but not with killing. Only when the local militia retaliated with force, assuming that this was another armed uprising, did such an occurrence actually take place."[462] Conversely, free wage labourers used action methods which are usually associated with other groups of subaltern workers, such as lynching, rioting, arson, and bombing.[463]

460. Mixter 1991, pp. 294-340.
461. Martin 1996, p. 51.
462. Schuler 1970. Reprinted in: Beckles and Shepherd (eds) 1991, pp. 373-386, here 382-383.
463. Rightly, Cloward and Fox Piven remark: "[...] some forms of protest are more or less universally available. Arson, whether in the fields of the preindustrial world or in the streets of the urbanized world, requires technological rather than organization resources, and not much of the former, either. Riots require little more by way of organization than numbers, propinquity, and some communication. Most patterns of human settlement, whether te preindustrial village or modern metropolis, supply these structural require-

Towards new concepts

The reflections above show that the boundaries between the "free" wage labourers and other kinds of subaltern workers in capitalist society are vague and gradual. In the first place, there are extensive and complicated grey areas full of transitional locations between the "free" wage labourers and the slaves, the self-employed and the lumpenproletarians. Secondly, almost all subaltern workers belong to households that combine several modes of labour.[464] Thirdly, individual subaltern workers can also combine different modes of labour, both synchronically and diachronically. And finally, the distinction between the different kinds of subaltern workers is not clear-cut. The implications are far-reaching. Apparently, there is a large class of people within capitalism, whose labour power is commodified in various ways. In this context, I refer to this class as *subaltern workers*. They make up a very varied group, which includes chattel slaves, sharecroppers, small artisans and wage earners. It is the historic dynamics of this "multitude" that we should try to understand.

The first question that catches our attention is what all these different subaltern workers have in common. Where is the dividing line, the *fundamentum divisionis*, between them and the other party, of those who have more power? Taking Cornelius Castoriadis' idiom as a first guide, we could say that all subaltern workers are in a state of "instituted heteronomy." For this Greek-French philosopher, instituted heteronomy is the opposite of social autonomy; it manifests itself as "a mass of conditions of privation and oppression, as a solidified global, material and institutional structure of the economy, of power and of ideology, as induction, mystification, manipulation and violence." Instituted heteronomy expresses and sanctions "an antagonistic division of society and, concurrent with this, the power of one determined social category over the whole. [...] In this way, the capitalist economy – production, distribution, market, etc. – is alienating inasmuch as it goes along with the division of society into proletariat and capitalists."[465] We can become a bit more specific when we follow an indication by philosopher Gerald Cohen. He has argued that "lack of means of production is not as essential to proletarian status as is traditionally maintained. It is better to say that *a proletarian must sell his labour power in order to*

ments." Piven and Cloward 1995, pp. 137-167, here 148.
464. For a full argumentation see my "Introduction" and "Conclusion" in Kok (ed.), 2002, pp. 1-23 and pp. 230-242.
465. Castoriadis 1987, p. 109.

obtain his means of life. He may own means of production, but he cannot use them to support himself save by contracting with a capitalist."[466] Following Marx, Cohen understands the phrase "must sell his labour power" in this context as economic compulsion, but if we also include physical compulsion, we come close to a clear demarcation. *Every carrier of labour power whose labour power is sold or hired out to another person under economic or non-economic compulsion belongs to the class of subaltern workers, regardless of whether the carrier of labour power is him- or herself selling or hiring it out and, regardless of whether the carrier him- or herself owns means of production.* In a sense, this brings us back to the pre-Marxian concept of the "labouring classes". All aspects of this provisional definition require further research.[467]

Another question follows from the above. How can we conceptualise the internal differentiation of the subaltern class? As is well-known, the classical analysis focused on power in the production process. That process of production is of course characterised by a combination of three elements: "purposeful activity, that is work itself, the object on which that work is performed, and the instruments of that work."[468] The product of labour is the fourth element of this analysis. Together these elements define the most important dimensions of the classical analyses that should be retained in a modified approach:

> i The relationship between the employee and his or her *labour power* (is the employee in control of his or her body, or is it the employer or a third party?);
>
> ii The relationship between the employee and his or her *means of production* (to what extent does the employee own his or her objects and instruments of work and to what extent are these objects and instruments owned by the employer or by a third party?);
>
> iii The relationship between the employee and his or her *labour product* (to what extent does the output of his or her effort belong to the employee and to what extent does it belong to the employer or to a third party?).

466. Cohen 1978, p. 72.
467. The concept of "economic compulsion", for example, deserves further consideration because it involves an important collective dimension. Even if every individual proletarian can, in theory, escape his fate by upward mobility, there can still be collective compulsion and lack of freedom, because "each [proletarian] is free only on condition that the others do not exercise their similarly conditional freedom." Cohen 1988, p. 263.
468. Marx 1976, p. 284. See also Wittfogel 1929, pp. 17-51, pp. 485-522, pp. 699-735, here 506-522, and Balibar 1968, pp. 79-226, here 98.

iv The observations in this paper seem to suggest that, beside the classical dimensions, three additional dimensions are relevant:

iv The relationship between the employee and the other members of his or her *household* (what kind of social and economic dependencies do exist between the employee and the other household members?);

v The relationship between the employee and his or her *employer outside the immediate production process* (to what extent is the employee through debts, housing, etc. tied to the employer?);

vi The relationship between the employee and *other employees* within the labour relationship (what kind of social and economic dependencies do exist between the employee and his or her immediate colleagues?).[469]

These six dimensions should allow us to develop a subtle range of variations with which we can describe the class position of an *individual* employee *vis-à-vis* one employer.[470] If an employee combines several jobs, then we have to carry out several of these class determinations. Moreover, because an employee usually belongs to a larger unit (household), it seems advisable to extend the analysis further and include the class positions of the other household members. This may lead to interesting incongruencies if one household unites diverging class positions.[471] Finally, these analyses should, as much as possible, be done longitudinally, because all household members can change their "jobs" during the course of their lives – that is, if they have a certain degree of freedom.[472]

469. Naturally, dimensions may overlap. In the service sector, for instance, the means of labour and the labour product can be identical and in subcontracting the work team may consist of household members.

470. Looking at subaltern workers as instituted heteronomy, we might say that the degree of heteronomy is larger as the employee has less power over (i) his or her own labour capacity, (ii) means of labour, (iii) labour product, (iv) the fellow members of his or her own household, (v) the relationship with the employer outside the immediate labour process, and (vi) possible fellow workers in the labour process. In this sense women generally have less autonomy than men and the autonomy of wage earners is larger than the autonomy of slaves, but smaller than the autonomy of self-employed workers.

471. For a discussion of the problem of "cross-class families" see: Graetz 1991, pp. 101-118. Graetz proposes a "generic model for the joint classification of family class locations".

472. For subjective reasons, not everybody changes his or her type of labour relationship easily. When the US-American social scientist Bakke lived in the working-class neighbourhood of Greenwich (London) in the early 1930s, he observed an "unwillingness to launch out into some sort of independent enterprise". He explained this by "the inability of one who has been born and bred in the tradition of a wage-earner to visualize himself as an independent worker, his own boss." This "lack of imagination" resulted from the wage

A new typology could further differentiate the varieties distinguished in Table 1. We could, for example, distinguish three kinds of selling transactions of labour power according to whether they exclusively concern labour power, or also part of the means of production or all means of production. We should also take into account how the labour is paid. Immanuel Wallerstein once suggested a rudimentary typology, consisting of two main groups: those who must relinquish all the value that they produce and those who must relinquish part of that value. Both these groups can be subdivided further into those who receive either nothing, or goods, or money, or goods plus money in return. In this way, a matrix can be formed with eight categories, only one of which consists of "typical" wage labourers.[473]

We could incorporate this suggestion too.[474] But in whatever way we tackle this, to me several warnings seem justified. In the first place, we should resist the temptation of an empirically empty "Grand Theory" (C. Wright Mills); instead, we need to create typologies on the basis of detailed empirical knowledge. Secondly, we should not study the different kinds of subaltern workers separately, but consider the connections between them as much as possible. Sidney Mintz, for example, has cautioned us not to define "slave" and "proletarian" in isolation: "[These] two vast categories of toiler were actually intimately linked by the world economy that had, as it were, given birth to them both, in their modern form." We should take into account such links, since "a purely definitional approach leaves something to be desired."[475] In the third place, we should not regard subalterns as isolated individuals, because, in reality, they are better analysed

earner's work socialization: "The work routine, the regularity and simplicity of the routine outside working hours, the plodding necessities of the household economy – all of these enforce a discipline which trains for stability as a wage-earner but not for the independence and adaptability and personality necessary for success in an independent enterprise." Bakke 1935, pp. 126-127.

473. Wallerstein 1979, pp. 283-293, here 289-290. Wallerstein's approach as such is certainly not suitable for our purpose as his category " proletarian" is reduced to "the most general and therefore the most abstract determinant of class – the appropriation of surplus product – and is imposed from without upon the most diverse social relations. Classes are defined in relation to the products of labor rather than by their relation to one another in the processes of social production and reproduction. It is as if people's relations to things rather than to one another were decisive." Tomich 1997, pp. 287-311, here 290.

474, The work of political economists Robert W. Cox and Jeffrey Harrod might also prove stimulating. See Cox' programmatic article (1971), and the elaboration of their work in two books: Cox 1987, and Harrod 1987.

475. Mintz 1978, pp. 81-98, here 97-98.

as concrete human beings, who are part of families, systems of kinship, and other social and cultural networks. And finally, we should not look at subalterns primarily from the point of view of the nation state (as in "the Indian working class," etc.); it is better to regard the "national" aspect as something which has to be put into context and explained in itself. Breman and others made us face a broad and complex issue.

REFERENCES.

Adamic, Louis 1935, "The Great 'Bootleg' Coal Industry", *The Nation*, 40.

Aggarwal, S.C. 1952, *Industrial Housing in India*, New Delhi.

Allen, V.L. 1972, "The Meaning of the Working Class in Africa", *Journal of Modern African Studies*, 10 (2), pp. 169-189.

Ashton, T.S. 1928, "The Coal-Miners of the Eighteenth Century", *The Economic Journal*: Economic History Series, No. 3, January.

Avila, Cuauhtemoc Velasco 1985, "Labour Relations in Mining: Real del Monte and Pachuca, 1824-74", in: Thomas Greaves and William Culver (eds), *Miners and Mining in the Americas*, Manchester: Manchester University Press.

Bakke, Wight E. 1935, *The Unemployed Man: A Social Study*, London: Nisbet and Co.

Balibar, Etienne 1968, "Sur les concepts fondamentaux du matérialisme historique", in: Louis Althusser *et al.*, *Lire le Capital*. Vol. II, Paris: Maspéro.

Bergquist, Charles 1986, *Labor in Latin America. Comparative Essays on Chile, Argentina, Venezuela, and Colombia*, Stanford: Stanford University Press.

Bernstein, Irving 1960, *The Lean Years. A History of the American Worker, 1920-1933*, Boston.

Bolland, O. Nigel 1995, "Proto-Proletarians? Slave Wages in the Americas", in: Mary Turner (ed.), *From Chattel Slaves to Wage Slaves: The Dynamics of Labour Bargaining in the Americas*, Kingston: Ian Randle.

Breman, Jan 1974, *Patronage and Exploitation. Changing Agrarian Relations in South Gujarat*, Berkeley: University of California Press.

Breman, Jan 1985, *Of Peasants, Migrants and Paupers. Rural Labour Circulation and Capitalist Production in West India*, Oxford: Oxford University Press.

Breman, Jan 1993, *Beyond Patronage and Exploitation. Changing Agrarian Relations in South Gujarat*, Oxford: Oxford University Press.

Breman, Jan 1996, *Footloose Labour. Working in India's Informal Economy*, Cambridge: Cambridge University Press.

Burkhardt, Michael 1995, "Kritik der Marxschen Mehrwerttheorie", *Jahrbuch für Wirtschaftswissenschaften*, 46.

Casanovas, Joan 1998, *Bread, or Bullets! Urban Labor and Spanish Colonialism in Cuba, 1850-1898*, Pittsburgh: University of Pittsburgh Press.

Castoriadis, Cornelius 1987, *The Imaginary Institution of Society*. Trans. Kathleen Blamey, Cambridge: Polity Press.

Chesneaux, Jean 1968, *Chinese Labor Movement 1919-1927*. Trans. H.M. Wright, Stanford: Stanford University Press.

Cohen, G.A. 1978, *Karl Marx's Theory of History: A Defence*, Oxford: Clarendon Press.

Cohen, G.A. 1988, *History, Labour, and Freedom. Themes from Marx*, Oxford: Clarendon Press.

Collonges, Yann and Georges Randal, Pierre 1976, *Les autoréductions. Grèves d'usagers et luttes de classes en France et en Italie (1972-1976)*, Paris: 10/18.

Cox, Robert W. 1971, "Approaches to a Futurology of Industrial Relations", *International Institute of Labour Studies Bulleti*, No. 8.

Cox, Robert W. 1987, *Production, Power and World Order: Social Forces in the Making of History*, New York: Columbia University Press.

Crinson, Mark 1997, "Abadan: Planning and Architecture under the Anglo-Iranian Oil Company", *Planning Perspectives*, 12.

d'Sena, Peter 1989, "Perquisites and Casual Labour on the London Wharfside in the Eighteenth Century", *London Journal*, 14.

Ditton, Jason 1977, "Perks, Pilferage, and the Fiddle: The Historical Structure of Invisible Wages", *Theory and Society*, 4.

Eldred, Michael and Hanlon, Marnie 1981, "Reconstructing Value-Form Analysis", *Capital and Class*, No. 13 (Spring).

English, Martin Cheryl 1996, *Governance and Society in Colonial Mexico: Chihuahua in the Eighteenth Century*, Stanford, CA: Stanford University Press.

Evers, Hans-Dieter 1987 „Schattenwirtschaft, Subsistenzproduktion und informeller Sektor", in: Klaus Heinemann (ed.), *Soziologie wirtschaftlichen Handelns*, Opladen: Westdeutscher Verlag.

Fox Piven, Frances and Cloward, Richard A. 1995, "Collective Protest: A Critique of Resource-Mobilization Theory", in: Stanford M. Lyman (ed.), *Social Movements: Critiques, Concepts, Case-Studies*, Houndmills: Macmillan.

Freund William 1982, "Theft and Social Protest Among the Tin Miners of Northern Nigeria", *Radical History Review*, No. 26.

Gooptu, Nandini 2001, *The Politics of the Urban Poor in Early Twentieth-Century*

India, Cambridge: Cambridge University Press.

Graetz, Brian 1991, "The Class Location of Families: A Refined Classification and Analysis", *Sociology*, 25.

Green, Anna 1992, "Spelling, Go-Slows, Gliding Away and Theft: Informal Control over Work on the New Zealand Waterfront, 1915-1951", *Labour History*, No. 63. Smyth, Ines and Grijns, Mies 1997, "*Unjuk Rasa* or Conscious Protest? Resistance Strategies of Indonesian Women Workers", *Bulletin of Concerned Asian Scholars*, 29, 4.

Grüttner, Michael 1982, "Working-Class Crime and the Labour Movement: Pilfering in the Hamburg Docks, 1888-1923", in: Richard J. Evans (ed.), *The German Working Class 1888-1933. The Politics of Everyday Life*, London and Totowa: Croom Helm and Barnes & Noble.

Gunder Frank, André 1969, *Capitalism and Underdevelopment in Latin America: Historical Studies of Chile and Brazil*. Revised and Expanded Edition, New York: Monthly Review Press.

Harrod, Jeffrey 1987, *Power, Production, and the Unprotected Worker* (New York: Columbia University Press.

Hart, Gillian 1986, *Power, Labor, and Livelihood: Processes of Change in Rural Java*, Berkeley: University of California Press.

Hayes, Peter 1988, "*Utopia* and the Lumpenproletariat: Marx's Reasoning in 'The Eighteenth Brumaire of Louis Bonaparte'", *Review of Politics*.

Hicks John 1991, *A Theory of Economic History*, London: Oxford University Press. Rohwer, Götz 1991, "Kapitalismus und `freie Lohnarbeit'. Überlegungen zur Kritik eines Vorurteils", in: Hamburger Stiftung zur Förderung von Wissenschaft und Kultur (ed.), "*Deutsche Wirtschaft*". *Zwangsarbeit von KZ-Häftlingen für Industrie und Behörden*, Hamburg, VSA-Verlag.

Hilton, George W. 1960, *The Truck System Including a History of the British Truck Acts, 1465-1960*, Cambridge: Cambridge University Press.

Honhart, Michael 1990, "Company Housing as Urban Planning in Germany, 1870-1940", *Central European History*, 23.

Hüsken, Frans 1979, "Landlords, Sharecroppers and Agricultural Labourers: Changing Labour Relations in Rural Java", *Journal of Contemporary Asia*, 9.

Hussey, Stephen 1997, "Low Pay, Underemployment and Multiple Occupations: Men's Work in the Inter-war Countryside", *Rural History*, 8.

Jaeger, Christine 1982, *Artisanat et capitalisme: l'envers de la roue de l'histoire*, Paris: Payot.

Johnson, Lyman L. 1997, "The Competition of Slave and Free Labor in Artisanal Production: Buenos Aires, 1770-1815", in: Tom Brass and Marcel van der Linden (eds), *Free and Unfree Labour: The Debate Continues*, Berne: Peter Lang Academic Publishers.

Klopov, Eduard V. 1998, "Secondary Employment as a Form of Social and Labor Mobility", *Sociological Research*, 37, 2 (March-April).

Kok, Jan (ed.) 2002, *Rebellious Families. Household Strategies and Collective Action in the Nineteenth and Twentieth Centuries*, Oxford and New York: Berghahn.

Kuczynski, Thomas 2013, „What Is Sold on the Labour Market?", in Marcel van der Linden and Karl Heinz Roth (eds), *Beyond Marx. Theorising the Global Labour Relations oft he Twenty-First Century*, Leiden: Brill.

Linebaugh, Peter and Rediker, Marcus 2000, *The Many-Headed Hydra. Sailors, Slaves, Commoners, and the Hidden History of the Revolutionary Atlantic*, Boston: Beacon Press.

Lundkvist, Anders 1985, "Kritik af Marx' lønteori", *Kurasje*, No. 37 (December).

Machtan, Lothar 1982, „Die 'Elendsschächte' in Oberschlesien: Bergmännische Selbsthilfe-Initiativen zur Überwindung von Arbeitslosigkeit um 1930", *Jahrbuch Arbeiterbewegung C Geschichte und Theorie 1982*, Frankfurt/Main: EVA.

Mars, Gerald 1974, "Dock Pilferage: A Case Study in Occupational Theft", in: Paul Rock and Mary McIntosh (eds), *Deviance and Social Control*, London.

Marx, Karl 1951, *The Class Struggles in France, 1848-1850*, in *Marx and Engels Selected Works*, vol. I, Moscow.

Marx, Karl 1973, "Manifesto of the Communist Party", in: Karl Marx, *The Revolutions of 1848. Political Writings*, vol. 1. Trans. David Fernbach, Harmondsworth: Penguin.

Marx, Karl 1973, *Grundrisse. Foundations of the Critique of Political Economy (Rough Draft)*. Translated with a Foreword by Martin Nicolaus, Harmondsworth: Penguin.

Marx, Karl 1976, *Capital*, Vol. I. Trans. Ben Fowkes, Harmondsworth: Penguin.

Marx, Karl 1988, „Ökonomische Manuskripte 1863-1867", in *Marx-Engels Gesamtausgabe*. Second Edition, vol. II/4.1, Berlin: Dietz.

Marx, Karl 1968, "Theorien über den Mehrwert", in: Marx-Engels Werke, vol. 26/3,

McDonald, Angus W. Jr. 1978, *The Urban Origins of Rural Revolution: Elites and the Masses in Hunan Province, China, 1911-1927*, Berkeley: University of California Press.

Melling, Joseph 1981, "Employers, Industrial Housing and the Evolution of Company Welfare Politics in Britain's Heavy Industries: West Scotland, 1870-1920", *International Review of Social History*, 26.

Mintz, Sidney W. 1978, "Was the Plantation Slave a Proletarian?", *Review*, 2, 1 (Summer).

Mixter, Timothy 1991, "The Hiring Market as Workers' Turf: Migrant Agricultural Workers and the Mobilization of Collective Action in the Steppe Grainbelt of European Russia, 1853-1913", in: Esther Kingston-Mann and Timothy Mixter (eds), *Peasant Economy, Culture, and Politics of European Russia, 1800-1921*, Princeton: Princeton University Press.

Moore, John Hebron 1962, "Simon Gray, Riverman: A Slave Who Was Almost Free", *The Mississippi Valley Historical Review*, 49 (December), reprinted in: James E. Newton and Ronald L. Lewis (eds) 1978, *The Other Slaves: Mechanics, Artisans and Craftsmen*, Boston, MA: G.K. Hall & Co.

Oppenheimer, Franz 1912, *Die soziale Frage und der Sozialismus. Eine kritische Auseinandersetzung mit der marxistischen Theorie*, Jena: Verlag von Gustav Fischer.

Orchard, John E. 1930, *Japan's Economic Position: The Progress of Industrialization*, London: McGraw-Hill.

Parpart, Jane L. 1983, *Labor and Capital on the African Copperbelt*, Philadelphia: Temple University Press.

Pinches, Michael 1987, "'All That We Have Is Our Muscle and Sweat'. The Rise of Wage Labour in a Manila Squatter Community", in: Michael Pinches and Salim Lakha (eds.), *Wage Labour and Social Change: The Proletariat in Asia and the Pacific*, Monash University, Centre of Southeast Asian Studies.

Potts, Lydia 1990, *The World Labour Market: A History of Migration*. Trans. Terry Bond, London and Atlantic Highlands, N.J.: Zed Books.

Ramseyer, J. Mark 1991, "Indentured Prostitution in Imperial Japan: Credible Commitments in the Commercial Sex Industry", *The Journal of Law, Economics, and Organization*, 7.

Randall, Adrian J. 1990, "Peculiar Perquisites and Pernicious Practices. Embezzlement in the West of England Woollen Industry, c. 1750-1840", *International Review of Social History*, 35.

Resnick, Stephen A. and Wolff, Richard D., *Knowledge and Class. A Marxian Critique of Political Economy* (Chicago and London: University of Chicago Press, 1987), 161-162.

Ruben, Peter 1995, "Ist die Arbeitskraft eine Ware? Ein Beitrag zu einer marxistischen Marxkritik", in Heinz Eidam and Wolfdietrich Schmied-Kowarzik (eds), *Kritische Philosophie gesellschaftlicher Praxis* (Würzburg: Königshausen & Neumann).

Schuler, Monica 1991, "Akan Slave Rebellions in the British Carribean", *Savacou*, 1, 1 (June 1970). Reprinted in: Hilary Beckles and Verene Shepherd (eds), *Caribbean Slave Society and Economy: A Student Reader*, Kingston and London.

Simeon, Dilip 1995, *The Politics of Labour Under Late Colonialism: Workers, Unions and the State in Chota Nagpur, 1928-1939*, New Delhi: Manohar.

Smith, Adam 1991, *The Wealth of Nations*, London: Everyman's Library.

Thompson, Ruth 1992, "Trade Union Organisation: Some Forgotten Aspects", in: Jeremy Adelman (ed.), *Essays in Argentine Labour History, 1870-1930*, Houndmills and London: Macmillan.

Tipple, A. Graham 1981, "Colonial Housing Policy and the `African Towns´ of the Copperbelt: The Beginnings of Self-Help", *African Urban Studies*, 11.

Tomich, Dale 1997, "World of Capital / Worlds of Labor: A Global Perspective", in: John R. Hall (ed.), *Reworking Class*, Ithaca, NY: Cornell University Press.

Turner, Mary 1995, *From Chattel Slaves to Wage Slaves*, Bloomington: Indiana University Press.

Van der Linden, Marcel 2008, *Workers of the World. Essays toward a Global Labor History*, Leiden: Brill.

Van Onselen, Charles 1982, *Studies in the Social and Economic History of the Witwatersrand, 1886-1914*. Vol. 2: New Nineveh, Harlow: Longman.

Von Waltershausen, August Sartorius 1998, *The Workers´ Movement in the United States, 1879-1885*. Eds. David Montgomery and Marcel van der Linden, New York: Cambridge University Press.

Walby, Sylvia 1986, *Patriarchy at Work. Patriarchal and Capitalist Relations in Employment*, Cambridge: Polity Press.

Wallerstein, Immanuel 1979, "Class Conflict in the Capitalist World-Economy", in: Wallerstein, *The Capitalist World-Economy*, Cambridge: Cambridge University Press.

Wittfogel, Karl August 1929, "Geopolitik, geographischer Materialismus und Marxismus", *Unter dem Banner des Marxismus*, 3.

Wright, Tim 1981, "'A Method of Evading Management' – Contract Labor in Chinese Coal Mines before 1937", *Comparative Studies in Society and History*, 23.

GRAMSCI'S READING OF THE BASE/SUPERSTRUCTURE METAPHOR

Peter D. Thomas

The last 20 years have not been the happiest period in the history of Marxism, either as a political movement or scholarly research programme. While individual scholars working in the Marxist tradition have elaborated significant research programmes (e.g., Harvey, Eagleton, Jameson, Wood), Marxist approaches and methodologies in general have been subjected to sustained critique in the human and social sciences. More importantly, academic Marxist work has only occasionally been able to call upon energies and interlocutors beyond the academy in the way that marked so strongly the preceding period. The social and political struggles of the 1960s and 1970s were accompanied by a growth of interest in radical theoretical perspectives in the academy, among which various currents of Marxism enjoyed a particular pre-eminence, to different degrees in different national cultures. The onset of a long period of retreat for popular causes and the rise of neoliberal hegemony from the late 1970s onwards, however, witnessed a strong reaction against the spirit of the 'Sixties', in the universities just as elsewhere. Many members of the radical intelligentsia began to turn to alternative research paradigms, unencumbered by what were then thought to be irremediable weaknesses in the Marxist tradition. Historical materialism as a scholarly research programme found itself accused of a variety of sins: teleology, totalitarianism, the overweening theoretical pride of a grand narrative, an abstract indifference to the shouts on the street of real history, outmoded modernist prejudices, etc. If a focus upon modes of production and struggles between classes as the ultimately determining instances of social life had established a 'weak' form of hegemony in the preceding period, this new conjuncture witnessed the emergence of more modest narratives, often organized around themes of identity, correspondence or analogy. Their relationship to Marxism's claim to develop not merely an analysis of particular historical periods but a theory of historical development as such remained at best ambivalent; more often, antagonistic. This story of Marxism's most recent fall from grace, in the perspective of overcoming it through the integration of the most rational elements of new perspectives while insisting upon the enduring relevance of the 'hard core' of the historical materialist research programme, is well known from studies by such figures as, among others, Jameson, Eagleton and Callinicos.[476]

As all these studies have stressed, there were fundamentally political determinants behind the transition from Marxism to what came to be known for a period as postmodernism. Stated in a grossly oversimplified (and deliberately polemical) form, it was the transition from the radical hopes of the New Left to the (more or less resigned) acceptance of the new neoliberal status quo. Deprived of the social and political struggles that gives it its *raison d'être*, Marxism could only with difficulty appear as anything but antiquated, a memory of another epoch that could on occasion embarrass the present but was more often disregarded by it. In the midst of imperialist adventures internationally and the continuing down sizing of what remains of the social welfare state in most domestic spheres, it would be premature to declare that this conjuncture has come to a close. Nevertheless, there have been signs for some time now that a fundamental structure of feeling has changed: rebellion against neoliberal policies in both underdeveloped and overdeveloped countries; an anti-war movement that, while failing in its immediate objectives, nevertheless organized the largest day of international protest in world history and indirectly brought about the fall of at least one government; a crisis of legitimacy for the institutions of representative democracy in its heartland, accompanied by deepening frustrations with failed attempts to extend its reach; a 'movement of movements' practically negating the TINA ('There is No Alternative') complex of the 1980s with the slogan 'another world is possible'. If not different answers, then at least different questions seem to be 'blowing in the wind'. It would seem, therefore, that there are new opportunities for re-proposing the relevance and fertility of historical materialism as a scholarly research programme alongside and within these revivified political and social movements. With the return to general currency in scholarly debates of terms such as imperialism, such a process is already well underway.[477] An additional, more directly academic, reason can also be discerned: those currents of thought that proposed to replace historical materialism now find themselves in the position of their former antagonist, (graduate student) heterodoxies transformed into new (institutional) orthodoxies, the latest fashion inevitably going the way of the last when a new one arrives to

476. Cf. Jameson 1991; Eagleton 2003; Callinicos 1991.
477. Cf. Harvey 2003; Meiksins Wood 2003.

contest its dominance. Fragmented and fragmentizing modes of thought are slowly giving way to attempts at a new synthesis. The most notable of these projects to date, Hardt and Negri's *Empire*, has established what will arguably become an influential paradigm for future attempts: on the one hand, the integration of the conceptual and thematic gains of the previous season, drawing in particular upon the more fruitful insights of postmodernism; on the other hand, the inscription of these perspectives within an overarching framework or narrative that, at least at the level of rhetoric, can be identified as more or less 'Marxist'.[478]

In what follows, I want to suggest an alternative way in which the Marxist tradition may be able to make a contribution to a 'cognitive map' (to adopt one of Jameson's key concepts) of contemporary culture and society: namely, not by means of an attempted immediate 'fusion' with other schools of thought, but through a critical re-examination of some of the fundamental concepts of historical materialism itself. In this perspective, I will propose that the work of Antonio Gramsci could provide the basis for an historical materialist interdisciplinary research programme today that is capable of engaging productively in dialogue and debate with other currents, while respecting their (and its own) differences. In particular, I will argue that Gramsci provides fertile tools and concepts for research into the 'macro- or meta-narrative' of modernity and modernization. With the concept of 'passive revolution', Gramsci proposes a particular interpretation of the foundational concepts of historical materialism that both breaks with various 'determinist' deformations of Marx's thought while at the same time insisting upon the integrity of Marxist theory, as a tradition of thought capable of renewal through self-criticism.[479]

478. The success of a work such as *Empire*, a grand totalizing work based upon a (historiosophical) conception of transitions between modes of production (in some senses reminiscent of the stagism of the Second International) if ever there was one, represents merely the tip of the iceberg of more general synthetic disposition or orientation in contemporary intellectual culture. Alternative synthetic approaches have emerged in a wide variety of disciplines, but have perhaps been most strongly registered to date in intellectual and sociopolitical historical writing, as evidenced by the projects of figures such as, for example, David Harvey, Mike Davis and Domenico Losurdo. Cf. Hardt and Negri 2000; for a critique, cf. Turchetto 2003; Harvey 2005; Davis 2006; Losurdo 2005.

479. There have been various attempts over the last 20 years to 'stem the tide' and present a renovated Marxism as a viable academic research programme. 'The moment of Althusser', in Gregory Elliott's felicitous phrase, proposed to do just that in the France of the 1960s and early 1970s, by productively engaging with other traditions of modern French thought. It eventually produced significant reverberations in other cultures, the Anglophone in particular. If we are not 'all Althusserians now', as Elliott acknowledges, it is nevertheless undeni-

Gramsci, of course, is one of the Marxists whose work best weathered the storm of the 80s and 90s. The sheer range of the *Prison Notebooks* – ranging from political economy, history and historiography, literary and cultural criticism, comparative sociology, political theory, linguistics to folklore – coupled with the 'openness' of his elaboration of historical materialism or, in his specific sense, the philosophy of praxis, as an integral and non-reductive conception of the world, gave his thought a wide resonance in a period attuned to the diversity of 'micro-narratives'. If anything, there was an increase in the reception of Gramsci's thought, in the Anglophone world at least, in a broad range of academic disciplines in precisely the same period when other Marxist theorists who had been equally prominent in the prior years of political and social movements found themselves consigned to the dustbin of history.[480] Such popularity, however, arguably came at the cost of the simultaneous diffusion of a depoliticized and sometimes post-Marxist image of Gramsci, which bears little resemblance to the true historical picture of a militant of the early years of the Third International martyred by Fascism.[481] There is further (theoretical) irony to this reputa-

able that Althusserian Marxism inspired a significant part of a generation of scholars to pursue 'the class struggle in theory'. Cf. Elliott 2006. Similarly, the 'moment' of Analytical Marxism that grew from the publication of Cohen (2000), while no longer as vibrant as its early years, remains capable of inspiring attempts to articulate Marxism in new ways as a social theory, sometimes with the contribution of Althusserian perspectives. Cf. Levine 2003. Also drawing together these two strands and adding a critical realist dimension is Callinicos 2006. The proposal to (re)turn to Gramsci in order to outline a Marxism 'for our times' offered in this paper follows these attempts insofar as it suggests that a re-examination of significant moments in the Marxist tradition could offer resources for renewal; it differs from them by consciously limiting the basis for such a re-examination to perspectives from within the Marxist tradition, rather than those drawn from other currents of thought. It therefore aspires to the status of an immanent critique rather than reconstruction, in the sense in which Gramsci insisted that 'the philosophy of praxis' could be, at its best, "'sufficient unto itself'", containing 'all the fundamental elements needed to construct a total and integral conception of the world' (Q 11, 27).

480. Gramsci was a particularly prominent influence on British Marxism in this period. Cf. Forgacs 1989. Above all it was in cultural studies that Gramsci found an Anglophone home, particularly in the work of Stuart Hall. Cf. Hall 1992, p. 281.

481. The seminal text in this regard was Laclau's and Mouffe's *Hegemony and Socialist Strategy*; Cf. Laclau and Mouffe (1985), spawning an entire movement of 'soft' Gramscianisms. As Paggi had emphasised, however, such post-Marxist versions of Gramsci need to ignore the historical record of Gramsci's engagement with the debates of the 4th congress of the Third International, in particular, and their profound impact upon the researches of the *Prison Notebooks*. 'By means of participation in the debates of this international meeting, Gramsci was able for the first time to comprehend the sense and the profound implications ... of the slogan of the United Front' (Paggi 1984, p. 3). This concept and its practice subsequently became Gramsci's final recommendation to the working class movement in the *Prison Notebooks*.

tion, given that, of all the figures of so-called Western Marxism (Lukács, the Frankfurt School, Althusser and other derivatives), Gramsci perhaps remains the closest to what we could call the 'classical' historical material-ism of Marx and Engels. By this, I am not concerned to assert or deny Gramsci's 'orthodoxy'. Rather, of all these thinkers, Gramsci remains in the closest contact with 'canonical' or classical texts of Marx and Engels, such as *The German Ideology*, *The Communist Manifesto* and the 1859 'Preface' to the *Contribution towards the Critique of Political Economy*, upon which various Marxist orthodoxies (and heterodoxies) were subsequently constructed.

This is most evident in the case of the concept on which Gramsci's contemporary fame largely rests: that of hegemony. The particular ver-sion of this concept that Gramsci develops in the *Prison Notebooks*, building upon the pre-revolutionary debates of the Bolsheviks and Lenin's exam-ple in particular, is seen as his primary contribution to political, social and cultural theory.[482] Less noted, however, has been an equally important contribution, upon which his theory of hegemony integrally depends: a reformulation of the unpopular base/superstructure [*Basis/Überbau*] metaphor as a fundamental criterion of what Gramsci calls 'historical-political research' (Q 1, §44).[483] Contrary to a common misperception regarding Gramsci's supposed 'culturalism', he does not simply dispense with this metaphor as irremediably tainted by 'economism' and 'teleol-ogy'. Rather, he goes so far as to call it 'the crucial problem of historical materialism' (Q 4, §38). The *Prison Notebooks*, or at least one important line of research within them, can be regarded as effectively an extended com-mentary on one of the key texts in which Marx outlined the fundamental concepts of what later became 'historical materialism' (a phrase not used by Marx, who, in his early work at least, referred to his own thought as the 'materialist conception of history'): namely, the 1859 'Preface' to the *Contribution towards the Critique of Political Economy*. Alongside the *Theses on Feuerbach*, Gramsci had in fact translated the 'Preface' into Italian in an early phase of his incarceration. Concepts from these two works in par-ticular play an increasingly important role as his project unfolds during

482. Among the best recent studies of Gramsci's concept of hegemony, Peter Ives's *Gramsci's Politics of Language* has the additional merit of emphasizing the integration of 'traditional' Marxist references and insights drawn from Gramsci's university training in linguistics in his concept of hegemony. Cf. Ives 2004.

483. References are given to the Italian critical edition of Gramsci's prison writings: cf. Gramsci 1975. I have adopted the internationally accepted standard of citation in Grams-cian studies, giving the number of notebook (Q), followed by the number of the individual note. Thus, e.g., Q 1, §44, refers to the forty-fourth note of Gramsci's first notebook.

over 6 years of work under atrocious carceral conditions, a project that necessarily remained incomplete.[484]

In the case of the base/superstructure metaphor, this development is decisive, for as his research progresses, Gramsci gradually reformulates it – or rather, returns to its origins in Marx – as a theory not of first causes or ultimate ends, but of the dialectical interaction of different social practices. In so doing, he thus gives the lie simultaneously to a series of interpretative traditions within and outside Marxism: both second International and Stalinist instrumentalizations in the sense of a 'progressivist' ideology, as well as those leftist currents that have condemned the 1859 'Preface' as a residue of the supposed teleology and essentialism of the young Marx, but also attempts to define retrospectively a 'classical' Marxist theoretical model based on interpretations of the notion of a 'mode of production' and different articulations of 'relations of production' and 'productive forces'.[485] Gramsci demonstrates that this difficult metaphor does not have 'an inbuilt tendency to lead the mind towards reductionism' (as one of historical materialism's most able practitioners, E.P. Thompson, once argued), but rather, in at least one version, opens onto political practice as Marxism's Archimedean point.[486]

---

484. It is necessary to enter a caveat regarding the famed fragmentary and elliptical nature of Gramsci's texts, which has all too often been taken as a license to make Gramsci say whatever one wants him to say by cruelly ripping a citation from its context. Context is important when reading Gramsci – his ideas undergo transformation and refinement over the years, as he integrates new elements into his research project and articulates old ones in new ways, to such an extent that it is difficult to define any given position as definitively 'Gramscian' or his final say on the matter. What the *Prison Notebooks* do show, however, are lines of research and tendencies, overdetermined by the fundamental concerns that Gramsci derived from his reading of Marx's two seminal texts. An accurate reading of these texts needs to take into account this 'rhythm of development' of the *Prison Notebooks* considered as an unfinished (and ongoing) research project. C.f. Joseph Buttigieg's excellent introduction to the first volume of the English critical edition of the *Prison Notebooks*; i.e., Gramsci (1992). This complete multi-volume translation of Gerratana's Italian critical edition (with supplementary apparatus by the English language editor) remains incomplete at present. Its completion, scheduled for 2008-9, will make available to the English speaking reader for the first time the entirety of Gramsci's carceral production. It will undoubtedly mark the beginning of a new phase of Gramscian studies, philologically secured, in the Anglophone world.
485. In different ways, both Althusser's and Cohen's attempted reconstructions of Marx focused upon these categories and argued that they represented the hard core of the Marxist research programme, considered in its scientific dimensions. Cf. Althusser and Balibar 1970, particularly pp. 209-224; G.A. Cohen 2000.
486. Cf. Thompson 1979, p. 18. Thompson's position developed in the context of his long-

Against deterministic readings of the 'Preface', Gramsci understands conflicts within the economic structure of society as the 'content' for which the ideologies of the superstructure are the 'forms'. As Guido Liguori has emphasised, Gramsci employs the concept of ideology throughout the *Prison Notebooks* in different senses; nevertheless, his most important and pervasive meaning can be defined as a 'neutral' definition of ideology.[487] Ideology here signifies not falsity as opposed to a truth, but the way in which social groups (and not merely individuals, as the middle Althusser proposed) make sense of their world and construct themselves *as* social groups.[488] It is by means of these ideologies or superstructural forms that the content is comprehended and ratified or – crucially – transformed. It is important to stress this element: for Gramsci, all forms of socially efficacious knowledge, of both classes – and not merely institutionalized ones of the dominant class such as law, 'official' politics and so forth – have a 'superstructural' dimension.[489] In Marx's phrase from the 1859 'Preface' to the *Contribution towards the Critique of Political Economy*, the superstructure is the location of 'the ideological forms in which men become conscious of this conflict [in the economic structure of society] and fight it out'.[490] As both elements mutually determine and condition each other – no content without form, no form without content – Gramsci's reading escapes charges of economistic essentialism; but equally, as the relation of content and form ascribes particular qualities and capacities to each element, Gramsci avoids a reductive relativism that collapses the distinction between them (something that is explicitly done in certain 'discourse' oriented interpretations of the concept of hegemony, for instance).[491] Gramsci names the

term struggle against what he understood as Stalinism and the 'debts of 1956', reaching a crescendo in his influential critique of Althusser (1978). Perry Anderson later provided a nuanced discussion of the theoretical gains and losses of this move in *Arguments within English Marxism* (1980). Cf. for a more nuanced discussion also Palmer 1994.

487. Cf. Liguori 2004, pp. 131-149.

488. One of the definitions of ideology Althusser proposed in his famous ISAs essay is that 'Ideology represents the imaginary relationship of individuals to their real conditions of existence'. For Gramsci on the other hand, ideologies are such only when historically effective and operative in the organisation of a society that extends beyond merely individual ideas. Cf. Althusser, 1971 pp. 127-188.

489. Buci-Glucksmann developed the concept of a 'politico-gnoseological thesis' in order to comprehend this dimension of Gramsci's elaboration of the *Theses on Feuerbach*. Cf. Buci-Glucksmann 1981.

490. Marx and Engels 1975-2005, vol. 29, pp. 261-2.

491. The most detailed reading of Gramsci's different formulations of the base/superstructure metaphor is Cospito 2004, pp. 227-246.

dialectical unity of content and form – of an economic structure and its ratifying superstructure and ideologies – an 'historical block', the process of 'structuration' of a social formation that permits it to endure as that which it is, or to maintain the established state of affairs. Such an 'historical block' is not given as a permanent element, achieved once and for all. Rather, it is actively and continually forged by the 'hegemonic apparatus' of a class – the various institutions and practices by means of which it concretizes its hegemonic project and continues to secure both social and political leadership, that is leadership both in civil society and at the level of the state. Equally, it is by means of the elaboration of a counter-hegemonic apparatus (a term not used by Gramsci himself, however) that another class or alliance of classes comes to contest and ultimately transform a given historical block into another.

This reformulation of the base/superstructure metaphor had a decisive impact upon Gramsci's historiography, helping him to avoid the teleological and sometimes essentialist conceptions of historical progress that characterized the Marxism of many of his contemporaries formed in the late years of the Second International. Gramsci was well aware both of the risks of these 'sins' and also the limitations of these critiques. This was not only because he had himself thoroughly criticized the presence of these themes in certain versions of second International Marxism, but also because one central element of Gramsci's own project was to rebut precisely such critiques as they were purveyed in his own time. Foremost among these was his critique of Benedetto Croce. The importance that Gramsci assigns to Croce throughout the *Prison Notebooks*, not merely as a leading figure of Italian cultural and political life but as a grand intellectual of European and international stature, may appear to the contemporary Anglophone reader to be an arbitrary exaggeration, a projection of provincial concerns onto the world stage. Indeed, throughout the history of the reception of Gramsci's thought, particularly outside of Italy, his self-confessed youthful 'Croceanism' has often been met with puzzlement (if not outright hostility).[492] In the contemporary Anglophone world, Croce is largely remembered, if at all, as the author of the essay 'What is Living and What is Dead in the Philosophy of Hegel', a text that disappoints the interest aroused by its title. In Italy itself, Croce is today more often almost

492. For Perry Anderson, Gramsci's engagement with Croce was the origin of numerous weaknesses in his conception of Marxism, his State theory in particular. Cf. Anderson 1976, pp. 5-79, in particular, p. 39.

ritualistically invoked rather than seriously studied, as either a chief representative of the weakest elements of traditional Italian intellectual culture (its 'historicism', 'humanism', 'idealism', the weak implantation of modern scientific methods, etc.) or champion of a distinctive brand of Italian liberalism. Gramsci's extensive engagement with Croce in the *Prison Notebooks* would appear to have been merely his own idiosyncratic overestimation of the world historic importance of a passing phenomenon, or a concession to his own cultural-intellectual formation.

Yet Gramsci's assessment of Croce was not as wilful or provincial as it may at first sight appear. Croce was one of the major intellectuals of his time, on a European scale, producing major texts in logic, ethics, aesthetics, literary criticism and history, historiography, history, political theory, countless interventions in contemporary culture and politics and even collections of Neapolitan 'folklore'. He founded, with Gentile, *La Critica*, one of the major intellectual journals of the early twentieth century, and with his editorial collaboration with the publishing house Laterza he shaped an 'infrastructure' of Italian culture that arguably remains operative to this day. Neither was Croce's influence confined to the ivory tower, as such prodigious productivity might lead one to suspect; independently wealthy, he in fact never held a university post, coordinating his extramural activities for a significant period from his home base under the shadow of the bell tower of Santa Chiara in Naples. Appointed senator for life in 1910 and involved in planning significant educational reforms as Minister of Public Instruction in 1920-1, he remained officially a member of the state apparatus throughout the fascist period, despite his withdrawal from public life and open opposition to Mussolini's regime (after 1925, when he felt that fascism had outlived its usefulness as a strong hand against the left).

Significantly, Croce was also perhaps the first 'post-Marxist'.[493] Formed in the intellectual environment of the last great flowering of Hegelianism in the Nineteenth century (the current of Italian neo-idealism that emerged following the Risorgimento), the young Croce, under the influence

493. Croce is properly regarded as a post-Marxist *avant la lettre* rather than mere anti-Marxist because he explicitly admitted that Marxism had exerted a decisive impact on him and that he had incorporated its most rational 'residues' in his own thought. Increasingly, particularly after 1917, he took his distance from the school in which he was formed until he eventually could declare that 'from Marxism, properly so called [...] I obtained nothing theoretically, because its value was pragmatic and not scientific, and scientifically, it offered only a pseudo-economics, a pseudo-philosophy and a pseudo-history' (Croce 1968, p. 291).

of his teacher Antonio Labriola, briefly flirted with historical materialism. However, he soon repudiated it and argued it was a not-so-disguised metaphysics, for which the economy functioned as a 'hidden god'. Unlike some of his latter day avatars, Croce was not content to dissolve Marxism into an ultimately teleological narrative of philosophical superannuation, or to replace its 'regional distortions' (economism) by another, equally regional and perhaps more provincial focus (such as, for example, more recent versions of discourse theory). More combatively, he attacked it root and branch, thundering against Marxism's 'dogmatism', its metaphysical disregard for empirical variation and theoretical abstraction, which made it impossible for historical materialism to comprehend the true variety of real history (interesting, this did not, however, prevent Croce from openly admitting to having incorporated the more rational 'residues' of his youthful excesses into his mature practice, as 'canons' of historical research). At stake here was a wide-ranging struggle over the inheritance and 'reform' of Hegelianism, particularly in terms of its systematic philosophical claims. However, given the strongly 'historicist' dimensions of Hegel's thought, conceived not merely as a philosophical system but a representative moment of an entire movement of 'intellectual and moral reform' (which Gramsci argues culminated in Marx and Engels' 'reform' of Hegelianism itself; c.f. Q 4, §3), it necessarily had a direct impact upon Croce's concept of history and historiographical practice.

Croce's alternative to historical materialism's supposed determinism was a conception of history not as the history of class struggle or the rise and fall of modes of production and their corresponding political forms, but as a history of liberty.[494] What this perspective amounted to in concrete terms can be seen in such influential (in their time) works as *A History of Italy 1871-1915* and *A History of Europe in the Nineteenth Century*.[495] As Gramsci wryly noted, for an historian who claimed to have dispensed with metaphysical grand narratives and to have proposed an 'absolute historicism', these works left something to be desired. In each case, they conveniently began by excluding the periods of struggle that founded the periods they sought to comprehend: in the case of Italy, Croce's history begins only after the Risorgimento; in the case of Nineteenth century Europe, after the French Revolution and Napoleonic wars. Having dispensed with such moments of force and dislocation in the forging of a new 'historical block',

494. Croce 1962 and 1921 a work that Gramsci read and criticized closely in prison.
495. Croce, 1963 and 1934.

history could not but appear as the story of a pacifically unfolding and self-realizing liberty, which effectively meant, as Gramsci recognized, writing 'history from above', that is, from the perspective of the State and the class that dominated it. Rather than the 'interest free view of the eternal becoming of human history' (Q 8, §39) that Croce claimed, Gramsci argued that he had instead produced 'a speculative history' (Q 8, §240) that ratified the status quo.[496]

Alongside this moment of negative critique, Gramsci also proposed a positive alternative conception of the history of the 'long nineteenth century'. It is here that we arrive at the concept of 'passive revolution', one of Gramsci's central political concepts (closely tied to that of the famed 'war of position' or 'manoeuvre' cf. Q 15, §11). He develops this concept in relation to his reading of the base/superstructure metaphor of the 'Preface' to the *Introduction to the Critique of Political Economy*, as what he calls its 'necessary critical corollary' (Q 15, §62). As with all of Gramsci's most important and distinctive concepts, it undergoes significant transformations and precisions throughout the *Prison Notebooks*. In the early phases of his research, Gramsci appropriated this concept from Vincenzo Cuoco, the historian of the failed Neapolitan revolution of 1799.[497] He transformed it, in the first instance, in order to provide an analysis of the distinctive features of the Italian *Risorgimento* (Q 1, §44). In this context, the term 'passive revolution' was used to describe the 'historical fact of the absence of popular initiative in the development of Italian history' (Q 8, §25), in particular, the role of the moderates in the Risorgimento in actively preventing popular initiative in an organized political form. With this phrase Gramsci aimed to highlight the lack of the radical-popular 'Jacobin moment' that had distinguished the experience of the French revolution. The formation of the modern Italian nation State, according to Gramsci, had been a 'revolution without revolution', or in other terms, a 'royal conquest' and not a 'popular movement'. It was a transformation of political forms undertaken by elites, garbed in the rhetoric of previous revolutionary movements, but without the extensive involvement of subaltern classes that had led to the placing in question of social and economic relations in earlier transformations.

However, it soon became clear to Gramsci that the concept could have a more general significance as a criterion of historical research into

496. The speculative character of Croce's thought in general, in fact, is one the elements Gramsci most thoroughly criticizes, as contradicting his claims to realism and historical concretion. For the fullest discussion of this theme in English, cf. Finocchiaro 1988.
497. Cuoco 1998, pp. 325-26.

periods and countries that had been similarly lacking in an impetus to modernity 'from below' (Q 4, §57). Thus, in a second extension of the concept, Gramsci used it to describe the *Sonderweg* to modernity taken by other European nation states with experiences similar to those of Italy. Foremost among these was the formation of Bismarckian Germany, similarly characterized by transformations of the political forms of a society that nevertheless failed to place in question their economic contents. Here Gramsci's concept has undergone expansion by means of the identification of substantial similarities between the class-content of these different national experiences, despite their apparent differences. 'Passive revolution', as in the first instance, continues to refer to a specific historical event or ensemble of events.

In yet a third moment, Gramsci asked whether the concept of passive revolution might have a more general validity, as descriptive of an entire historical period in Europe as a whole: roughly, a period he characterized as the 'Restoration' that followed upon the exhaustion of the energies that had driven the French revolution, beginning in 1848 with the defeat of the Europe wide workers' revolts but intensifying after the defeat of the Paris commune and extending to his own day in the form of Fascism. In this version, passive revolution comes to signify the pacifying and incorporating nature assumed by bourgeois hegemony in the epoch of imperialism, particularly in its Western European heartlands but with determinant effects upon the colonial periphery. As Domenico Losurdo has argued, 'Beginning with the defeat of the workers and popular classes in June 1848 and further with that of 1871, a phase of passive revolution begins, identifiable neither with the counterrevolution nor, even less, with the political and ideological fall of the dominant class. The category of passive revolution is a category used in the *Prison Notebooks* in order to denote the persistent capacity of initiative of the bourgeoisie which succeeds, even in the historical phase in which it has ceased to be a properly revolutionary class, to produce sociopolitical transformations, sometimes of significance, conserving securely in its own hands power, initiative and hegemony, and leaving the working classes in their condition of subalternity'.[498] 'Revolution' here still refers to the capacity of the ruling class still to deliver substantive and real historical gains, producing real social transformations that could be comprehended, formally at least, as progressive; 'passive' continues to denote the attempt to produce these transformations without the extensive involvement of subaltern classes as classes, but by means of molecular absorption of their

498. Losurdo 1997, p. 155.

leading elements into an already established hegemonic project. However, 'passive revolution', as a concept, no longer refers primarily to a particular recognizable event. Rather, in this final usage, 'passive revolution' has taken on a more general significance, as a 'logic' of (a certain type) of modernization. In a certain sense, the concept has almost become synonymous with modernity as such, which is now viewed as a melancholy tale in which the mass of humanity is reduced to mere spectators of a history that 'progresses' without its involvement (cf. Q 15, §9).[499]

Why could a concept originally derived from a rather limited national experience – the year 1799 in Naples, in Cuoco's original formulation, a decade or so in Gramsci's analysis of the Risorgimento – be adequate to comprehend European-wide processes, for an entire epoch? Has Gramsci's expansion of this concept led him to promote merely a mirror image of precisely the type of abstract, metaphysical grand narrative to which he had objected so strongly in Croce? Except that rather than a utopian narrative of the onward march of progress and freedom, Gramsci's presents a dystopian vision of modernity as continual degeneration?

Gramsci's response to these doubts, which he himself expressed in later phases of his research, was to return to the concepts of the 1859 'Preface'. He argued, paraphrasing key phrases from Marx's text, that 'the concept of passive revolution needs to be rigorously deduced from two fundamental principles of political science: 1) that no social formation disappears until the productive forces that have been developed in it find a way to make an ulterior progressive movement; 2) that society doesn't pose itself tasks for the solution of which there are not already the necessary conditions' (Q 15, §17). The historical fact of passive revolution, according to one reading of these theses taken on their own, would seem to be proof that the capitalist mode of production that had not yet been superannuated by reaching its own limits – the objective conditions for the emergence of

499. Despite such an expansion of reference (from limited event, to nation state, to Europe as a whole), Gramsci nevertheless insists on gradations and differentiations that prevent the degeneration of this concept into a *passe partout* of the type arguably present in Adorno's and Horkheimer's *Dialectic of Enlightenment* or even Lukács's *Destruction of Reason*. He distinguished between at least two phases of passive revolution on a European scale (not to mention its reverberations in the colonial periphery). In its early phases, the passive revolution proceeded as a cautious, defensive measure, molecularly absorbing leading figures of the subaltern classes and oppositional social movements into a consolidating state apparatus and its 'representative' organs in civil society. Confidence slowly returning to the ruling class and the new institutions hardening into durable forms, entire organizations were subsequently integrated (cf. Q 8, §36).

an alternative mode of production, such as socialism, would then appear to be 'unripe'. Yet immediately following these lines, Gramsci insisted that 'One must understand that these principles first need to be developed critically in all of their significance and cleansed of any residue of mechanism and fatalism' (ibid.).

As he went on to argue, nothing had been pre-determined in the adoption of the 'passive revolution' as a hegemonic strategy of a now moribund bourgeoisie, striving to maintain the 'historical block', the fusion of economic structure and ideological superstructure, it had forged in its previously revolutionary phase. There were indeed objective conditions, common to all the European capitalist societies, that had led to its emergence at around the same time: namely, the threat of militant working class movements demanding that the continual revolutionizing of the mode of production and the new forms of collective social life in modernity – in the labour process, in urbanization and so forth – were extended to include substantial equality at the level of the economic structure of the society. However, passive revolution had not been necessitated by this economic structure or inscribed in modernity as its telos. Rather, its successful imposition had involved conscious, political choices: on the one hand, the choice of the ruling classes to develop strategies to disaggregate those working classes and confine them to an economic-corporative level within the existing society; on the other, the political choices of the subaltern classes that had resulted in a failure to elaborate their own hegemonic apparatuses capable of resisting the absorptive logic of the passive revolution. In other words, the working classes – for different reasons in different countries, but with the same result – had not been able to socialize the ideological forms that corresponded to their own experiences of the conflicts within the economic structure of bourgeois society and thus lay the foundations for transforming it. They had remained subaltern to the superstructural elements of the existing 'historical block', unable to find 'a way to make an ulterior progressive movement'. Modernity had indeed become a 'history of (bourgeois) freedom'.

Therefore, rather than emphasising 'structure' – to use a more recent terminology – Gramsci's alternative history from below ultimately places the accent upon 'agency', or more precisely, it analyses the formation of determining structures through the activity of determinate social actors. How could the rigorous deduction of the concept of passive revolution from 'two fundamental principles of political science' that have often been read in a deterministic way have resulted in such a seemingly 'voluntaristic' valorisation? Marx's precise formulations read as follows: 'No social order is ever destroyed before all the productive forces for which it is sufficient have been developed, and new superior relations of production never replace older ones before the material conditions for their existence have matured within the framework of the old society'.Mankind thus inevitably sets itself only such tasks as it is able to solve, since closer examination will always show that the problem itself arises only when the material conditions for its solution are already present or at least in the course of formation'.[500] As we have seen, Gramsci reproduces these lines almost verbatim, before adding that these perspectives first need 'to be developed critically in all of their significance and cleansed of any residue of mechanism and fatalism' (Q 15, §17), if they are to be made adequate for the 'deduction' of the concept of passive revolution. Why does Gramsci feel the need to make this addition, and on what basis does he claim that this represents a critical development of Marx's propositions?

Here Gramsci is implicitly referring to one of the other texts by Marx that he translated alongside the 'Preface', namely, the *Theses on Feuerbach*.[501] Specifically, he is referring to the break enacted in these notes with both idealism and previous versions of materialism by means of an emphasis upon 'the significance of 'revolutionary', of 'practical-critical', activity' (1st thesis) and Marx's proposition that 'the coincidence of the changing of circumstances and of human activity or self-change [*Selbstveränderung*] can be conceived and rationally understood only as *revolutionary practice*' (3rd thesis).

In other words, Gramsci is here appropriating the orientation towards praxis, and therefore towards the active role of human agency, in one of Marx's texts and using it in order to read the orientation towards social determinations, or 'structures', in another, which then permits him to appropriate this latter text and integrate it with his independently developed new concept of passive revolution. This is not a case of one Marx opposed to an other Marx (youthful 'humanist' vs. mature 'economist', as both Althusser and Thompson proposed, in different ways); rather, it is a question of reading the 'Preface' as itself an instance of 'revolutionary practice', that is, not a 'question of theory', but a 'practical question' (2nd thesis),

500. Marx and Engels 1975-2005, vol. 29, pp. 261-2.
501. Marx and Engels 1975-2005, vol. 5, p. 3. Giuseppe Cospito provides a sophisticated analysis of Gramsci's integration of themes from both of Marx's texts, with particular emphasis upon the significance of this operation for his formulation of the base/superstructure metaphor as a 'unity in distinction' cf. Cospito 2004, pp. 227-246.

specific analyses undertaken in a determinate period as a contribution to the workers' movement's comprehension of the 'structural' challenges it faced. Gramsci was thus able to give due weight to two constitutive dimensions of the Marxist tradition that are not always easily articulated: on the one hand, the critique of political economy, or those elements that tend towards a 'science' of the capitalist mode of production; and on the other hand, a political theory of the working class movement, or what Gramsci famously described as the philosophy of praxis's status as a 'conception of the world'. The former *describes* the conditions confronted by the latter; but ultimately, Gramsci insists, it is only the latter that can *explain and justify* the former, in both theoretical and practical forms.

It was in this perspective, finally, that Gramsci was able to judge Croce's historiography not only as tendentious and partisan, but also, crucially, as an *effect* of the passive revolution, or rather, an active contribution to it. For Croce, 'history of freedom' in fact merely provided a speculative description of the existing state of affairs, without being able to reveal its determining mechanisms. Viewed from a perspective that excluded the moments of struggle in which the economic and political structures were forged and modified, the history of (European) modernity did indeed seem to be one of tranquil development and pacific integration (Q 10, §1, n.9). Because Croce had posited the idea of liberty as the telos of modern history, events that contradicted it, such as Fascism, could only be explained as, strictly speaking, irrational and unhistorical. For Gramsci, on the other hand, Fascism, as one of the extreme forms of the passive revolution, its 'actual' form in his time (cf. Q 8, §236), was entirely comprehensible, as one of the historical possibilities that arose on the basis of a given economic structure of society, within determinant relations of forces between classes. Equally comprehensible for Gramsci, of course, even from his Fascist jail cell, remained the possibility of a revolution of a very different type. Acknowledging this, however, depended upon the re-introduction of the political moment, both theoretically and practically, that would allow a genuinely historical narrative to *explain*, rather merely *describe*, both the causes and effects of this development and integration.

The full development of Gramsci's concept of passive revolution thus provides an example of the capacity of the Marxist tradition for both productive engagement with non-Marxist thought and critical self-renewal. Both moments are integrated in Gramsci's dialectical analysis. Initially appropriating the concept of passive revolution from outside the Marxist tradition, he then deployed it for the study of concrete historical case studies, testing and modifying it in accordance with the findings of his research; in a third moment, he measured his new concept against theoretical criteria of the critique of political economy that were foundational for the materialist conception of history; and in a final move, he supplemented these criteria with another, equally foundational concept of praxis, as their 'necessary critical corollary' (Q 15, §62), or as a 'lens' that allowed them to be read in a new and politically enabling way. Marx's texts and therefore the Marxist tradition that derives from them are thus subjected to an act of immanent critique. Perhaps more importantly, by returning to the concept of praxis as the self-critique of Marxism itself, Gramsci proposes a conception of Marxism that is neither an attempted synthesis of competing doctrines nor one theory ranged alongside others. Rather, Gramsci's vision of Marxism insists upon its constitution as a political moment capable of explaining the historical emergence of all 'ideologies', including itself. It is precisely in that sense, in terms of making the possibilities for social and political transformation that are immanent to existing forms of thought comprehensible, that an historical materialist interdisciplinary research programme still perhaps has a contribution to make today.

REFERENCES

Althusser, Louis 1971, 'Ideology and Ideological State Apparatuses' in *Lenin and Philosophy and Other Essays*, NLB: London.
Althusser, Louis and Balibar, Étienne 1970, *Reading Capital*, London: NLB.
Anderson, Perry 1976, 'The Antinomies of Antonio Gramsci' in *New Left Review* 100.
Anderson, Perry 1980, *Arguments within English Marxism*, London: Verso.
Buci-Glucksmann, Christine 1981, *Gramsci and the State*, London: Lawrence and Wishart.
Callincos, Alex 2006, *Resources of Hope*, Cambridge: Polity Press.
Callinicos, Alex 1991, *Against Postmodernism: A Marxist Critique*, Cambridge: Polity.
Cohen, G.A. 2000, *Karl Marx's Theory of History: A Defence*, Oxford: Oxford University Press.
Cospito, Giuseppe 2004, 'Struttura-superstruttura', in Fabio Frosini and Guido Liguori, *Le parole di Gramsci: per un lessico dei "Quaderni del carcere"*,

Rome: Carocci.

Cospito, Giuseppe 2004, 'Struttura-superstruttura' in Fabio Frosini and Giudo Liguori, *Le parole di Gramsci: per un lessico dei Quaderni del carcere'*, Rome: Carocci.

Croce, Benedetto 1921, *Theory and History of Historiography*, London: George G. Harrap & Co.

Croce, Benedetto 1934, *History of Europe in the Nineteenth Century*, London: Allen & Unwin.

Croce, Benedetto 1962, *History as the Story of Liberty*, London: Allen & Unwin.

Croce, Benedetto 1963, *A History of Italy 1871-1915*, New York: Russell & Russell.

Croce, Benedetto 1968, 'Come nacque e come mori il marxismo teorico in Italia (1895-1900). Da lettere e ricordi personali', in *Materialismo storico ed economia marxistica*, Bari: Laterza.

Cuoco, Vincenzo 1998, *Saggio storico sulla rivoluzione di Napoli*, critical edition by A. De Francesco, Bari: Lacaita.

Davis, Mike 2006, *Planet of Slums*, London: Verso, 2006.

Eagleton, Terry 2003, *After Theory*, New York: Basic Books.

Elliott, Gregory 2006, *Althusser: the Detour of Theory*, Leiden: Brill.

Finocchiaro, M.A. 1988, *Gramsci and the History of Dialectical* Thought, Cambridge, Mass.: CUP.

Forgacs, David 1989, 'Gramsci and Marxism in Britain,' *New Left Review* 176 (July-August)

Gramsci, Antonio 1975, *Quaderni del carcere*, ed. Valentino Gerratana, Rome: Einaudi.

Gramsci, Antonio 1992, *Prison Notebooks Vol. 1*, tr. Joseph A. Buttigeig and Antonio Callari, New York, Columbia UP.

Hall, Stuart 1992, 'Cultural Studies and its Theoretical Legacies', in L. Grossberg, C. Nelson and P. Treichler (eds.), *Cultural Studies*, New York: Routledge.

Hardt, Michael and Negri, Antonio, *Empire*, Cambridge, Mass.: Harvard University Press.

Harvey, David 2003, *The New Imperialism*, Oxford; Oxford University Press.

Harvey, David 2005, *A Brief History of Neoliberalism*, Oxford; OUP.

Ives, Peter 2004, *Gramsci's Politics of Language: Engaging the Bakhtin Circle and the Frankfurt School*, Toronto: University of Toronto Press.

Jameson, Fredric 1991, *Postmodernism, or, The Cultural Logic of Late Capitalism*, Durham, N.C.: Duke University Press.

Laclau, Ernesto and Mouffe, Chantal 1985, *Hegemony and Socialist Strategy: Towards a Radical Democratic Politics*, London: Verso.

Levine, Andrew 2003, *A Future for Marxism? Althusser, the Analytical Turn and the Revival of Socialist Theory*, London: Pluto Press.

Liguori, Guido 2004, 'Ideologia', in Guido Liguori and Fabio Frosini, *Le parole di Gramsci: per un lessico dei "Quaderni del carcere"*, Rome: Carocci.

Losurdo, Domenico 2005, *Controstoria del liberalism*, Rome: Laterza.

Losurdo, Domenico, 1997, *Antonio Gramsci: dal liberalismo al "comunismo critico"*, Rome: Gamberetti.

Marx, Karl and Engels, Frederich 1975-2005, *Marx Engels Collected Works*, London: Lawrence and Wishart.

Meiksins Wood, Ellen 2003, *Empire of Capital*, London; Verso.

Paggi, Leonardo 1984, *Le strategie del potere in Gramsci: tra fascismo e socialismo in un solo paese 1923-1926*, Rome: Riuniti, 1984.

Palmer, Bryan 1994, *E.P. Thompson: Objections and Oppositions*, London: Verso.

Thompson, E. P. 1978, *The Poverty of Theory and Other Essays*, London: Merlin Press.

Thompson, E. P. 1979, 'Folklore, Anthropology and Social History', Brighton: Studies in Labour History.

Turchetto, Maria 2003, 'The Empire Strikes Back: On Hardt and Negri', *Historical Materialism* 11.1.

FEMINIST AND
QUEER MARXISMS

'WORKERS OF THE WORLD, WHO WASHES YOUR SOCKS?'

Second wave feminist critiques of Marxism in Italy, France and Yugoslavia

Chiara Bonfiglioli

> *Men, women's liberation*
> *Will let you drown*
> *Under your pile of soil*
> *Beware!*[502]

The slogan 'Workers of the world, who washes your socks?' seems to have its origin in the French feminist movement (*Travailleurs de tous les pays, qui lave vos chaussettes?*) and expresses the main critique addressed by neo-feminist movements to Marxist theory and communist organisations in the period that followed May 1968.[503] Feminist critiques argued that most of Marxist analyses 'absorbed feminism into class struggle', and treated women's oppression as 'another aspect of class oppression', without recognizing its specificities.[504] This slogan also expresses the fact that while workers organised collectively and fought against their exploitation on the labour market, women were left to cope individually with everyday domestic work and with other forms of exploitation in the private sphere. This slogan echoes a phrase by Engels that was also popularised as a feminist slogan: 'Within

---

502. ("UOMINI LA LIBERAZIONE DELLE DONNE VI LASCERA' AFFOGARE SOTTO IL VOSTRO MUCCHIO DI LORDURA FATE ATTENZIONE!") from a leaflet of Movimento Femminista Romano, quoted in Frabotta 1973, p.164.
503. This is a very general reconstruction. Therefore, I do not deal here with distinctions between radical, socialist, and liberal feminism, nor with the specificities of feminist movements in each of the country taken into consideration (Italy, France, SFRY). The political stances taken into account in this paper range from Marxist and socialist feminism to radical feminism, even if these categories seem to me too limited in respect to the multiple references to Marxist theory that were to be found within different strands of feminist thought in the 1970s.
504. Hartmann 1981, pp. 97-99.

the family he – the man – is the bourgeois and the wife represents the proletariat'.[505]

In this paper I will briefly introduce the theme of the 'Woman Question' in Marxist texts. Next, I will look at the way in which Marxist texts influenced the practices of communist parties and organisations in Western and South-Eastern Europe in terms of 'women-friendly' policies or 'state feminism'. I will then explore second wave feminist critiques of Marxism within capitalist and socialist countries, taking as a case study the international feminist conference 'Comrade Woman. The Woman Question: A New Approach?', held in Belgrade in 1978. I will refer in particular to the Italian, French and Yugoslav context in the 1970s.

The 'Woman Question' in Marxist texts and in practice

A text has been foundational for the way in which international socialist movements and parties had envisioned women's emancipation from the end of the 19th century onwards. *The Origins of the Family, Private Property and the State* was published by Engels in 1884, elaborating the late Marx's notes on an anthropological essay, Morgan's *Ancient Society* (1877). Following Morgan, Engels argues that the organisation of the family in so-called primitive societies was radically different from its form in the industrialised world, with matriarchy and common ownership being gradually replaced by patriarchy and private property. Engels sees the patriarchal monogamic family as a product of the capitalist order, and as a means to transmit and maintain private property. This reversal in the 'division of labour within the family' – because of the primacy of 'social productive labour' and not of domestic labour in a context of industrialisation – caused the devaluation of women's status, connected to the recent lack of importance of domestic labour. According to Engels, woman can thus become 'the equal of man' by 'taking part in production on a large, social scale' and by the reduction of the time required for domestic work to an 'insignificant amount'.

This will be facilitated by 'modern large-scale industry', which demands women's participation, and whose technical advances make it possible to end private domestic labor by turning it into 'a public industry'.[506] We find here some of the major ideas sustaining policies towards women implemented by communist organisations both in Western and Eastern Europe: women's emancipation is to be reached through legal equality and

505. Engels 1884.
506. Engels 1884.

318

entrance into the realm of production, as well as via the socialisation of domestic labor and childcare. Engels' fundamental thesis that 'the family is not static but reacts to changes in the way people earn their livelihood'[507] had a very important impact on anthropological and political studies of the family, and was also very radical in a political sense, as it contested the structure of the family and argued that this structure could be changed. At the same time, the literal application of these theories 'encouraged the belief that women would be 'returned' to a position of equality by the destruction of the private property system' and presupposed 'a direct and simple connection between economic change and a crucial reversal of woman's position'.[508]

Within the German Social Democratic party, Auguste Bebel and Clara Zetkin played a leading role in putting women's emancipation on the socialist agenda. Bebel's *Woman Under Socialism*, published illegally in 1879, and revised until 1909, was extremely popular, and became 'the handbook for several generations of socialists and Communists before and after the First World War.'[509] Bebel's book, utopian in tone, elaborates Engels's insights from an historical perspective. Following Engels's position, Bebel takes an empirical stance and acknowledges the advent of women's equality through the inevitable access to the labor market, while supporting protective measures against exploitation that causes the disruption of 'the family life of the working class'.[510] Clara Zetkin, who started her militancy within German Social Democracy at the end of the 19th century, dedicated her life to winning working-class women for socialism. After the October Revolution, she was appointed as the head of the International Women's Secretariat of the Comintern from 1924. There she promoted a program assuring legal rights, marriage reform, struggle against illiteracy, protection of mothers, socialised domestic work and childcare, and protective working legislation. The latter followed the example of the Soviet *Zhenotdel*, the Women's Section of the Central Committee of the Communist Party of the Soviet Union founded by Alexandra Kollontai in 1919. While incessantly raising the 'Woman Question' within the party and within the international socialist movement, both Kollontai and Zetkin were nevertheless opposed to women's suffragist or-

507. Scott 1976, p. 28.
508. Scott 1976, p.42.
509. Scott 1976, p.57.
510. See Bebel 1879.

ganisations, seen as an expression of counter-revolutionary and 'bourgeois' interests. This division between 'bourgeois feminism' and women's socialist organisations would prove to be a long-lasting historical legacy, influencing the narratives and the practices of Eastern European socialist regimes in the Cold War period.[511]

The main socialist guidelines on the 'Woman Question' had been drawn between the end of the 19th century and the Russian Revolution, and were connected to working class struggles and revolutions.[512] However, since the late 1920s and during the 1930s Stalinism put an end to 'creative Marxist thinking' on this issue.[513] In the Soviet Union, the increasingly difficult economic context and political dogmatism combined to strengthen the socialist family in a conservative sense, while the rise of pro-natalist and Fascist regimes in Europe had a profoundly reactionary impact on gender roles.

The Second World War modified these configurations: communist parties and movements in Eastern and Western Europe acquired a great political legitimation in their struggle against Nazi-fascism. In Eastern and South-Eastern Europe, all the new communist regimes faced a similar task of post-war reconstruction and mass mobilisation, in countries that were mainly agricultural and where the majority of the population, and women in particular, were illiterate, with big differences between rural and urban areas. The entry of women in the labour market in the late 30s and during the war period was accompanied by legislation that enhanced rights and favoured participation, starting with women's right to vote.

In Eastern and South-Eastern Europe, new values and norms were imposed, but were also interiorised among male and female citizens, due to the access of a formerly uneducated population to education and cultural facilities, universal social and medical care, full employment in the administration and political bureaucracy, low-cost housing, progressive family law and so on. At the same time, this resulted in women's characteristic 'double burden' (domestic work at home and paid work outside the home). The family as an institution – and gender and sexual roles within the family - were only rarely questioned.

511. Scott 1976, pp.58-71. On the resilience of the concept of 'bourgeois feminism', elaborated during the Second International, see also Psarra, 2007, pp.207-213.
512. For the important debates on the status of women and on the family that took place during the 1917 Revolution and afterwards, see the writings of Alexandra Kollontai. For an overview of the relations between socialist and feminist movements in Europe between the two World Wars, see Gruber and Graves 1998.
513. Scott 1976, p.69.

The political control exercised by socialist regimes also limited the range of possible debates, with different degrees of coercion and censorship according to the various national contexts. Official socialist organisations that were in charge of implementing policies on the 'Woman Question' in Eastern Europe left very little space for autonomous initiatives and discourses, which were immediately defined as 'bourgeois' whenever they deviated from the party line. Even in Yugoslavia, where political control was less severe than in the Soviet bloc, important women's movements such as the Anti-Fascist Women's Front in Yugoslavia were dissolved in the 1950s, with the argument that women's status should not be treated as a separate question from class and labour.[514]

Feminist critiques of 'state feminism' and 'emancipationism'

The assessment of 'women-friendly' policies promoted by socialist systems in Eastern and South-Eastern Europe, as well as the relationship between feminist and communist ideas and practices are still matters of contemporary debate. The feminist journal *Aspasia* recently hosted a forum titled: 'Is 'Communist Feminism' a *Contradictio in Terminis?*' There Mihaela Miroiu provocatively argues that we should rather talk of 'state patriarchy' than of 'state feminism'. The communist system, she contends, never promoted women's autonomy as such, but rather adopted the discourse of women's emancipation opportunistically.[515] Other authors respond with a more nuanced stance, stressing the need to contextualise and historicise abstract categories such as 'communism' and 'feminism'.

According to Natalia Novikova, 'feminism appears as an umbrella term for a variety of ideologies and strategies aimed at women's individual freedom and liberty of choice, and national histories vividly show that women saw different, sometimes conflicting ways to gain their autonomy'.[516] Krassimira Daskalova prefers to speak of 'state socialism' rather than "communism", to stress the fact that the ideal communist state was never achieved.[517] She rejects binary thinking that would depict state socialist countries as 'unfree' and Western democracies as 'free' places without state patriarchy. She points out of the absence of women's rights in Eastern

---

514. For a more extensive discussion of this subject and for further references see Bonfiglioli 2008.
515. Miroiu 2007, pp.197-201.
516. Novikova 2007, pp.202-06.
517. For recent discussions on the idea of communism, see Badiou et al. 2010.

Europe prior to 1945. 'Women-friendly' policies and 'state patriarchy' in socialist systems should instead be investigated, Daskalova argues, through cross-cultural and transnational historical comparisons, in order to avoid stigmatising of state socialism per se.[518]

Even more challenging are Harriet Evans' questions, based on her fieldwork in China. She underlines that feminism and communism are 'contested concepts' and asks:

'Do we accept that there is a multiplicity of feminisms, defined in different and shifting cultural, social and political spaces, and that do not correspond with the epistemological understandings of the individual embedded in the European origins of Western feminism? And how do we fit the commitments and self-identifications of women who spend their lives working to empower women in diverse fields of practice, but who reject feminism as an ideological agenda alien to their own cultural and political agenda'?[519]

The debate hosted by *Aspasia* indeed shows, in the words of Angelika Psarra, that 'it is worth investigating the changing relations between communism and feminism, in shifting political and social contexts'.[520]

In 1970s Western Europe, the rhetoric on the 'Woman Question' employed by communist parties was surprisingly similar to that of their homologues in Eastern Europe, apart from the fact that Western European communist parties were oppositional parties and weren't exercising state power through one-party systems. Women's emancipation was related primarily to the possibility of entering the labour market, to the defence of working mothers and of motherhood as a social value, as well as to alphabetisation and legislative equality. However, each political context had its specificities, and for instance in Italy the Communist Party in the 1970s still had a very moderate position on divorce and abortion, as it was searching to establish a compromise with the Christian-Democrats.[521] The gendered structure of the family was also rarely questioned, and neither was the division of labour within the family.

Second wave feminist movements and groups that emerged after 1968 and in the early 1970s often criticized the contradictory stance of communist leaders themselves, and pointed out the fact that the leaders eas

518. Daskalova 2007, pp. 214-19.
519. Evans 2007, p.222.
520. Psarra 2007, p.207.
521. Caldwell 1978.

322

ily forgot their revolutionary standpoint when dealing with women's issues. In France, feminist Marxist scholar Christine Delphy linked Lenin's revolutionary recommendations (*'The real emancipation of women, real communism, will begin only where and when an allout struggle begins (led by the proletariat wielding state power) against this petty housekeeping, or rather when its wholesale transformation into a largescale socialist economy begins'*) with the PCF's call to 'make domestic appliances available for all households which can lead to the mechanisation of domestic labour' in order to 'enable the working woman to fulfil her role as mother of a family'.[522]

The French and Italian feminist movements were often constituted by women who inhabited different political spaces and identities. In Italy the term 'double militancy' (*doppia militanza*) was coined: it referred to women's multiple political engagements: in the communist party, in the 'extra-parliamentary' radical left, and in feminist groups.[523] At the time clear generational divides appeared between women who were members of the UDI (Unione Donne Italiane, the women's organisation affiliated to the PCI) and the new wave of women engaged in students', workers' and extra-parliamentary movements after 1968. Younger women had directly experienced the subordination of women's problems to more urgent, more revolutionary matters.

The experience of double militancy often shed light on the double moral standards that were present within leftist groups, where male comrades often used the rhetoric of sexual liberation to impose their choices and desires on female comrades. Women rebelled against this subaltern role, refusing to be the 'angels of the stencil printer' (*angeli del ciclostile*). Like other political groups within the New Left, however, radical feminists rejected the reformist policies praised by communist parties and communist women's organisations and stressed the need for revolutionary struggle.[524]

On the 8th of March 1972 in Rome women marched under the banner: 'There is no revolution without women's liberation, there's no women's liberation without revolution'.[525] Second wave feminist groups preferred the term 'women's *liberation*' to 'women's *emancipation*', used by left-wing parties and organisations.[526] The emancipationist perspective of the

522. Delphy 1984, p. 73.
523. Slaughter 2007, pp. 236-40.
524. For an excellent overview of the Italian feminist movement in the 1970s, see Vandelac 1978. See also: Frabotta 1973; Bono and Kemp 1991; Chiavola Birnbaum 1986.
525. Frabotta 1973, p. 14.
526. See Chiavola Birnbaum 1986.

PCI and UDI was read as an attempt to integrate women in an all-male system, without criticising the mechanisms that reproduced this same system. The PCI and UDI reformist stance, according to feminist groups, led to the eternal postponement of women's needs and desires. *Liberation*, instead, signified the need for an immediate process of consciousness raising, in order to deconstruct internalised structures of oppression.

Women-only consciousness-raising groups (*gruppi di autocoscienza*) became a collective space where women would share personal experiences, practicing the idea of 'starting from one's self'" (*partire da sé*) in order to transform society as a whole. The Italian feminist movement – formed by a myriad of groups and collectives – therefore adopted a stance of *autonomy* in relation to other political forces. The issues of health, the body and sexuality, violence against women, and the critique of the private sphere coexisted with practices of visibility in the public sphere, developed in the course of the long battle for divorce and abortion rights.[527]

The 1978 Belgrade meeting between Yugoslav and Western European feminists

Within the socialist Federation of Yugoslavia, second wave feminists started to formulate their ideas explicitly in the late 1970s, after more than a decade of student and dissident movements. These movements denounced the gap between revolutionary discourses and lived realities, criticizing the 'red bourgeoisie' who had seized power in 1945 and who had grown more and more bureaucratic and distant from socialist ideals. This position was developed particularly by humanist Marxist philosophers who gathered around the internationally renowned journal, *Praxis*.[528] The Yugoslav system, being more open than other socialist regimes of Eastern Europe, allowed the so-called democratic 'struggle of opinions', as long as the official socialist discourse was not contested openly. This included the theme of women's emancipation, with the difference that the question was considered to be even more resolved than the issues of revolution and socialism.

527. See Vandelac 1978.
528. The *Praxis* school started a critique of the Yugoslav system from a Marxist perspective, arguing for instance that self-management tended to be implemented from above and not reflected upon, that workers' alienation had not been eliminated, and that the increased decentralisation of economic resources towards the republics favoured the interests of a new middle class of bureaucrats. 'Socialism is propagated, popularly explained, and its faithful gather in the newspaper columns, but no one thinks about it, since it has long ago been proclaimed as being beyond doubt', wrote Milan Miric in *Praxis* n.43-4, 1971. Quoted in Sher 1977, p.187.

324

The main official organisation – the Conference for the Social Activity of Women – was often composed of former Partisan women who had been engaged in the Women's Alliance or the Anti-Fascist Women's Front, and had later become official representatives of the party line.[529]

During the 1960s and 1970s, nonetheless, Yugoslavia's self-management, Non-Alignment and open border policy made the country a meeting point for different artistic, political and intellectual avant-gardes, contributing to the circulation of international feminist texts and ideas. Neo-feminist texts from Western Europe and the United States circulated among Yugoslav women who had travelled abroad and who had participated in student and dissident movements. These texts resounded with their everyday experiences of patriarchy and women's subordination, even within leftist dissident circles. Inspired by this atmosphere, a group of women – mostly young academics, journalists and artists from Belgrade, Zagreb and Sarajevo – decided to organise an international feminist meeting at the Belgrade Students' Cultural Center (SKC). They aimed to gather firsthand information on Western European feminist movements, and to raise awareness of the issue of women's social inequality in Yugoslavia, in defiance of the official discourse that stated that women's parity had already been reached through legal rights and the entrance into the labour market. [530]

The fundamental difference between Western Europe and Yugoslavia, however, was that the official socialist discourse about the accomplished revolution limited and constrained the discursive range of possible political interventions.[531] During the international feminist meeting held in Belgrade in October 1978 and significantly titled 'Comrade Woman. The Woman Question: A New Approach?', Yugoslav and Western European participants articulated very different political and theoretical positions, even if all of them were criticising Marxist theory from a feminist standpoint.[532] In their introductory document, Yugoslav feminists developed a critique of the socialist system without completely dismissing the legal and material achievements brought by socialism. Patriarchy was depicted as an anachronism, as a remnant of bourgeois morality. In this way, the feminist critique was legitimated in Marxist terms, showing that the 'woman's ques-

---

529. See Jancar-Webster 1990.
530. See Bonfiglioli 2008.
531. For a discussion on official socialist narratives and feminist history in Yugoslavia, see Sklevicky 1989.
532. For a reconstruction of the discussions taking place during the 1978 conference, see Bonfiglioli 2008.

tion' hadn't been solved despite the 'victory of the socialist revolution'. The argument with which the organisers founded a feminist reflection on Yugoslav society could thus be summarized as follows: feminist movements and theories have a universal progressive value as an attempt to struggle against human alienation. If society wants to live up to its socialist premises, it cannot ignore this struggle without being irremediably caught in contradiction.[533]

This internal critique of the Yugoslav system – feminist but not anti-socialist – is a very specific one, and can also be explained by the fact that socialist ideology was far more popular and open to critique in Yugoslavia than in Eastern Europe. This was the major point of cultural and political difference between the Yugoslav and the international participants. Western European feminists – closer to radical feminism, psychoanalysis and theories of sexual difference and having elaborated their analyses for almost a decade – were very doubtful about communist parties' ability to enforce women's emancipation through state intervention and without democratic participation. Moreover, Yugoslavia was seen as another country 'behind the Iron Curtain', so that Yugoslav feminists, although dissident in their own context, were mistaken as representative of the official party line.

Carla Ravaioli – an Italian journalist who had worked on the 'Woman Question' within the PCI[534] – prepared a long report once she came back from Belgrade. She wrote at the time that Yugoslav analyses appeared to be 'based on the old emancipationist line: work, laws, services, social integration, political participation, construction of socialism' and so on. The interventions of the women coming from abroad dealt instead with 'oppressing machismo, expropriated sexuality, symbolical elaboration, unconscious, daily life, autonomy, materialist theory that has to be constructed starting from the body'. These interventions, thus, sounded like 'voices from another planet, or even as provocations.'[535]

This profound difference in political languages led to a deep tension at the end of the second day, and to polemical exchanges. Carla Ravaioli

---

533. See the original preparatory brochure to the Belgrade conference contained in the Appendix, ibidem. For similar Marxist humanist arguments in the Italian context, see the positions developed by the PCI, UDI and Il Manifesto in the early 1970s, and in particular the documents collected in Castellina 1974. 'Marxism is thus total revolution, foundation of a different society and therefore of a different relationship between man and woman, man and man, parents and sons, man and society.' Castellina 1974, p. 36.
534. Ravaioli 1976.
535. Ravaioli 1978.

reported that after a series of interventions by foreign guests one of the Yugoslav organisers exclaimed: 'Don't come here to give us lessons, what do you know of our reality?' To this Western European feminists replied: 'If you keep on talking of economic development and self-management, you will get nowhere'.[536] Italian and French reports on the Belgrade conference underlined the reciprocal misunderstandings and the feeling of displacement experienced by Western European guests. Christine Delphy explained this by acknowledging that the tools for feminist struggle were necessarily different in a society where revolution had been declared as accomplished and women's emancipation as realised. Delphy thus arrived at the following question: 'how to struggle against a system when women's liberation is part of its principles?'[537]

While Italian and French feminist movements were building their mass campaigns on themes such as divorce, abortion, and the right to health, in Yugoslavia all these rights existed already, or at least middle class women living in urban areas took them for granted, although the situation was very different in rural areas and in poorer regions. In the presence of a hegemonic discourse that stated that women's emancipation had been already granted, which portrayed neo-feminism as "bourgeois" or imported from the West, and in the absence of major social conflicts, the conditions for the development of a wide feminist movement were unfavorable.

In this difficult context, feminists such as Zarana Paric, Lydia Sklevicky, Blaženka Despot, Slavenka Drakulic, Vesna Kesic and Rada Ivekovic started to unravel the internal contradictions and patriarchal structures of the socialist system, introducing their ideas to the mainstream through academic essays, novels, art, and the media. Grassroots feminist movements grew only in the following decades in Yugoslavia, particularly in the late 1980s and during the wars of the 1990s, when they were connected to anti-war and anti-nationalist movements. The second wave or neo-feminist generation of the 1970s, however, played a fundamental role within these movements and laid the basis for an in-depth critique of nationalism, ethnicization and wartime gendered violence.[538]

With these examples in mind, I have attempted to highlight the specificity, complexity and multiplicity of feminist theories and practices in

536. Ibidem.
537. Delphy 1979.
538. For an introduction to the subject of feminist ideas in South-Eastern Europe, see Blagojevic, Kolozova, and Slapsak 2006. See also Pejic 2009.

different historical and political contexts, and in relation to contextual political articulations and hegemonic discourses. I have tried to trace the debt of second wave feminist critique towards Marxist analyses, showing that Marxist theories and practices both constrained and enabled feminist theories and practices. At the same time, women's feminist engagements were constantly questioning and transforming Marxist theories and practices, articulating women's autonomous revolutionary strategies, and asking unorthodox and uncomfortable questions, just like the one about the workers' dirty socks.

REFERENCES

Badiou, Alain et al. 2010, *L'idée du communisme*, Paris: Lignes.

Bebel, August 1910 [1879], *Woman and Socialism*, available at www.marxists. org/archive/bebel/1879/woman-socialism/index.htm

Blagojevic, Jelisaveta, Katerina Kolozova, and Svetlana Slapšak (eds.) 2006, *Gender and Identity: Theories From and/or On Southeastern Europe*, Belgrade: ATHENA.

Bono, Paola and Sandra Kemp (eds.) 1991, *Italian Feminist Thought : A Reader*, Oxford: Basil Blackwell.

Bonfiglioli, Chiara 2008, *Belgrade, 1978. Remembering the conference «Drugarica Žena. Žensko Pitanje – Novi Pristup?»/ «Comrade Woman. The Women's Question: A New Approach?» thirty years after*, available at http://igitur-archive.library. uu.nl/student-theses/2008-1031-202100/UUindex.html

Caldwell, Leslie 1978, 'Church, state, and family: the women's movement in Italy' in *Feminism and Materialism* edited by Annette Kuhn and AnnMarie Wolpe, London: Routledge and Kegan Paul.

Castellina, Luciana (ed.) 1974, *Famiglia e società capitalistica*, Roma: Il Manifesto/Alfani.

Chiavola Birnbaum, Lucia 1986, *liberazione della donna, feminism in Italy*, Middletown:Wesleyan University Press

Daskalova, Krassimira 2007, 'How Should We Name the 'Women-Friendly' Actions of State Socialism?', *Aspasia*, 1.

Delphy, Christine 1979, '...de Yougoslavie', *Questions Féministes*, 5.

Delphy, Christine 1984, *Close to Home. A materialist analysis of women's oppression*, London: Hutchinson & Co.

Engels, Friedrich 1942 [1884], *The Origins of the Family, Private Property and the State*, available at: www.marxists.org/archive/marx/works/1884/origin-family/index.htm

Evans, Harriet 2007, 'Chinese Communism and Chinese Feminism', *Aspasia*, 1.

Frabotta Biancamaria (ed.) 1973, *Femminismo e Lotta di Classe in Italia (*1970-1973*)*, Roma: Savelli.

Gruber, Helmut and Pamela Graves (eds.) 1998, *Women and Socialism/Socialism and Women: Europe Between the Two World Wars*, New York:Berghan Books.

Hartmann, Heidi 1997 [1981], 'The Unhappy Marriage of Marxism and Feminism. Towards a More Progressive Union' in *The Second Wave: A Reader in Feminist Theory* edited by Linda Nicholson, New York: Routledge.

Jancar-Webster, Barbara 1990, *Women & revolution in Yugoslavia, 1941-1945*, Denver: Arden Press.

Kollontai, Alexandra 1907-1946, *The Alexandra Kollontai archive*, available at: <www.marxists.org/archive/kollonta/index.htm>

Miroiu, Mihaela 2007, 'Communism was a State Patriarchy, not State Feminism', *Aspasia*, 1.

Novikova, Natalia 2007, 'Communism as a Vision and Practice', *Aspasia*, 1.

Peji, Bojana et al. 2009, *Gender Check: Femininity and Masculinity in the Art of Eastern Europe* (catalogue of the exhibition held at MUMOK, Wien, November 13, 2009 – February 14, 2010), Koln: Verlag der Buchhandlung Walther Konig.

Psarra, Angelika 2007, 'Feminism and Communism. Notes on the Greek Case', *Aspasia*, 1.

Ravaioli, Carla 1976, *La questione femminile:Intervista col PCI*, Milano:Bompiani.

Ravaioli, Carla 1978 'Ufficiale ma non troppo', *Il Messaggero di Roma*, 5/11/1978.

Scott, Hilda 1976, *Women and socialism: Experiences from Eastern Europe*, London: Allison & Busby.

Sher, Gerson 1977, *Praxis : Marxist criticism and dissent in socialist Yugoslavia*, Bloomington: Indiana University Press.

Sklevicky, Lydia 1989,'More Horses Than Women: On the Difficulties of Founding Women's History in Yugoslavia', *Gender & History*, 1:1.

Slaughter, Jane 2007, 'Communist Feminism. The Unfulfilled Possibilities of A Difficult Relationship', *Aspasia*, 1.

Vandelac, Louise 1978, *L'Italie au féminisme*, Paris: Tierce.

SOCIALIST FEMINIST QUESTIONS ABOUT QUEER ACTIVISM

Peter Drucker

Beginning in the 1990s in the US, a 'queer' activist current has gradually spread to other countries, including in recent years in Western Europe. In decades when the prevailing trend in LGBT movements has been to orient to legal reforms by parliamentary means, queer activism has constituted a third wave of sexual radicalism,[539] emphasising visibility, difference, direct action, refusal to assimilate to the dominant culture, and the fluidity and diversity of sexual desire. What are the social origins of queer? Does this current have a vision (implicit or explicit) of sexual liberation, and if so, what is it? What is its relationship to such emancipatory projects as feminism, antiracism, global justice and socialism?

I come to these questions as a socialist, whose own socialist activism and LGBT activism have been linked for 30 years. The year I came out as a gay man, 1978, was also the year I became active on the socialist left – more specifically, the socialist-feminist left. The two things were closely linked in my mind and in my life, and still are. So the questions I bring to queer activism are very much the questions of a socialist and feminist gay man. There are also, for better or worse, the questions of an outsider. Although I was active in ACT UP, the milieu that the queer current first emerged from, in San Francisco and New York in the late 1980s and early 1990s, this current didn't exist in the Netherlands when I moved here in 1993. In recent years, when a queer activist current has emerged in the Netherlands, I have related to it as a sympathetic observer and occasional support, but not as a real participant.

I would like to emphasise that the questions I'm posing really are *questions*. I don't claim to know the answers; I'm not sure anybody has definitive answers yet. I think queer activists will have to come up with the answers as their politics continue to evolve. My hope is that asking the questions will help stimulate discussion on them within the queer current.

539. The first two waves were the sex reform movements of the late nineteenth and early twentieth century – see e.g. Lauritsen and Thorstad 1995 – and the lesbian/gay liberation movement of the 1960s and '70s.

Another point I'd like to stress is that my questions concern queer activism, *not* the body of largely academic thought that's called 'queer theory'. My impression is that queer activism emerged a few years before the key works of queer theory were published. In later years some queer activists have been influenced by queer theory; but many queer activists are not particularly theoretically minded, and those who are can be influenced by other approaches besides queer theory. Queer theory is itself a complex, contradictory, evolving body of thought, on which I don't have any claim to be an expert. I do think there are criticisms to be made of queer theory,[540] but I don't think they all necessarily apply to queer activism.

Although queer activism has emerged only recently in the Netherlands, internationally it is almost 20 years old. The first queer group, Queer Nation, was founded in New York in 1990.[541] In fact the first wave of Queer Nation groups in the US rose and receded within a few years. Only a few groups, like OutRage! in London (founded only a month after Queer Nation in New York) around its controversial leader Peter Tatchell, have managed more or less to survive through the intervening years. Some of the most active queer-identified groups today are in Southern Europe, like the French and Portuguese Pink Panthers, and emerged only in the past decade. This lack of organisational continuity makes the current hard to pin down. Although there are various international queer events, like the annual 'queeruption' that took place each year from 1998 to 2007 in a different country and city, the queer current is also very decentralised, with no permanent national or international structures or decision-making bodies. Many queer activists define themselves as anarchists, leaning towards the tendency within anarchism that is suspicious of organisation; DIY ('do it yourself') is widely seen as a queer principle. This too contributes to the difficulty in defining queer politics. Finally, queer-identified activity sometimes raises the question of how 'politics' should be defined, since much of it consists of cultural and sexual events that make little or no effort to reach non-queer-identified people.

The contemporary shape of queer activism probably has something to do with its social origins. Before discussing the strengths and limitations of queer activism, therefore, I would like to analyze the emergence of the queer scene more generally.

540. For a cogent and balanced Marxist appreciation and critique of queer theory, see Girard 2009.
541. For a critical analysis of early queer nationalism, see Drucker 1993.

From Fordist to post-Fordist gay identities

The emergence of queer can be explained to a great extent in class terms, I think, starting from John D'Emilio's analysis of the emergence of gay identity under capitalism.[542] Roughly following his analysis, I would argue that modern lesbian and gay communities are largely a product of the development of capitalism in the 19th and 20th centuries, and on a mass scale particularly a product of the long expansive wave of capitalism from 1945 to 1973.

It is by now nothing new to link the rise of what might be called classic lesbian/gay identity to the rise of a 'free' labour force under capitalism. This has been a centuries-long process, and historians have generally looked at it as a long process. But gay identity as we know it, particularly on a mass scale, is in fact amazingly recent, more a question of decades than of centuries. On closer examination the emergence, consolidation and spread of gay identity took place to a large extent during what some Marxist economists refer to as the expansive long wave of 1945–73. It emerged gradually from the waves of political and social repression (in Europe fascism and Stalinism; in the US the aftermath of Prohibition followed by McCarthyism[543]) that had begun with the 1930s depression. Gay identity was dependent on the growing prosperity of the working and middle classes, catalysed by profound cultural changes from the 1940s to the 1970s (from the upheavals of the Second World War[544] to the mass radicalisation of the New Left years) that prosperity helped make possible. This means that gay identity was shaped in many ways by the mode of capitalist accumulation that some economists call 'Fordism': specifically by mass consumer societies and welfare states.

After 1945, working class living standards in capitalist countries went up dramatically under the Fordist order, in which increases in labour productivity were matched to a large extent with increasing real wages that sustained increasing effective demand, and many forms of social insurance cushioned the blows that hit working people during dips in the business cycle. As a result, for the first time masses of working class people as well as students and others were able to live independently of their families. Working class family structures and gender roles also changed. For the first time since the family wage became a cherished ideal, and sometimes a reality,

542. D'Emilio, 1983.
543. See e.g. Chauncey 1994, pp. 334–46.
544. See Bérubé 1983.

for broad working class layers in the mid- to late nineteenth century, the Second World War made waged work at least temporarily normal for even respectable working class and middle class women.

This made a dent in the pronounced gender polarisation that had been characteristic of both working class heterosexuality and homosexuality in the first decades of the twentieth century. Higher funding for education and expansion of a social safety net (in the imperialist countries at least) decreased people's economic dependence on parents to support them as students or young people, on spouses to help pay the rent, and on children to save them from poverty in old age. Rapid growth of service and leisure industries in developed countries created more jobs, for men if not for women, in which gender expectations were in some cases less rigid than in blue collar sectors.

The combination of increased economic possibilities and more questioning of gender roles helped many more people in the 1950s and '60s defy convention and form lesbian/gay couples and communities. What remained to prevent people from living openly lesbian/gay lives were the constraints of the law, police, employers, landlords, and so on. The lesbian/gay movements of the 1960s and '70s rebelled against these constraints, inspired by a wave of other social rebellions: black, youth, anti-war, feminist, and (at least in some European countries) working class. The second wave of feminism was key in virtually finishing off (or at least driving underground) the butch-femme patterns that were still largely hegemonic in 1950s lesbian subcultures. The first lesbian/gay legal victories in the 1970s made mass, open lesbian/gay communities possible in the imperialist countries for the first time in history.

Yet the conditions that initially shaped emerging lesbian/gay identities did not last. The depressive long wave that began by 1974–75 was met by the late 1970s with a neoliberal offensive. This offensive has included (to be incredibly schematic): a shift to 'Toyotist' production techniques and to 'lean production' generally; economic globalisation, liberalisation and deregulation; an increase in the wealth and power of capital at labour's expense; an increase in inequality among countries (through the debt crisis and structural adjustment policies) and within countries (through regressive tax and welfare 'reforms' and attacks on unions), and luxury consumption that has increasingly replaced mass consumption as a motor of economic growth. This offensive has among other things fragmented the world's working classes. Big differences have grown between better- and worse-paid workers, permanent and temporary workers, native-born and immi-grant, employed and unemployed. The relatively greater homogeneity of national working classes in the 1960s, which was the backdrop to the rise of lesbian/gay identity, is a thing of the past.

Like the rise of Fordism, its decline has had implications for LGBT identities, communities and politics. There is of course no one-to-one correspondence between economic and social developments and shifts in sexual, cultural and political identities. In lesbian/gay communities as in the world at large, there is a whole set of institutions that produce (among other things) lesbian/gay ideology and identity and mediate the underlying class and social dynamics. But there are some trends that correspond to changing class dynamics in lesbian/gay communities and are expressed in a shifting relationship of forces within them.

On the one hand, commercial gay scenes and sexual identities com-patible with these scenes have advanced and been consolidated in many parts of the world. Particularly among some middle class and upper work-ing class social layers that prospered in the 1980s and '90s, especially but not only in the imperialist countries, commercial gay scenes continued to grow, continuing to undergird lesbian/gay identities.[545] Market-friendly les-bian/gay identities have prospered in commercialised spaces, in the con-struction of two-income households among better-off gays and to a lesser extent lesbians, and in the tolerant public space fostered by gay rights vic-tories. Many relatively better paid lesbian/gay people who have benefited from both economic success and gay rights reforms have some cause to be contented with the progress they have made: 'inside a cosy brownstone, curled up next to a health-insured domestic partner in front of a Melissa Etheridge video on MTV, flipping through *Out* magazine and sipping an Absolut and tonic, capitalism can feel pretty good'.[546]

The ideological and cultural sway of gay identities in LGBT com-munities extends beyond the more privileged social layers in which peo-ple's lives fit these identities most comfortably. In the imperialist countries, despite the proliferation of websites and zines defining identities and sub-cultures for minorities within the minorities, the most widely circulated books, periodicals and videos tend to be those most closely linked to the new, predominantly middle class gay mainstream. Even poor transgender and queer people whose lives are most remote from the images of the

545. See Altman 1982, pp. 79–97.
546. Gluckman and Reed 1997, p. xv.

gay mainstream often incorporate aspects of gay mainstream culture into their aspirations and fantasies. Three aspects of the lesbian/gay identity that stabilised by the early 1980s fit well with the increasingly conservative social climate: the community's self-definition as a stable minority, its increasing tendency towards gender conformity, and marginalisation of its own sexual minorities.

Lesbians and gay men's self-definition as a minority group expressed a profound social fact about lesbian/gay life as it took shape in the 1970s. To the extent that lesbians and gays were increasingly defined as people who inhabited a certain community (went to certain bars, bathhouses and discos, patronised certain businesses, and in the US at least even lived to some extent in certain neighbourhoods), they were more 'ghettoised' than before, more clearly demarcated from a majority defined as straight. The tendency of many early theorists of lesbian/gay liberation to question the categories of heterosexuality and homosexuality, emphasise the fluidity of sexual identity and speculate about universal bisexuality tended to fade away with time as the community's material reality became more sharp-edged. The lesbian/gay rights movement accordingly ran less risk of seeming sexually subversive of the broader sexual order.

The decline of butch/femme role-playing among lesbians and of camp culture among gay men also contributed to normalising lesbian/gay identity. The drag queens who had played a leading role in the 1969 Stonewall rebellion found that as social tolerance of lesbians and gays in general began to increase in the 1970s, social tolerance for gender nonconformity in many queer spaces if anything decreased. Drag often seemed anomalous and even embarrassing in the context of androgynous imagery that was in vogue in the early 1970s. Despite growing levels of consciousness and self-expression among transgender people, lesbian/gay communities increasingly defined themselves in ways that placed transgender people and other visible nonconformists on the margins if not completely out of bounds. The decline of Fordism was accompanied early on by a shift among gay men from the largely androgynous imagery of the early 1970s to the more masculine 'clone' culture that took hold by the early '80s, while feminine forms of self-presentation that lesbian feminists once frowned on had become more common and acceptable among 'lipstick lesbians' by the 1990s. A higher degree of gender conformity among lesbian/gay people has fit with their incorporation into a neoliberal social and sexual order.

The social origins of queer

However, commercial scenes have not been equally determinant for the lifestyles or identities of all people with open same-sex sexualities. In the dependent world many poor people simply have a hard time taking part in commercial gay scenes. In the imperialist countries, while commercial scenes are more accessible to even lower-income queers, growing economic inequality has meant increasingly divergent realities in lesbian and gay people's lives. Criticism has mounted among LGBT people of the over-consumption increasingly characteristic of many aspects of the commercial gay scene, which inevitably marginalises many LGBT people and alienates many others. Alternative scenes of various sorts (not always less commercial) have proliferated, creating space for queer identities more or less outside the mainstream commercial scene.

Contrary to much right wing anti-gay rhetoric, the prosperous couples focused on by glossy lesbian/gay magazines were never typical of queers in general. Data gathered by the US National Opinion Research Centre's General Social Survey in the 1990s suggested that lesbian and bisexual women were still far less likely than other women to have professional or technical jobs and more likely to have service or craft/operative jobs, while gay and bisexual men were more likely than other men to have professional/technical, clerical/sales or service jobs but less likely to have managerial jobs.[547] Whatever the causes (less ability or willingness to meet gendered job expectations, migration to more competitive job markets, discrimination), the net result (contrary to unfounded claims made not only by anti-gay ideologues but also by some gay publications) was that at least in the US both gay men and lesbians were and are underrepresented in the higher income brackets (with family incomes of $50,000 or more), while gay men in particular are over-represented in the lower income brackets (with family incomes of $30,000 or less). Another set of data showed that after taking differences in education, age and other factors into account, gay and bisexual men earned 11 to 27 per cent less than comparable straight men.[548]

The expansion of queer communities centred on gay commercial scenes has not improved the situation of lower-income queers. Particularly in imperialist countries like the US and to a lesser extent Britain, the welfare state has been shredded by Reaganism and Thatcherism, unions have been very much weakened, and inequality has grown rapidly. Economic

547. Badgett 1997, p. 81.
548. Badgett and King 1997, pp. 68–9.

inequality is presumably as characteristic of LGBT communities as of the broader societies they exist in. Lower-income queers, transgender people, street youth and queer people of colour have been under assault in various ways, as attacks on poor people and minorities have become more prominent in politics and society generally in recent decades. Queers are also more likely to be cut off from broader family support networks, and as the social safety net frayed inequalities resulting from wage differentials affected queers with particular intensity.

A queer social milieu has grown up since the mid-1980s, made up to a large extent of young people on the bottom of the unequal social hourglass that has resulted from economic restructuring. One aspect of the underlying social reality is that the lower young queers' incomes are and the more meagre their job prospects, the less on average they identify with or want to join the lesbian/gay community that has grown up since the 1960s and '70s. Particularly in English-speaking imperialist countries — the ones where social polarisation first took flight in the 1980s — young queers resisted disco culture and a bar-centred ghetto. In some ways English-speaking queer scenes have been echoed by queers in squatters' milieus in continental Western Europe. This generation had also grown up in far more diverse and changeable family structures, which made the notion of modelling lesbian/gay households on traditional straight ones all the more implausible for them. Economic marginalisation and cultural alienation were closely interlinked in the emergence of a queer milieu, making it hard in many cases to say to what extent poverty was a cause of alienation, to what extent the choice for a queer lifestyle contributed to more or less voluntary poverty, and to what extent some queers are middle class gays dressing and talking like down-and-outs. But the correlation between lower incomes and queer self-identification seems unmistakable.

As we have seen, the dominant trend during the 1980s and '90s, based particularly on the reality of more prosperous lesbian/gay people's lives, was for the lesbian/gay community to define itself as a stable and distinct minority, tend increasingly towards gender conformity, and marginalise its own sexual minorities. By contrast, the nonconformist same-sex identities that have grown up among more marginalised layers have tended to identify with broader communities of oppressed or rebellious people and to resist dominant gender norms.

Queer identities defined by marginalisation on the basis of age, class, region and/or ethnicity overlap with the growth or persistence of various subcultures that have been marginal in the commercial scene because they constitute (sometimes extensive) niche markets at best and illicit ones at worst. The relationship between queer identities and marginalised sexual practices is elusive, but there does appear to be some kind of correlation. There are of course many queers who limit their sexual rebellion to the safety of a particular brand of bar. But the more attached people are to their sexual identities, the more reluctant many of them become to give them up at work or in public.

Not coincidentally, the more visible transgender or leather people are, the less likely they are to get one of the well-paid, permanent, fulltime jobs that have become scarcer and more coveted commodities in post-Fordist economies. Moreover some people are virtually or entirely incapable of hiding aspects of their identities, particularly effeminacy in men or butchness in women, that are often rightly or wrongly associated with queer sexualities. Voluntary or involuntary, tell-tale signs of sexual deviance often lead to management excluding people from professional or service jobs or to fellow workers' hostility that impels people to avoid or flee certain workplaces. The result is not a straightforward correlation between queer identity and working class affiliation; on the contrary, working class lesbians and gays have sometimes reacted against self-defined queer groups when such groups demanded visibility of them that would make their lives more difficult in particular workplaces or communities. But there does seem to be a correlation between queer identities and particular sectors of the working class — on average younger, less skilled, less organised and lower-paid — that have expanded since the 1970s.

Part of the younger queer generation has taken up and to some extent recast claims for stigmatised sexual practices that were made during the sex wars of the early 1980s. For example, younger transgender people seem more likely to take on gender identities that are difficult to subsume at all under existing feminine or masculine roles. These more flexible and ambiguous forms of transgender associated with queer milieus contrast with the forms of transsexuality promoted by a wing of the medical establishment.

Queer politics and its limits

This account of the social roots of queer can help us understand several positive aspects of queer politics as well as some of its limitations. To begin with the positive aspects:

Reflecting queer alienation from the ghettoised lesbian/gay mainstream, queer politics is anti-assimilationist, inclusive and diverse. It refuses to fit into any model of gay or lesbian respectability. It is a space where many of the LGBT people who are least welcome in other LGBT spaces – such as trans and intersexed people, bisexuals and SM practitioners – are welcome and visible. Queer is not seen as a single way of being, but rather as a dissident stance with great respect and room for difference.

Queers do not have any of the access to the political power structure that the lesbian/gay establishment has built up over the years. So when they take political action, they do so militantly, keeping up the tradition of direct action pioneered by ACT UP (and to a great extent borrowed, though rarely acknowledged, by the global justice movement).[549] They do not engage in the kind of lobbying and parliamentary work that has come to predominate in mainstream LGBT political groups, but instead use more confrontational and creative tactics. Peter Tatchell's attempt to do a citizens' arrest of homophobic Zimbabwean President Robert Mugabe was an internationally notorious example. The early Queer Nation groups applied these kinds of tactics at the most local level, for example by highlighting the dictatorship of the heterosexual norm by holding same-sex kiss-ins in non-gay bars and responding to homophobic violence with the slogan 'Queers bash back!' (though as far as I know this remained at the level of a slogan). My impression though is that there have been fewer such militant queer actions in recent years.

Rejecting ghettoisation, queers reaffirm the fluidity of sexual desire and identity that was proclaimed by the pioneers of lesbian/gay liberation in the 1960s and '70s – what was then often defined as a universal bisexual potential or an aspiration to universal 'polymorphous perversity' (a Freudian term picked up by Herbert Marcuse[550]). Queers therefore reject the vision of lesbian and gay people as a fixed, static minority of the population, which some of the most moderate currents in lesbian/gay movements take as the basis for their claim for equal rights ('we can't help it, we were born this way, so it's not fair to discriminate against us – and not necessary to discriminate against us, since there won't be any more of us if you tolerate us'). Queers also refuse to let their sexual difference and visibility be confined to a gay ghetto, insisting that the whole world should be – as the expression goes – 'queered': that is, opened up to queer possibilities.

549. See Shepard and Hayduk 2002.
550. Marcuse 1955.

Reflecting the international character of the neoliberal offensive that gave rise to the queer scene, queer politics is in principle internationalist. The list of the 10 queeruption sites from 1998 to 2007 give a sense of the scope and limits of this internationalism, however. 5 of the 10 were in Europe, three in North America, one in Australia and one in Israel. That is to say, they all took place in the richest one-fifth of the world. 6 of the 10 took place in cities where the dominant language is English. This is in fact a narrower geography than the geography of the open, visible LGBT world; many Latin American countries have vibrant, visible LGBT communities and movements, as do South Africa and several Asian countries. Like its internationalism, the geographical limits of queer are probably no accident; they reflect the fact that sexual dissidence takes very different forms in imperialist and dependent countries. For example, the World Social Forum in Mumbai in 2004 showed that thousands of India's transgender *hijras* identified with the global justice movement's rebellion against neoliberalism, and were prepared to resort to militant tactics similar to European and North American queer activists'; but they did so on the basis of the subculture that they had been developing over the course of decades or even centuries.

So what are the factors that make it harder for queer activists to link up with many of other rebellious LGBTs in the world, let alone with labour, feminist and other movements?

The sexual conservatism of other social movements clearly makes it difficult for queer activists to ally with them. In many countries the labour and even feminist movements reflect the open heterosexism of their societies. In other countries where open anti-LGBT prejudice is less accepted, mainstream social movements often link up with middle class, moderate lesbian/gay organisations rather than with radical groups. This sexual conformism can dovetail with the political and social moderation of mainstream leaderships. LGBT activists in broader social movements sometimes adapt to those leaderships' moderation and sexual conservatism; as noted above, working class LGBTs, LGBTs of colour and other specially oppressed LGBTs sometimes feel obliged to downplay their own sexualities in order to blend more easily into broader communities. This makes many LGBTs hesitate to associate themselves with queers. Moreover, in many cases queer groups simply do not have the size or institutional weight to make them interesting as allies or interlocutors for big social organisations.

In addition, there are other factors isolating queer activists that sometimes reflect their own political limitations. For example:

The anti-organisational, DIY leanings of some queer groups can re-inforce their social homogeneity. Spontaneous, informal styles of action are easier to sustain when activists have roughly similar backgrounds, lifestyles and social situations. When people need to unite in action who face differ-ent forms of oppression and lead very different lives, they need structures to help them discuss their differences in depth, make joint decisions and carry out their decisions over the longer term. More structures mean a greater risk of bureaucracy and authoritarianism; but the way to minimise these risks is to consciously make structures as grassroots and democratic as possible, not to avoid structure altogether.[551]

The social marginality that queer people experience sometimes seems to lead queer activists to choose political marginality, cutting themselves off from other LGBT people who might sympathise with queer politics if they encountered it. For example, the commercialisation and depoliticisation of lesbian/gay pride events help explain the allergy that many queer activists seem to have to them; but staying away from pride marches can deprive queer groups of access to a big potential audience. Pride marches of hun-dreds of thousands of people in several countries helped put the issue of same-sex marriage and civil union on the political agenda. Again, many queer activists' allergy to the institution of marriage and the assimilation-ism that the demand for access to it can reflect may be understandable and even justified. But thousands of working class and poor LGBTs have very practical concerns that lead them to demand equal access to marriage. Failing to address these concerns is another way that some queer radicals may cut themselves off from a potential base of support.[552]

Queer political activism can flow almost imperceptibly into subcul-tural events. This can be a source of strength, inasmuch as the politics is rooted in the life of a community. But it can sometimes lead queer activists to stress the aspects of LGBT identity that are cultural and chosen, rather than those that are socially constructed and involuntary. Many of the most oppressed LGBT people do not feel that there's anything chosen about their identities. This is reflected for example in the differences between queer-oriented transgender people who may say that they transcend gen-

---

551. For a comparable argument made during the second wave of feminism, see Freeman 1973.

552. For an approach to the issue of same-sex marriage that tries to be both nuanced and radical, see FI 15th World Congress 2003, point 17.

der and more traditional transgender people who strongly identify with a gender different from the one they were assigned to as children. This is one way in which queer activism sometimes takes on the suspicion of identity practiced by queer theory. It is important to recognise that an identity can be fluid and malleable and yet at the same time very strong and stable — and essential as the basis for a movement. The emphasis on cultural rather than material aspects of identity may also make queer politics less appealing to some LGBT blacks and immigrants, who are more likely to contend with material oppression in their daily lives.[553]

Queer activists rarely seem to have a very well worked out vision of the society they would like to see. This is understandable, given that the decades in which queer politics emerged were ones in which traditional conceptions of socialism seemed largely discredited. But given that queer politics expresses a deeply felt rebellion against the lives that queer people are forced to live under patriarchal capitalism, it seems incomplete if it does not include an explicit rejection of patriarchal capitalism. This suggests that radical queers should take up and develop the analyses that an earlier radical generation made during the lesbian/gay liberation movement, of the roots of gender and sexual oppression in the capitalist family and the way it helps reproduce labour and authoritarian social hierarchies.

The use of the words 'some', 'sometimes', 'can', 'tend to' and so on in these remarks is not simply an attempt to soft-pedal criticism. It reflects the real diversity of queer activists. For every group that shares these weaknesses, there may be another one somewhere that has overcome them, or is at least trying to. This is a reason to hope for the emergence of a radical queer current that is better organised, more oriented to the broader range of LGBT people, more ethnically diverse, more genuinely global in its politics, more materialist and profound in its analysis — and that thus can lay the basis for a powerful queer anti-capitalism and feminism.

553. One French participant in the Returns of Marxism discussion mentioned that there is in fact an LGBT Muslim group called Queer Jihad, and that the French queer group Pink Panthers has had a working relationship with the radical immigrant group Indigènes de la République.

REFERENCES

Altman, Dennis 1982. *The Homosexualization of America, The Americanization of the Homosexual*, New York: St. Martin's Press.

Badgett, M.V. Lee, 'Beyond biased samples: challenging the myths on the economic status of lesbians and gay men', in Glucksman and Reed (eds.).

Badgett, M.V. Lee and Mary C. King 1997, 'Lesbian and gay occupational strategies', in Glucksman and Reed (eds.).

Bérubé, Alan 1983, 'Marching to a different drummer: lesbian and gay GIs in World War II', in Snitow et al. (eds.), *Powers of Desire: The Politics of Sexuality*, New York: Monthly Review Press.

Chauncey, George 1994, *Gay New York: Gender, Urban Culture, and the Making of the Gay Male World, 1890–1940*, New York: Basic Books.

D'Emilio, John 1983, 'Capitalism and gay identity', in Ann Snitow et al. (eds.), *Powers of Desire: The Politics of Sexuality*, New York: Monthly Review Press.

Drucker, Peter 1993, 'What is queer nationalism?' *Against the Current* 43 (Mar./Apr.).

FI 15th World Congress 2003, 'On lesbian/gay liberation', <www.internationalviewpoint.org/spip.php?article177>.

Freeman, Jo 1973, 'The tyranny of structurelessness', *Ms. Magazine* (July).

Girard, Gabriel 2009, 'Théories et militantismes queer: réflexion à partir de l'exemple français' (<www.europe-solidaire.org/spip.php?article14760>); abridged English translation: 'Queer theories and militant practices' (<www.europe-solidaire.org/spip.php?article14759>).

Glucksman, Amy and Mary Reed (eds.) 1997, *Homo Economics: Capitalism, Community and Lesbian and Gay Life*, New York: Routledge.

Lauritsen, John and David Thorstad 1995, *The Early Homosexual Rights Movement (1864–1935)*, Ojai: Times Change Press.

Marcuse, Herbert 1955, *Eros and Civilization: A Philosophical Inquiry into Freud*, Boston: Beacon.

Shepard, Benjamin and Ronald Hayduk eds. 2002, *From ACT UP to the WTO: Urban Protest and Community Building in the Era of Globalization*, London: Verso.

MANY MARXISMS

THE COMING COMMUNISM ON THE POST-WORKERIST READING OF MARX

Katja Diefenbach

In this text, a single question is central: how does post-workerism think the act of politics? This question leads directly on to the next ones: how, therefore, does post-workerism unite diverging theses under the concept of living labour to identify production, being and politics in the instance of potentiality?[554] And does this operation succeed in separating Marxism from its idealising and historico-philosophical figures of argumentation? By short-circuiting economico-critical, ontological and political approaches, post-workerist authors integrate the following positions into a new model of political and ontological materialism: firstly, the Marxian idea of the real subsumption of labour under capital and labour-power as radically expropriated but creative potentiality; secondly, the feminist thesis of the productivity of reproductive and affective labour; thirdly, the Deleuzian idea of creative forces that express an impersonal life that neither belongs to a subject nor comprises an object but presents a 'desire desiring self-creating';[555] and fourthly, the Foucauldian thesis that the capitalist mode of production is preceded by the inclusion of life in power mechanisms that subsequently co-exist along side it. In the course of integrating these positions, post-workerist authors partially revert their order of argumentation to adapt them to one key hypothesis: the ontological primacy of what Negri calls 'living abstract labor' and determines to be the 'substance' of the 'new figure of the proletariat'.[556] Abstract labour is conceived here as general labour, labour-power reduced to a mere generic capacity the definition of which Negri finds in *The Grundrisse*: 'Labour as absolute poverty: poverty

---

554. The Latin concept of *potentia* used by Spinoza and the French concept *puissance* used by Negri are translated as *potentiality*, not understood in the sense of Aristotle's *dynamis*, a potentiality that has to be realised, but rather in the anti-Aristotelian sense of a degree of differentiality that will be expressed.
555. Agamben 1999, p. 119.
556. Negri 1996, p. 167.

not as shortage, but as total exclusion of objective wealth. [...] Labour not as an object, but as activity, not as itself value, but as the living source of wealth.'[557] Particularly, Negri has elaborated, during the last thirty years, a 'metaphysics of productive force'[558] by linking the idea of generic forces in the *Parisian Manuscripts* and of subjective wealth in *The Grundrisse* with the idea of *conatus* in Spinoza's *Ethics*. I explore the question of how politics is thought in post-workerism because the authors gathered under this name emerged in the 1980s with the promise of combining the analysis of the relation between valorisation, bio-power and law in imperial capitalism with a new idea of communist militancy and a new materialism in the line of Machiavelli, Spinoza and Marx. Where did this theoretical synthesis lead them?

Reading Marx

Let's begin with the question of what it means to actualise Marx's thought. To align oneself with Marx means accepting a heterogeneous, theoretically aporetic and politically dramatic legacy. What we are used to calling Marxism is composed of the constitution of an international workers' movement, a revolutionary promise, a scientific critique of the political economy, and an open framework of philosophical problems. This encounter is historically marked by the fact that it led to the construction of a productivist, police-based social order. The acceptance of the Marxian legacy consequently necessitates a distance in relation to the idealisations in Marx's texts, the violence of his theoretical and political blockades, and a positioning in relation to Stalinism. Here, Foucault's argumentation still sets the example. Foucault calls for an analysis of Stalinism that does not operate in terms of error, but in those of reality. Instead of searching Marxism for something that might serve to criticise and condemn the camp system, productivism and the bureaucratisation of the political, one should search for what these developments made possible.[559]

If one rejects the purifying idea of an epistemological break in Marx's work along the seam of scientificity that Althusser recanted in 1973 as a 'theoreticist error'[560] since it implies an equating of science with truth

557. Marx 1993, p. 296.
558. Negri 1991b, p. 218.
559. Cf. Foucault 1980, p. 201.
560. In *For Marx*, Althusser took up Bachelard's concept of the epistemological break and divided Marx's works into early works, works of the break, works of transition and mature works (cf. 2005, pp. 33–9). He contrasts the ideological early works with the scientificity of the texts after 1845, cf. Althusser 1976, p. 119.

and ideology with error, the polyvalence of Marx's theoretical work becomes evident. In his short and essayistic text 'Reading Marx', Blanchot emphasises the unrelated juxtaposition of three voices: firstly, a direct, long, both philosophical and anti-philosophical voice in which Marx, in terms of a historico-philosophical thought, gives answers to questions that remain indeterminate ('alienation, the primacy of need, history as process of material practice, the total man');[561] secondly, a political voice that is brief, direct and a call to participate in the struggle, announcing the immediate dissolution of bourgeois society through the praxis of the proletariat, and expressing the urgency of what it announces; thirdly, the indirect speech of a scientific, economico-critical discourse that analyses the value-form as self-processing contradiction and the reproduction of capitalist relations of production, a scientific speech that undermines itself by, as Blanchot says, 'showing itself as radical transformation of itself, as a theory of mutation always in play in practice, just as in this practice the mutation is always theoretical.'[562] Even if Blanchot ignores the developments and breaks in Marx's works by limiting himself to the thesis that science and philosophy do not emerge from Marx's work unscathed and that his productivity consists in the multiplicity of his perspectives, he provides us with two references that are particularly valuable for an investigation of the post-workerist reading of Marx: on the one hand, to pay attention to the questions found in relation to Marx's answers; and on the other, to investigate how the relationship between economy and politics is understood. This relationship oscillates precariously in Marx between a formal economico-critical and a political perspective that are – like all form-content-arguments – reversible into one another. Either the economic conditions convert, at a certain moment of their contradictory unfolding, into hindrances, or the working class, by being not reducible to a commodity and possessing the generic capacity for free, all-sided self-activity, resists on an ever increasing scale to its universal exploitation. Both perspectives result into a negation of negation, in which they find their historical solution. Therefore, post-Marxism in all its divergences is characterised by the attempt to elaborate a complex dialectic from which the synthesising function of negativity and the figure of the negation of negation have been subtracted.

By examining the question that is answered by Marx, Blanchot varies the motif of Althusser's symptomal reading formulated in the foreword

561. Blanchot 1997, p. 145.
562. Blanchot 1997, p. 146.

to *Reading Capital*. The key question, which Marx, in Althusser's view, still put in the old Hegelian terms of inner essence and outer appearances, is the question of the effect of a structure on its elements.[563] According to Althusser, Marx shows in multiple ways the presence of a concept that is decisive for his thought and lacking in the context of his discourse: namely, that of the social formation as complex structured whole in which the economic is determinant 'in the last instance'[564] – i.e. not directly, not in a pre-definable or prescriptive way, but constantly deferred, displaced, distorted in the translation of its effectivity to other instances of the social.

With the hypothesis that the structure expresses itself in the displacement of degrees of effectivity between relatively autonomous elements, Althusser takes up Marx and Engels's idea of a totality of social relations that reaches far beyond the economic, and consists in the interaction of really distinguished elements, which are only determined 'in the last instance' through the realisation of surplus value. So as not to withdraw to á relativist position of infinitely mutating interactions, Althusser claims it would be necessary to take up the idea of a primacy of determination by the economic that unifies the play of differences between social elements by determining the displacements of their degrees of effectivity.[565] In other words, the economic determines nothing but the relation which becomes prevalent in the overall structure; it determines the relational logic in which the degrees of effectivity vary in the structure. Althusser thus works with an immanent mode of causality with which he wants to reinforce Spinoza's position in Marxism, and which he also terms, with Jacques-Alain Miller, metonymic causality.[566] However, the problem of this position is the following: If the genesis of the social structure is explained by the dislocation of degrees of effectivity through a complex movement of partial reflection, against his own intuition, Althusser refers to an idea developed by Hegel, not by Spinoza. Already in 1969 Hyppolite pointed out to him that it would not be easy to separate Marx's from Hegel's idea of determination by attributing to one 'the complexity of an *effective overdetermination*', and to the other 'the complexity of a cumulative *internalization*'.[567] The partial

563. Althusser and Balibar 2006, vol. 1, p. 35.
564. Engels 1934, pp. 81–5.
565. See 'Is it Simple to Be a Marxist in Philosophy?' in Althusser 1976, p. 183.
566. For Althusser's remarks on this subject, cf. Althusser and Balibar 2006, pp. 32–5, 228–34, 248–61 and the chapter 'Structure in dominance' in Althusser 2005, pp. 251–256; cf. in addition Miller 2009.
567. lthusser 2005, p. 101.

reflexivity through which Althusser still defines overdetermination relates, for Hyppolite, to precisely the idea of structures that Hegel develops in the *Science of Logic*, especially in 'The Doctrine of Essence': 'There he describes structures in which the essential and unessential are reflected in one another, in which the existential condition of a dominant contradiction are an element in the contradiction itself.'[568] Thus, the decisive concept, coined by Spinoza, of a positive determination that does not limit and negate what it determines is not taken up by Althusser in his model of immanent causality.

Beyond Marx

What question, then, does post-workerism find to the answers given by Marx? How does it go beyond Marx's dialectic and teleological idealisations? Let's begin by clarifying what it means, with Marx, to go beyond Marx. This is a challenge that Negri himself signed in *Marx beyond Marx*,[569] and which, as Balibar pointed out in the 1980s, has in relation to the status of materialist thought at least two methodological dimensions: firstly, Marxism participates in the transgressing of its future perspectives since it assumes the historical specificity of a discourse, including its own, and is thereby able to reflect the temporal conditionality of its thought, while on a non-discursive level, the labour movement, class struggle, the development of the Soviet Union and the real-socialist states contributed to the way capitalist strategies of government and valorisation have changed and no longer correspond to the conditions that Marx analysed in the mid nineteenth century. Secondly, Marxian theory provides a number of supports for the deconstruction of its own dialectical fictions. Especially Marx's institutional and historical analyses on the legislation of labour time, the creation of large-scale industry and the socialisation of production in the fourth part of *Capital* manifest a thought that is neither based on an evolutionary development of predetermined forms nor on collective generic forces immanent to the history of being, expressing the universal content that explodes the capitalist form. Instead, one encounters a theory that investigates the complex and mutual effectivity of antagonistic strategies: 'strategies of exploitation, domination and resistance constantly being deferred and renewed as a consequence of their own effects.'[570]

568. Hyppolite 1973, p. viii.
569. Cf. Negri 1991a, and Balibar's 1991 reference to 'Negri's beautiful expression' 'Marx beyond Marx' (p. 207).
570. Balibar 1991, p. 202. On Marxism's transgression of its own future perspectives, cf. Balibar 1991, pp. 192.

It is precisely this aspect of displacing interactions between management, accumulation and law that Foucault radicalises in his works on biopower and governmentality. It is not difficult to realise how far Foucault, despite his anti-Marxist rhetorics, is inspired here by Althusser's model of a complex structured whole without closure. In *Security, Territory, Population* Foucault explains that in post-Fordism the dispositif of discipline has not been replaced by the dispositif of security. What has changed from one to the next is only the 'system of correlation' between social mechanisms ordered in 'complex edifices' in which nothing but the 'dominant characteristic' is displaced.[571] In relation to Marxism, Foucault tends to strengthen the relative autonomy of the different social instances, already emphasised by Althusser, to an extreme limit-point by relativising the concept of contradiction. As Balibar suggests, both authors, Marx and Foucault, share common ground insofar as they strive to pass from a 'philosophy of history' to a 'philosophy in history',[572] but Foucault presents historicity in terms of a historicity of an event. That is why he differs from Marx in thinking the action of structure: In Foucault, contradiction is 'at best one particular configuration' in a diagram of power mechanisms. In Marx, in contrast, the power relation is only 'a strategic moment'[573] in the logic of contradiction. Hence, Foucault brings Althusser's operation to separate the model of a complex and differential determination of relationships from the model of their cumulative internalisation that Hyppolite judged to be difficult to uphold to a maximum. Consequently, the concept of antagonism is given a historically non-necessary and a politically non-primary status. Particularly in the first volume of *The History of Sexuality*, Foucault translated his considerations on a strategic concept of power into a series of methodological rules: the immanence of knowledge and power, the constant variation of their distributions, the double conditionality of their micro- and macro-political mechanisms, the polyvalence of governmental practices that are discontinuous and transformative in their effects and enter into various total strategies.[574] For Foucault, political practices coexist with these power relations; it is a matter of two practices that mutually provoke, propel, elude, penetrate and in some cases attack each other. A social break is the improbable and eventual result of a particular conjunction of heterogeneous political practices, an idea that Balibar defined in relation to a 'becoming-

571. Foucault 2007, p. 8.
572. Balibar 1992, p. 54.
573. Balibar 1992, p. 52.
574. Cf. Foucault 1990, pp. 113–124.

necessary of freedom' as a 'becoming-contingent of resistances'.[575] With Marx, to go beyond Marx, means for Foucault to distance from a mode of dialectics that conceptualises the progression of social antagonisms on the base of a movement, by which the terms of a relationship internalise the relationship itself, 'in such a way that the antagonist terms become the function or the bearers of the relationship,'[576] that is to say, that the entire process subjectivises. This implies to end all attempts at grasping the social as a totality, and to detect, in the interplay of its parts, a constitutive political cause (labour-power) or a constitutive economic law (value-form) which would re-introduce – not in terms of the life of the spirit, but in terms of the real of productive forces – the Hegelian idea that the whole fulfils itself by the immanent arrival of its own truth.

The conditions of communism

So how is the post-workerist discourse to be inscribed into the post-Marxist field? Workerism itself came out of the encounter between new types of Marxist *intelligentsia* and new types of factory activism, the latter playing an initiating role. As Bologna put forth, workerism emerged from organised micro-systems of factory struggle that had broken with union and party structures, and, at the beginning of the 1960s, appeared in divisions of Fiat, Pirelli, Innocenti, Olivetti.[577] Their practices were drawn on by a heterogenous group of theorists working on a rewriting of Marx's theory. After a wave of severe political and theoretical disagreements, post-workerism is particularly characterised through the attempt of ontologically reformulating the primacy of the working class or the multitude. Politics is thought through two conceptual genealogies: in the line of Spinoza-Deleuze in the category of potentiality, and in the line of Marx-Foucault in the category of biopolitical labour-power. In the post-workerist reading of Marx, two texts have a central position. While the reading of *The Paris Manuscripts*, in which the young Marx, inspired by Feuerbachian and Hegelian themes, understands labour as self-generation, as 'life-engendering life',[578] remains with few exceptions[579] implicit, the re-interpretation of 'The Fragment on Machines'[580] in *The Grundrisse*, which was already central

575. Balibar 2002, p. 30.
576. Balibar 1992, p. 52.
577. Cf. Bologna 2000, p. 92.
578. Marx 1975a, p. 76.
579. Cf. for example Virno 2008, p. 39, cf. Negri and Hardt 2009, pp. 22–37, 249.
580. Cf. Marx 1993, pp. 590–609.

for the development of workerist theory in the 1960s, is dealt with explicitly and represents the most visible Marxian point of reference. With this divergent reading, the ontological theses of the young Marx on the creative vitality of practise and the historico-critical theses of the later Marx on the socialisation of production are combined and projected into one another. It is precisely at this point that the question post-workerism found to Marx's answers becomes evident which Blanchot with Althusser demanded to examine if one wants to understand how Marx is read in a specific discourse: it is the question of the conditions of communism in being emerging in the historical development of modes of production. Post-workerism operates with the basic assumption that, with the post-Fordist mode of accumulation, a mass intellectual, cooperative and affective productive force was formed that embodies the human of the human being, its ontological determination, its creative potentiality, and thus the force of politics to produce the new, a change of change of the world The projection of an ontological potentiality into a historical development leads to a circle typical for an anthropological variant of the philosophy of history, where that what comes about is what was latently present.

In the 1960s, Tronti had insisted that the working class can only become political by destroying its economic function, negating its own productive force. For him, labour-power had to remove itself from capital, stop being its variable expression, and refuse to carry out capital's needs. In this way he developed the idea of a political entrepreneurship: 'Here, we are happy to see Schumpeter's figure of the entrepreneur, with his initiative of innovation, being reversed in the permanent initiative of struggle of the great working masses. In this way, labour-power can – indeed must – become a power of struggle. This is the political transition from labour-power to working class.'[581] Already in the mid-1970s, Negri started to level the difference between the technical and the political composition of class by introducing the notion of the social worker, initially coined by Alquati, to present a new class subjectivity that is no longer produced in the factory, but in the process of the becoming-productive of every activity through the subsumption of the entire society under capital. This new and heterogenous class, for Negri, was 'already completely separated' and 'autonomous'[582] from capital. Hence, he suggested, that there is no need any more to 'define a line of division between the social and the political'.[583]

581. Tronti 1966, p. 177 [author's translation].
582. Negri 1996, p. 171.
583. Negri 1996, p. 174.

Ultimately, post-workerist authors like Negri, Lazzarato or Virno, in the 1990s, conceptualised another entrepreneurial class figure, this time animated by the generic force coming from life's plasticity.

Onto-technology

In other words, the post-workerist reading of Marx is structured by an 'onto-technological trick'[584] that consists in combining two arguments: firstly, contrary to the assumption of their non-totalisability, complex historical processes are reduced to the fulfilment of an ontological determination; secondly, the instance of potentiality is identified as medium of this fulfilment in which processes of being can be linked to processes of production. This instance is analysed, inconsistently, as non-corporeal potentiality of the brain (memory and attention in Lazzarato),[585] general pre-individual properties of the subject producing the human of the human being (capacity for speech, abstraction, improvisation, and self-reflection in Virno),[586] or flesh, in the sense of an incarnation of the productive means in a first element (in Negri).[587]

The determination of an onto-technological instance, oscillating between disembodiment and incarnation in which post-workerist authors link being and production, can be traced back to different interpretations of the Marxian concept of the 'general intellect' used in the sixth and seventh notebooks of *The Grundrisse*[588] to designate the transition from the labour process to the production process. In these notebooks Marx diagnosed a final crisis of industrial capital, since the productive deployment of the totality of knowledge available in society and the efficiency of machinery created an effect that subverted the logic of valorisation – objectively as well as subjectively. In relation to machine capacity, the expenditure of labour-power becomes secondary, the necessary labour time to produce a commodity decreases, the value of the commodity sinks, the dimension of

584. Rancière 2005, p. 25.
585. Cf. Lazzarato 2007, p. 186; Cf. also the chapter 'Brain machine' in Negri 1998.
586. Cf. Virno 2004, pp. 136; 151f. In his 2008 book on the multitude, Virno, in an examination of Plessner and Schmitt, suggests that man is a dangerous animal, distinguished by language and an indeterminate potentiality to act that is not proto-communist, but can be expressed in both a reactionary as well as emancipatory way, cf. especially 'So-called "Evil" and Criticism of the State', pp. 9–66.
587. Negri 2002, pp. 115 passim.
588. Cf. Marx 1993, pp. 590–609; this chapter is designated in workerism as 'The Fragment on Machines'.

freely available time becomes accessible, the all-sided unfolding of the individual can be anticipated. Marx writes: 'Capital is itself a moving contradiction in that it presses to reduce labour time to a minimum, while it posits labour time, on the other side as the sole measure and source of wealth.'[589]

Like Marx, who in *The Grundrisse* oscillates between the analysis of the self-contradiction of capital and the announcement that the social potentialities subsumed under the total process of the machinery, serving as its organs and links, are in reality the conditions to 'explode' capital,[590] post-workerist authors recognise in the 'general intellect' a proto-communist instance that is constantly reintegrated into capitalist relations of production and reproduction. However, the major changes that occurred in the relationship between capital and labour-power since then are interpreted in terms of the separation and self-valorisation of the masses: following the struggles of 1968, post-workerist authors recognise a process in which living labour separated itself from capital by incorporating the knowledge and the productive means to manage production: 'Historically, capital provided the worker with the instrument of labour; as soon as the human brain re-appropriates this instrument of labour, capital loses the ability to articulate the command by means of the instrument.'[591] Consequently, capital is conceived of having mutated into an exterior mechanism of value extraction and police control, realising value by acts of immediate expropriation (land grabbing, etc.) or on an abstract niveau distant to the production process (financial speculation, rent, etc.).

For Negri, this autonomy of a mass-intellectual labour-power represents the culmination of the socialisation of production. Living labour does not create the means of social life, but social life itself. Economy, politics and trans-individual being coincide. The productive forces are immediately translated into relations of production.[592] Labour is substantialised; capital derealised as nothing more than a parasitic mechanism appropriating creative productivity. Hence, the multitude as embodiment of this productivity is defined in a circular way. It represents both the condition and the result of social change. It embodies the active dissolution of the existing order and the production of the new. Its radical subjectification is carried out at the precise point at which the processes of social change change. Its labour

589. Marx 1993, p. 601.
590. Marx 1993, p. 602.
591. Negri 2007, p. 21.
592. Cf. Negri 1996, p. 152: 'There is an immediate translatability between the social forces of production and the relation of production themselves.'

potentiality is given in post-Fordism the highest actuality, introducing the transition to communism. In short, it is the last class, the last content of the capitalist form. It is the ontological and biopolitical entrepreneur of itself and of communism, 'the entrepreneur of fullness, who seeks essentially to construct a productive fabric'.[593] With this analysis, developed in the 1990s and 2000s, post-workerism seems to formulate a positive or vitalist variant of the idealised idea of practice that we can find in the young Marx, when he thought class struggle in the imminence of the revolution. Vis à vis all forms of abstractions – the abstractions of mind, law, property, state and religion – the proletariat occupied the opposite and anti-ideological pole of the real: Denuded of all properties, robbed of all possessions, universally disappropriated and universally suffering, the proletariat was to Marx that exceptional class which is not a class of civil society but its active dissolution.[594]

Which Spinoza?

Negri's interpretation of the 'Fragments on Machines' in *The Grundrisse* communicates with his reading of Spinoza. In *The Savage Anomaly*, written in prison in 1979 and 1980, he grafts Spinoza's idea of the *conatus* from the third and fourth part of the *Ethics* onto the idea, that Marx developed in the *Grundrisse*, of living labor as form-giving capacity subsumed under the production process. The *conatus* is defined by Spinoza as the striving immanent to the existing thing or mode, insofar as it is in itself, to 'persevere in its being'[595] and to increase it. Departing from the 18th proposition of the fourth book of the *Ethics* – 'Desire arising from joy is, other conditions being equal, stronger than desire arising from sadness' – Negri conceives of the conatus as a kind of jumping board of existence, a force that, as also Deleuze emphasises, links mechanical (persisting, preserving), dynamic-organisational (increasing, favoring) and antagonist capacities (opposing that which opposes).[596] In Spinoza, the *conatus* as a self-organising, self-accumulating force capacitates us to graduate from joyful passions to an increased potentiality to act, to insight into the reasons for this increase, and finally to arrive at active affects and intellectual self-possession of the singular potentiality that distinguishes a being in its essence (knowledge of

593. Negri 1998.
594. Cf. Marx 1975b.
595. Spinoza 1985, E3p6, p. 498.
596. Cf. Deleuze 1988, p. 101.

the third kind, union in the love of God):[597] 'For Spinoza, in other words, love is a production of the common that constantly aims upward, seeking to create more with ever more power, up to the point of engaging with the love of God, that is, the love of nature as a whole, the common in its most expansive figure.'[598] In this perspective, Negri's reading of Spinoza enables him to imagine the project of communism as an infinitely creative production, which starts from below, through a force imminent to life, through local, corporeal affections, and is impelled by joyful passions: it is the joy arising from a positive chance encounter, which pushes the accumulation movement of *conatus* from persistence to increase. It enables one to form an adequate idea of why elements are positively composed, because adequate ideas (common notions or knowledge of the second kind) emerge, according to Spinoza, from the intellectual appropriation or the genetic conceptualisation of the experience of having something in common. These first common notions catalysed by joy put people and groups into the situation of being able to organise their encounters, no longer leaving them to chance, to the permanent oscillation between composition (joy) and decomposition of their elements (sadness). It is from here, on the open path of '*conatus-potentia-mens*',[599] that Negri sees the creative and proto-communist process of being set in.

If we compare this reading with the one put forth by Balibar we detect a major difference. Instead of short-circuiting economic, ontological and political theorems, Balibar distinguishes the political from the ethical position in Spinoza by a minimal shift in perspective. Where Negri focused in his reading on the joyful passions and the ascending path striving-potentiality-intellect, Balibar emphasises the oscillation of affects and the fear of the masses, which can become ever more intemperate, the more the masses are terrorised through religion and oppression, so that their fear increases to nationalist and theological hatred.[600] Balibar does not read Spinoza's theory of affects through the medium of joy as Negri does, but through the differentiation of hatred and joy, through their increase and decrease, through the very points of transition where they revert into each other.

Once Spinoza not only explains imaginations and passions on the basis of object choices (what you like, what you do not like), but on the

597. Cf. Spinoza 1985, E5p15: 'Who clearly and plainly understands himself and his affects, loves God and all the more so, the more he understands himself and his affects.'
598. Negri, 1991b, p. 176.
599. Negri 1991b, p. 228.
600. Cf. Balibar 1994, pp. 3–37.

basis of the relationships individuals imagine to have to their objects, the entire problem of affective socialisation dramatically changes. Sociality is no longer understood in terms of a social bond between human beings, but in terms of the real-imaginary production of the images that one makes oneself of the relationships one has established. This imaginary production of the others works by a mechanism that is called affect imitation with which we respond to things we perceive as being similar to us.[601] We feel joy about that of which we think similar beings feel joy, we are sad about that of which we imagine them to be sad, and we oscillate when they reject what we love. To avoid these ambivalences which characterise all imaginary identifications testifying that all of these similar things are indeed different ones, we tend to an affect that Spinoza calls ambition and consists in doing something in order to appeal to the imaginary other, to be recognised and loved by her or him.[602] From these introjection and projection mechanisms might emerge a field of provisionary social agreements but if those agreements do not include occasions for a radical change to political rationality, this field will decompose itself into pieces of hatred and resentment. This is why Balibar determines the question of politics in Spinoza to be the question of the transition points in the affectivity of the masses. The lowest level of imagination is reached when a society is based on affect imitation and the identification with what is perceived to be similiar, i.e. on the fear of difference. As Spinoza has shown with regard to the ruin of the ancient Hebrew state, fear of difference will lead to social and religious hatred and might escalate into terror. Affectivity and thought, in contrast, arrive at a maximal level in a republic that is built on friendship, egality and cooperation. But Spinoza knows that the question of politics is not friendship, egality and cooperation themselves, but their production which spans between minimal and maximal thresholds, between reactionary and emancipatory expressions. .

In a realist tradition that rejects Morus' utopianism, Spinoza demands neither to ridicule nor to exclude negative, decreased or depotentialised affects but to grasp them as expression of the social conditions, in which, not against which, politics has to be made. Centuries before Nietzsche and Foucault, Spinoza thinks that the forces that pass through the individuals are catalysers both of liberation and oppression. The production of society through the affects spans through a field that knows a vec-

601. Cf. Spinoza 1985, E3p27–31, and Balibar 1998, pp. 105–13.
602. Cf. Spinoza 1985, E3p29s, E3p31c, E5p4s.

tor of potentialisation and of becoming reactionary. To think politics is to relate both processes to one another and to change their relationship.

This non-idealised relationality of politics imminent to Spinoza's ontology is neglected in Negri's reading.

REFERENCES

Agamben, Giorgio 1999, 'Absolute Immanence', in *Potentialities. Collected Essays in Philosophy*, Stanford: Stanford University Press.
Althusser, Louis 2005, *For Marx*, translated by Ben Brewster, London: Verso, <http://www.marx2mao.com/Other/FM65i.html>.
Althusser, Louis 1976, 'Elements of Self-Criticism', in *Essays in Self-Criticism*, translated by Grahame Lock, London: NLB. <http://www.marx2mao.com/Other/ESC76NB.html>
Althusser, Louis and Étienne Balibar 2006, *Reading Capital*, translated by Ben Brewster, London: Verso. <http://www.marx2mao.com/Other/RC68i.html>.
Balibar, Étienne 1991, 'From Class Struggle to Classless Struggle', in Étienne Balibar and Immanuel Wallerstein, *Race, Nation, Class*, translated by Chris Turner, London and New York: Verso.
Balibar, Étienne 1992, 'Foucault and Marx. The question of nominalism', in T.J. Armstrong (ed.), *Michel Foucault, philosopher*, London and New York: Harvester Wheatsheaf.
Balibar, Étienne 1994, 'Spinoza, the Anti-Orwell: The Fear of the Masses', in *Masses Classes, Ideas*, translated by James Swenson, London and New York: Routledge.
Balibar, Étienne 1994, *Spinoza and Politics*, translated by Peter Snowdon, London and New York: Verso.
Balibar, Étienne 2002, 'Three Concepts of Politics', in *Politics and the other Scene*, translated by Daniel Hahn, London and New York: Verso.
Bologna, 2000, 'For an Analysis of Autonomia. An Interview led by Patrick Cuninghame', in *Left History*, Vol. 7, No. 2,
Blanchot, Maurice 1997, 'Marx's Three Voices', in *Friendship*, translated by Elisabeth Rottenberg, Stanford: Stanford University Press.
Deleuze, Gilles 1988, *Spinoza. Practical Philosophy*, translated by Robert Hurley, San Francisco: City Lights Books.
Engels, Friedrich 1934, 'A Letter to J. Bloch (London, 21 September 1890)'

in 'Four Letters on Historical Materialism', *New International*, Vol. 1, No. 3.

Foucault, Michel 1990, *The History of Sexuality. An Introduction*, translated by Robert Hurley, London: Penguin Books.

Foucault, Michel 1980, 'Power and Strategies', in Colin Gordon (ed.), *Michel Foucault. Power/Knowledge*, Harvester: Hemel Hempstead.

Foucault, Michel 2007, *Security, Territory, Population, Lectures at the Collège de France, 1977–78*, translated by Graham Burchell, edited by Michel Senellart, Basingstoke: Palgrave.

Hyppolite, Jean 1973, *Studies on Marx and Hegel*, translated by John O'Neill, New York: Harper & Row.

Lazzarato, Maurizio 2006, 'The Concepts of Life and the Living in the Societies of Control', in Martin Fuglsang and Bent Meier Sørensen (eds.), *Deleuze and the Social*, Edinburgh: Edinburgh University Press.

Marx, Karl 1975a, 'Economic and Philosophical Manuscripts of 1844', MECW, vol. 3, New York: International Publishers.
<http://www.marxists.org/archive/marx/works/1844/manuscripts/labour.htm>

Marx, Karl 1975b, 'Introduction to A Contribution to the Critique of Hegel's *Philosophy of Right*', MECW, vol. 3, Moscow: Progress Publishers.

Marx, Karl 1993, *The Foundations of the Ctitique of Political Economy(Rough Draft)*, translated by Martin Nicolaus, London: Penguin.

Miller, Jacques-Alain 2009, 'Action of Structure', in *The Symptom* Nr. 10.
<http://www.lacan.com/thesymptom/?p=423>

Negri, Antonio 1991a, *Marx beyond Marx. Lessons on the Grundrisse*, London and New York: Autonomedia/Pluto.
<http://libcom.org/files/Negri%20-%20Marx%20Beyond%20Marx%20-%20Lessons%20on%20the%20Grundrisse.pdf>

Negri, Antonio 1991b, *Savage Anomaly: The Power of Spinoza's Metaphysics and Politics*, translated by Michael Hardt, Minneapolis: University of Minnesota Press.
<http://www.generation-online.org/p/fpnegri17.htm>

Negri, Antonio 1996, 'Twenty Theses on Marx. Interpretation of the Class Situation Today', in Saree Makdisi et al. (eds.), *Marxism beyond Marxism*, London and New York: Routledge.

Negri, Antonio 1998, 'Back to the future', English translation of a video interview, published in an extended version as *Exil*, Paris: Editions Mille et Un Nuits.
<http://www.generation-online.org/p/fpnegri19.htm>

Negri, Antonio 2002, 'Towards an Ontological Definition of the Multitude', in *Multitude*, No. 9, <http://multitudes.samizdat.net/spip.php?article269>.

Negri, Antonio 2007, 'Zur gesellschaftlichen Ontologie. Materielle Arbeit, immaterielle Arbeit und Biopolitik', in Thomas Atzert et al. (eds.), *Empire und die biopolitische Wende*.

Negri, Antonio and Michael Hardt 2009: *Commonwealth*, Cambridge, Massachusetts: Harvard University Press.

Rancière, Jacques 2005, 'From the Actuality of Communism to its Inactuality', unpublished English manuscript, p. 2, German translation published in *Indeterminate Kommunismus. Texte zu Ökonomie, Politik und Kultur*, Münster: Unrast.

Spinoza, Baruch de 1985, *The Ethics*, in *The Collected Works of Spinoza*, vol. 1, translated and edited by Edwin Curley, Princeton: Princeton University Press.

Tronti, Mario 1974, A*rbeiter und Kapital*, Frankfurt/ M.: Neue Kritik.

Virno, Paolo 2004, *The Grammar of the Multitude. For an Analysis of Contemporary Forms of Life*, translated by Isabella Bertoletti, James Cascaito and Andrea Casson, New York: Semiotexte, <http://www.generation-online.org/c/fcmultitude3.htm>.

Virno, Paolo 2008, *Multitude. Between Innovation and Negation*, New York: Semiotexte.

OPERAISMO AND ITS ACTUALITY TODAY

Steve Wright

Given its importance as a European Marxist tendency of the late twentieth century, there is still not a great deal that is known about the Italian workerism (*operaismo*) of the sixties and seventies. If anything, it continues to be overshadowed by the subsequent work and activities of some of the individuals and currents that emerged from its defeat. When I first read some workerist texts for the first time, more than thirty years ago, I was fascinated above all by their challenge to the common sense of orthodox marxism, starting with their affirmation of the struggle against work as a working class practice. Celebrating experiences that tried to ground a revolutionary mass politics in the shifting structure of the working class, the *operaisti* made some entertainingly provocative statements: for example, regarding the history of the American working class, Mario Tronti had once asserted that 'The smaller the contribution of leftist culture, the more the class pregnancy of a given social reality comes forward'[603].

Back in the seventies, I wanted to make sense of the history of the working class where I lived, in Australia, and texts such as Tronti's, alongside others by Sergio Bologna and Romano Alquati, offered a new interpretative key, a new way of reading social processes as part of that interpreting of history. These texts seemed attentive to the rhythms of class struggle, and provided a framework for establishing the relationships between cycles of struggle and cycles of accumulation. The British historian E. P. Thompson had famously written of the 'making' of the English working class: *operaismo* instead spoke of the class' continual making and remaking, with each iteration bringing new political projects, organisational forms, and class demands in its wake: what the workerists called 'class composition'. As I dug further into the few workerist texts then in translation, it was evident that *operaismo* itself contained significant internal fissures, and that the only way to explore these was to examine its outpourings in the original Italian. What Guido Borio, Francesca Pozzi and Gigi Roggero have called workerism's 'multiple pathways with their roots in a common theoretical

603. Tronti 1971.

matrix'[604] may have developed closely together at first, but the divergences that followed were often dramatic, as can be seen in the marked differences in outlook that today separate many of its former adherents. As I came to discover, *operaismo* at its worst tended to replicate the stage-ist logic of so-called 'historical materialism', trying to force social processes to conform to its own processional logic of class figures: professional worker, mass worker, socialized worker. Often this went hand in hand with hasty organizational 'solutions' that belied the tendency's original attentiveness to class composition: whether it was as born-again Communist party members, or 'militants within 'organised Autonomy', the answer to most questions was too often 'build the party'. In its better moments, however, the discourse on class composition attempted to explain class behaviour in terms that critically interrogated Marx's *Capital* through the lenses of contemporary capitalist production, laying the bases for innovative experiments in working class self-organisation, whether at FIAT during the wildcat strikes of 1969, or in the petrochemical factories outside Venice.[605]

One outcome of this digging through the outpourings of the *operaisti* was the discovery of the workerist history journal *Primo Maggio*, founded in the early seventies. The writings of the historians associated with that journal (from Sergio Bologna to Peppino Ortoleva, from Marco Revelli to Bruno Cartosio) proved intriguing: more self-critical than earlier worker-ist historical research, it was all the richer and more suggestive as a result. Joined by some of the pioneers of Italian oral history, such as Sandro Portelli and Cesare Bermani, the editors of *Primo Maggio* had not simply celebrated the struggles of the past (starting with those of the IWW), but attempted to understand the long years of apparent silence on the front of open class conflict. More than this, in examining the past through the eyes of the present, they had also sought to engage directly with the political problems of their own time, working with workers collectives in a number of industries (especially transport) in an effort to understand and defeat the industrial restructuring unleashed in response to the proletarian gains that followed 1969. Along with *Collegamenti*, a journal founded by class struggle anarchists and libertarian marxists involved in workplace and neighbourhood organising (and still extant today), *Primo Maggio* quickly became my favourite Italian publication of the period.

604. Borio, Pozzi & Roggero 2005, pp. 34-5.
605. For insights into the latter case, see the film *Porto Marghera, The Last Firebrands* – Pellarin 2004.

All of which derailed my original interest in Australian working class history, and led instead to a prolonged study of Italian workerism, eventually published as a book.[606] When the first draft of that text was completed, at the end of the eighties, the political circles in which I then moved were burdened less by the collapse of 'actually existing socialism' – a series of events that, on the contrary, filled us with delight, since it seemed to indicate the return of open class struggle in the 'East' – than by the apparent faltering of the workplace revolts which had shaken Australia and other 'Western' social formations in the prior decade. Examining the experience of the Italian *operaisti* during the sixties and seventies, then, was one way of trying to understand that previous wave of class conflict, and what could be learned from its defeat.

The roots of workerism itself lie in efforts to understand an earlier class defeat, which led in turn during the fifties to Italy's so-called economic 'miracle' of industrialisation and urbanisation. The 'miracle' greatly expanded and reshaped that country's working class, even as it apparently tamed and 'embourgeoisified' the latter. *Operaismo* was also one response to the incapacity of most sections of the local workers' movement – both parties and unions – to understand and engage with these new workers, and with their cultures and needs, so often distant from the sensibilities of the traditional left. Together with other circles within the new left of the late fifties and sixties, the proto-workerists attempted to map the power relationships within factories such as FIAT, conducting 'co-research' with small groups of worker militants keen to rebuild an antagonistic class presence within industry. According to Bologna,

> In the sixties – co-research, to my mind, is functional to what I'm about to say – we were convinced that within the body of the working class there was already, whole, the knowledge of liberation, the awareness of solidarity, of cohesion, of rebellion. We were convinced that in the genetic inheritance of the working class lay conflict as a form of social identity, but that there was also a memory of hard defeats and therefore, you could say, a 'prudence' that had to be respected.[607]

The encounter between worker militants and intellectuals within

606. Wright 2002.
607. Bologna 2001, p. 12.

the context of workplace organizing shaped both parties profoundly. As Augusto Finzi states in the film *The Last Firebrands*, remembering his initial contacts with the likes of Toni Negri, Guido Bianchini, Luciano Ferrari Bravo and Massimo Cacciari,

> It was the first time that I understood what a picket meant, what it meant to make demands, what alternatives there might be to piece-work, what an enquiry might be, what professional skills might be. All those things which I had heard of, which nobody had ever ex-plained, because neither the party nor the union was able to explain these things.[608]

As Riccardo Bellofiore and Massimiliano Tomba have since pointed out, often 'the workerism of male and female workers was more advanced than the reflections of the current's theoreticians'.[609] That the most astute of the *operaisti* were themselves more than aware of this emerges clearly within a recent anthology entitled *The workerism of the sixties*, edited by Giuseppe Trotta and Fabio Milana. This book is a very rich resource for all those who want to understand how the *operaista* laboratory functioned during that decade, containing as it does the minutes of meetings, letters, leaflets, and other primary source material. In one text from 1962, Romano Alquati is quoted at the end of a meeting affirming that 'We have always studied *Das Kapital*, but we haven't studied how workers organize and move'.[610] The ef-forts to redress this failing would launch the workerists upon some of their most important political experiments, particularly in Northern cities such as Turin, Milan and Venice. In fact, as Mario Tronti would acknowledge in an interview reprinted in the same volume,

> [Our] Roman group, like the Northerners, arrived at the notion of the political centrality of the working class and the factory. But the difference consisted in this: they arrived at this because they had that working class in front of them. They saw it, they studied it, whereas we arrived at that point by following a theoretical path, reading Marx'.[611]

Perhaps *operaismo* began as an enterprise set in motion by intellectuals, but

608. In Pellarin 2004.
609. Bellofiore and Tomba 2008, p. 304.
610. In Trotta and Milana, p. 252.
611. In Trotta and Milana, p. 600.

in some important cases, such as in Porto Marghera, it became a project where militant workers engaged in self-organised struggles, and continued to build workplace organizations even when abandoned by their earlier allies. Back in the mid seventies, Bologna had asserted that the process of working class autonomy was in permanent contradiction with the construction of the party. With hindsight, it can be said that much of the confusion that descended upon the Italian workerists in the early seventies stemmed from the 'failure' of militant workers to follow the path that had been prescribed by them. For it was precisely after the euphoria of the Hot Autumn of 1969 that many of the *operaisti* were to discover that the forces of self-organisation which they had championed in the factories, and had in turn come to impose their egalitarian programme upon the working class as a whole (and with it much of the union movement), were in large part now developing their own agendas, separate and in part antagonistic to those of the majority of workerists. It is in this period that it becomes possible to begin to distinguish between what Primo Moroni would later call the 'rational' and the 'irrational' workerists: between those who wanted to force the process of working class autonomy towards some pre-ordained path, and those who chose, for better or worse, to support that autonomy as it sought to challenge capital and the state.

Operaismo would produce a series of distinctive categories, from the refusal of work to passivity as an elementary form of organisation. But the most innovative workerist category by far remains that of class composition. Why? Because it draws attention to changes within the process of production as seen from a working class point of view, in terms of the implications of these changes for demands and forms of struggle. Beginning as a sensitivity to those 'young forces' within workplaces that most traditional sections of the labour movement proved unable to understand, the category class composition became increasingly sophisticated with use. By the end of the sixties, it had come to mean a process of struggle against the divisions imposed by capital, and the attempts to overcome this fragmentation ('decomposition') through a process of recomposition. At that point in time, the privileged class figure for the *operaisti* was the mass worker: a 'rude pagan race' (Tronti) of seemingly interchangeable drones who were able to defy the dictatorship of the assembly line, and challenge not only the boss, but the cult of work itself. The rise of the so-called new social movements, and attacks upon the mass worker itself, would further complicate the picture, accentuating the differing prognoses for political activity advanced by the various camps within *operaismo* as a political tendency.

If the most useful thing that remains from the workerist experience is the centrality given to deciphering class composition as the foundation of anti-capitalist politics, it is precisely this distinctive discourse of reading class composition that has suffered most from the defeat thirty years ago of *operaismo* and the broader revolutionary movement of which it was part. Certainly a discourse has continued since that time of looking to new social figures, from the 'precariat' to self-employed workers or the 'multitude'. But for the most part, there has not been much discussion amongst the ex-workerists concerning the relationship between all the various sections that together comprise the proletariat: at most, there has been some reflections about a given stratum deemed hegemonic, or of interest for some other reason. More than this, the categories particular to the original discourse used in the past to interpret working class figures – above all, the relationship between structures and behaviours (to use workerist jargon, between the class' technical composition and its political composition) – is almost never deployed in such analyses.

There is still a lot to learn from *operaismo*'s insistence upon trying to view modern social relations through the prism of shifting patterns of class composition and recomposition. Unfortunately (or perhaps fortunately), no neat class figure akin to the mass worker is evident today as a privileged reference point for recomposition. In an age of multiple subjects in struggle, just what recomposition now means seems equally hard to determine. Surely the capital relation and state form will not die through a thousand pinpricks? As usual, theory will likely have to chase behind the practices that concrete singularities evolve. And if we look back with care, we find that, even (especially!) in the time of the mass worker's glory, there were 'multiple subjects' in struggle, and that neither simple-minded 'unity', let alone submission to the hegemony of one layer of the class, were appropriate ways of understanding or practicing recomposition …

If class composition analysis has often been in disarray since the defeat of Italy's mass worker in the early eighties, important work has nonetheless been done in the meantime. A few years ago, for example, the work around call centre workers conducted by Kolinko has – not without some controversy – sparked a renewed discussion of the *operaista* practice of workers' enquiries, and the ways in which these might be relevant today.[612] In a similar vein, Hardt and Negri's *Empire* can be said, at the very least, to have

612. Kolinko 2002; Aufheben 2004.

laid bare the inadequacies of many commonplace leftist suppositions concerning imperialism. For those less than convinced by *Empire*'s explanation of contemporary global capitalism, there is a surfeit of alternative explanatory frameworks on offer. The problem, as Ferrari Bravo once pointed out, is that we live in a period when 'the same series of facts offer different and "untranslatable" readings'.[613] Then again, by looking at the world through lenses rather different from those developed by *operaismo*, Beverly Silver's study of the *Forces of Labor* offers some useful working hypotheses for understanding some of the possibilities facing us all. Whether this or some other framework will prove most suitable will have to be seen: the best that we can do (to quote Ferrari Bravo again) is to test the adequacy of each in terms of its ability 'to provide meaning to the prospect of liberation from oppression and exploitation'.[614]

In this spirit, it was a pleasure to read an article not so long ago by Mario Tronti, in which he underlined the need to '[bring] the theme of work back on the political agenda. How? With whom? The answer to the last question seems obvious: with the workers themselves. Getting to know them again, these unknowns. Getting them to speak again, these mutes'. According to Tronti, there is less need for 'the immaterial, the cognitive, the politics that is bios', and more for 'women and men of flesh and bone who organise themselves for the struggle'.[615] In attempting this task, it will be necessary to draw upon the work of a range of tendencies that place workers' self-organisation at the heart of their political project. As part of that process, we may well find that, while their original answers may no longer suffice, many of the questions raised by the workerists of the sixties and seventies remain urgent and relevant.

REFERENCES

Aufheben 2004, 'Review Article – Hotlines: "We have Ways of Making you Talk!"', *Aufheben* 12.
Bellofiore, Riccardo and Massimiliano Tomba 2008, 'Postfazione', in Wright, Steve *L'assalto al cielo. Per una storia dell'operaismo*, Rome: Edizioni Alegre.

613. Ferrari Bravo 2000, p. 358.
614. Ferrari Bravo 2000, p. 344.
615. Tronti 2008.

Bologna, Sergio 2001, 'Intervista 21 febbraio 2001', now in the CD-ROM accompanying Borio, Guido, Francesca Pozzi & Gigi Roggero, *Futuro anteriore. Dai "Quaderni Rossi" ai movimenti globali: ricchezze e limiti dell'operaismo italiano*, Rome: DeriveApprodi.

Borio, Guido, Francesca Pozzi and Gigi Roggero (eds.) 2005, *Gli operaisti*, Rome: Derive Approdi.

Ferrari Bravo, Luciano 2001, *Dal fordismo alla globalizzazione. Cristalli di tempo politico*, Rome: Manifestolibri.

Hardt, Michael and Antonio Negri 2000 *Empire*, Cambridge, Mass.: Harvard University Press.

Kolinko 2002, *Hotlines*, http://www.nadir.org/nadir/initiativ/kolinko/lebuk/e_lebuk.htm

Pellarin, Manuela (dir.) 2004 *Porto Marghera, The Last Firebrands*, http://libcom.org/files/firebrands_booklet_2_horizontal.pdf

Silver, Beverly 2003, *Forces of Labor: Workers' Movements and Globalization since 1870*, Cambridge: Cambridge University Press.

Tronti, Mario (1971) 'Workers and Capital', http://libcom.org/library/workers-and-capital-mario-tronti

Tronti, Mario (2008) 'The Politics of Work', http://conjunctural.blogspot.com/2008/10/old-guard-on-new-crisis-pt-2-mario.html, translated by Alberto Toscano.

Trotta, Giuseppe and Fabio Milana (eds.) 2008 *L'operaismo degli anni Sessanta*. Rome: DeriveApprodi.

Wright, Steve 2002, *Storming Heaven. Class composition and struggle in Italian Autonomist Marxism*, London: Pluto Press.

A DIFFICULT LOVE AFFAIR?
ON THE RELATION BETWEEN
MARXISM AND THEOLOGY

Roland Boer

The relationship – often difficult and rancorous – between Marxism and theology continues to fascinate me. Why are Marxism and theology so close, I wonder? Why do they argue so much? Is it something that weakens each one, holding the other back? Or are they, perhaps, stronger and sharper because of that tense connection? In fact, I was so enthralled by this liaison that I have written a book series on it, called *The Criticism of Heaven and Earth*. This essay gives me the chance to reflect upon what I am doing with the project. For, as one of my former teachers once said to me, you need to know what you are talking about, since if you don't, how on earth are you going to communicate that to anyone else? So, I will say a little about the first book in the series, *Criticism of Heaven*, as well as the other four. However, so that this essay does not become an exercise in pure self-indulgence, I will soon enough turn to three questions. Why are theology and Marxism so close? Why do they argue so much? And what does it mean for both of them?

The 'Criticism' series

As for the books themselves, let me begin with an enticing statement by the early Marx that keeps coming back to me. In his 'Contribution to the Critique of Hegel's Philosophy of Law' he writes:

> Thus the criticism of heaven turns into the criticism of earth, the *criticism of religion* into the *criticism of law* and the *criticism of theology* into the *criticism of politics*.[616]

This text comes in the midst of the famous and much-discussed section where Marx begins by saying that the criticism of religion is the beginning of all criticism and moves onto his well-known metaphors of flowers, chains and opium. Now, I do not want to offer yet another opinion about

616. Marx 1975, p. 176.

opium, sighs of oppressed creatures and chains here (that is for the study of Marx and Engels). What we have in this quotation from Marx is what might be called poetic parallelism.[617] In fact, we have a triple parallelism: from the criticism of heaven to the criticism of earth, from religion to law, and from theology to politics. On the one side are heaven, religion and theology, while on the other there are earth, law and politics. The strange thing is that, for all their desire for a criticism of earth, law and politics, Marxists have a knack of devoting a good deal of attention to matters of heaven, religion and theology. I must admit that I am one of them.

Initially, I adopted the phrase *Criticism of Heaven* for the first book. I had no plans for any further volumes. I knew that some Marxists had written on religion, that Marx and Engels's scattered comments on religion had generated much debate, and I was aware that one or two other Marxists had even written on the Bible, for I had first encountered Ernst Bloch more than twenty years ago. But as I read, searched and studied further, I was continually surprised by how much Marxists have written on the Bible and theology. I do not mean religion in a general sense (which is all too often interchanged with 'theology' in ways that still bother me), but the disciplines of biblical studies and theology, which have their own histories. My focus was squarely on theology, partly because of my background, and partly because most treatments of religion and Marxism do so from the perspective of the sociology of religion, a discipline for which Marx is one of the founders along with Durkheim and Weber.[618] Initially I tried to contain my study to Ernst Bloch,[619] Walter Benjamin[620] and Theodor Adorno (who wrote his first book on philosophy, his *habilitation* on Kierkegaard, under the direction of the theologian Paul Tillich).[621] I sent the manuscript off in 2003, but was unhappy with it. So I pulled it and began working on it again. It grew and grew: Henri Lefebvre had been part of the Roman Catholic Church, albeit with the heretical Jansenists (his mother was

---

617. The term comes from the study of poetry in the Hebrew Bible, poetry in which the usual signs of poetry (at least by our own limited standards), such as rhythm and rhyme, are absent. Instead, one of the crucial features is the exercise of parallelism, where a text will say roughly the same thing in a different way in the next line. Here is one example: 'They shall build up the ancient ruins, they shall raise up the former devastations; they shall repair the ruined cities, the devastations of many generations' (Isaiah 61:4).

618. For instance Goldstein 2006; Ott 2007.

619. See especially Bloch 1972; 1985, Vols. 1, 4 and 5; 1995.

620. Benjamin 1974–89, Vols. 1, 2 (pp. 62-74) and 5; 1996; 1998; 1999.

621. Adorno 1973; 1986, Vols. 2, 3 and 6; 1989; Adorno and Horkheimer 1999.

one) only to undertake a lifelong flight from it;[622] Louis Althusser wrote a number of early theological essays before turning to Marxism[623] and the themes from those early essays permeate his later work; Antonio Gramsci wrote extensively on the Roman Catholic Church in Italy, the Reformation and so on;[624] Terry Eagleton had been a left theologian (and wrote some theological books) before becoming a Marxist, only to return to the theology in the new millennium;[625] Slavoj Žižek had thrashed his way to the New Testament via, of all people, Lenin.[626] By the time I had finished the manuscript of *Criticism of Heaven* it contained 290,000 words, which would have been a book of over 700 pages. I talked to a few publishers, but when I mentioned how long it was, they looked the other way. I sent it to Verso, it fell into the hands of Sebastien Budgen, who wrote to me to say it was too long for Verso, but that the Historical Materialism Book Series with Brill may well be interested. And then, after the poor referees had to wade through it, Peter Thomas wrote to me and said, yes, they would publish it, but perhaps I could try to 'shave off' 100,000 words. Over two weeks in Sofia, Bulgaria, I did so.

By this time I had written a few odd pieces and occasional essays on other Marxists. But that is it, I thought. I'm not going to write any more on this theme. Yet before I knew it, I had another book in hand. There were more Marxists dealing with theology, the Bible and even the Church! Rosa Luxemburg had written a booklet called Socialism and the Churches, where she argued for an early Christian communism and freedom of conscience on religious matters.[627] Karl Kautsky had not only written his fascinating but problematic *Foundations of Christianity*,[628] but also a massive unfinished study called *Vorläufer des neueren Sozialismus*,[629] of which only one volume and half have been translated as; 'Communism in Central Europe in the Time of the Reformation'.[630] Here he explored the various heretical sects in the Middle Ages and then the socialist dimensions of the Protestant Reforma-

622. Lefebvre 1991, pp. 201-27.
623. Althusser 1994; 1997.
624. Gramsci 1992; 1995; 1996.
625. Eagleton 1966; 1970; 2003a; 2003b.
626. Žižek 2000; 2001; 2003.
627. Luxemburg 1982; 2004.
628. Kautsky 1908; 2001.
629. Kautsky, 1976, Kautsky and Lafargue 1977
630. Kautsky 2002a.

tion, including his hero Thomas More.[631] Fredric Jameson has written a few essays on theological themes, such as those on Milton and St Augustine,[632] but theological questions that go back to Feuerbach lie behind sections of his recent 'Archaeologies of the Future'.[633] Lucien Goldmann remained fascinated by the theological dialectics of Pascal and Jansenism;[634] Alain Badiou[635] and Giorgio Agamben[636] sought to resuscitate Paul in the *New Testament* as a revolutionary; Raymond Williams had more to say than most of us would think on the Baptist Chapel of his native Wales; even George Lukács was given to curious theological arguments (such as that the novel is the genre of the world abandoned by God)[637] and spent his lifetime trying to eradicate what he saw as his messianic utopianism.[638] On and on it goes: Negri makes use of *New Testament* ideas such as the *kairos*[639] and has written a study of Job in the *Bible*;[640] E.P. Thompson became fascinated by the heretical British religious sects such as the Muggletonians;[641] Michael Löwy[642] has been working with liberation theology for some years now…

I have tried to keep the list concise, but you get the picture: it was more than enough for another book, so the manuscript for *Criticism of Religion* took shape. In light of the parallelism between the criticism of heaven and the criticism religion in the Marx text that I quoted a little earlier, these two books operate on the same basis: they explore and in some respects establish a Marxist tradition of engagements with theology and the Bible. It is all very well to list what these Marxists of different shades have done. The deeper question is what I am doing with these books. What are my aims? How do I go about it? The catch is that the answers to these questions have really emerged only as I have been writing. At the risk of being formulaic, I list the aims as I see them now. I seek:

To provide a comprehensive critical commentary on the interaction

631. Kautsky 1947; 2002b.
632. Jameson 1986; 1996.
633. Jameson 2005.
634. Goldmann 1959; 1964.
635. Badiou 1997; 2003.
636. Agamben 2000; 2005.
637. Lukács 1971; 1994.
638. Lukács 1968, p. 30; 1988, p. xxvii. See also Lukács 1973, pp. 308–26; 1983.
639. Negri 2003.
640. Negri 2002.
641. Thompson 1993.
642. Löwy 1988; 1996.

between materialism and theology within the work of the leading Marxist thinkers of the twentieth and twenty-first centuries.

To set the current surge of interest in the *Bible* and theology by Marxist critics such as Slavoj Žižek, Alain Badiou and Giorgio Agamben within historical perspective.

To explore, where possible, unknown and neglected theological writings by these critics.

To assess the implications of their theological engagements for the thought of each thinker as a whole.

To compare with each other the various theological engagements by these figures.

To produce my own coherent body of thought in response, with a specific focus on the question as to why Marxists are so interested in theology.

Each of these aims addresses something that has not been done. Apart from pointing out that there is no comprehensive commentary and assessment of what is really a tradition in its own right – the relationship between Marxism and theology – we also have a rather curious lack of historical perspective. What I mean is that for many, the recent spate of writings by Marxist philosophers focusing on Paul and the New Testament itself seems to been created *ex nihilo*. I have already mentioned the major interventions by Alain Badiou, Giorgio Agamben and Slavoj Žižek, but there has also been Hardt and Negri's evocation of a collective Christian love,[643] as well as Terry Eagleton's recovery of his days in the Catholic left. More are now being pulled into this debate, such as Sichère[644] and Trigano,[645] and the assessment of this development has itself begun.[646] However, what these studies lack is a distinct historical perspective, namely, that the Bible and theology have always been constant companions for Marxist thought and politics. By contrast, this project sets the interaction between materialism, theology and the Bible within the context of a longer historical tradition.

In light of such a deeper historical perspective, it soon becomes apparent that the flurry of interest in the theological engagements of Badiou, Agamben and Žižek is an anomaly. Indeed, going back to look at the

643. Hardt and Negri 2004, pp. 351-2, 358.
644. Sichère 2003.
645. Trigano 2004.
646. Blanton and De Vries forthcoming.

tradition before the current rush, I have been constantly surprised at the neglect of the writings on theology by many of the critics on whom I focus. These writings include monographs (Adorno, Bloch, Goldmann, Eagleton, Kautsky and Luxemburg), sections of monographs (Kristeva, Gramsci, Lukács, Williams), essays (Althusser, Eagleton, Lefebvre, Jameson, Luxemburg) and even the odd novel (Williams). The same should be said of Marx and Engels: for all the avalanche of commentary and engagement, they have not been subjected to an analysis of what they do with the Bible and theology.

A further problem is that where there has been critical discussion of these figures, in nearly all cases (the exception is really Walter Benjamin) it fails to assess their writings on theology in light of their *oeuvres* as a whole. This is especially the case with the spate of recent responses to Badiou, Agamben and Žižek. So I am interested in precisely this question: what is the implication for their work as a whole? Is it a peripheral concern, or is it more central? Two lines have opened up so far: either the wider principles of someone's work will also be applied to theology (a key example, here, is Rosa Luxemburg), or theological categories make their way into other parts of their work. Adorno and Althusser are good examples of this second process: Adorno makes the *Bilderverbot*, drawn from the ban on images of the second commandment in Exodus 20/Deuteronomy 5, into a basic motif of his work; Althusser's effort to banish the Church from his later work (it is central to his early essays) turns it into an absent cause of that work.

There are two final areas where no work has been done at all – a comparative critique of the various engagements with theology and a constructive response to those engagements. Now, one would hardly expect to find such work, since there has been no exploration of the whole tradition. All the same, it seems to me that both are necessary. Apart from assessing the role of theology in the *oeuvres* of each critic, what is also needed is a weighing and assessment of the work of each figure in light of the others. Here, I can assess whether one position criticises another, whether it is a step back or an improvement, why theology is so enticing for materialist critics, and so on. For example, if one sets out to secularise theological terms for political analysis (a rather common feature in the tradition), then I am very interested in any sustained critique of such secularised theology (Adorno is the key, here).

Finally, it is all very well to comment on the work of others, however critical one might be. But there is a time and a need for one to come clean and risk putting one's own position forward. I have, after all, gathered quite a collection of ideas that have developed in response to the sundry figures of this tradition – ideas such as necessary fables, theological suspicion, the critique of classicism, and the passing moment of theology. I am keen to knit them into a coherent body of thought, not least because theology has been and remains an important element of materialism. Indeed, it seems to me that materialism and theology are two sides of the same coin, or, in more rigorous terms, they are engaged in a dialectical relation that lies at the heart of this whole project.

To sum up, I would say that my approach in the *Criticism of Heaven and Earth* series is intimate, immanent, comparative, historical and con-structive. In other words, I seek to read patiently and carefully, refusing to rush over texts, to ask what the implications might be for the whole body of thought of each critic, to compare, weigh and assess each contribution in light of the others, to develop a sense of the distinct history of this tradi-tion, and then to construct my own creative and coherent body of thought in response.

By now, it should be obvious that there really had to be some further volumes. One was *Criticism of Theology*,[647] which dealt with Max Horkhe-imer, E. P. Thompson, G. E. M. de Ste. Croix, Michael Löwy, Roland Bar-thes, Deleuze and Guattari, and Antonio Negri. The fourth was *Criticism of Earth*,[648] focusing on the engagements with theology and the Bible in the works of Marx and Engels. These engagements are more extensive than one might think. While Marx was given to perpetual allusions from the Bible, theology and the Church, often with an ironic twist, Engels knew his Bible rather well. Able to read Koine (New Testament) Greek, having re-nounced with difficulty his evangelical (in the old German sense) faith, and keeping up with biblical studies, Engels was no amateur on these matters. He is even the source of a central element in the history of early Chris-tianity, namely its beginnings among the exploited classes in the Roman Empire. The famous observation from his *On the History of Early Christianity* reads: 'Christianity was originally a movement of oppressed people: it first appeared as a religion of slaves and freedmen, of poor people deprived of all rights, of peoples subjugated or dispersed by Rome'.[649] This position is not merely a staple of some strains of Marxist work, but is also a debated

647. Boer 2010.
648. Boer 2012.
649. Engels 1990, p. 447

377

matter in New Testament studies and Church history. So, *Criticism of Earth* will offered a patient reading and critique of Engels's theological works, along with an analysis of the extensive theological engagements in Marx's work, including his criticisms of the Young Hegelians (Bruno Bauer, Max Stirner and Ludwig Feuerbach), the theme of the fetish, and the political ambivalence of theology.

The final volume was *In the Vale of Tears*,[650] where I put forward my own position in light of the other three volumes. Let me see if I can state its argument in a few sentences: in exploring the dialectic of materialism and theology, I develop the category of theological suspicion out of the Marxist practice of ideology-critique in order to tackle the prevalent tendency to secularise theological terms for political debate. However, rather than a futile search to eradicate any trace of theology in materialist thought, I argue that theology provides one shape for such terms; they may equally well take on other forms, as they indeed have done and will do. Further, it seems to me that Marxism has done and must continue to construct what I call necessary fables, or rather viable political myths.[651] Finally, in light of a distinct definition of secularism – as the program of drawing one's terms from this world and this age – I explore what a new secularism might look like, where religion is its necessary flip-side, and then argue that Marxism, like religion, is an anti-secular program insofar as it draws its terms from another age beyond this one of capitalism. I do not have the space, here, to unpack these sentences, but at least they provide an idea of where my thought is at the moment concerning this volume.

Why are theology and Marxism so close?

That is more than enough on the five-volume series. Let me turn now to the three questions I mentioned earlier. A stock answer to the first question is that the two are so close since Marxism borrows some deep assumptions from theology, especially its prophetic criticism of the present world order (capitalism) and its eschatological projection of a future world that is qualitatively different (which usually goes under the name of communism). I am hardly saying anything new in pointing out that this has been a standard move to debunk Marxism as some secular religion – the 'church of communism' as it has been called. You would think that critics had become tired of such polemic, but you still find it in various places,

650. Boer 2014.
651. Boer 2008.

such as Rothbard's argument that all the totalitarian evils of Marxism are due to its secular version of theological eschatology, due, in short, to its effort to replace God.[652]

Others, such as Jameson[653] and Žižek,[654] argue that Marxism gains from the interaction, which has been going on at least since Engels. One might recast the relationship as one of forerunner and fulfilment in which various theological expressions are an imperfect foreshadowing of Marxism. For example, one might argue that Calvinist predestination is an earlier and inchoate way of expressing the ultimately determining instance of the market.[655] Or one might argue that early Christianity was a less complete form of communism, based on consumption rather than production; for a full realisation, we have to wait for a proper communism.[656] The various heretical and breakaway religious movements of the medieval and Reformation eras, such as the Taborites or Thomas Müntzer's peasants, also become forerunners of socialism, as Kautsky would have it.[657]

While I have at various moments endorsed such a view, it now seems to me that it makes only a few light scratches on the hard surface of this problem. Rather, it seems to me that Marxism and theology are so close because they occupy the same space. And it is a contested space, one that I would like to name political myth. As soon as I mention this term in various contexts it immediately becomes the focus of much debate, for more than one materialist and more than one theologian shies away from the term. It conjures up all too readily fictional stories, childhood fantasies, pre-scientific beliefs and the supposedly ignorant and superstitious phase of our human development. So let me offer a brief definition of political myth: an important story. In a little more detail: since myth is an alternative language saturated with images and metaphors, and since we use myth to speak about what cannot be spoken of in everyday terms, then myth is an extraordinarily powerful political medium. Political myth is then an important story with – as Georges Sorel argued[658] – motivational power that offers a political vision or an image of a better economic and political system.

652. Rothbard 1990.
653. Jameson 1971, pp. 116–18; 1981, p. 285
654. Žižek 2003.
655. Jameson 1986.
656. Luxemburg 1982; 2004.
657. Kautsky 1976; 2002; Kautsky and Lafargue 1977.
658. Sorel 1961, pp. 124, 127.

Let me use the example of Christian communism that has been so important for characters as diverse as Gerrard Winstanley, Rosa Luxemburg and Karl Kautsky, as well as the Christian Socialist movement today. Such a myth has, I would suggest, an enabling and virtual power with historical consequences. In other words, the myth of Christian communism may initially be an image, using figurative and metaphorical language that expresses a hope concerning communal living, but once it becomes an authoritative and canonical text, it gains a historical power of its own. It becomes the motivation for repeated and actual attempts at Christian communism. In this sense, it is possible to say that the myth of Christian communism will have been true at some future moment.

Or, in its Marxist version: the political myth of communism may initially be an image, often making use of figurative language that expresses a hope concerning communal living. However, once it has become an actual lived experience, however fleeting and fraught with problems, it becomes an authoritative and even canonical story that gains a historical power of its own, one that generates various plans and programs to bring it about. It becomes the motivation for repeated and actual attempts at such communism. So the political myth of communism will also have been true at some future moment.

I have made my point, it seems to me, that Marxism and theology lay claim to the same ground. Let me try a simple exercise I have undertaken before. If I ask people to describe the Marxist project in a simple sentence, we might come up with something like this: understanding the world in order to change it; or even more simply, socio-economic transformation. In that brief description we find the beginnings of a political myth as the crucial story for those who gather, in various ways, under the Marxist banner.

Why do they argue so much?

All too often, a very close and long relationship is marked by perpetual arguing and bickering. It seems as though those arguments were there right at the beginning. It is not so well known that when Marx and Engels wrote the 'Manifesto of the Communist Party' they did so at the request of a group that had not long beforehand been known as the *League of the Just*.[659] The curious thing about the *League of the Just*, which had been formed by German workers in Paris in 1836, was that it was an organisation with a substantial religious flavour, propagating utopian-socialist and

659. On what follows, see Struik 1986; and the classic Riazonov 1996, especially Chapter 4.

communist ideas and practices on the basis of the *Bible*. Marx and Engels were invited to join it in 1847, by which time the organisation numbered over a thousand members in many different countries. The relationship soon became testy. The old slogan of the *League of the Just* was distinctly biblical: it was to work towards 'the establishment of the Kingdom of God on Earth, based on the ideals of love of one's neighbour, equality and justice'. Marx and Engels didn't let it remain so for long: it became 'Working men of all countries, Unite!' And within a few months, they managed to get the new organisation to adopt the name of the *Communist League*. As they did so, they attacked some of the leading figures of the old *League of the Just*, such as Wilhelm Weitling and Bruno Bauer. Now, the journeyman Weitling was the author in 1842 of the central text for the old league, called 'Garantien der Harmonie und Freiheit' (*Guarantees of Harmony and Freedom*), in which he argued for a violent communist revolution and pictured not merely Christ as the forerunner of communism, but communism as Christianity without all its later developments. Despite his early admiration, Marx soon took a distinct stand against Weitling's near-prophet status. Indeed, the letters between Marx and Engels repeatedly discuss the need to counter Weitling's influence. As for the rather complex Bruno Bauer – Young Hegelian, *New Testament* scholar and political theorist – he of course came in for a sustained attack in 'The German Ideology'. A difficult relationship right from the start, it seems.

But why do Marxism and theology argue so much? I have partly answered this second question in the preceding section, for Marxism and theology argue with each other – breaking up for a time, only to be reconciled once again – precisely because they have a different take on that crucial question of what a better global future might look like (it is difficult to avoid such a phrase becoming either syrupy or corny). While a conventional theological answer would work from the world above to the world to come, the former inaugurating the latter, a Marxist answer begins with the world to come and then explores what might follow in any other domain. To stay with our well-tried spatial metaphor, theology operates with a top-down approach, whereas Marxism works from the bottom up.

The catch is that such a contrast is far too simplistic; so let us start again and answer the question from a different angle. It seems to me that Marxism and theology are both anti-secular programs. Responses I have had to this statement invariably assert that Marxism is secular because it takes its stand against religion. The problem with such a response is that secularism is understood as necessarily anti-religious. So let me take a step back and ask what the definition of secularism is: it is a system of thought and action, if not a way of living, that draws its terms purely from this age and from this world (*saeculum*) and not from some world above or future age. Other, popular senses of secularism may derive from this basic sense, especially the idea that secularism is an anti-religious program, that it entails the separation of church and state, and that one must keep theology well and truly away from the proper scientific disciplines. Yet these are but secondary meanings (and therefore not necessary ones) that may flow from the primary sense of secularism.

In this light, we can see that Marxism and theology are both thoroughly secular and anti-secular. But let me stay with the prime meaning of secularism: as a way of acting and thinking that draws its terms from this world, the implication is that a fully secular program does not draw its reference point from something beyond this world, whether that is a god or the gods above, or a better society and economic system in the future. On the first count, theology is disqualified; on the second count, Marxism is ruled out of order. So we have a delectable paradox: Marxism is thoroughly secular in one sense (did not Marx develop his deepest insights by immersing himself in the study of capitalism?), but in another it is not (it takes as its reference point a better society beyond capitalism). So too with theology: while it is vitally concerned with this age and this world, with its concerns regarding anthropology (the term is originally a theological one) and the history and shape of human collectives, it seeks to draw its terms of analysis from a realm beyond this secular one.

I am most interested in the anti-secular side of the equation, for it is here that Marxism and theology struggle over the same territory. While Marxism works towards a transformation (the usual term is revolution) of capitalism in favour of whatever communism might be, theology has its New Jerusalem that marks the end of one history and the beginning of an entirely new one. It is no wonder they argue so much, for the stakes are high: what will be the shape of this new society, this new socio-economic system? Will it draw its terms from above (the New Jerusalem descends from heaven) or from the new era of communism (what I have called elsewhere a temporal transcendence)?

At the risk of over-stressing my point, the quarrels between Marxism and theology arise not because Marxism has plagiarised theology, but because they contest the same historical and ideological space.

382

What does it mean for both of them?

My answer to this question is twofold: it means that historical materialism and theology are dialectically connected, and one strategy that makes the most of this connection is what may be called a politics of alliance. As far as the first answer is concerned, I pointed out earlier that the whole project of the *Criticism of Heaven and Earth* series may be summed up as a detailed exploration of the dialectic between historical materialism and theology. I used to think it rather strange that Marxism and theology should be engaged in an on-again off-again affair. No longer is that the case. The number of Marxists who have engaged with theology is but one pointer to that dialectic. If I stay with the Hegelian terminology (and I am following rather a good example, here), then Marxism might be viewed as the sublation or *Aufhebung* of theology: it both negates and draws up the questions that theology raises to a completely new level. But the converse is also true, although it has not yet been realised. So, I will put in terms of a question: what might theology as the *Aufhebung* of Marxism look like? However, for a long time I have been taken with Adorno's reworking of the dialectic: eschewing the formulaic process of *Aufhebung*, Adorno sought to push each side of the dialectic as far as it would go until it gave out into its other side. So, if we take Marxism as far as it will go, then theology keeps turning up, as I have found time and again in this project. But so too with theology: it is just that too many theologians fall back on the old frameworks of theology, seeking to assert its prior status. I wish to take a very different path.

Such theory is all very well, but what does it mean in practice? This is where the politics of alliance comes into play. In a nutshell, it seems to me that since the religious left has been marginalised with the rise of all manner of fundamentalisms, and since what I call the old secular left is on the rise, we need a politics of alliance between the religious left and the old secular left. I call this alliance the 'worldly left'.

By 'religious left' I mean those who struggle within the Synagogue and Church for justice and who find the Bible an inspiration for their struggles. They include both the reformers and the revolutionaries. It will come as no surprise that my preferences lie with the revolutionaries – the sundry Christian and Jewish socialists, communists and anarchists. But for a politics of alliance, the religious left also includes the reformers, those who prefer to tinker with the system in order to improve it in one way or another. This is where many of those who struggle for queer, gender, indigenous and environmental justice may be found. By '(old) secular left' I mean the various socialists, communists and anarchists who are deeply suspicious of religion of any stripe, let alone theology or the *Bible*. They still follow the old model of secularism which they understand as anti-religious, indeed as atheistic. Such a position may have been fine in nineteenth century politics, but it cuts off some extremely valuable allies and hobbles the programs of the left today.

In light of such an alliance, the old antagonism between materialism and religion, once seemingly set in cement, should be a thing of the past. We can well understand how those antagonisms came to be so. For instance, following the criticism of Christian socialism in *The Communist Manifesto* – as 'but the holy water with which the priest consecrates the heart-burnings of the aristocrat'[660] –socialism and communism since the time of Marx became largely anti-religious movements. And popular opinion followed suit, so much so that if a religious person declared she or he had become a socialist, then the assumption was that that person had lost his or her faith. It doesn't help matters when the major churches also declared communism to be 'Godless'. But these are, or at least should be, things of the past.

Finally, a politics of alliance recognises the diversity and pluralism of the left. Rather than the long tradition of one small group on the left feeling as though it is the keeper of the grail, spending all its energy condemning other groups as revisionists, deviationists, or heretics, the sheer diversity of the left is one of its great achievements. Within this diversity, a religious left has a legitimate and crucial role to play. Let me give one example: at the protests against the World Economic Forum in Melbourne in 2000 and then again at the G20 meeting in 2006, we found anarchists, environmentalists, socialists, feminists, various elements of the loopy left, and some elements of the religious left.

REFERENCES

Adorno, Theodor W. 1973, *The Jargon of Authenticity*, Translated by K. Tarnowski, and Frederic Will. Evanston: Northwestern University Press.
— 1986, *Gesammelte Schriften*. 23 vols. Frankfurt: Suhrkamp.
— 1989, *Kierkegaard: Construction of the Aesthetic*, Translated by R. Hullot-Kentor. Vol. 61, *Theory and History of Literature*. Minneapolis: University of

660. Marx and Engels 1967, p. 108.

Minnesota Press.

Adorno, Theodor W., and Max Horkheimer 1999, *Dialectic of Enlightenment*, Translated by J. Cumming. London: Continuum.

Agamben, Giorgio 2000, *Il tempo che resta. Un commento alla Lettera ai Romani*, Turin: Bollati Boringhieri.

— 2005 [2000], *The Time That Remains: A Commentary on the Letter to the Romans*, Translated by P. Dailey. Stanford: Stanford University Press.

Althusser, Louis 1994, *Écrits philosophiques et politiques, Tome 1*. Paris: Éditions Stock/IMEC.

— 1997, *The Spectre of Hegel: Early Writings*, Translated by G. M. Goshgarian. London: Verso.

Badiou, Alain 1997, *Saint-Paul: la fondation de l'universalisme*, Paris: Presses universitaires de France.

— 2003, *Saint Paul: The Foundation of Universalism*, Translated by R. Brassier. Stanford: Stanford University Press.

Benjamin, Walter 1974–89. *Gesammelte Schriften*. Edited by R. Tiedemann and H. Schweppenhäuser. Frankfurt: Suhrkamp.

— 1996, *Selected Writings. Volume 1: 1912–1926*. Edited by M. Bullock and M. W. Jennings. Cambridge, MA: Belknap.

— 1998, *The Origin of German Tragic Drama*, Translated by J. Osborne. London: Verso.

— 1999, *The Arcades Project*, Translated by H. Eiland and K. McLaughlin. Cambridge, MA: The Belknap Press of Harvard University Press.

Blanton, Ward, and Hent De Vries (eds.) Forthcoming, *Paul in Philosophy and Culture*. Chicago: University of Chicago Press.

Bloch, Ernst 1972, *Atheism in Christianity: The Religion of the Exodus and the Kingdom*, Translated by J. T. Swann. New York: Herder and Herder.

— 1985, *Werkausgabe*, Frankfurt: Suhrkamp Verlag.

— 1995, *Principle of Hope*, Cambridge, MA: MIT Press.

Boer, Roland 2007. *Criticism of Heaven: On Marxism and Theology, Historical Materialism Book Series*. Leiden and Chicago: Brill and Haymarket .

— 2008, *Political Myth*, Durham, NC: Duke University Press.

— 2009. *Criticism of Religion: On Marxism and Theology II Historical Materialism Book Series*. Leiden and Chicago: Brill and Haymarket .

— 2010. *Criticism of Religion: On Marxism and Theology III. Historical Materialism Book Series*. Leiden and Chicago: Brill and Haymarket.

— 2012. *Criticism of Earth: On Marx, Engels and Theology. Historical Materialism Book Series*. Leiden and Chicago: Brill and Haymarket.

— 2014. *In the Vale of Tears: On Marxism and Theology V. Historical Materialism Book Series.* Leiden and Chicago: Brill and Haymarket.

Eagleton, Terry 1966, *The New Left Church*, London: Sheed and Ward.

— 1970, *The Body as Language: Outline of a 'New Left' Theology*, London: Sheed and Ward.

— 2003a, *Sweet Violence: The Idea of the Tragic*, Oxford: Blackwells.

— 2003b, *After Theory*, New York: Basic Books.

Engels, Friedrich 1990 [1894], 'On the History of Early Christianity', in *Marx and Engels Collected Works*, Vol. 27, London: Lawrence & Wishart.

Goldmann, Lucien 1959, *Le Dieu cache: Études sue la vision tragiques dans les Pensées de Pascal et dans le theatre de Racine*, Paris: Éditions Gallimard.

— 1964, *The Hidden God: A Study of the Tragic Vision the Penséés of Pascal and the Tragedies of Racine*, Translated by P. Thody. New York: The Humanities Press.

Goldstein, Warren S. (ed.) 2006, *Marx, Critical Theory and Religion: A Critique of Rational Choice, Studies in Critical Social Sciences*, Leiden: Brill.

Gramsci, Antonio 1992. *Prison Notebooks*, Translated by J. A. Buttigieg, and Callari, Antonio. Edited by L. D. Kritzman, and Wolin, Richard. Vol. 1, *European Perspectives*. New York: Columbia University Press.

— 1995, *Further Selections from the Prison Notebooks*, Translated by D. Boothman. Minneapolis: University of Minnesota Press.

— 1996, *Prison Notebooks*, Translated by J. A. Buttigieg. Edited by L. D. Kritzman. Vol. 2, *European Perspectives*. New York: Columbia University Press.

Hardt, Michael, and Antonio Negri 2004, *Multitude: War and Democracy in the Age of Empire*, New York: Penguin.

Jameson, Fredric 1971, *Marxism and Form: Twentieth-Century Dialectical Theories of Literature*, Princeton, New Jersey: Princeton University Press.

— 1981, *The Political Unconscious: Narrative as a Socially Symbolic Act*, Ithaca, New York: Cornell University Press.

— 1986, *Religion and Ideology: A Political Reading of Paradise Lost. In Literature, Politics and Theory: Papers from the Essex Conference* 1976-84, edited by F. Barker. London: Methuen.

— 1996, 'On the Sexual Production of Western Subjectivity, or, Saint Augustine as a Social Democrat'. In *Gaze and Voice as Love Objects*, edited by R. Salecl and S. Žižek. Durham, North Carolina:Duke University Press.

— 2005, *Archaeologies of the Future: The Desire Called Utopia and Other Science Fictions*, London: Verso.

Kautsky, Karl. 1908, *Der Ursprung des Christentums: Eine Historische Untersuchung*, Stuttgart: J.H.W. Dietz.

— 1947 [1888], *Thomas More und seine Utopie: mit einer Historischen Einleitung*, Third edition, Berlin: J.W.H. Dietz.

— 1976 [1895–7], *Vorläufer des neueren Sozialismus*, 2 vols. Berlin: J.H.W. Dietz.

— 2001. *Foundations of Christianity*. Translated by H. F. Mins: marxists.org. Original edition, German, 1908. London: Russell and Russell, 1953.

— 2002a [1897], *Communism in Central Europe in the Time of the Reformation*, Translated by J. L. Mulliken and E. G. Mulliken. London: T. Fisher Unwin.

— 2002b [1888], *Thomas More and His Utopia*, Translated by H. J. Stenning. London: Lawrence and Wishart.

Kautsky, Karl, and Paul Lafargue 1977 [1922] *Vorläufer des neueren Sozialismus III*. Stuttgart: J.H.W. Dietz.

Lefebvre, Henri 1991, *Critique of Everyday Life*, Translated by J. Moore. London: Verso.

Löwy, Michael 1988, *Marxisme et théologie de la libération, Cahiers d'étude at de recherche*, Amsterdam: IIRE.

— 1996, *The War of Gods: Religion and Politics in Latin America*, London: Verso.

Lukács, Georg 1968, *Geschichte und Klassenbewusstsein*, Vol. 2, *Georg Lukács Werke*. Neuwied und Berlin: Hermann Luchterhand.

— 1971 *Theory of the Novel: A Historico-Philosophical Essay in the Forms of Great Epic Literature*, Translated by A. Bostock. Cambridge, MA: MIT.

— 1973, *Marxism and Human Liberation*, New York: Delta.

— 1983, *Record of a Life: An Autobiographical Sketch*, Translated by R. Livingstone. London: Verso.

— 1988, *History and Class Consciousness: Studies in Marxist Dialectics*, Translated by R. Livingstone. Cambridge, MA: MIT.

— 1994, *Die Theorie des Romans: Ein geschichtsphilosophischer Versuch über die Formen der grossen Epik*, Munich: Deutscher Taschenbuch Verlag.

Luxemburg, Rosa 1982 [1905], *Kirche und Sozialismus*, Frankfurt: Stimme-Verlag.

— 2004 [1905]. Socialism and the Churches. *Rosa Luxemburg Speaks*. Ed. Mary-Alice Waters. Translated by J. Punto. New York: Pathfinder Press.

Marx, Karl 1975 [1844], 'Introduction' to 'Contribution to the Critique of Hegel's Philosophy of Right', in *Marx and Engels Collected Works*, Vol. 3, London: Lawrence & Wishart.

Negri, Antonio 2002, Job, la force de l'esclave. Paris: Bayard.

— 2003, *Time for Revolution*, Translated by M. Mandarini. London: Continuum.

Ott, Michael R. (ed.) 2007, *The Future of Religion: Toward a Reconciled Society, Studies in Critical Social Sciences*, Leiden: Brill.

Riazonov, David 1973 [1937], *Karl Marx and Frederick Engels: An Introduction to Their Lives and Work*, Translated by J. Kunitz. New York: Monthly Review Press.

Rothbard, Murray N. 1990, *Karl Marx: Communist as Religious Eschatologist. The Review of Austrian Economics*, 4:123-79.

Sichère, Bernard 2003, *Le jour est proche: la révolution selon Paul*, Paris: Desclée de Brouwer.

Sorel, Georges 1961, *Reflections on Violence*, Translated by T. Hulme and J. Roth. New York: Collier.

Struik, Dirk J. 1986, *The Birth of the Communist Manifesto*, New York: International Publishers.

Thompson, Edward P. 1993, *Witness against the Beast: William Blake and the Moral Law*, Cambridge: Cambridge University Press.

Trigano, Shmuel 2004, *L'E(xc)lu: Entre Juifs et chrétiens*, Paris: Denoël.

Žižek, Slavoj 2000, *The Fragile Absolute, or, Why Is the Christian Legacy Worth Fighting For?*, London: Verso.

— 2001, *On Belief*, London: Routledge.

— 2003, *The Puppet and the Dwarf: The Perverse Core of Christianity*, Cambridge, MA: MIT.

NOTES ON CONTRIBUTORS

Sara R. Farris (editor) is a Lecturer in the Sociology Department at Goldsmiths, University of London. She has published on social and political theory, migration and feminism. Her most recent publications include *Max Weber's Theory of Personality. Individuation, Politics and Orientalism in the Sociology of Religion* (Brill 2013). She is a fellow of the IIRE, International Book Review Editor for *Critical Sociology* and serves on the editorial board of *Historical Materialism*.

Guglielmo Carchedi is a retired professor at the University of Amsterdam. Presently, he is Adjunct Professor at York University, Toronto. He has been writing widely in the fields of Political Economy, Sociology, Epistemology and European Integration. His latest book is *Behind the Crisis. Marx's Dialectics of Value and Knowledge* (Haymarket 2011).

Riccardo Bellofiore is a professor of monetary economics and history of economic thought at the University of Bergamo. He is the author of numerous articles and books in Marxist political economy. Most recently he co-edited *In Marx's Laboratory. Critical Interpretations of the Grundrisse* (Brill 2013, with Peter D. Thomas and Guido Starosta).

Michael Heinrich teaches economics at Hochschule für Technik und Wirtschaft, Berlin. Recent publications include *An Introduction to the Three Volumes of Karl Marx's Capital* (Monthly Review Press 2012); "The 'Fragment on Machines': A Marxian Misconception in the *Grundrisse* and its Overcoming in *Capital*", in: Riccardo Bellofiore et al. (eds.), *In Marx's Laboratory. Critical Interpretations of the Grundrisse* (Brill 2013).

Geert Reuten taught at the School of Economics of the University of Amsterdam, where is currently a guest professor in political economy. From 2007 he is a member of the senate of the Netherlands for the Socialist Party. He wrote two monographs and 60 articles in academic journals and books, including 20 on Marx's *Capital*, on which he also coedited two books.

Frieder Otto Wolf is Professor of Philosophy at the Freie Universität Berlin, and a former member of the European Parliament. He is the translator and editor of the complete works of Louis Althusser in German. His books include *Die Neue Wissenschaft des Thomas Hobbes* (Frommann-Holzboog 1969) and *Radikale Philosophie* (Westfälisches Dampfboot 2002) and – as co-author – *Europe's Green Alternative: A Manifesto For a New World* (Black Rose 1992 and 1996).

Tom Rockmore is Distinguished Humanities Chair Professor at Peking University. He is the author of numerous books including, more recently, *Kant and Idealism* (Yale 2007) and *Hegel, Idealism and Analytic Philosophy* (Yale 2005). His most recent book is *Art and Truth After Plato* (Chicago Unversity Press 2013).

Wei Xiaoping is professor of History of Marxist Philosophy in the Philosophy Institute of Chinese Academy of Social Sciences, Author of *The Reflection on the Historical Subject and Historical Object* (1999), *On the Tracks of Karl Marx* (2005), *German Ideology, re-read and analysis from MEGA* (2010), *Rethinking China's Economic Transformation* (2010), *The Road Towards "Capital":On the track of Marx' Labor Theory of Value* (2013).

Joost Kircz is a Marxist activist since the late sixties, and since 1982 member of the IIRE board. After an academic education and research period in physics, he became international science publisher for 16 years. Hereafter he started research in the field of electronic knowledge transfer and electronic publishing, lately as research professor at the University of Applied Sciences Amsterdam.

Jan Drahokoupil, is senior research fellow at the Mannheim Centre for European Social Research (MZES), University of Mannheim. His research deals with politics and political economy of Eastern Europe, Russia, and Central Asia as well as with the European integration. His most recent book publication is *Transition economies*, co-authored with Martin Myant (Wiley-Blackwell 2010).

Bastiaan van Apeldoorn, is a reader in International Relations at the Vrije. Universiteit Amsterdam, the Netherlands. His most recent publications include *The State-Capital Nexus in the Global Crisis* (Routledge 2014) edited with Naná de Graaff, and Henk Overbeek, and *Neoliberalism in Crisis* (Palgrave Macmillan 2012, with Henk Overbeek).

Laura Horn is Associate Professor at the Department of Society and Globalisation at Roskilde University, Denmark. Her work focuses on the political economy of European integration from a critical political economy perspective. Her publications include *Contradictions and Limits of Neoliberal European Governance* (2008, Palgrave, with Bastiaan van Apeldoorn and Jan Drahokoupil) and *Regulating Corporate Governance in the EU* (2011, Palgrave).

Gal Kirn is currently Humboldt Stiftung Fellow at the Humboldt Universität in Berlin. He is a co-editor of *Encountering Althusser* (Continuum 2012); *Yugoslav Black Wave Cinema and Its Transgressive Moments* (JVE 2012) and editor of *Postfordism and its discontents* (JVE, B-Books and Mirovni Inštitut 2010). He comments on politics in the Slovenian weekly *Objektiv*. In his hometown Ljubljana, he participates in the Workers'-Punks' University.

Jeff Webber is a Senior Lecturer in the School of Politics and International Relations at Queen Mary University of London and a member of the editorial board of *Historical Materialism*. He is the author most recently of *Red October: Left-Indigenous Struggles in Modern Bolivia* (Haymarket 2012).

Bertel Nygaard is associate professor at the Department of Culture and Society, Aarhus University (Denmark). He specializes in European history during the long 19th Century. His most recent publications include "French Revolution and Communist Future. Historical Time and Agency in European Labour Movements at the End of the First World War", in: Hagen Schulz-Forberg (ed.), *Zero Hours* (Peter Lang 2013).

Marcel van der Linden is Senior Research Fellow at the International Institute of Social History, Professor of Social Movement History at the University of Amsterdam, and President of the International Social History Association (2010-15). He has published extensively on labor and working-class history and on the history of ideas. He is the author of *Workers of the World* (Brill 2010) and *Western Marxism and the Soviet Union* (Haymarket 2009).

Peter D. Thomas lectures in the History of Political Thought at Brunel University, London. He is the author of *The Gramscian Moment: Philosophy, Hegemony and Marxism* (Brill, 2009), co-editor of *Encountering Althusser* (Bloomsbury 2012), and *In Marx's Laboratory. Critical Interpretations of the Grundrisse* (Brill 2013). He serves on the Editorial Board of *Historical Materialism. Research in Critical Marxist Theory*.

Chiara Bonfiglioli (PhD, Utrecht University) is currently NWO Rubicon Research Fellow at the University of Edinburgh. She is particularly interested in issues of transnational gender history, post-socialist studies, and post-colonialism, and is the authors of several publications on feminist and gender history in twentieth century Southern and South Eastern Europe.

Peter Drucker is a Fellow and former co-director of the IIRE, an editorial board member of the Dutch socialist website Grenzeloos, a longtime LGBT activist, and author of the book Warped: Gay Normality and Queer Anti-Capitalism (forthcoming from Brill/HM, 2015).

Katja Diefenbach is a philosopher and cultural theorist based in Berlin. She has been a reader in Cultural Studies at Universität der Künste and Humboldt Universität (Berlin), Hochschule für Bildende Künste (Hamburg) and Jan van Eyck Academy (Maastricht). Her publications include *Encountering Althusser* (co-editor, Bloomsbury 2013) and *Politics of potentiality. Post-Marxist Readings of Spinoza* (forthcoming in 2015).

Steve Wright is in the Caulfield School of IT, Monash University. He is the author of Storming Heaven: class composition and struggle in Italian autonomist marxism (Pluto Press 2002).

Roland Boer researches and writes in the area of Marxism and religion, having published a large number of books and articles in the area. The core of this work is the five-volume work, *The Criticism of Heaven and Earth* (Brill 2007-14). He is also Professor of Literary Theory at Renmin University of China and research professor at the University of Newcastle, Australia.

ABOUT THE INTERNATIONAL
INSTITUTE FOR RESEARCH AND EDUCATION

The IIRE is an international foundation, recognised in Belgium as an international scientific association by Royal decree of 11th June 1981. The International Institute for Research and Education (IIRE) provides activists and scholars worldwide with opportunities for research and education in three locations: Amsterdam, Islamabad and Manila.

Since 1982, when the Institute opened in Amsterdam, its main activity has been the organisation of courses. Our seminars and study groups deal with all subjects related to the emancipation of the world's oppressed and exploited. It has welcomed hundreds of participants, most participants have come from the Third World.

The IIRE has become a prominent centre for the development of critical thought and exchange between activists. Our sessions give participants a unique opportunity to step aside from the pressure of daily activism. During a session, they have the time to study, reflect upon their involvement in social movements, unions, students organisations, etc. and exchange ideas with people from other countries.

Our website is being expanded with downloadable publications in four languages, audio files and video recordings. The recordings can be downloaded from this site - as can the audiotapes of the talks given by founding Fellows such as Ernest Mandel and Livio Maitan, dating back to the early 1980s.

The IIRE publishes Notebooks for Study and Research to focus on themes of contemporary debate or historical or theoretical importance. Lectures and study materials given in sessions in our Institute, located in Amsterdam, Manila and Islamabad, are made available to the public in large part through the Notebooks.

Different issues of the Notebooks have also appeared in languages besides English and French, including German, Dutch, Arabic, Spanish, Japanese, Korean, Portuguese, Turkish, Swedish Danish and Russian.

For a full list of the Notebooks for Study and Research visit our website at **www.iire.org**. Notebooks can be ordered through our website.